Critical Research on Scalability and Security Issues in Virtual Cloud Environments

Shadi Aljawarneh
Jordan University of Science and Technology, Jordan

Manisha Malhotra
Chandigarh University, India

A volume in the Advances in
Information Security, Privacy, and
Ethics (AISPE) Book Series

Published in the United States of America by
   IGI Global
   Information Science Reference (an imprint of IGI Global)
   701 E. Chocolate Avenue
   Hershey PA, USA 17033
   Tel: 717-533-8845
   Fax: 717-533-8661
   E-mail: cust@igi-global.com
   Web site: http://www.igi-global.com

Library of Congress Cataloging-in-Publication Data

Names: Aljawarneh, Shadi, editor. | Malhotra, Manisha, 1987- editor.
Title: Critical research on scalability and security issues in virtual cloud
   environments / Shadi Aljawarneh and Manisha Malhotra, editors.
Description: Hershey, PA : Information Science Reference, [2018] | Includes
   bibliographical references and index.
Identifiers: LCCN 2017012047| ISBN 9781522530299 (hardcover) | ISBN
   9781522530305 (ebook)
Subjects: LCSH: Cloud computing--Security measures. | Computer
   networks--Scalability.
Classification: LCC QA76.585 .C75 2018 | DDC 004.67/82--dc23 LC record available at https://
lccn.loc.gov/2017012047

This book is published in the IGI Global book series Advances in Information Security, Privacy, and Ethics (AISPE) (ISSN: 1948-9730; eISSN: 1948-9749)

British Cataloguing in Publication Data
A Cataloguing in Publication record for this book is available from the British Library.

All work contributed to this book is new, previously-unpublished material.
The views expressed in this book are those of the authors, but not necessarily of the publisher.

For electronic access to this publication, please contact: eresources@igi-global.com.

Advances in Information Security, Privacy, and Ethics (AISPE) Book Series

ISSN:1948-9730
EISSN:1948-9749

Editor-in-Chief: Manish Gupta, State University of New York, USA

MISSION

As digital technologies become more pervasive in everyday life and the Internet is utilized in ever increasing ways by both private and public entities, concern over digital threats becomes more prevalent.

The **Advances in Information Security, Privacy, & Ethics (AISPE) Book Series** provides cutting-edge research on the protection and misuse of information and technology across various industries and settings. Comprised of scholarly research on topics such as identity management, cryptography, system security, authentication, and data protection, this book series is ideal for reference by IT professionals, academicians, and upper-level students.

COVERAGE

- Global Privacy Concerns
- CIA Triad of Information Security
- Privacy-Enhancing Technologies
- Security Classifications
- Risk Management
- Device Fingerprinting
- Privacy Issues of Social Networking
- IT Risk
- Electronic Mail Security
- Telecommunications Regulations

IGI Global is currently accepting manuscripts for publication within this series. To submit a proposal for a volume in this series, please contact our Acquisition Editors at Acquisitions@igi-global.com or visit: http://www.igi-global.com/publish/.

Titles in this Series

For a list of additional titles in this series, please visit:
https://www.igi-global.com/book-series/advances-information-security-privacy-ethics/37157

Algorithmic Strategies for Solving Complex Problems in Cryptography
Kannan Balasubramanian (Mepco Schlenk Engineering College, India) and M. Rajakani (Mepco Schlenk Engineering College, India)
Information Science Reference • ©2018 • 302pp • H/C (ISBN: 9781522529156) • US $245.00

Information Technology Risk Management and Compliance in Modern Organizations
Manish Gupta (State University of New York, Buffalo, USA) Raj Sharman (State University of New York, Buffalo, USA) John Walp (M&T Bank Corporation, USA) and Pavankumar Mulgund (State University of New York, Buffalo, USA)
Business Science Reference • ©2018 • 360pp • H/C (ISBN: 9781522526049) • US $225.00

Detecting and Mitigating Robotic Cyber Security Risks
Raghavendra Kumar (LNCT Group of College, India) Prasant Kumar Pattnaik (KIIT University, India) and Priyanka Pandey (LNCT Group of College, India)
Information Science Reference • ©2017 • 384pp • H/C (ISBN: 9781522521549) • US $210.00

Advanced Image-Based Spam Detection and Filtering Techniques
Sunita Vikrant Dhavale (Defense Institute of Advanced Technology (DIAT), Pune, India)
Information Science Reference • ©2017 • 213pp • H/C (ISBN: 9781683180135) • US $175.00

Privacy and Security Policies in Big Data
Sharvari Tamane (MGM's Jawaharlal Nehru Engineering College, India) Vijender Kumar Solanki (Institute of Technology and Science Ghaziabad, India) and Nilanjan Dey (Techno India College of Technology, India)
Information Science Reference • ©2017 • 305pp • H/C (ISBN: 9781522524861) • US $210.00

Securing Government Information and Data in Developing Countries
Saleem Zoughbi (UN APCICT, UN ESCAP, South Korea)
Information Science Reference • ©2017 • 307pp • H/C (ISBN: 9781522517030) • US $160.00

For an enitre list of titles in this series, please visit:
https://www.igi-global.com/book-series/advances-information-security-privacy-ethics/37157

701 East Chocolate Avenue, Hershey, PA 17033, USA
Tel: 717-533-8845 x100 • Fax: 717-533-8661
E-Mail: cust@igi-global.com • www.igi-global.com

Table of Contents

Section 3
Approach of Cloud Towards Internet of Things

Chapter 11
Inderbir Kaur, Khalsa College, India

Section 4
Networks and Energy Efficiency in Virtual Cloud

Chapter 12
Samia Chehbi Gamoura, Université de Strasbourg, France

Chapter 13
Muneer Bani Yassein, Jordan University of Science and Technology, Jordan

Mohammed Shatnawi, Jordan University of Science and Technology, Jordan

Nesreen l-Qasem, Jordan University of Science and Technology, Jordan

Chapter 14
Shivani Bajaj, Chandigarh University, India

Detailed Table of Contents

Section 1
Scalability Issues of Cloud Environment: Scope and Case Study

Chapter 1

Mohan Murthy M. K., Nitte Meenakshi Institute of Technology, India
Sanjay H. A., Nitte Meenakshi Institute of Technology, India

Scalability is one of the reasons behind the popularity of the Cloud. In the real IT world, resource requirement of an application varies over the time. Elastic and scalable nature of the Cloud makes it more suitable for such situation. By scaling the resources as per the resource demand, efficient resource utilization can be achieved. Vertical scaling and horizontal scaling are two different types of scaling. In vertical scaling, the virtual machine resources are scaled, and in horizontal scaling, infrastructure is scaled by adding or removing new virtual machines to it. This chapter focuses on scaling in Cloud environment, especially resource scaling for applications. The chapter starts with a brief introduction to Cloud and scaling in the cloud. After the introduction, related literature is visited. The chapter explains the necessity of scaling with real life examples. The chapter covers virtualization and some important hypervisors from the scaling perspective. The chapter also explains vertical scaling and horizontal scaling in detail.

Chapter 2

Manisha Malhotra, Chandigarh University, India
Aarti Singh, Guru Nanak Girls College, India

Cloud computing is a novel paradigm that changes the industry viewpoint of inventing, developing, deploying, scaling, updating, maintaining, and paying for applications and the infrastructure on which they are deployed. Due to dynamic nature of cloud computing it is quite easy to increase the capacity of hardware or software, even without investing on purchases of it. This feature of cloud computing is named as scalability which is one of the main concern in cloud environment. This chapter presents the architecture of scalability by using mobile agents. It also highlights the other main issues prevailing in cloud paradigm. Further it presents the hybrid architecture for data security which is also the one of major concern of it. This chapter mainly highlights the solution for scalability and security.

Chapter 3

The Copperbelt University Computer Centre runs five physical servers 24/7 throughout the academic year calendar. These machines consumed a lot of resources such as electricity used to run and cool them. In addition, the Computer Centre employed a lot of technicians to run, maintain and service the named servers. All the discussed costs were incurred throughout the year including the idle workload period when there was very little work to be processed. It was against that background the Computer Centres Resource Cloud Elasticity-Scalability (CRECES) was envisaged to only use one physical server during idle workload period. It was at such periods when the Computer Centre carried a rapid elasticity to scale down on the huge server resource utilisation. Similarly, at peak workload time the centre carried a rapid elasticity to scale up by producing many virtual hardware and software resources just from a single server to five virtualised ones. Hence, the capacity of the Centre to scale up and down resources acted as a cost serving measures in utilising the hardware and software resources.

Section 2
Security and Trust Issues of Cloud Paradigm

Chapter 4

Information dispersal is a technique in which pieces of data are distributed among various nodes such that the data can be reconstituted from any threshold number of these pieces. Information dispersal algorithms employ a method in which a file F needs to be dispersed among n nodes such that any m pieces will be sufficient to reconstruct the whole file F. The size of each piece is |F/m|. We must also ensure that the complete knowledge of any m-1 pieces is insufficient to reconstruct the complete file F. The ideas for accomplishing this have been given in many literatures in the past. A discussion and comparison of some of these is covered in this chapter.

Shivani Jaswal, Chandigarh University, India
Manisha Malhotra, Chandigarh University, India

Cloud computing is a rising paradigm in today's world. In this, users can send his or her request to any CSP, i.e., cloud service provider, of their choice. In return, the CSP reverts him back with that particular service. Now, while communicating from various two locations, the data transferred is not passed through that much amount of security and privacy as expected. So, there are lots of parameters in the environment that are taken care of while sending, receiving or just passing data over the network. This chapter presents various security issues that are underlying in cloud computing. This chapter has illustrated various issues such as Trust, Encryption, Authenticity, Confidentiality and Multi Tenancy. Also, some of the proposed solutions have also been discussed later in the chapter.

Thangavel M, Thiagarajar College of Engineering, India
Narmadha N, Thiagarajar College of Engineering, India
Deepika B, Thiagarajar College of Engineering, India

Cloud computing is a technology for complex computing, it eliminates the need to have computing hardware, storage space and software. Multi tenancy is considered as important element in which same resources will be shared by multiple users. The users are named as tenants in the cloud environment. The tenants may run their applications in their own cloud environment which will have some vulnerability. These vulnerabilities will cause some attacks to the tenant virtual machine. In general, the cloud providers will not provide that much security to the cloud tenants. So, it is the duty of the tenant to make some countermeasures to avoid these attacks. In a cloud environment, there may be multiple tenants in that there is a possible of malicious tenant also present in the cloud environment. The attacker will do sniffing attack by monitoring all the user traffic. In the cloud, it is a fact that all the user data will resides in same hardware so the attacker monitor the activities of all the user and observes the type of traffic.

Cloud computing is growing with a giant pace in today's world. The speed with which it is growing, the same speed is taken over by the insecure data transfer over the cloud. There are many security issues that are underlying in cloud computing. This chapter presents how a trust is built between any user and a cloud service provider. Various techniques have been adopted to calculate the value of trust and further how it can be strength. This chapter has also explained various trust models based on the necessities of a user. This chapter has also thrown some light over the concept of TTP, i.e., Trusted Third Party which further helps in maintaining trust over the cloud environment.

Chapter 8

IaaS, PaaS, and SaaS models collectively form the Cloud Computing Infrastructure. The complexity of interrelationship of service models is very high and so security issue becomes essentials and must be developed with utmost care. Distributed DOS attacks are a major concern for different organization engaged in using cloud based services. The denial of service attack and distributed denial of service attacks in particular in cloud paradigms are big threat on a cloud network or platform. These attacks operate by rendering the server and network useless by sending unnecessary service and resource requests. The victims host or network isn't aware of such attacks and keeps providing recourses until they get exhausted. Due to resource exhaustions, the resources requests of genuine users doesn't get fulfilled. Severity of these attacks can lead to huge financial losses if, they are able to bring down servers executing financial services. This chapter presents DOS threats and methods to mitigate them in varied dimensions.

Section 3
Approach of Cloud Towards Internet of Things

Internet of Things (IoT) is one of the most active and hot topics these days in which most of our everyday objects are connected with each other over internal and external networks. As in any data communication paradigm there are security aspects that should be taken care of. The traditional security mechanisms are usually not applicable in IoT because there are different standards involved, this make the security preservation is one of the main challenges in IoT. According to previous surveys, there are many of security issues in regards to IoT. In this chapter, five issues from the security issues in IoT are discussed; Access Control, Authentication, Privacy, Policy Enforcement, and Trust. After that, major proposed solutions from the literature is listed and compared according to the strength and weakness points for each of them.

Chapter 10

Big data refers to the huge amount of data that is being used in commercial, industrial and economic environments. There are three types of big data; structured, unstructured and semi-structured data. When it comes to discussions on big data, three major aspects that can be considered as its main dimensions are the volume, velocity, and variety of the data. This data is collected, analysed and checked for use by the end users. Cloud computing and the Internet of Things (IoT) are used to enable this huge amount of collected data to be stored and connected to the Internet. The time and the cost are reduced by means of these technologies, and in addition, they are able to accommodate this large amount of data regardless of its size. This chapter focuses on how big data, with the emergence of cloud computing and the Internet of Things (IOT), can be used via several applications and technologies.

Chapter 11

Cloud computing is an upcoming IT approach that presents various new economic benefits, effective rapid deployment of services to achieve ultimate benefits and goals. Cloud computing reveals an effective connection of internet and computing technologies with personal or business computing that is changing the environment of computing process by providing solutions which are designed, delivered and managed. This model is a remarkable shift from the traditional model of computing.

The cloud is an attractive technology solution as it enables to reduce the total cost of ownership and giving "green computing" environment by energy saving concept. Use of Cloud computing technology in different areas provides greater opportunities in the overall development of world, especially India. This chapter throw lights on various dimensions in which cloud computing concept is used . This paper also reviews the potential and opportunities for cloud computing in the healthcare industry, tourism, defence and military applications and various another aspects.

Section 4
Networks and Energy Efficiency in Virtual Cloud

Chapter 12

With the democratization of Data management through Big Data and Cloud Computing, and the proliferation of business lines into complex networks, industries are ever more subject to disasters than ever. It is practically impossible to forecast their happening and degree of damages. Consequently, companies try to collaborate in integrating risk management in their information systems against downtimes. This chapter addresses this problem by outlining and discussing insights from the extensive literature review to produce a generic approach for cross-management. A set of prerequisites of disaster planning is also provided with comparative analysis and arguments. The proposed approach is focused on risk assessment methodology based on Fuzzy Cognitive Map. The method is able to aggregate all assessment variables of the whole stakeholders involved in the business network. The key findings of this study aim to assist enterprises in improving risk readiness capability and disaster recovery. Finally, we indicate the open challenges for further researches and an outlook on our future research.

Chapter 13

Mobile ad hoc networks (MANETs) is a collection of wireless mobile devices that dynamically communicates with each other as a self-configuration without the need of centralized administration or fixed infrastructure. In this paper, we interested to introduce the different broadcast methods based on the probabilistic scheme which is simple implement code with speed broadcast and to reduce a storm broadcast problem effects and to alleviate redundancy through rebroadcast by using different routing protocols such as (AODV, DSR, LAR, PAR) that we interested in MANETs.

Chapter 14

Energy Efficiency can be defined as reduction of energy used by a given service or level of activity. In spite of scale and complexity of data centre equipment it can be highly difficult to define the proper activity that could be examined for the efficiency of energy. So there can be four scenarios which may define within the system where the energy is not utilised in an efficient manner. The main goal of Cloud service providers is creation of usage of Cloud computing resources proficiently for efficient cloud computing. Cloud computing has many serious issues such as load manager, security and fault tolerance. This chapter discusses the energy efficient approaches in cloud computing environment. The energy efficiency has become the major concern for the service providers. In this chapter, the major concern is the high lightly of resource allocation challenges and there are some which will be given in the data center energy consumption. The focus is done on the power management task and even the virtualization of saving the energy.

A book is the only place in which you can examine a fragile thought without breaking it. – Edward P. Morgan

Preface

Cloud basically stands for Common Location-independent Online Utility service, available on-Demand. It's a pool of virtualized computer resources which supports large variety of different workloads, including batch-style back-end jobs and interactive, user-facing applications. Cloud computing thus offers computing technologies being offered at cloud. Cloud computing offer lots of advantages over traditional computing such as online resources, offline access, flexibility, and savings. It is distributed into three segments namely, applications, platforms and infrastructure. Majorly, the definition of cloud computing specifically revolves round the terms like scalability, pay-per use model, and virtualization. In fact, enablers supporting cloud computing are interoperability, portability, integration of components, ease of deployment, pay as per use, economic, rapid provisioning and elasticity and so on. Because of the appealing features mentioned above, cloud computing is becoming a temptation for all business organizations. Due to dynamic nature of cloud computing it is quite easy to increase the capacity of hardware or software, even without investing on purchases of it. From last few years, cloud computing has become a promising business concept. All existing business applications are complicated in nature and much too expensive. To run these applications there is a need of data centers having supporting staff and infrastructure like bandwidth, networks and server etc. along with a dedicate team for its execution. For deploying such kind of applications, organizations have to invest large amount of funds which makes it difficult for small businesses to establish themselves. Therefore, cloud computing provides a simple alternative to start IT based business organization with much less initial investment.

OBJECTIVE OF THE BOOK

The purpose of this book is to present the concept of cloud computing and explore the various shortcomings of cloud. The background of assorted issues that arises in the field of cloud computing is to be discussed. It also highlights the comparison among the existing techniques of various problems. Furthermore, the future work will be provided to pursue the research in the same field. The main aim of this book is to provide the information to research community, students, practitioners and academician also in the form of various aspects.

ORGANIZATION OF THE BOOK

This book contains 14 chapters arranged in different four sections. Section 1 comprises three chapters and mainly focuses on scope and issue of scalability in cloud environment and a case study on it. This section describes that how mobile agents deployed in cloud environment. Section 2 consists of five chapters which provide the sensitive area of cloud, i.e., security and trust management in cloud paradigm. It also provides the different security algorithm by which the providers and users can secure their data. Section 3 depicts an approach of cloud towards the new era of internet, i.e., Internet of things (IOT) and big data. It consists of three chapters which represent the security issues of IOT and new rising of big data. Section 4 detailed the concept of networks and energy efficiency in cloud computing. The summary of book organization is as follows:

SECTION 1: SCALABILITY ISSUES OF CLOUD ENVIRONMENT – SCOPE AND CASE STUDY

This section highlights the scalability issues occurred in cloud computing along with a case study of Copperbelt University in Zambia.

Chapter 1: This chapter focuses on scaling in Cloud environment, especially resource scaling for applications. Authors have started with a brief introduction to Cloud and scaling in the cloud. After the introduction, related literature is visited. It explains the necessity of scaling with real life examples. It also covers virtualization and some important hypervisors from the scaling perspective. Vertical scaling and horizontal scaling is also addressed by authors.

Chapter 2: This chapter presents the architecture of scalability by using mobile agents. It also highlights the main issues prevailing in cloud paradigm. Authors have presented the hybrid architecture for data security which is also the one of major concern of it. This chapter mainly highlights the solution for scalability and security.

Chapter 3: This chapter insight the case study of Copperbelt University in Zambia. The Copperbelt University Computer Centre runs five physical servers 24/7 throughout the academic year calendar. These machines consumed a lot of resources such as electricity used to run and cool them. In addition, the Computer Centre employed a lot of technicians to run, maintain and service the named servers. All the discussed costs were incurred throughout the year including the idle workload period when there was very little work to be processed. Author focuses on the capacity of the Centre to scale up and down resources acted as a cost serving measures in utilizing the hardware and software resources.

SECTION 2: SECURITY AND TRUST ISSUES OF CLOUD PARADIGM

This section throws a light on security issues and provides the mechanisms so that no one can breach the security. It also highlights the trust issue and its management in cloud computing.

Chapter 4: This chapter discussed the Information Dispersal technique in the field of cloud computing. It is a technique in which pieces of data are distributed among various nodes such that the data can be reconstituted from any threshold number of these pieces. Information Dispersal Algorithms employ a method in which a file F needs to be dispersed among n nodes such that any m pieces will be sufficient to reconstruct the whole file F. The size of each piece is |F/m|. Authors have ensured that the complete knowledge of any m-1 pieces is insufficient to reconstruct the complete file F. The ideas for accomplishing this have been given in many literatures in the past. A discussion and comparison of some of these is covered in this chapter.

Chapter 5: This chapter presents various security issues that are underlying in cloud computing. Authors have exemplified various issues such as Trust, Encryption, Authenticity, Confidentiality and Multi Tenancy. Also, some of the proposed solutions have also been addressed by the authors.

Chapter 6: In this chapter, the authors explain the deployment model of cloud computing. Authors have also discussed the different attacks, i.e., DOS, Malware Injection, Wrapping, Authentication, Insider Attacks. After that authors explains the concept of sniffing, its working and how it is custom in cloud computing.

Chapter 7: This chapter presents how a trust is built between any user and a cloud service provider. Various techniques have been adopted to calculate the value of trust and further how it can be strength. Authors have also explained various trust models based on the necessities of a user. This chapter has also thrown some light over the concept of TTP, i.e., Trusted Third Party which further helps in maintaining trust over the cloud environment.

Chapter 8: This chapter presents DOS threats and methods to mitigate them in varied dimensions. DOS attacks are a major concern for different organization engaged in using cloud based services. The denial of service attack and distributed denial of service attacks in particular in cloud paradigms are big threat on a cloud network or platform. The author explained that how attacks operate by rendering the server and network useless by sending unnecessary service and resource requests.

SECTION 3: APPROACH OF CLOUD TOWARDS INTERNET OF THINGS

Technologies are changing day by day. This is the time that researchers have to think about the data stored on cloud. To manage this thing, researchers are moving towards big data, Internet of Things. This section depicts the approach of cloud towards the new era.

Chapter 9: This chapter explains the five issues from the security issues in IOT are discussed; Access Control, Authentication, Privacy, Policy Enforcement, and Trust. After that, major proposed solutions from the literature is listed by the authors and compared according to the strength and weakness points for each of them.

Chapter 10: This chapter focuses on how big data, with the emergence of cloud computing and the Internet of Things (IOT), can be used via several applications and technologies.

Chapter 11: This chapter throws light on various dimensions in which cloud computing concept is used and reveals that cloud computing drives various firms to become more customer centered and focused by enabling them quickly respond needs. The author has described the potential and opportunities for cloud computing in the healthcare industry, tourism, defense and military applications and various another aspects.

SECTION 4: NETWORKS AND ENERGY EFFICIENCY IN VIRTUAL CLOUD

This section describes the concept of network and energy efficiency in cloud computing. It also explains the broadcast method based on probabilistic scheme, disaster plan in networked enterprises and provides the solution for optimum utilization of energy consumption.

Chapter 12: This chapter addresses the described problem by outlining and discussing insights from the extensive literature review to produce a generic approach for cross-management. A set of prerequisites of disaster planning is also provided with comparative analysis and arguments. The proposed approach is focused on risk assessment methodology based on Fuzzy Cognitive Map. The method is able to aggregate all assessment variables of the whole stakeholders involved in the business network. The key findings of this study aim to assist enterprises in improving risk readiness capability and disaster recovery. Finally, the author indicates the open challenges for further researches and an outlook on our future research.

Chapter 13: In this chapter, the authors are interested to introduce the different broadcast methods based on the probabilistic scheme which is simple implement code with speed broadcast and to reduce a storm broadcast problem effects and to alleviate redundancy through rebroadcast by using different routing protocols, such as AODV, DSR, LAR, PAR, that we interested in MANETs.

Chapter 14: This chapter discusses the energy efficient approaches in cloud computing environment. The energy efficiency has become the major concern for the service providers. In this chapter, the major concern is the high lightly of resource allocation challenges and there are some which will be given in the data center energy consumption. The focus is done on the power management task and even the virtualization of saving the energy.

This book is expected to assist academicians, IT professionals, researchers, industry people, advanced-level students, government officials who are working in the field cloud computing. The book is expected to serve as a reference for the postgraduate students as it offers the requisite knowledge for understanding the security, scalability issues along with different solutions. This book is based on a research studies carried out by experienced academicians and is expected to shed new insights for researchers; academicians, students and improves understanding of cloud computing.

Shadi A. Aljawarneh
Jordan University of Science and Technology, Jordan

Manisha Malhotra
Chandigarh University, India

Acknowledgment

Writing a book is a rigorous task that contains lots of attention and dedication. Firstly, we would like to pay our sincere gratitude to God for making things possible at the right time always. A word of special thanks to our family members for their constant support.

We would like to acknowledge the help of all the people involved in this book and, more specifically, to the authors and reviewers that took part in the review process. Without their support, this book would not have become a reality.

First, we extend our sincere thanks to each one of the authors for their contributions. Our sincere gratitude goes to the chapter's authors who contributed their time and expertise to this book.

Second, we wish to acknowledge the valuable contributions of the reviewers regarding the improvement of quality, coherence, and content presentation of chapters. Most of the authors also served as referees; we highly appreciate their double task.

We are very grateful to IGI Global team for giving this opportunity and believe in us. We extend our heartiest thanks and appreciate the team for providing constant technical and moral support and resources time to time. Without them this project cannot be completed.

Last but not the least we are thankful to our reader for choosing this book. We wish it would be an abundant resource for you in its domain.

Shadi A Aljawarneh
Jordan University of Science and Technology, Jordan

Manisha Malhotra
Chandigarh University, India

Section 1
Scalability Issues of Cloud Environment: Scope and Case Study

Chapter 1
Scalability for Cloud

Mohan Murthy M. K.
Nitte Meenakshi Institute of Technology, India

Sanjay H. A.
Nitte Meenakshi Institute of Technology, India

ABSTRACT

Scalability is one of the reasons behind the popularity of the Cloud. In the real IT world, resource requirement of an application varies over the time. Elastic and scalable nature of the Cloud makes it more suitable for such situation. By scaling the resources as per the resource demand, efficient resource utilization can be achieved. Vertical scaling and horizontal scaling are two different types of scaling. In vertical scaling, the virtual machine resources are scaled, and in horizontal scaling, infrastructure is scaled by adding or removing new virtual machines to it. This chapter focuses on scaling in Cloud environment, especially resource scaling for applications. The chapter starts with a brief introduction to Cloud and scaling in the cloud. After the introduction, related literature is visited. The chapter explains the necessity of scaling with real life examples. The chapter covers virtualization and some important hypervisors from the scaling perspective. The chapter also explains vertical scaling and horizontal scaling in detail.

INTRODUCTION

Cloud computing is the distributed computing model which provides software and hardware resources to the users in an on-demand way (Buyya, Yeo, Venugopal, Broberg, & Brandic, 2009). Most of the time cloud providers use pay-as-you-go

DOI: 10.4018/978-1-5225-3029-9.ch001

model where users will pay only for what they have used. Users are moving towards cloud because it offers several benefits such as scalability, elasticity, maintenance free, cost effectiveness, etc. It provides a better QoS than a traditional computing model with less initial investment.

In the cloud paradigm, based on the type of services provided, three important service models are defined: Software as a Service (SaaS), Infrastructure as a Service (IaaS), and Platform as a Service (PaaS). SaaS is a software delivery model where software and its associated data are hosted centrally and are typically accessed by users using a thin client, normally using a web browser over the Internet (Wikipedia, 2017). SaaS model is also called as "on-demand software" model. Ex – Salesforce. In infrastructure as a Service (IaaS) model, computer hardware (servers, network, storage, and data center space) are delivered as service. It may also include the delivery of operating systems and virtualization technology to manage the resources. The IaaS customer rents computing resources instead of buying and installing them in their own data center. Most of the IaaS vendors support dynamic scaling of the resources where if the customer needs more resources than expected, he/she can get them immediately, probably up to a given limit (Hurwitz, Bloor, Kaufman, & Halper, 2010), e.g., Amazon, RackSpace. Platform as a Service (PaaS), is one rank higher to IaaS in which the provider delivers more than infrastructure. PaaS offers an integrated environment to design, develop, test, deploy and support custom applications (Hurwitz et al., 2010), e.g., Windows Azure, Google App Engine.

Four important deployment models are possible in the cloud. They are Private, Public, Community, and Hybrid clouds. Private cloud is specific to an organization where within organization users can access the cloud. Public cloud is open to the large user community, where computing resources, software, storage space, etc. are given to the end users as metered services. There is a possibility that two or more organizations can set up their own cloud infrastructure. This kind of cloud is called as community cloud. The combination of private, public or community cloud is called as hybrid cloud.

Irrespective of the service or deployment models the fundamental infrastructure setup of a Cloud will be as shown in Figure 1.

Many big companies like Amazon, Rackspace have set up their data center using the model shown in Figure 1. A virtualization software is installed on top of the enormous amount of the hardware. The virtualization software helps in creating and managing the Virtual Machines (VM). Virtualization is the creation of a virtual (rather than actual) version of something, such as an operating system, a server, a storage device or network resources (Rouse, 2017). There are many virtualization applications available in the market. Some of the important virtualization software are VMware, Xen, KVM.

Figure 1. Cloud setup

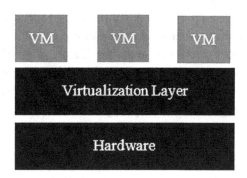

Cloud offers many benefits to the users. Some of the important benefits are listed below:

- **Less Capital Investment:** With a very little amount, users can set up the infrastructure to access the cloud services. The cloud services offered by a public cloud service provider are easily accessible by a normal desktop machine with a good internet connection.
- **Cost Effectiveness:** In the cloud world, many flexible pricing models and pricing schemes are available (Mohan Murthy, Sanjay, & Ashwini, 2012). This gives the users to choose the pricing scheme which is cost effective to them. Users will be paying only for what they use. For example, in traditional software model even though the user is going to use the software for short period of time, he should buy the full license which costs huge amount of money for software like Microsoft Office, but in cloud model the user will pay only for the duration he has used the software (Mohan Murthy et al., 2013). Though the Pay-as-you-go model is popular in cloud, user can also go for the subscription based model if he/she is interested in long term usage of cloud services.
- **Security:** In most cases, the security offered by the cloud vendors are far superior when compare to the in-house infrastructure setup.
- **Software Maintenance:** In the case of the Software as a Service model, end users need not worry about the software maintenance. Applying a patch, upgrading the software, fixing defects everything will be handled by the service provider with minimum or not interrupt in the services offered.
- **Easy Access:** A decent desktop with a good internet connection, that's all needed to access a cloud service offered by a service provider. Users can access the services from anywhere in the world around the clock.

- **Increased Availability:** More than 99.5% of availability is offered by almost all the cloud service providers. A formal SLA (Service Level Agreement) is signed with the user before services offered which make sure the QoS (Quality of Service) metrics are met. Service providers also pay the penalty, if they are not able to meet the QoS metrics which are defined in the SLA.
- **Flexibility:** The change in demand for resource requirement is easy to address in cloud computing. The cloud capacity can be easily increased or decreased based on the demand for resource requirement.

A cloud-based application's resource requirement may vary over time. To accommodate the change in resource requirement the underlying infrastructure must be scaled as per the requirement or otherwise, it might result in application performance degradation or resource wastage. Elastic nature of the cloud makes it scalable in both ways. Increasing or decreasing the cloud capacity are called as scaling up or scaling down respectively. A VM will have three main resources: Memory, CPU and Storage space. It is possible to scale these resources individually. The capacity of the virtual machine can be increased or decreased by dynamically increasing or decreasing the memory or CPU or storage space of the VM. This type of scaling is called as vertical scaling. Another type is horizontal scaling, in which the capacity of the cloud is increased or decreased by adding or removing VMs to the cloud. Horizontal scaling is more popular compare to the vertical scaling.

Along with computing resources, most of the IaaS providers also provide storage space as service ex – Amazon Simple Storage Service (Amazon S3). Massively scalable storage space is ideal for taking backup of the enormous amount of data. which is produced over time. This chapter explains the computing resources scaling in the cloud in detail.

BACKGROUND

The roots of cloud computing go back to 1950s. During that time, large mainframe computers were accessed by multiple users using dumb terminals. This arrangement is no surprise considering the cost of the mainframes during that time. Cloud computing evolved gradually from 1950. The concept of virtual machines (VM) first created during the 70s. Multiple VMs are created on a single physical hardware which allowed the multiple users to share the same hardware. By 90s telecommunication companies started offering virtualized private network (Neto, 2014). As the speed of the internet increased, accessing a remote desktop was no different from accessing an in-house desktop machine. The evolution of the cloud computing started with grid computing which is used to solve large and complex problems with parallel computing. In most cases, the grid computing was used by scientists. The concept of utility computing is also an important milestone in the evolution of the cloud computing. In utility computing, computing resources are offered as metered service. Network based subscriptions to software applications are possible because of the growth of the internet. This lead (network-based subscription) to the birth of SaaS (Software as a Service).

Cloud scalability is reflected by its capability to dynamically increase or decrease the number of server instances assigned to an application depending on the usage demand of application (Wu, Liang, & Bertino, 2009). There are research studies on application scaling prior to cloud computing. One such study (Doyle, Chase, Asad, Jin, & Vahdat, 2003) focuses on model-based resource provisioning in which single-tier applications are considered. The idea is to predict the value of candidate resource allotments under changing load using internal models of service behavior. Further studies consider multi-tier applications. In the works Urgaonkar, Shenoy, Chandra, and Goyal (2005) and Urgaonkar, Shenoy, Chandra, Goyal and Wood (2008), multi-tier applications are considered. In these works, to determine the resources needed by each tier, authors propose a queuing model based dynamic provisioning technique and a combination of predictive and reactive methods are proposed to determine when to provision these resources. To reduce provisioning overheads, authors also propose a novel data center architecture based on virtual machine monitors.

The emergence of cloud computing introduced new aspects for scalability. The workload on the enterprise applications in virtualized environments varies over time with multiple seasonal patterns and trends (Spinner et al., 2015). Even though the traditional scaling models can be used with little or no modification the nature of the cloud demanded new types of models. There are many works related to scaling in a cloud environment. Some important works are briefly explained in the next few paragraphs.

In Bi, Zhu, Tian, and Wang (2010), the authors have considered the response time of a multi-tier applications. Each tier is scaled by adding additional virtual machines to achieve the response time target. Authors consider a cluster-based virtualized multi-tier application and present a novel dynamic provisioning technique to determine the number of virtual machines at each tier in a virtualized application. The dynamic provisioning technique employs a flexible hybrid queueing model. In Iqbal, Dailey, Carrera, and Janecek (2011), to automatically detect and resolve bottlenecks in a multi-tier web applications which are hosted on a cloud, authors propose a methodology. Authors also propose a method for identifying and retracting over-provisioned resources in multi-tier cloud-hosted web applications. In the work, a working prototype system is presented.

In the study by Gong, Gu, and Wilkes (2010), the authors present a scheme called Predictive Elastic reSource Scaling (PRESS), which adjust application resource allocation automatically by extracting fine-grained dynamic patterns in application resource demands. In Shen, Subbiah, Gu, and Wilkes (2011) authors present a system called CloudScale. CloudScale automates fine-grained elastic resource scaling for multi-tenant cloud computing infrastructures. In this work by using online resource demand prediction and prediction error handling, adaptive resource allocation is achieved. In Mao, Li, and Humphrey (2010), auto-scaling of the VM instances with respect to the load, where the load is defined as the number of jobs submitted and the deadline and budget to complete the submitted jobs are considered. In the proposed system, the VM must be rebooted after scaling it. In Hung, Hu, and Li (2012), a cloud computing architecture is developed. The architecture consists of a front-end load balancer which manages the user requests by routing them to cloud services deployed in a virtual cluster. As the name suggests front-end load balancer also balances the load. The cloud architecture also consists of a virtual cluster monitor system and an auto-provisioning system. The statistics of the usage of physical resources in each virtual machine in the virtual cluster are collected using the virtual cluster monitor system. Auto-provisioning system dynamically provisions the virtual machines. It considers the number of the active sessions or the use of the resources in the virtual cluster to dynamically provisioning the virtual machines. In Dougherty, White, and Schmidt (2012), a model-driven engineering approach is presented to optimizing the configuration, energy consumption, and operating cost of cloud auto-scaling infrastructure. The main motivation here is to create greener computing environments. In de Assunção, Cardonha, Netto, and Cunha (2016), to reduce costs with resource allocation, authors propose a scheduling algorithm and auto-scaling triggering strategies considering user patience as a QoS metric.

Compare to horizontal scaling vertical scaling is more sophisticated. There are a couple of efforts related to vertical scaling. In Sedaghat, Hernandez-Rodriguez, and Elmroth (2013), the authors investigate the problem of when and how a set of allocated VMs should be repacked to a new optimal set of VMs. In work by considering cost authors propose a model to provide the required capacity. In Mohan Murthy, Sanjay, and Jumnal (2014), a threshold based auto scaling system is developed. Memory and CPU of the VM are up-scaled or down-scaled when the utilization crosses predefined threshold values. The main motivation of this work is to keep the utilization of VM in the optimal range. Spinner et. al. (2015) propose a proactive approach to memory scaling for virtualized applications. Using statistical forecasting, future workload is predicted and the virtual machine's memory size is reconfigured accordingly. Dutta, Gera, Verma, and Viswanathan (2012) proposes a hybrid model. In work, authors propose an auto-scaling framework called as SmartScale. The framework uses a combination of vertical and horizontal scaling. The main motivation is to optimize the resource usage and reducing the reconfiguration cost incurred due to scaling.

Vertical scaling can be further classified into static scaling and dynamic scaling. In static scaling, the running VM is stopped, and it is reconfigured to increase its capacity, but in dynamic scaling, the resources of a VM are scaled without stopping it. Dynamic scaling is possible only if the virtualization software supports it.

Another important solution for changing resource requirement of an application in a cloud environment is live migration. In live migration, an application hosted on a VM is migrated to a more suitable VM in terms of resources. There are couple studies related to live migration, but it is out of the scope of this chapter. This chapter focuses on scaling in the cloud.

WHY SCALING?

A simple example of an online retail shop explains the need for scaling. An online retail (for ex - Amazon) sells many items (needle to a drone) to its customers. The number of purchases will not be same in all the months. During the festive and holiday season, purchasing orders will be much more compare to the rest of the months. This is true all over the world. The vendors also organize special events to promote their sales. Black Friday in USA and Big Billion Day in the Indian subcontinent are such events. During Black Friday or Big Billion Day, the number online transactions related to online purchases will be very high. The vendors should process an enormous amount of purchasing requests. To process such a vast number of requests the vendors should scale up their infrastructure. Also during the offseason, the vendors should scale down the infrastructure as the number online orders are less. Otherwise, it results in inefficient usage of resources. The resources include computing resources as well as electricity (power).

Consider another example of airline passengers. In most cases, the airline passengers use online services to book the flight tickets. Airline service providers are using sophisticated software to manage ticket bookings. The number of online requests for booking tickets in a time period is directly proportional to the number of passengers travelling in that period. Figure 2 gives the number of passengers on all scheduled US based flights from 2003 to 2015 (Bureau of Transportation Statistics, 2016).

Figure 2 shows a steady increase in the number of passengers every year except 2008 and 2009. During 2008-2009 there is a decline in passengers because of the recession. It is evident that the number passengers traveling over the time is never a

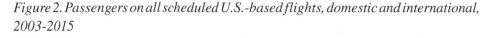

Figure 2. Passengers on all scheduled U.S.-based flights, domestic and international, 2003-2015

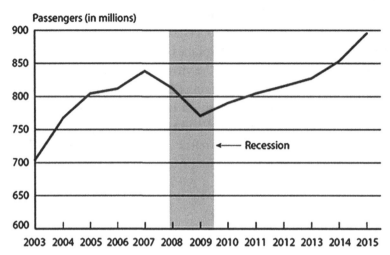

constant. As the number of passengers increases, airlines can expect an increase in online requests for booking flight tickets. To accommodate the increase in requests the underlying infrastructure which is used to process these requests must be scaled or otherwise it will result in long processing time for a request. After some threshold level, the server might crash. It creates a bad reputation for the airlines and eventually airlines will run out of business.

The online retail and airline examples clearly explain the necessity of the scaling. In traditional computing model scaling up is done by adding more resources to the infrastructure. However, in some cases, the infrastructure will have an upper limit on how much it can be scaled. The cost of expanding the infrastructure is higher in this model. Scaling down is always a big problem in traditional computing model because it results in unused hardware. This ultimately affects the ROI (return on investment). Cloud computing addresses these issues successfully. Upscaling has virtually no limit in public cloud, and downscaling is done within no time. The cloud service provider charges only for what end users have used. In the examples explained if the online retail vendor and airlines have hosted their software on the cloud, they can easily upscale and downscale the underlying infrastructure as per their requirement. The reduced power consumption which results from downscaling helps the data center/ cloud to become environment-friendly.

HYPERVISORS

In computing, virtualization refers to the act of creating a virtual (rather than actual) version of something, including virtual computer hardware platforms, storage devices, and computer network resources (Wikipedia, 2017). In virtualization, hypervisor plays an important role. A hypervisor which is also called as virtual machine monitor is a software which creates and runs the virtual machine. There are two types of hypervisor: Type 1 hypervisor and Type 2 hypervisor. Type 1 hypervisors are also called as bare metal hypervisors. They are directly installed on top of the hardware as shown in Figure 3. Type 2 hypervisors are installed on top of the host operating system as shown in Figure 4. During the initial days of virtualization, Type

Figure 3. Type 1 hypervisor

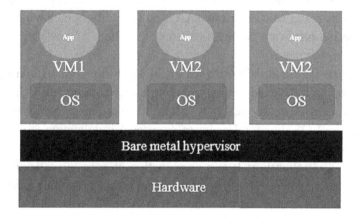

Figure 4. Type 2 hypervisor

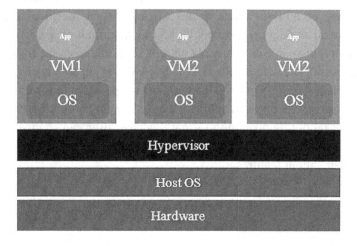

2 hypervisors were popular. Later Type 1 hypervisors started gaining popularity because of their efficiency.

The virtual machine created is also called as virtual guest, the operating system installed in the VM is called as guest OS. The actual machine which is virtualized to created multiple VMs is called as host machine. The OS installed in host machine is called as host OS.

There are different types of virtualization: para virtualization, full virtualization, hardware assisted virtualization, and hybrid virtualization.

- **Para Virtualization:** In para virtualization, the guest OS is aware that it is running in a virtualized environment and it will have necessary drivers to interact with the hardware. The hardware commands are directly issued to the host OS.
- **Full Virtualization:** In full virtualization, the guest OS is not aware that it is running in virtualized environment. Guest OS will not be having the drivers to issue the hardware commands it takes the help of host OS to issue the hardware commands.
- **Hardware Assisted Virtualization:** In hardware assisted virtualization, hardware will have additional capabilities to support full virtualization. Usually microprocessor supports special instructions set which can be used by the guest OS directly. Hardware Assisted Virtualization is very efficient compare to other types of virtualizations.
- **Hybrid Virtualization:** It is a combination of para virtualization and full virtualization, where part of guest OS is aware that it is running in a virtualized environment and other part is unaware of it.

From the scaling perspective whether it is horizontal scaling or vertical scaling, hypervisor plays an important role. It provides necessary API/tools to add additional virtual machine or add resources to an existing virtual machine in horizontal scaling or vertical scaling respectively. In scaling an admin or a user instructs the hypervisor by typing some command or clicking on some icon, the hypervisor will take care the rest of the action. Most of the hypervisors support horizontal scaling and static vertical scaling. Only few hypervisors support dynamic vertical scaling. For example, Xen server gives an option of dynamic memory control (DMC). Using DMC, without rebooting a running virtual machine, user can change the amount of host physical memory assigned to it. Table 1 lists some important hypervisors along with their salient features.

Table 1. Hypervisors and their features

#	Hypervisor Name	Virtualization Types Supported	Support for Dynamic Resource Allocation	Support for Live Migration	Open Source/ Proprietary
1	Xen Hypervisor	Paravirtualization, Hardware Assisted Virtualization, Full Virtualization	Yes	Yes	Open Source
2	KVM	Paravirtualization, Hardware Assisted Virtualization, Full Virtualization	No	Yes	Open Source
3	VMWare VSphere enterprise edition	Paravirtualization, Hardware Assisted Virtualization	Yes	Yes	Proprietary
4	IBM PowerVM enterprise edition	Full Virtualization	Yes	Yes	Proprietary
5	Microsoft Hyper-V Server 2008 R2 SP1	Operating System Virtualization, Hardware Assisted Virtualization, Full Virtualization	Yes	Yes	Proprietary
6	Linux V-Server	Operating System Virtualization	Yes	Yes	Open Source

HORIZONTAL SCALING

In horizontal scaling resources are scaled by adding or removing VMs. Figure 5 shows the horizontal scaling (upscaling).

Horizontal scaling is more suitable for cloud based enterprise applications. For example, consider a cloud based enterprise application which processes the online reservation requests for flight tickets. The number of such requests varies over the time.

Figure 5. Before and after horizontal scaling

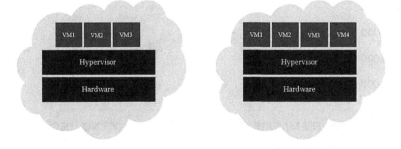

Figure 6 shows the number of US citizens travelling to international region each month from 2011-2016. As mentioned earlier the number of online requests to book flight tickets in a period is directly proportional to the number of air passengers travelling in that period. From the Figure 8 we can conclude that during the June to August time frame the number of requests are highest and during February it is lowest. Usually, enterprise application which processes web requests are hosted on application servers. As the number of requests processed by these application servers increases they need more resources to process them, otherwise response time will start growing. In cloud when the number of requests is larger, by adding VMs the response time can be kept under check. During the lower requests time one or more VMs can be removed to minimize the resource wastage.

Horizontal scaling is also done to meet the QoS criteria. For example, to minimize the response time in case of an enterprise web application which is hosted on the cloud, horizontal scaling is done. In case of a N tier application, each tier can be horizontally scaled by allocating or deallocating virtual machines to that tier.

Horizontal scaling is always limited to the actual resources available in the physical host. The distribution of the actual resources among the virtual machines plays an important role in the performance of the host applications. Prior knowledge of the resource utilization statistics of a virtual machine helps in proper allocation of the resources to that virtual machine. Hypervisors provides various control mechanisms using which one can control the allocation of resources to the virtual machines.

Figure 6. US citizens travelling to international region each month (2011-2016)

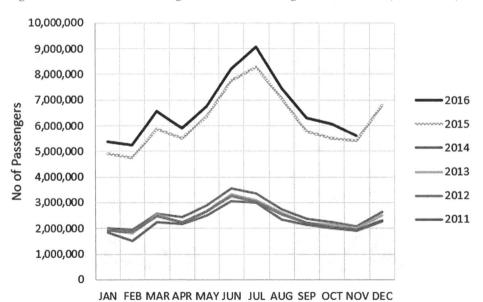

VERTICAL SCALING

Vertical scaling is more suitable when the resource requirement of the application does not change dramatically. It is also very useful in a private cloud environment where multiple users are given access to VMs. The resource requirement of the application which is hosted on the VM may vary over time, also user may run different types of application (a simple MS word to a sophisticated account software) in a VM. In such cases if the VM instance capacity is fixed there is a high possibility of mismatch between the VM capacity and application resource requirement. If the allocated resources to a VM are more than the application resource requirements, then resources will be wasted, on the other hand if the allocated resource to a VM are less than the application resource requirements, then the application performance will degrade. In such cases, vertical scaling is very useful. Instead of creating a new VM, if an existing VM is scaled, the unnecessary overhead of creating a new VM and the resources which are used to manage the new VM can be avoided. This type of individual VM scaling is called as vertical scaling. Figure 7 depicts vertical scaling. VM1 is up-scaled by adding new resources to it. The bigger VM signifies it is having more capacity in terms of resources (CPU, Memory, Storage).

As mentioned earlier there are two types of vertical scaling: static and dynamic vertical scaling. Both are limited by the availability of the actual underlying hardware resource. Almost all the hypervisors support static vertical scaling and only few support dynamic vertical scaling. Usually hypervisor provides special command set to support vertical scaling. Using these commands user can increase or decrease resources allocated to a VM. For example, Xen Server (Xenserver, 2017) provides special commands under Dynamic Memory Control (DMC), using them users can dynamically increase or decrease memory of a VM within specified limits.

Xen Server supports two types of memories: static and dynamic. Both are having minimum and maximum range. The static memory maximum is the upper limit of

Figure 7. Before and after vertical scaling

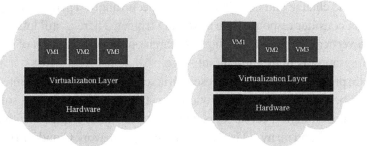

13

the physical memory which can be accessed by the guest operating system from the time the guest boots up until the time the guest shuts down again. It is not possible to change static memory when the VM is running. But the dynamic memory can be changed when the VM is running provided that the static max memory is always greater or equal to dynamic max memory.

In Xen Server, CPU scaling can be done by modifying the CPU cap or CPU weight. The CPU cap optionally fixes the percentage of CPU cycles a virtual machine will be able to consume. The cap is expressed in percentage of one physical CPU: 100 is one physical CPU, 50 is half a CPU, 200 is 2 CPUs, etc. The default value of CPU cap is 0 which means there is no upper cap. The allocation of the physical CPU to a virtual machine can also be controlled by CPU weight parameter. CPU weight of a VM decides how much CPU is allocated to that VM. A virtual machine with a weight of 512 will get twice as much CPU as a virtual machine with a weight of 256 on the host machine. Valid range for CPU weight is from 1 to 65535. The default value is 256. The CPU can also be scaled by adding additional virtual cores to it. The CPU cap and weight controls the actual physical CPU time/ cycles allocated to the virtual machine adding the virtual core simply adds a virtual core to the CPU of the virtual machine. If there enough resources are not available on the host machine adding virtual cores will not improve the performance of the hosted applications, in-fact it may degrade the performance of the hosted applications due to the resources required to manage the additional core.

RESEARCH DIRECTIONS

Whether it is vertical or horizontal scaling, there are two important questions to answer. 1) When to scale? 2) How much to scale? It is in this direction most of the research works are focused. Utilization, SLA, QoS, Profit are the major factors considered by the researchers as scaling triggers. When the utilization or load on the VM or the actual physical hardware crosses a predefined threshold, it is used as a trigger for scaling. In horizontal scaling after scaling the load balancer should take care of the change and distribute the load accordingly. There are few research works which consider response time as scaling trigger. There is still lot of scope for research in vertical and hybrid scaling. Research on the combination of the scaling with live migration is in its early infant stage.

The main problem with the cloud research is setting up the environment. A simple desktop can be set up as a private cloud by installing a virtualization software in it but that is not enough if researchers want to conduct experiments with multiple physical machines and many VMs. The simulation framework CloudSim (2017) can be used to conduct experiments in such cases. CloudSim is an extensible, generalized, java based simulation framework that enables seamless modelling and simulation of app performance. An improved version of CloudSim called as CloudSim Plus (2017) can also be used to conduct cloud related experiments.

CONCLUSION

Scalability and elasticity are two important features of Cloud. Scaling the resources up or down as per the user requirement is easy in Cloud. The resource requirement of an application varies over time in the real IT world. This may lead to resource wastage or application performance degradation if the resources are fixed. This issue can be addressed by scaling the resources as per the requirement. The ability to scale on demand is one of reasons for the popularity of cloud computing. Even in a private cloud, scaling plays an important role in minimizing the resource wastage without compromising the application performance. In horizontal scaling resources are scaled by adding or removing VMs and in vertical scaling individual VM is scaled by adding more resources to it. Both are having their own advantages and disadvantages. Hypervisor plays an important role in both types of scaling. Only few hypervisors support dynamic vertical scaling. Whether it is horizontal scaling or vertical scaling, triggering factors for scaling are important. Utilization, SLA, QoS, Profit are considered as major factors to trigger the scaling.

There are many research works related to scaling in cloud. Most of them are focused on horizontal scaling. There are couple of efforts related to vertical scaling and hybrid scaling. There is a lot of research scope in the hybrid models where hybrid models constitute of the different combinations of horizontal scaling, vertical scaling, and live migration. In this chapter, a brief history of Cloud computing is discussed and the necessity of scaling is explained with real life examples. Some important works in the area are covered and a brief introduction to virtualization and different types of hypervisors are given in the chapter. Horizontal and vertical scaling are explained in detail. Finally, the research directions related to cloud scalability are discussed.

REFERENCES

Aljawarneh, S., Aldwairi, M., & Yassein, M. B. (2017). Anomaly-based intrusion detection system through feature selection analysis and building hybrid efficient model. *Journal of Computational Science*. doi:10.1016/j.jocs.2017.03.006

Aljawarneh, S., Yassein, M.B. & Talafha, W.A. (2017). A multithreaded programming approach for multimedia big data: Encryption system. *Multimed Tools Appl.* <ALIGNMENT.qj></ALIGNMENT>10.1007/s11042-017-4873-9

Aljawarneh, S. A., Alawneh, A., & Jaradat, R. (2017). Cloud security engineering: Early stages of SDLC. *Future Generation Computer Systems*, *74*, 385–392. doi:10.1016/j.future.2016.10.005

Aljawarneh, S. A., Moftah, R. A., & Maatuk, A. M. (2016). Investigations of automatic methods for detecting the polymorphic worms signatures. *Future Generation Computer Systems*, *60*, 67–77. doi:10.1016/j.future.2016.01.020

Aljawarneh, S. A., Vangipuram, R., Puligadda, V. K., & Vinjamuri, J. (2017). G-SPAMINE: An approach to discover temporal association patterns and trends in internet of things. *Future Generation Computer Systems*, *74*, 430–443. doi:10.1016/j.future.2017.01.013

Bi, J., Zhu, Z., Tian, R., & Wang, Q. (2010). Dynamic Provisioning Modeling for Virtualized Multi-tier Applications in Cloud Data Center. In *3rd International Conference on Cloud Computing* (pp. 370-377). Miami, FL: IEEE. doi:10.1109/CLOUD.2010.53

Buyya, R., Yeo, C. S., Venugopal, S., Broberg, J., & Brandic, I. (2009). Cloud computing and emerging IT platforms: Vision, hype, and reality for delivering computing as the 5th utility. *Future Generation Computer Systems*, *25*(6), 599–616.

Dias de Assunção, M., Cardonha, C. H., Netto, M. A. S., & Cunha, R. L. F. (2016). Impact of user patience on auto-scaling resource capacity for cloud services. *Future Generation Computer Systems*, *55*, 41–50. doi:10.1016/j.future.2015.09.001

Dougherty, B., White, J., & Schmidt, D. C. (2012). Model-driven auto-scaling of green cloud computing infrastructure. *Future Generation Computer Systems*, *28*(2), 371–37. doi:10.1016/j.future.2011.05.009

Doyle, R. P., Chase, J. S., Asad, O. M., Jin, W., & Vahdat, A. M. (2003). Model-based resource provisioning in a web service utility. In *4th conference on USENIX Symposium on Internet Technologies and Systems* (vol. 4, pp. 5-5). Seattle, WA: ACM.

Dutta, S., Gera, S., Verma, A., & Viswanathan, B. (2012). SmartScale: Automatic Application Scaling in Enterprise Clouds. In *3rd International Conference on Cloud Computing* (pp. 221-228). IEEE. doi:10.1109/CLOUD.2012.12

Gong, Z., Gu, X., & Wilkes, J. (2010). PRESS: PRedictive Elastic ReSource Scaling for cloud systems. In *International Conference on Network and Service Management* (pp. 9 – 16). IEEE.

Hung, Hu, & Li. (2012). Auto-Scaling Model for Cloud Computing System. *International Journal of Hybrid Information Technology, 5*(2).

Hurwitz, J., Bloor, R., Kaufman, M., & Halper, F. (2010). *Cloud Computing for Dummies*. Wiley.

Iqbal, W., Dailey, M. N., Carrera, D., & Janecek, P. (2011). Adaptive resource provisioning for read intensive multi-tier applications in the cloud. *Future Generation Computer Systems, 27*(6), 871–879. doi:10.1016/j.future.2010.10.016

Kalpana, G., Kumar, P. V., Aljawarneh, S., & Krishnaiah, R. V. (2017). Shifted Adaption Homomorphism Encryption for Mobile and Cloud Learning. *Computers & Electrical Engineering*. doi:10.1016/j.compeleceng.2017.05.022

Mao, M., Li, J., & Humphrey, M. (2010). *Cloud Auto-scaling with Deadline and Budget Constraints*. Brussels: IEEE. doi:10.1109/GRID.2010.5697966

Mohan Murthy, Ameen, Sanjay, & Yasser. (2013). Software licensing models and benefits in Cloud Environment: A Survey. In *International Conference on Advances in Computing* (*vol. 174*, pp. 645-650). Springer. doi:10.1007/978-81-322-0740-5_76

Mohan Murthy, M. K., Ashwini, J. P., & Sanjay, H. A. (2012). Pricing Models and Pricing Schemes of IaaS Providers: A Comparison Study. In *International Conference on Advances in Computing, Communications and Informatics* (pp. 143-147). ACM. doi:10.1145/2345396.2345421

Mohan Murthy, M. K., & Sanjay, H. A., & Anand, J. (2014). Threshold Based Auto Scaling of Virtual Machines in Cloud Environment. In Lecture Notes in Computer Science: Vol. 8707. *IFIP International Conference on Network and Parallel Computing* (pp. 247-256). Springer. doi:10.1007/978-3-662-44917-2_21

Neto. (2014). *A brief history of cloud computing*. Retrieved on December 16, 2017, https://www.ibm.com/blogs/cloud-computing/2014/03/a-brief-history-of-cloud-computing-3/

Rouse, M. (n.d.). *Virtualization*. Retrieved on March 1, 2017, from http://searchservervirtualization.techtarget.com/definition/virtualization

Sedaghat, M., Hernandez-Rodriguez, F., & Elmroth, E. (2013). A Virtual Machine Re-packing Approach to the Horizontal vs. Vertical Elasticity Trade-off for Cloud Autoscaling. In *Proceedings of the ACM Cloud and Autonomic Computing Conference*. Miami, FL: ACM. doi:10.1145/2494621.2494628

Shen, Z., Subbiah, S., Gu, X., & Wilkes, J. (2011). CloudScale: elastic resource scaling for multi-tenant cloud systems. In *2nd ACM Symposium on Cloud Computing*. Cascais, Portugal: ACM doi:10.1145/2038916.2038921

Singh, A., Juneja, D., & Malhotra, M. (2015). A Novel Agent Based Autonomous Service Composition Framework for Cost Optimization of Resource Provisioning in Cloud Computing. In JKSU-CIS. Elsevier Publisher.

Singh, A., & Malhotra, M. (2015). Evaluation of a Secure Agent based optimized Resource Scheduling Framework in Cloud Environment. IJCAR, 188-198.

Singh, A., & Malhotra, M. (2016). Hybrid Two Tier Framework for Improved Security in Cloud Environment. India-Com, 1601-1606.

Singh, A., & Malhotra, M. (n.d.). A Novel Agent Based Framework for Cost Optimization in Cloud Computing Environment. *International Journal of Cloud Applications*, 53–61.

Spinner, S., Herbst, N., Kounev, S., Zhu, X., Lu, L., Uysal, M., & Griffith, R. (2015). Proactive Memory Scaling of Virtualized Applications. In *8th International Conference on Cloud Computing* (pp. 277-284). New York: IEEE.

Urgaonkar, B., Shenoy, P., Chandra, A., & Goyal, P. (2005). Dynamic provisioning of multi-tier internet applications. In *Second International Conference on Autonomic Computing* (pp. 217 – 228). Seattle, WA: IEEE. doi:10.1109/ICAC.2005.27

Urgaonkar, B., Shenoy, P., Chandra, A., Goyal, P., & Wood, T. (2008). Agile dynamic provisioning of multi-tier Internet applications. *ACM Transactions on Autonomous and Adaptive Systems*, *3*(1), 1–25. doi:10.1145/1342171.1342172

Wikipedia. (n.d.). *Software as a Service*. Retrieved on December 1, 2016, from http://en.wikipedia.org/wiki/Software_as_a_service

Wu, J., Liang, Q., & Bertino, E. (2009). Improving Scalability of Software Cloud for Composite Web Services. In *International Conference on Cloud Computing* (pp. 143 - 146). Bangalore, India: IEEE. doi:10.1109/CLOUD.2009.75

Chapter 2
Role of Agents to Enhance the Security and Scalability in Cloud Environment

Manisha Malhotra
Chandigarh University, India

Aarti Singh
Guru Nanak Girls College, India

ABSTRACT

Cloud computing is a novel paradigm that changes the industry viewpoint of inventing, developing, deploying, scaling, updating, maintaining, and paying for applications and the infrastructure on which they are deployed. Due to dynamic nature of cloud computing it is quite easy to increase the capacity of hardware or software, even without investing on purchases of it. This feature of cloud computing is named as scalability which is one of the main concern in cloud environment. This chapter presents the architecture of scalability by using mobile agents. It also highlights the other main issues prevailing in cloud paradigm. Further it presents the hybrid architecture for data security which is also the one of major concern of it. This chapter mainly highlights the solution for scalability and security.

INTRODUCTION

Cloud Computing incorporates virtualization, on-demand deployment; Internet based delivery of services and use of open source software. In contrast to the use of already established concepts, approaches and best practices, Cloud Computing is a novel

DOI: 10.4018/978-1-5225-3029-9.ch002

paradigm that changes the industry viewpoint of inventing, developing, deploying, scaling, updating, maintaining, and paying for applications and the infrastructure on which they are deployed. Due to dynamic nature of cloud computing it is quite easy to increase the capacity of hardware or software, even without investing on purchases of it. From last few years, cloud computing has become a promising business concept. All existing business applications are complicated in nature and much too expensive. To run these applications there is a need of data centers having supporting staff and infrastructure like bandwidth, networks and server etc. along with a dedicate team for its execution. For deploying such kind of applications, organizations have to invest large amount of funds which makes it difficult for small businesses to establish themselves. Therefore, cloud computing provides a simple alternative to start IT based business organization with much less initial investment. Although cloud computing offers significant edge of the traditional computing methods but the data which is being continuously transferred to cloud is actually *Big Data* (Chen et al., 2014). In fact, in order to handle the data received cloud owners need to have skilled analytics and also they must ensure that all clients get their due resources well in time and should satisfy the need. In order to automate the data centers, cloud owners are now moving towards deploying mobile and intelligent agents. The current work has thus been motivated by the emergent requirements of improving resource scheduling and cost optimization algorithms in cloud computing. The work aims to exploit mobile agents to overcome the barriers.

The chapter is therefore structured into three major parts. It begins by providing brief overview of cloud computing and issues prevailing in the cloud computing. The promises of mobile agents have been highlighted justifying them as enablers to the barriers so far projected in the success of cloud computing. Finally, it provides the solution for stringent security in cloud environment.

CLOUD COMPUTING

Cloud basically stands for **C**ommon **L**ocation-independent **O**nline **U**tility service, available on-**D**emand. It supports huge amount of virtual workload of resources including communicative environment for user. Cloud computing thus offers computing technologies being offered at cloud. Cloud computing offer lots of advantages over traditional computing such as online resources, offline access, flexibility, savings, just to name a few (see Figure 1).

Cloud computing includes everything that already exists (Armbrust et al., 2009). It is distributed into three segments namely, applications, platforms and "infrastructure". Majorly, the definition of cloud computing specifically revolves round the terms like scalability, pay-per use model, and virtualization.

Figure 1.

In fact, enablers supporting cloud computing are interoperability, portability, integration of components, ease of deployment, pay as per use, economic, rapid provisioning and elasticity and so on. Because of the appealing features mentioned above, cloud computing is becoming a temptation for all business organizations.

Besides the various features that cloud computing supports, there are few barriers also that are acting as hurdles towards the complete adoption of cloud computing by the business community. For instance, cloud computing architecture (Armbrust et al., 2010) is service based architecture, i.e., it offers Software as a Service (SaaS), Platform as a Service (PaaS) and Infrastructure as a Service (IaaS). While SaaS allows the consumer to use desired software from the cloud infrastructure, the PaaS provides resources such as operating system and software development frameworks. On the other hand, IaaS provides the facility of virtual environment having virtual machines, storage, virtual networks and essential computing resources. Now, each service layer is equipped with certain inherent issues such lack of transparency about storage and security and integrity of data at software as well as platform level. Although IaaS provides primary security in the form firewall, load equilibrium. The design issues presented above majorly highlight the concerns related to security in cloud computing. Therefore, one of the prime objectives of this research work is to address these security issues pertaining to each layer.

ISSUES IN ADOPTION OF CLOUD COMPUTING

Referring to the literature (Armbrust et al., 2010), we could identify that there are many issues such as technological issues, business issues, performance issues and few miscellaneous issues are prevailing in the wide adoption of cloud computing. Figure 2 depicts the issues and are being discussed as follows.

Technological Issues

This domain highlights on technological issues of cloud computing. The main focus is on some inherent issues which involve some following areas:

Figure 2.

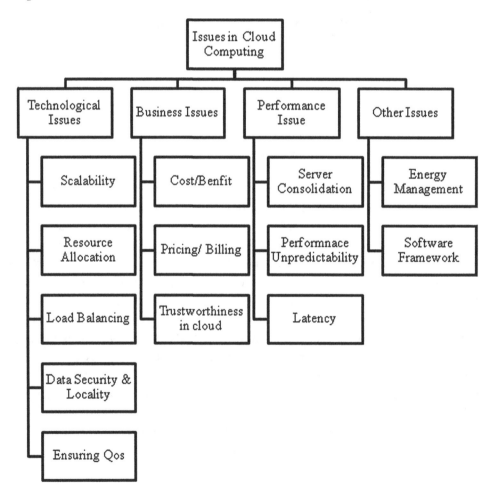

- **Scalability in Cloud Computing:** Cloud Computing delivers scalability platform. Cloud scalability has the capability to vigorously scale up and scale down the number of server instances which is assigned to a request depending on the demand of user. Whenever any cloud service will deploy on server, it can be extent on multiple servers.
- **Resource Allocation:** In cloud computing, according to user demands, the resources will provide as a service which is led by service level agreement (SLA) (Zhang & Cheng, 2010). Due to wastage of resource, there is a need of resource allocation technique because of high demand of resources which is definitely will share and most of requests are heterogeneous. Therefore, resource allocation and scheduling is one of the major issue of cloud computing.
- **Load Balancing:** Load Balancing is one of the key research areas which make resources effectively distributed. Many load balancing algorithms have been developed in this field; still there is need of improvement in lacking part.
- **Data Security and Locality:** Whenever customers use cloud application, his major concern is about the data storage and its locality. Data assurance must be there that no one accesses the customer's data without legitimate permission (Yang & Tate, 2009).
- **Ensuring Quality of Service by Migration of Virtual Machines:** It ensures that service providers deliver better quality of services. It mainly concerned about the allocation of virtual machines (VM) to job assigned by user. Effective QOS outcomes can be in the form of minimum processing time of the data center, virtual machine cost, data transfer cost and overall response time. There should be an optimized algorithm which considers minimum processing time and total VM cost.

Business Issues

As it is well known that cloud computing is the business model, so during its implication there are many issues which need to be considered. It mainly involves:

- **Return on Investment (ROI) Cost/Benefit:** It is mainly focus on user's side. The main of researchers is to optimize the cost and benefit for migrating computing tasks over the clouds (Yang & Tate, 2009). Such efforts can further help users while choosing cloud services.
- **Pricing/Billing:** It mainly focuses on providers' side. Researchers focus on developing pricing and billing models for cloud providers in order to retain customers at the same time guarantee profits for the providers (Armbrust et al., 2009, 2010).

- **Trustworthiness in the Cloud:** Cloud brokers are the bridge between the customers and cloud service providers. Customer depends heavily on the cloud broker and deciding the right cloud broker and evaluating its trustworthiness are major challenges.

Performance Issues

This issue is regarding the performance of a data center which further depends on servers and operators handling the requests.

- **Server Consolidation:** For taking maximum benefits of resource utilization, server consolidation is an effective way by minimizing the energy consumption. In case of single server, all VMs set to an energy saving state except the executing VM. Due to this, resource congestion takes place by changing footprints in VM on data center and by sharing of resources. It can be helps to select the effective server consolidation. Whenever the resource congestions are occurred in server, it works fast and effectively.
- **Performance Unpredictability:** In cloud computing with the help of virtualization, VM can easily share CPU, and memory, but it is quite difficult to share I/O. again using virtualization, I/O interrupts is the best solution to improve the performance of operating system. Multiple VMs are hold workload of I/O interrupts randomly. So, it is quite difficult to check the performance especially in a batch processing.
- **Latency:** It is also one of the important research issues of cloud computing that affect the performance of a server. Latency increases with the rapid use of cloud based applications.

Other Issues

- **Energy Management:** Performance of server depends upon the energy efficiency. Cost of powering and cooling is 53% of total operational cost (Foster et al., 2008). Infrastructure provider must reduce the energy consumption as well as cost for accounting energy. The main aim is to achieve the good performance of a data center by reducing energy.
- **Software Framework:** Cloud computing is the better option for hosting data intensive applications. It uses Hadoop architecture for scalable applications and use Map Reduce architecture for fault tolerance. Although Map Reduce architecture supports heterogeneous nodes but design of a suitable job scheduling algorithm which works for every node is still an open challenge.

All above unfolded challenges reveals that there is an ample of scope in the field of cloud computing. This chapter considers resource allocation, load balancing, data security issues and have made an attempt to propose solutions adjacent to these issues.

As already mentioned that business organizations i.e. the cloud providers are now making a shift towards deploying mobile agents to improve the performance of cloud technology. Next section provides an overview of mobile agents and also describes the feasibility of mobile agents in cloud computing.

MOBILE AGENTS: AN OVERVIEW

A Mobile Agent (MA) is a software module that performs a desirable task in a heterogeneous network by migrating autonomously from one machine to another. MAs are being used as mediators between users and devices (Danny, 1998). Figure 3 illustrates interaction of mobile agents with their environment.

A mobile agent inherits features from distributed computing and artificial intelligence fields. Mobile agents have already been deployed successfully in many distributed and web based tasks because of their appealing attributes such as mobility, dynamic, portable etc. Table 1 delineates the features of mobile agents.

Characteristics of MAs reveals that these can be used anywhere in any technology. Some of the most pertinent applications of mobile agents in different fields are shown in Figure 4.

Multi agent system (MAS) referred as comprising of multiple interacting intelligent agents within an environment. MAS is used to perform difficult problems for an individual agent or a monolithic system. Intelligence may include some methodic,

Figure 3.

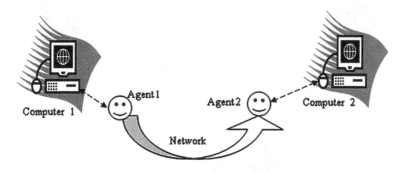

Table 1.

Attributes	Description
Overcomes Network Delay	Only one time connection has to be established when agents have to migrate first time. Thus agents can work on limited bandwidth and reduce network delay.
Autonomous	Agents can operate without interference of user.
Asynchronous	Once mobile agents have been initialized and assigned a specific task, they leave their source location computer system and roam freely through internet.
Dynamic	They can initiate and destroy themselves.
Cooperative	Agents can cooperate with each other in cyberspace to achieve their goals and to provide services to their beyond their specified capabilities.
Robust	Agents can cooperate with each other in cyberspace to achieve their goals and to provide services to their beyond their specified capabilities.
Fault Tolerant	Due to usage of multiple agents, agent system has a tolerance for failure of limited number of agents. If an agent is being lost during execution then system can reproduce another copy of that agent or can assign the same task to another agent.
Protocol Encapsulation	Agents can make their own protocol and encapsulate the data.
Social	Agents interact with each other by agent technologies like Tool Command Language (TCL), Jade etc.
Reactive	Agents perceive their environment and react according to command given by user
Proactive	Agents can take initiative and make changes in their environment.
Veracity	Agents are expected to communicate with each other without floating false information.

Figure 4.

functional, procedural or any algorithmic approach. Agents in MAS may choose to cooperate, direct other agents and migrate from machine to machine.

Due to the features and applications of mobile agents mentioned above, these are widely deployed in different field like distributed computing, grid computing, artificial intelligence, wireless sensor networks and semantic web. Incorporation of mobile agents improves the efficiency of system in different field as well as in different concerns. Authors have (Singh & Malhotra, 2012) amalgamated the mobile agents in cloud computing, since by deploying mobile agents the network traffic got reduced and at the same time response time could also be reduced. In contrast to this, in traditional system of cloud, every request is sent directly on WWW which leads to increase in network traffic, the amalgamated replica of mobile agent was created which could be migrated from one end to another. Figure 5 shows the amalgamation of mobile agents in cloud computing.

SCALABILITY IN CLOUD ENVIRONMENT

This work concentrates on guaranteeing adaptability in cloud computing in circumstances where either the assets of the cloud have been depleted or it cannot give administrations to more client or the asked for assets are not accessible with it. This work is being proficient in two sections: first is to look another group cloud to

Figure 5.

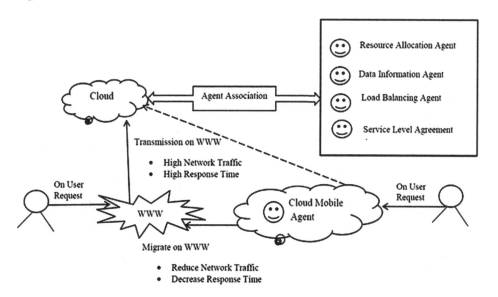

fulfill the demand close by and besides to scan for nearest datacenters with minimum reaction time of virtual machines (VM). The proposed system makes utilization of mobile agents to accomplish the objective. The proposed structure connects a mobile agent with every open/private cloud, which contains the data about that cloud, for example, different assets accessible with the cloud and it additionally monitors free and designated assets. Consequently, at whatever point an administration ask for lands to a cloud, agent checks the accessible free assets to choose whether the demand can be served or not. The proposed structure involves cloud mobile agent and directory agent as appeared in Figure 6.

- **Cloud Mobile Agent (MA$_C$):** It is related with each cloud and is in charge of keeping up asset data and also their status anytime, whether it is free or allocated.
- **Directory Agent (DA$_C$):** DA$_C$ keeps record of all MA$_C$ enlisted with it, alongside abilities of the mists. At whatever point a cloud is made its MAc should get enrolled with a DAc, which keeps up their database fundamental for giving versatility in administration.

Initially the MAc sends an enlistment demand to closest DAC alongside data of the cloud with which it is related, accordingly the DAC sends back an affirmation flag showing that the MAc has got enlist with it. Figure 7 clarifies this procedure.

Presently at whatever point a public/private cloud turns out to be excessively over-burden, making it impossible to deal with another client ask for then the versatility highlight is practiced to give administrations to the client through some

Figure 6.

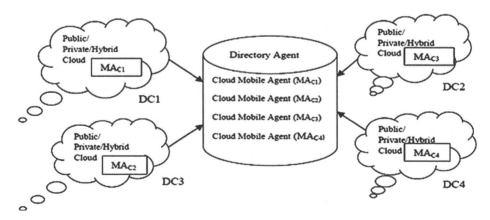

Figure 7.

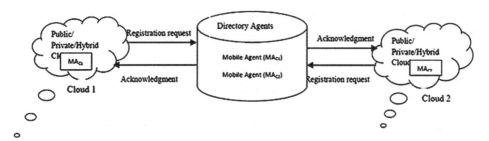

other cloud. In such circumstance MAc gets enacted and sends demand to registry specialist requesting for the rundown of other MAc equipped for giving the coveted administration. The catalog operator on getting this demand seeks its database and gives the rundown of able MAcs. On getting the rundown from the DAC the initiator MAc sends benefit demand to them and sits tight for their reaction. In the event that some cloud having the required assets ends up noticeably prepared to give the administrations, it reacts back to the initiator MAc. Initiator MAc checks all the got reactions, performs transaction with concerned MAcs and afterward at long last doles out the close in response to popular demand to the MAc most appropriate both, as far as less cost and quicker administrations.

As we know cloud computing research is still in its initial stages and there are many challenges still prevailing in it. The issues highlighted earlier need attention from research community and mobile agents may be instrumental in solving some

Figure 8.

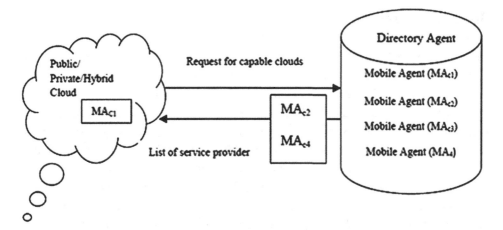

of those issues. This research work has deployed mobile agents in cloud computing and this is unique contribution of this research work. Next section discusses the various security issues prevailing in cloud computing.

SECURITY ISSUES AND RESOLUTIONS

Infrastructure as a Service (IaaS), particularly data storage is one of important service given by a cloud. Single client and business associations are moving their data on cloud as a result of simple accessibility and lessened cost offered by it. Be that as it may, sparing information at a remote server is much the same as giving your cash to somebody, since in today's computerized period, information is the foundation of handling. In this manner, with all the adaptability offered by cloud, genuine security concerns have additionally been produced. Security concerns are creating impediment for business associations to move altogether to open mists.

Recently, there is expanded consideration from research and business community towards developing an effective security measures in cloud environment. Some association like Cloud Security Alliance (CSA), European Network and Information Security Agency (ENISA) (Funmilade et al., 2012), Cloud Computing Interoperability Group and Multi-Agency Cloud Computing Forum are working towards giving viable and proficient controls to give data security in cloud condition. Some imperative security concerns winning in this area are information security, protection, data accessibility, trust management and so on. Be that as it may, as of late parcel of specialists have proposed systems for enhancing data security yet at the same time there is degree for research toward this path. This work investigates security issues in cloud paradigm and exemplifies existing algorithms for the same.

Security Issues Unveiled

Cloud is a web based administration worldview where clients get to different administrations from Cloud service provider (CSP) through web. At whatever point client signs in a cloud and begins getting to different administrations, data trade begins amongst client and CSP. To the extent security of data traded is concerned, just distributed storage is not concerned. There are in certainty different levels where security rupture may occur and trustworthiness of data might be bargained.

Figure 9 outlines different levels of security worries in cloud condition.

Each level focused on some key issues. All levels have their own significance and need measure up to consideration for guaranteeing general hearty security in cloud situations. Figure 10 highlights different levels requiring security alongside concerns basic.

Figure 9.

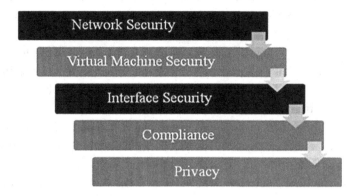

Figure 10.

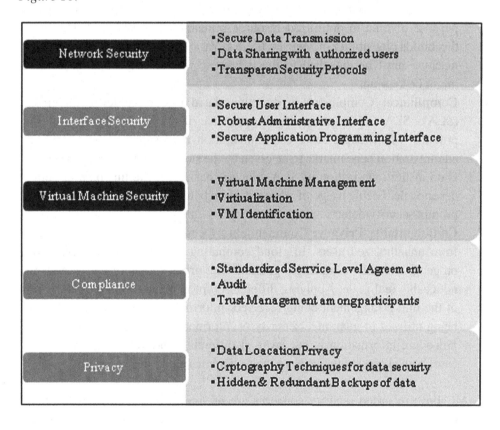

- **Network Security:** While transferring data from one network to another, cloud service providers must ensure about robust and secure communication protocol to avoid network attack on data.

- **Interface Security:** It is concerned with the interface given by cloud suppliers and level of security offered by it. VM interface influences the inalienable security elements, for example, IBM Blue Mix is a cloud benefit in view of Linux and Microsoft Azure depends on Windows operating system. Linux working framework is more secure when contrasted with Microsoft Windows. In this way interface security would be better with Linux based interface. Hence interface offered by CSP ought to send secure working environment.

- **Virtual Machine Security:** VM security is of most extreme worry among all security concerns. Clients make utilization of VM for their processing assigned jobs. Further, a cloud makes utilization of Multi-tenancy strategy, i.e., same VM and assets are being utilized by various clients at various purpose of time to optimized resource utilization and VM cost. However, this builds plausibility of security breaks. Various clients of a solitary virtual machine must be detached to the degree so that secrecy of an individual might be kept up.

- **Compliance:** Compliance is directly related to service level agreement (SLA). SLA is the main legal certificate between the client and the provider which expresses the administration necessities of the client and administration benchmarks to be given by the supplier. Be that as it may, there is no institutionalization of SLA which is basic to make this plan of action dependable. Feeble usage of administration benchmarks by the supplier may prompt security defects.

- **Confidentiality/Privacy:** Confidentiality focuses on preventing client data from unauthorized users. In cloud computing all information is put away on geographically accordingly guaranteeing privacy of information ends up noticeably real issue. Applying different cryptographic techniques is the run of the mill arrangement being received. Information part is another method being utilized to guarantee security of information at supplier's end. In this procedure information is put away at different non-interfacing has. In any case, both above strategies have their own intrinsic issues.

All above recorded security concerns are of significance at various levels of correspondence with cloud. CSP needs to guarantee security at all levels, which is an extreme undertaking. Next segment investigates existing answers for above security concerns.

THE SECURITY ALGORITHMS: RELATED WORK

In concentrated on system mindfulness and reliable streamlining of asset allotment procedures and highlighted the exploration issues winning in this field. Creators stressed that more endeavors are required to make the current execution models prescient and responsive. Safiriyu et al. (2011) proposed a client character administration convention (UIDM) in cloud worldview. It suits all partners, i.e., end clients and suppliers. It gives validation, encryption and key administration component. They have tried frail, solid and extremely solid client personality and watched more disappointment if there should arise an occurrence of powerless IDM. Zhen et al. (2013) proposed a community oriented system security model framework utilized as a part of a multi-inhabitant server farm. They have utilized a brought together community oriented plan alongside bundle review at various levels of security. It shields the server farm from all conceivable system assaults. This unified security focus can convey security principles and gather information from the systems. In any case, the proposed model needs in recognition of system arrangement infringement.

Philipp et al. (2013) has built up a stage which guarantees the incorporated security and enhanced information handling known as Virtual Fort Knox. This item is reasonable for little and medium ventures. It gives physical security like get to control, assurance from altering of physical server and in addition insurance against disappointment of chairman.

The instrument introduced in a design which builds the security of virtual machine. The engineering is partitioned into two sections one is refresh checker design and another is online entrance suite engineering appeared in Figure 11. Refresh checker distinguishes the obsolete data introduced on virtual machine. Second one sweeps every single virtual machine and boot them if there is requirement for it. Assist, report generator is another part which produces the consequences of defects (as far as hazard level) in the wake of gathering all reports from scanner.

With the assistance of this report the blunder can undoubtedly be recognized and expelled. However, both these designs can be correlated just on Linux condition. Be that as it may, there is need of a nonspecific engineering which can chip away at each condition.

Sapuntzakis et al. (2008) built up a component which allots virtual machines naturally. The proposed conspire has averted security breaks however does not permit updation of all bundles of virtual machines. Qian et al. (2011) proposed a cloud information stockpiling engineering that gives open auditable cloud component which serves to looks at capability and capacities of information proprietor to

Figure 11.

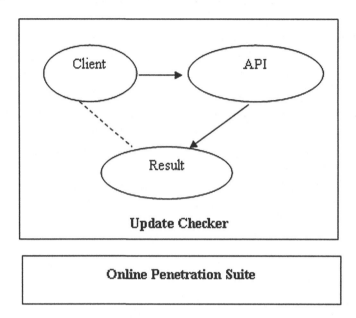

survey the danger of outsource information with the assistance of outside review party. The proposed engineering involves four segments viz., information proprietor, client, cloud server and Third Party Auditor (TPA). It gives a component in which information proprietor delegate TPA to review the cloud server in successful and cost productive route for end clients, when it is required. With regards to security, it is not totally secure as it appears in light of the fact that the examining totally depends on TPA and information proprietors. Here the question emerge that if the proprietor and TPA are not conveying right answer to client, then will's identity in charge of that.

These systems (Yassa et al., 2012) proposed a dynamic information driven design which is equipped for limiting the SLA infringement by discharging asset arrangement. In the proposed design, the creators have concentrated just on asset discharging yet consideration towards security is lacking. Cloud Security Alliance checks all administration systems and review approaches for guaranteeing great security in distributed computing. It discharges new strategies with the assistance of National Institute of Standards and Technology (NIST) and Information Systems Audit and Control Association (ISACA).

Ryoo et al. (2013) exhibited a review on need of security in distributed computing. As of now, the greater part of the offices are chipping away at HDFS engineering which depends on ace slave hub. Ace hub is named as namenode and slave hub is named as datanodes. All information is recreated thrice and put away on datanodes.

As per this review, all get to control of datanodes are overseen by a solitary point i.e. namenode which can be a reason for disappointment. They gave a model three lines of barrier as appeared in Figure 12. These are validation security at first level, encryption and security insurance at second level and quick recuperation at third level.

Authentication layer is utilized for client check with the assistance of advanced mark and encryption calculation is conveyed at second layer. Third layer utilizes quick recuperation calculation for recouping the information.

Huiqi et al. (2014) proposed Random Space Perturbation (RASP) strategy and Nearest Neighbor (kNN) which address the four primary perspectives information classification, inquiry security, proficient question handling and low preparing cost. Creators played out a trial under a danger model and found the outcomes giving more productivity at diminished cost. In any case, this strategy experienced information spillage and frail question security.

Hossein et al. (2013) introduced Encryption as a Service (Eaas) for guaranteeing the security at CSP. In this approach, a private cloud is being made by utilizing Message Authentication Code (MAC) for uprightness. This approach depends on multi-threading forms. Each single string hits proportionately on a parallel area and produces group of strings after encryption. Notwithstanding, this system works effectively just if the program had been composed in multi-threading style, generally the execution gets diminished. The portrayal of this model is appeared in Figure 13.

Xu et al. (2005) proposed an operator based trust display which guarantees the unwavering quality and validity. As appeared in Figure 14, the Trustworthy Agent Execution Chip (TAEC) engineering gives high security and deals with sensor hub by utilizing operator innovation. Before sending the information from hub A to hub B, it encodes the information by applying TAEC. Initially hub A gets the trust testament from TAEC Manufacturer (TAECM) which contains open key, security

Figure 12.

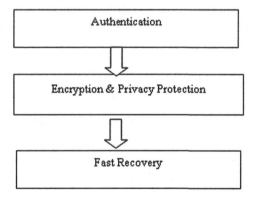

Figure 13.

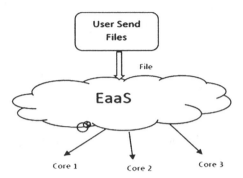

Figure 14.

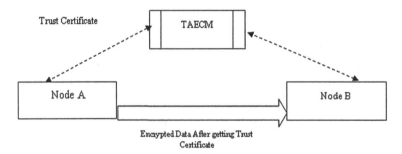

technique, and TAEC sort. After check of computerized mark, information is exchanged to hub B. Because of osmosis of specialists the proposed demonstrate moves toward becoming stage autonomous, however the use of advanced mark diminish the effectiveness of model.

Wang et al. (2013) proposed an examining instrument in cloud condition known as Public Auditing for shared information (PANDA) with productive client repudiation. The reason behind the client disavowal is that if a similar client would approach the cloud in denial period, the private key is produced and the information must be re-marked with private key. Due to this registering, time increments and productivity diminishes.

Authors have illustrated that with the help of virtualization (Quan et al., 2015) how we can increase the security of cloud. Virtualization protects the integrity of VM and IaaS components. A new intrusion detection system has been proposed as a security business flow language (Doelitzscher et al., 2012). It is the first prototype which provides the cloud security. This mechanism uses autonomous agents and made the SaaS architecture very flexible. The protocol that has been used for providing services is user identity management protocol (UIDM). It provided the security after checking the authenticity and authorization of user in networks.

Few other works concerning the security issues and solutions are available in Zissis et al. (2012). The authors have tried to mention all aspects of security that were need to be concerned. They have designed a framework which cures all kind of vulnerabilities and threats. They have migrated all kind protection to a third party which took care of all these things. Orellana et al. 2010 proposed a new transparent layer which encrypts the data before storing it on google server. The authors have presented a solution particularly for google server to store google docs. The user can select the security algorithm. After selecting the algorithm, the data would be converted into cipher text and would be stored in google server. Results shows that blowfish has smaller key size and faster speed as compared to other algorithms. However, all algorithms discussed are symmetric algorithms which are less secure than asymmetric algorithms.

Villalpando et al. (2014) proposed a methodology for detecting the different kind of attack that can be related to co-residency and network stress. These attacks could harm the kernel layer of cloud environment. To detect the above said attack, the method has implemented Smith Waterman Genetic Algorithm. Another author has proposed tracing the kernel layer of VM where each VM is traced simultaneously. The algorithm could detect the interaction between threads of VM on a core machine. For ensuring security, user authentication protocol is also quite promising. The protocol is based on identity based cryptography overcoming the weaknesses of its descendants.

A critical look at the literature reflects that there is strong need of a novel model which could address the open issues in cloud especially resource optimization, load balancing and a strong security mechanism to ensure security, integrity and authorization of user data stored on cloud. It also indicates that limited research had been carried out towards various security issues dominant in cloud. Thus, there is still ample scope of research in this dimension.

PROPOSED ARCHITECTURE

This architecture provides strong security of data placed in cloud and to ensure that even CSP can't breach this security. Literature survey highlighted that Blowfish and ECC techniques are best in symmetric and asymmetric key cryptography segments. These techniques make use of much small key sizes compared to existing techniques. This work proposes the combined use of above two encryption algorithms having smaller key sizes to provide stronger security than existing. Cryptography is traditionally accepted method of ensuring data security. It is the mechanism to secure data by converting it into non-readable form. There are two types of cryptography algorithms: symmetric and asymmetric key algorithms. Symmetric algorithms use only one key i.e. private key which is used for both encryption and decryption of data. In asymmetric algorithm, there are two keys, one is private and another is public key. Public key is used for encrypting the data and private key is used for decryption of data. Asymmetric algorithms are more secure than symmetric algorithm because in asymmetric algorithms both keys are different and leakage of one single key can't cause harm to the encrypted data. Presently cloud service providers are making use of triple DES technique for security which is symmetric key cryptography technique. There are two major agents used in this architecture whose description is as follows:

- **Crypto Agent (CA):** This agent is responsible for encryption and decryption of data at client end. It is equipped with user's set of keys. Whenever a user gets registered with a cloud service provider (CSP), CA exchanges its Elliptic Curve Cryptography (ECC) public Key with ECC public key of cloud service provider agent. When user sends some data to cloud data center, CA encrypts it using encryption mechanism adopted, on receiving some data from DC, CA decrypts it before providing it to user.
- **Cloud Service Provider Agent (CSPA):** This agent is responsible for interacting with CA of user. It receives encrypted data from the user, places it in cloud data base. It also keeps record of user ECC public key in server key log file. Whenever user requests for its data, it authenticates user, performs necessary encryption decryption process and then sends data to the user.

As far as threat of security breach from CSP is concerned, security mechanism must provide data decryption control to user only, even CSP should not be able to decrypt data in any way; it is possible with use of symmetric key cryptography; however, in case of symmetric key technique, algorithm complexity is less but security is also low. Whereas in case of asymmetric key algorithms complexity is more and security of data while travelling in network is also more. However, if asymmetric key mechanism is opted in CC, then one part of key would be saved with CSP, which is a constant threat for the users.

This architecture presents hybrid two tier security engine henceforth termed as HT2SE, it is an agent based framework which uses both types of encryption i.e. symmetric and asymmetric in combination, before sending data to CSP. This mechanism has two layers, first layer makes use of symmetric key algorithm i.e.

Blowfish to encrypt data, this key would only be known to the user. Output of the first layer would be processed by second layer, which would again encrypt it with asymmetric key ECC, for this layer ECC private key will be with user and corresponding public key will be with CSP.

Figure 15 provides high level view of HT2SE architecture where first layer makes use of symmetric key algorithm BF and second layer makes use of asymmetric key algorithm ECC.

Whenever a user wants to keep his/her data on the cloud, the user will need to get encryption keys from the standard authorities. Every user will receive a set of two keys as shown in equation below:

$$Key_i = \left\{ BF_i, \left\{ ECC_{prti}, ECC_{pubi} \right\} \right\}$$

Here BF_i refers to symmetric key of ith user, this key is known and used by user only. ECC_{prti} refers to asymmetric private key of ith user, this key is known and used by user only. ECC_{pubi} refers to asymmetric public key of ith user, this key is known and kept with the CSP.

In the same way, a CSP will also acquire the above set of keys for it, to be used at its end. Now whenever user has to save his/her data on cloud, it will first encrypt it with its BF_i, ciphertext obtained after encryption is again encrypted using ECC_{prti} before sending it to CSP. ECC_{pubi} of the user is available with the CSP, however even if CSP wishes to decrypt data for some reason, it can only decrypt data to one level only, because first level symmetric key of the user is unknown to the CSP.

Figure 15.

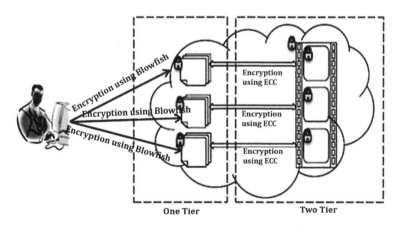

39

This way threat of security decreases and data security threats due to multi-tenancy in cloud may be resolved.

Figure 16 provides detailed architecture of proposed HT2SE framework and illustrates working of crypto and CSP agents, which are responsible for encryption / decryption at user and cloud service provider's end respectively:

After user registration, whenever data is received from the cloud user for storage on cloud database, CA gets activated. It first applies Blowfish algorithm for converting original data into cipher form in level 1 and then it applies ECC private key to encrypt cipher text obtained from level 1 to encrypt it for the second time. It then sends this data for travel in the network and its subsequent storage in cloud database. When data reaches cloud data center, CSPA gets activated, it fetches user ECC public key stored in Server key log and decrypts data to level1 and then saves it in cloud data center data base. Whenever data is required by a particular user, CSPA fetches requested data, encrypts it for the second time using its own ECC private key and sends it on the network. This way data is always double protected while travelling in the network and both encryption keys can't be hacked as they are distributed. Further, CSPA encrypts its Server key log file using its own BF symmetric key which is kept with this agent only. This is an additional safety measure, however since CSP is an agent, it is also vulnerable to attack possible for other software components. But even compromising CSP can't solve purpose of the hacker since data placed in data center data base is still encrypted by BF keys of various users which are unknown to CSP. This way security of user data placed in cloud data centre is enhanced to a high level.

The algorithms of Crypto agent and Cloud Service Provider Agent are presented in Table 2 and 3.

Figure 16.

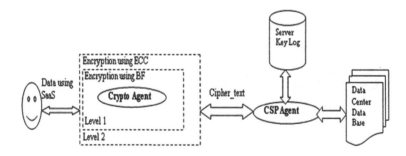

Table 2.

Crypto Agent (CA)
Input: Ordinary Data from User/ Cipher Text from DC; Set of user keys $Key_i = \left\{ BF_i, \left\{ ECC_{prti}, ECC_{pubi} \right\} \right\}$; *Output:* Cipher Text/ Ordinary Data

CA ()
{
If (incoming_data == ordinary data)
{
CA applies BF_i (Plain_text);
CA applies ECC_{pubi} (cipher_text$_1$);
Forward cipher_text$_2$ to CSPA();
}
Else
{
Decrypt cipher_text$_2$ with $ECC_{pub\text{-}csp}$;
Decrypt cipher_text$_1$ with BF_i of user;
}
}

Table 3.

Cloud Service Provider Agent()
Input: Cipher Text *Output:* Store Data into DC Database; Fetch Data from DC Database;

CSPA ()
{
Receive <cipher_text, ECC_{pubi} >;
Store <cipher_text> in database;
Update server_key_loag_file;
If(user_demands_data)
{
CSPA checks authenticity;
If (successful)
{
Apply ECC_{pubi} for decyption;
CSPA apply $C_{prt\text{-}csp}$;
Convert data into cipher form;
Forwards cipher text to CA();
}
Else
Send message<unsuccessful> to CA ;
}
}

CONCLUSION

This chapter exemplifies the concept of cloud in the era of academia and industry. it express the various applications of cloud computing which can be application in different areas. Apart from it, this chapter lights on the various issues like technological, business, performance and other miscellaneous issues prevailing in cloud environment. Further it illustrates the concept of mobile agents and their benefits of adoption of them in different technologies. It also explains the incorporation of mobile agents in cloud computing. This chapter explains that how agents can ensure scalability in cloud computing environments. Scalability is one of the main feature if cloud which can be employing mobile agents. Algorithm for implementing the agents involved is also provided. The second part of this chapter focused on security issue of cloud. Data security is one of the most debated and important issue in Cloud computing. Although cloud service providers claim of providing high level of security but still there are increasing number of incidents of security breaches in cloud environments. For increasing trust of user in cloud, there is dire need of robust security mechanism. However, cloud service providers are still using traditional symmetric key algorithms for data security and not providing much transparency on the security algorithms being deployed. This work presents a hybrid two tier security engine which combines symmetric and asymmetric key algorithms, further the algorithms deployed have already proved their excellence for lesser time and better speed of encryption. Future work aims to focus on providing security solutions for other levels of cloud computing.

REFERENCES

Aljawarneh, S., Aldwairi, M., & Yassein, M. B. (2017). Anomaly-based intrusion detection system through feature selection analysis and building hybrid efficient model. *Journal of Computational Science*. doi:10.1016/j.jocs.2017.03.006

Aljawarneh, S., Yassein, M.B., & Talafha, W.A. (2017). A multithreaded programming approach for multimedia big data: encryption system. *Multimed Tools Appl.* <ALIGNMENT.qj></ALIGNMENT>10.1007/s11042-017-4873-9

Aljawarneh, S. A., Alawneh, A., & Jaradat, R. (2017). Cloud security engineering: Early stages of SDLC. *Future Generation Computer Systems*, *74*, 385–392. doi:10.1016/j.future.2016.10.005

Aljawarneh, S. A., Moftah, R. A., & Maatuk, A. M. (2016). Investigations of automatic methods for detecting the polymorphic worms signatures. *Future Generation Computer Systems*, *60*, 67–77. doi:10.1016/j.future.2016.01.020

Aljawarneh, S. A., Vangipuram, R., Puligadda, V. K., & Vinjamuri, J. (2017). G-SPAMINE: An approach to discover temporal association patterns and trends in internet of things. *Future Generation Computer Systems*, *74*, 430–443. doi:10.1016/j.future.2017.01.013

Armbrust, M., Fox, A., Griffith, R., Joseph, A., Katz, R., Konwinski, A., . . . Stoica, M. (2009). Above the Clouds: A Berkeley View Of Cloud Computing. UC Berkeley Reliable Adaptive Distributed Systems Laboratory, 1-23.

Armbrust, M., Fox, A., Griffith, R., Joseph, A. D., Katz, R. H., & Konwinski, A. (2010). A View of Cloud Computing. ACM Communication, 53(4), 50–58.

Banerjee, C. (2012). Framework ON Service Based Resource Selection In Cloud Computing. *International Journal of Information Processing and Management*, *3*(1), 17–25. doi:10.4156/ijipm.vol3.issue1.2

Chen, K., Shen, M., & Zheng, W. (2005). Resources Allocation Schemas For Web Information Monitoring. *Tsinghua Science and Technology*, *10*(3), 309–315. doi:10.1016/S1007-0214(05)70074-2

Chen, M., Mao, S., & Liu, Y. (2014). Big Data: A Survey. *Mobile Networks and Applications*, *9*(2), 171–209. doi:10.1007/s11036-013-0489-0

Danny, B. (1998). Mobile Objects And Mobile Agents: The Future Of Distributed Computing. *12th European Conference on Object-Oriented Programming*, *1445*, 1-12.

Doelitzscher, F., Reich, C., Knahi, M., Passfall, A., & Clarke, N. (2012). An Agent Based Business Aware Incident Detection System For Cloud Environments. *Journal of Cloud Computing: Advances Systems and Applications*, *1*(9), 239-246.

Flavio, L., & Roberto, D. P. (2011). Secure Virtualization For Cloud Computing. *Journal of Network and Computer Applications*, *41*(1), 45–52.

Foster, I., Yong, Z., Raicu, I., & Lu, S. (2008). Cloud Computing And Grid Computing 360-Degree Compared. *Workshop on Grid Computing Environments*, 1-10. doi:10.1109/GCE.2008.4738445

Funmilade, F., Rami, B., & Georgios, T. (2012). A Dynamic Data Driven Simulation Approach For Preventing Service Level Agreement Violations In Cloud Federation. *International Conference on Computational Science Procedia of Computer Science*, 1167-1176.

Gebai, M., Giraldeau, F., & Dagenais, M. R. (2014). Fine Grained Preemption Analysis for Latency Investigation Across Virtual Machines. *Journal of Cloud Computing: Advances System and Applications*, *3*(23), 1–15.

Gonzalez, N., Miers, C., Redigolo, F., Carvalho, T., Naslund, M., & Pourzandi, M. (2012). A Quantitative Analysis Of Current Security Concerns And Solutions For Cloud Computing. *Journal of Cloud Computing: Advances, System and Applications*, 1-11.

Goyal, O., Pandey, A., & Sahai Waters, B. (2006). Attribute-Based Encryption For Fine-Grained Access Control Of Encrypted Data. *ACM Conference Computer Communication Security*, 89–98. doi:10.1145/1180405.1180418

Hossein, R., Elankovan, S., Zulkarnain, M. A., & Abdullah, M. Z. (2013). Encryption As A Service As A Solution For Cryptography In Cloud. *International Conference on Electrical Engineering and Informatics indexed in Science Direct*, 1202-1210.

Huiqi, X., Shumin, G., & Keke, C. (2014). Building Confidential And Efficient Query Services In The Cloud With Rasp Data Perturbation. *IEEE Transactions on Knowledge and Data Engineering*, *26*(2), 322–335. doi:10.1109/TKDE.2012.251

Jungwoo, R., Syed, R., William, A., & John, K. (2013). Cloud Security Auditing: Challenges And Emerging Approaches. *IEEE Security and Privacy*, 1–13.

Kalpana, G., Kumar, P. V., Aljawarneh, S., & Krishnaiah, R. V. (2017). Shifted Adaption Homomorphism Encryption for Mobile and Cloud Learning. *Computers & Electrical Engineering*. doi:10.1016/j.compeleceng.2017.05.022

Kumarswamy. (2009). Cloud Security And Privacy: An Enterprise Perspective On Risks And Compliances. Academic Press.

Lamb, C. C., & Heileman, G. L. (2012). Content Centric Information Protection In Cloud Computing. *International Journal of Cloud Computing and Services Science*, *2*(1), 28–39.

Li, Chinneck, Wodside, & Litoiu. (2009). Fast Scalable Optimization To Configure Service System Having Cost And Quality Of Service Constraints. *IEEE International Conference on Autonomic System Barcelona*, 159-168 doi:10.1145/1555228.1555268

Loke, S. W (1999). A Technical Report On: Mobile Agent Technology For Enterprise Distributed Applications: An Overview And An Architectural Perspective. *CRC for Distributed Systems Technology*, 1-45.

Matos, M., Sousa, A., Pereira, J., & Oliveira, P. (2009). Clon: Overlay Network For Clouds. *Third Workshop on Dependable Distributed Data Management*. doi:10.1145/1518691.1518696

Moharana, S. S., Ramesh, R. D., & Powar, D. (2013). Analysis Of Load Balancers In Cloud Computing. *Computing in Science & Engineering*, *2*(2), 101–108.

Morikawa, T., & Ikebe, M. (2011). Proposal And Evaluation Of A Dynamic Resource Allocation Method Based On The Load Of Vms On Iaas. *4th IFIP International Conference on New Technologies, Mobility and Security, 5*(6), 1–6.

Orellana, L., Silva, D., & Castineira, F. (2010). Privacy For Google Docs: Implementing A Transparent Encryption Layer Cloud Views. *International Conference on Cloud Computing*, 41-48.

Philipp, H., Rolf, W., Joachim, S., & Thomas, B. (2013). Virtual Fort Knox: Federative Secure And Cloud Based Platform For Manufacturing. *46th Conference on Manufacturing System indexed in Science Direct*, 527-532.

Qian, W., Cong, W., Kui, R., Wenjing, L., & Jin, L. (2011). Enabling Public Auditability And Data Dynamics For Storage Security In Cloud Computing. *IEEE Transactions on Parallel and Distributed Systems*, *22*(5), 847–859. doi:10.1109/TPDS.2010.183

Quan, Z., Chunming, T., Xianghan, Z., & Chunming, R. (2015). A Secure User Authentication Protocol For Sensor Network In Data Capturing. *Journal of Cloud Computing: Advances System and Applications*, *4*(6), 1–12.

Ryoo, J., Rizvi, S., Aiken, W., & Kissell, J. (2013). Cloud Security Auditing: Challenges And Emerging Approaches. *IEEE Security and Privacy*, 1–13.

Safiriyu, E., Olatunde, A., Ayodeji, O., Adeniran, O., Clement, O., & Lawrence, K. (2011). A User Identity Management Protocol For Cloud Computing Paradigm. *Int J Commun Network Syst Sci*, *1*(4), 152–163.

Sapuntzakis, C., Brumley, D., Chandra, R., Zeldovich, N., Chow, J., Lam, M., & Rosenblum, M. (2008). Virtual Appliances For Deploying And Maintaining Software. *17th USENIX Conference on System Administration*, 181–194.

Singh, A., Juneja, D., & Malhotra, M. (2015). A Novel Agent Based Autonomous Service Composition Framework for Cost Optimization of Resource Provisioning in Cloud Computing. In JKSU-CIS. Elsevier.

Singh, A., & Malhotra, M. (2012). Analysis For Exploring Scope Of Mobile Agents In Cloud Computing. *International Journal of Advancements in Technology*, *3*(3), 172–183.

Singh, A., & Malhotra, M. (2015). Analysis Of Security Issues At Different Levels In Cloud Computing Paradigm: A Review. *Journal of Computer Networks and Applications*, *2*(2).

Singh, A., & Malhotra, M. (2015). Evaluation of a Secure Agent based optimized Resource Scheduling Framework in Cloud Environment. IJCAR, 188-198.

Singh, A., & Malhotra, M. (2016). Hybrid Two Tier Framework for Improved Security in Cloud Environment. India-Com, 1601-1606.

Singh, A., & Malhotra, M. (n.d.). A Novel Agent Based Framework for Cost Optimization in Cloud Computing Environment. *International Journal of Cloud Applications*, 53–61.

Villalpando, L. E. B., April, A., & Abran, A. (2014). Performance Analysis Model For Big Data Applications In Cloud Computing. *Journal of Cloud Computing*, *4*, 3–19.

Wang, B., Li, B., & Li, H. (2013). Panda: Public Auditing For Shared Data With Efficient User Revocation In The Cloud. *IEEE Transaction*, 1-14. Retrieved from http://www.thinkgrid.com/docs/computing-whitepaper.pdf

Wiese, L. (2014). Clustering Based Fragmentation And Data Replication For Flexible Query Answering In Distributed Databases. *Journal of Cloud Computing*, *2*, 3–18.

Yang, H., & Tate, M. (2009). Where Are We At Cloud Computing? A Descriptive Literature Survey. Association for Information System, 807-819.

Yang, K., & Jia, X. (2013). An Efficient And Secure Dynamic Auditing Protocol For Data Storage In Cloud Computing. *IEEE Transactions on Parallel and Distributed Systems*, *24*(9), 1717–1726. doi:10.1109/TPDS.2012.278

Yassa, M. M., Hassan, H. A., & Omara, F. A. (2012). New Federated Collaborative Network Organization Model (FCNOM). *International Journal of Cloud Computing and Services Science*, *1*(1), 1–10.

Yuefa, D., Bo, W., Yaqiang, G., Quan, Z., & Chaojing, T. (2009). Data Security Model For Cloud Computing. *International Workshop on Information Security and Application New York*, 141-144.

Zhang, C., & Sterck, H. D. (2009). Cloudwf A Computational Workflow System For Cloud Based For Hadoop. *Lecture Notes in Computer Science, 5391*, 393–404. doi:10.1007/978-3-642-10665-1_36

Zhang, Q., & Cheng, L. (2010). Cloud Computing: State-Of-The-Art And Research Challenge. *Raouf Boutaba J Internet Serv Appl*, 7-18.

Zhen, C., Fuye, H., Junwei, C., Xin, J., & Shuo, C. (2013). Cloud Computing-Based Forensic Analysis For Collaborative Network Security Management System. *Tsinghua Science and Technology, 18*(1), 40–50. doi:10.1109/TST.2013.6449406

Zissis, D., & Lekkas, D. (2012). Addressing Cloud Computing Security Issues. *Future Generation Computer Systems, 28*(3), 583–592. doi:10.1016/j.future.2010.12.006

Chapter 3
Computer Centres Resource Cloud Elasticity– Scalability (CRECES):
Copperbelt University Case Study

Jameson Mbale
Copperbelt University, Zambia

ABSTRACT

The Copperbelt University Computer Centre runs five physical servers 24/7 throughout the academic year calendar. These machines consumed a lot of resources such as electricity used to run and cool them. In addition, the Computer Centre employed a lot of technicians to run, maintain and service the named servers. All the discussed costs were incurred throughout the year including the idle workload period when there was very little work to be processed. It was against that background the Computer Centres Resource Cloud Elasticity-Scalability (CRECES) was envisaged to only use one physical server during idle workload period. It was at such periods when the Computer Centre carried a rapid elasticity to scale down on the huge server resource utilisation. Similarly, at peak workload time the centre carried a rapid elasticity to scale up by producing many virtual hardware and software resources just from a single server to five virtualised ones. Hence, the capacity of the Centre to scale up and down resources acted as a cost serving measures in utilising the hardware and software resources.

DOI: 10.4018/978-1-5225-3029-9.ch003

INTRODUCTION

The larger capital expenditure of the Copperbelt University comes from the running of the Computer Centre, which provides the information communication technology (ICT) or information technology (IT) services to the entire institution community. Currently the Centre has five (5) physical servers that have been consuming a lot of expenditure on electricity which is used to power on the machines 24/7. The electricity is also used to cool the five servers and room ventilation. In addition, the Computer Centre employed a lot of technicians to run, maintain and service the named servers. All the discussed costs are incurred throughout a twelve month academic year calendar including the idle workload period. All this causes overheard costs even when the same number of machines is running whilst there is less workload being processed. It is in view of that the Computer Centres Resource Cloud Elasticity-Scalability was envisaged and in this work referred to and abbreviated as CRECES. The CRECES scales up or down the hardware and software resources either during the peak or idle workload periods to reduce the cost of production. For instance during the idle period that stretches from April to October, the Computer Centre shall only use one server in this case referred to as host server. In this way, fewer resources shall be used, hence very little electricity will be required to run a single machine. During the peak workload period, the host server shall be virtualised, to yield five guest servers that will process all the institution workloads at a low cost of production.

The CRECES has an 'inthahs' which is composed of the Host Operating System, Type 2 Hypervisor, and Guest Operating System. These technologies during the peak period produce five virtual guest servers that process huge amount of workload. These guest servers operate imitating the host machine. At this time, all the university workload is simultaneously processed. The other benefit of the CRECES, is that less manpower shall be maintained and this shall reduce the labour costs. As currently, the university still pays same salaries to the large workforce even during the idle workload period.

Problem Statement

The Coperbelt University like any other academic institutions in the sub-Saharan region is none profit making organisation. The institution is experiencing a lot of overhead costs to run the everyday operations of the Computer Centre. The Computer Centre is an university unit which provides the institution with Information Technology (IT) services such as Internet resources, systems for processing examinations, salaries, student registration and printing. Other functions include processing teaching, tutorial and research materials. However to accommodate the storage of the university's huge data, the Centre requires a number of hardware equipment such as mail, SQL, Salaries, examination, human resource and security servers. To maintain the capacity of such data in terabytes under the traditional system is very costly. As the University spent a lot of money to run and maintain just a single server and what more on several of them as listed above. As a result, most of the university's budget goes to run the services of the Computer Centre. It is against this background that the University envisaged on CRECES, a system whose hardware and software resources are either scaled up or down depending to the size of the workload. The CRECES uses the technologies of elasticity, scalability, virtualisation and Type 2 Hypervisor to produce and increase the number of virtual guest servers during the peak workload period. These resources process the large volume of workload at a very minimal cost of production. Similarly, when the workload reduces, the virtual guest servers are scaled down to a single host machine. In that way the cost of production is reduced drastically hence managing the hardware and software resources at a low cost of production. The CRECES yields a number of benefits that include affordable university operation budget, efficiency in processing of examination, registration, and research data. Others benefits include the capacity building, but to mention a few. Others include upgrading of technician, technology acquisition and capacity building.

Objectives of CRECES Model

The CRECES model was developed in accordance with the following objectives:

- Design and build the CRECES model.
- Purchase and install only a single high-quality host server.
- Install the Type 2 Hypervisor software into host server to facilitate the functionalities of the hardware and operating system.
- Configure the 'inthahs' to facilitate the functionality of the elasticity, scalability and virtualisation.
- Configure the host server to adapt to the scaling up and down of the hardware and software resources either during peak workload or idle workload periods to reduce the cost of production.
- Automate the scaling up and down of the hardware and software resources during the peak workload and idle workload periods.
- Automate the scheduling of scaling up and down of the workload resources on the academic calendar.
- Identify the occurrence of idle and peak workloads in a twelve-month academic year calendar.

- Virtualise the existing single server into five guest virtual resources that include: examination, registration, web, research and mail servers.
- Use the five virtualised guest servers to reduce the production costs during the peak workload periods.
- Use only the host server during the idle workload periods for cost serving measures.
- Employ only a few technicians to manage a single host server, as this will reduce the high labour expenditures.
- Add hardware and software resources during operation in order to improve throughput.
- Install the anti-virus to protect the host server from malicious attack.
- Train or upgrade the Computer Centre technicians to manage the CRECES.

Organisation of the Chapter

The reset of the Chapter is organised as follows: the next Section is the Literature Review which looks at similar technologies that deals with the scaling up and down of the resources during pick and idle workload period. This Section is presented by discussing the highlights of the following technologies: elasticity, scalability, virtualisation, Comparison Between Elasticity and Scalability, Comparison Between Virtualisation and Hypervisor and hypervisor. This is followed by the Section The CRECES Model which demonstrates the functionalities of all the components involved. Its inner component the 'inthahs' has the capacity to produce and replicate virtual guest resources utilising its virtualisation mechanism. The next is Implementation of CRECES Section which describes the source of the information that is processed by CRECES and it emanates from the respective schools and institute of the university. This is followed the Section Discussion which analyses the volume and percentage of workloads that are processed either during the peak or idle periods. The Conclusion Section summarises the functions and benefits of using the CRECES Model.

LITERATURE REVIEW

The cloud elasticity, scalability and virtualisation as an effort to dynamically reduce the deployment of many hardware resources that are costly to maintain, has also been discussed by other researchers. These three key concepts are very close in giving the interpretation of the cloud phenomena or mechanism in the form of adaption processes.

Elasticity

Herbst et al. (2013) described elasticity as "The degree to which a system was able to adapt to workload changes by provisioning and deprovisioning resources in an autonomic manner, such that at each point in time the available resources matched the current demand as closely as possible." They further illustrated the basic factors to consider when evaluating elasticity and these included:

First, the autonomic scaling, which was dealt with adaptation processes used for autonomic scaling; second, the elasticity dimensions, that considered the set of resource types scaled as part of the adaptation process, third, the resource scaling units, that was the varied amount unit of the allocated resources, and fourth, scalability bounds, that was the upper bound on the amount of resources that were allocated. (Herbst et al., 2013)

Similarly to the views of these authors, the envisaged CRECES would provision and deprovision the Copperbelt University's registration and examination work load that is heavily processed only at the beginning and end of semesters. The CBU system would also deal with the cloud factors that involves the autonomic scaling, elasticity dimension,

The ODCA Report (2012) defined elasticity as "The configurability and expandability of the solution based on subscriber workload." The Report further illustrated the same concept in reference to the Infrastructure-as-a-service (SaaS) highlighting on the following elasticity's attributes:

Ability to scale both up and down, responsiveness on the speed of dynamic scaling, policies that control how the cloud subscriber's application should be scaled, execution of additional tasks on trigger, automatable via an application interface (API) and exception handling. (ODCA Report, 2012)

In accordance to the ODCA Report, the CRESES would also formulate the policies that would facilitate how the CBU's application should be scaled up and down.

Mell et al. (2012) defined rapid elasticity as "The capabilities that can be elastically provisioned and released, in some cases automatically, to scale rapidly outward and inward commensurate with demand." They further explained that "To the consumer, the capabilities available for provisioning often appeared to be unlimited and could be appropriated in any quantity at any time." Whereas, Wolski (2011) pointed out that "Elasticity measures the ability of the cloud to map a single user request to different resources." Consequently to the authors, the CRECES would have the capability to scale rapidly outward and inward commensurate with demand of the registration and examination workload. In addition be in a position to map from a single server to virtual ones.

Shawish et al. (2013) they explained that "Elasticity was an ability to quickly scale up or down one's resource usage, and was an important economic benefit of Cloud Computing as it transferred the costs of resource over provisioning and the risks of under-provisioning to Cloud providers." They further cited a real-world example of elasticity, which was an "Animoto.com whose active users grew from twenty five thousand (25,000) to two hundred and fifty (250,000) in three days after they launched their application on Face book." Such an example from these authors is very encouraging in the sense that it will motivate the CRECES work.

Agrawal et al. (2011) defined elasticity as "a desirable property of a system, which indicated its ability to either handle growing amounts of work in a graceful manner or its ability to improve throughput when additional resources, such as hardware are added." They further defined the same concept as "The ability to deal with variations by adding more resources during high load or consolidating the tenants to fewer nodes when the load decreases, all in a live system without service disruption, is therefore critical for such systems". From these definitions, it's what CCRECS is envisaging to equip the Computer Centre with an ability to virtually scale-up its servers when the load is increases especially during the processing of student registration and results. Around this period all the virtual servers would be in use.

Whereas, IITE Policy Report highlighted that a key feature of cloud computing was its rapid elasticity that allowed for sudden peaks in demand and giving the customer the impression that the services were infinitely scalable. The Report further emphasised that elasticity allowed for rapid escalations in demand at peak times such as at the start of the academic year or during examination periods. Others, such as Shawish et al. (2009) explained that Clouds were a large pool of easily usable and accessible virtualized resources such as hardware, development platforms and/or services. They further illustrated that those resources could be dynamically reconfigured to adjust to a variable load or scale), allowing also for an optimum resource utilization. This was also supported by Grimes et al. (2014) who with efficiency and economics of scale, Cloud Computing services are becoming not only a cheaper solution but a much greener one to build and deploy IT services.

Scalability

White Paper (2012) pointed out that "In search for a more scalable approach to IT infrastructure, a growing number of schools see cloud-based computing as a tremendous opportunity to achieve large-scale efficiencies without sacrificing performance". The Paper gives the CCRECS confidence by assuring that elsewhere a number of schools have embarked on scalable approach to run the Computer Centre

IT services. In fact, Computer Centres as IT service providers of the university need to ensure that during low activity, to minimise the operation costs. On the other hand, during the peak hour to automatic increase the virtual servers.

Falatah (2014) described virtualisation as a technique which integrated resources from a huge computation and storage network, such that users only needed one low-cost device for accessing the network. He also discussed cloud computing as a scalable and easy way for users to access a large pool of virtualized resources that could be dynamically provisioned to adjust to a variable workload. Other scholars such as Lakshminarayanan et al. (2014) pointed out that the cloud computing was a new style of computing in which dynamically scalable and often virtualized resources were provided as a service over the Internet. They further emphasised that the need for servers, storage and software were highly demanding in the universities, colleges and schools.

Comparison Between Elasticity and Scalability

Herbst et al. (2013) in comparison stated that:

Scalability was the ability of the system to sustain increasing workloads by making use of additional resources, and therefore, in contrast to elasticity, it was not directly related to how well the actual resource demanded were matched by the provisioned resources at any point in time.

Agrawal et al. (2011) also went to make a comparison between elasticity and scalability. They distinguished elasticity as "dynamic property that allowed the system's scale to be increased on-demand was on operational, whereas, scalability was a static property of the system on a static configuration." The CRECES is designed to operate simultaneously utilising elasticity and scalability phenomena.

Galante et al. (2012) distinguished scalability and elasticity as:

The former was the property that described the systems' ability to reach a certain scale, such as a thousand servers or a million requests per minute. On other hand, the later was the dynamic property that allowed the system to scale on-demand in an operational system.

That was supported by Agrawal et al. (2011) who stated that "Scalability was the ability of the system to be enlarged to a size which was expected to accommodate a future growth or its ability to improve throughput when additional resources were added." Agrawal et al. (2011) further described the two ways in which a system could scale by adding hardware resources and they related them, the first as "vertically, which added resources to a single node in a system, which also involved the addition of processors or memory to a single computer". The second was the "horizontally, which added more nodes, such as adding a new computer to a distributed software application. This is where there was scaling out from one web-server to three web-servers." Others like Badger (2012) defined:

Elasticity as the ability for customers to quickly request, receive, and later release as many resources as needed. They further argued that elasticity implied that the actual amount of resources used by a user may be changed over time, without any long-term indication about the future resources demands.

Virtualisation

Virtualisation is a new technology where a single hardware and software are configured such that they result into a logical view of several resources. In that way, the users may see several images of the virtualised resources such as servers, desktop computers, storage devices, networks, but to name a few. Having yielded several logical resources, the users can access them and use them for their intended applications.

Gouda et al. (2014) described virtualisation as "the use of software and hardware to create the perception that one or more entities existed although not physically present." They illustrated that "in applying virtualization one server appear to be many, desktop computer appear to be running multiple operating system simultaneously or a vast amount of disk space or drives to be available." They also cited the most common forms of virtualization that included "server virtualization, desktop virtualization, virtual networks, and virtual storage." The authors also discussed the hypervisor or virtual machine monitor (VMM) as "computer software that created and run virtual machines." They highlighted that "the hypervisor that run one or more virtual machines was called host machine, whereas each of the virtual machine were called guest machines." The authors also gave an example of an:

x86 machine, a virtualization layer which was added between the hardware and operating system, and such a layer helped in running multiple operating system simultaneously within the virtual machines in a single computer. The layer dynamically divided and shared the available resources basically physical such as storage, CPU, memory and others.

Eisen (2011) described server virtualisation as that "created multiple isolated environments, allowed multiple operating system's (OS's) and workloads to run on the same physical hardware and solved the problem of tight coupling between OS's and hardware." The author also outlined that:

Virtual machines provided the following: first, hardware independence, that's, guest virtual machine (VM) sees the same hardware regardless of the host; second, isolation, where the VM's operating system is isolated from the host; and third, encapsulation, when the entire VM is encapsulated into a single file.

He further gave the economic reasons for virtualization, such as, "reduce physical infrastructure cost; reduce data-center operating cost, like heavy power consumption and cooling; and minimize lost revenue due to downtime."

Malhotra et al. (2014) and Krishnatej et al. (2013) discussed virtualisation as:

Basically making a virtual image or version of something such as server, operating system, storage devices or network resources so that they can be used on multiple machines at the same time.

They also highlighted the main aim of virtualisation was "to manage the workload by transforming traditional computing to make it more scalable, efficient and economical." The authors emphasised that "Virtualization could be applied to a wide range such as operating system virtualization, hardware-level virtualization and server virtualization".

Hypervisor

Bauman et al. (2015) and Popek and Goldberg (1974) described a hypervisor also known as virtual machine monitor (VMM) as that "enabled a computing environment to run multiple independent operating system at the same time in a single physical computer, which lead to more effective use of the available computing power, storage space, and network bandwidth." The authors further identified the two classifications of hypervisor and these included:

Type 1, the bare metal hypervisors, which run directly on the host's hardware to control the hardware and monitor the guest operating system (OS); and Type 2, the hosted hypervisors, which run within a traditional OS. In other words, a hosted hypervisor adds a distinct software layer on top of the host OS, and the guest OS becomes a third software layer above the hardware.

Mogul et al. (2015) stated that "Hypervisor allocated and rescheduled central processing unit (CPU) and memory resources to virtual machines (VMs) and when multiple of them shared a server's CPU cores and DRAM." They further explained that hypervisor "in a cloud, only needed to control access to the local disk: space allocation, isolation between the blocks accessed by VMs, and perhaps disk-bandwidth management and disk de-duplication." Whereas, the PCI Report (2011), VMWare (2007), Gu et al. (2012), Fayyad-Kazan et al. (2013), and Obasuyi and Sari (2015) discussed that:

Hypervisor mediated all hardware access for the VMs running on the physical platform and that it was in two types these included: Type 1 hypervisor also known as, native or bare metal, which was a piece of software or firmware that ran directly on the hardware and was responsible for coordinating access to hardware resources as well as hosting and managing VMs.

The other one was "Type 2 hypervisor known as host which ran as an application on an existing operating system and it emulated the physical resources required by each VM." The major function of hypervisor was to enable more than one guest machine to utilize the hardware resources of a single host machine. On these technologies, a path is created by the hypervisor which allowed multiple of the same operating system to run on the host machine as well with the hypervisor managing the resources among the various operating system hardware requirements.

Comparison Between Virtualisation and Hypervisor

The JKCS Report defined virtualisation as "an abstraction layer of software called the Hypervisor, which sat between hardware and the operating system and it allowed multiple operating systems and applications to cohabitate on a physical computing platform." The JKCS Report also explained how the virtualization works that "It was accomplished by the use of a hypervisor to logically assigned and separated physical resources". The Report further highlighted that "The hypervisor allowed a guest operating system, running on the virtual machine, to function as if it were solely in control of the hardware, unaware that other guests were sharing it." In fact, the Report emphasised that the cloud computing required "the use of virtualisation which was the separation of the hardware and software such as V Mware's vSphere." It also stressed that virtualisation meant that:

The services provided by a hardware device were abstracted from the physical hardware such that if a disk provided the service of storing data for a server, the virtualization abstraction layer separated the server's access to the storing data service from the physical disk on which the data was stored.

The Report finally stressed that:

Virtualization technology, combined with advances in processor, I/O and other technology will make it possible for high volume, industry standard systems to be deployed for everything from decision support to collaborative environments to high volume transactional applications to high performance modelling.

THE CRECES MODEL

The CRECES Model demonstrated in Figure 1 is composed of the inner triangular hypervisor abstraction host server, in this work referred to, and abbreviated as "inthahs", and pronounced as 'intazi'. The 'inthahs' has the capacity to produce and replicate virtual guest resources utilising its virtualisation mechanism. These guest resources include: virtual web, research, registration, examination, and mail servers.

Figure 1. The CRECES model

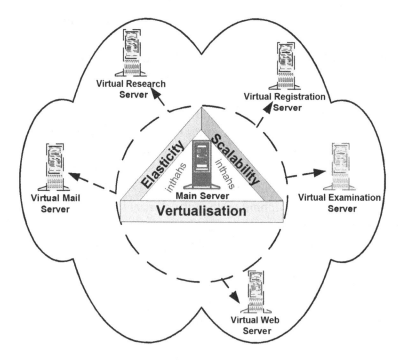

Similarly, the 'inthahs' has the elasticity capability to adapt and handle either the sudden increase or decrease of the workload being processed at that particular time. In addition, the 'inthahs' has also the scalability capacity to sustain an increase of institutional workloads by utilising the additional guest resources. That's the capacity to handle and improve the throughput when more guest resources are added.

The 'inthahs' can be virtualised to produce guest resources which are enhanced with elasticity capabilities as discussed above. The virtualised resources can be scaled either up or down to accommodate more or into less resources. It should be noted that more guest resources can be created as much as the system administrator configures it to yield the virtualised guest resources as indicated in Figure 1. Once the operation is accomplished the resources are scaled down and back into the host server.

The resource mechanism of 'inthahs' is composed of the Host Operating System, Type 2 Hypervisor, and Guest Operating System. The other components are the produced virtual resources that include: mail server, registration server, examination server, research server and web server as demonstrated in Figure 2. The main server which is the host machine runs Type 2 Hypervisor which resides and interfaces the Host and Guest Operating Systems. However, much of the Type 1 and Type

Figure 2. Resource mechanism of 'inthahs'

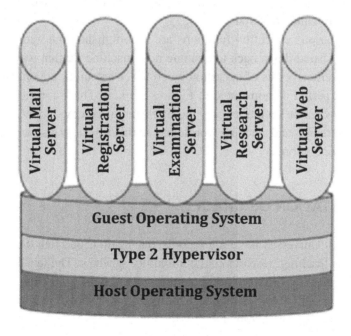

2 Hypervisors have been adequately discussed in the earlier Sections. The Type 2 Hypervisor is the software which co-habits between hardware and operating system and this facilitates the complete functional of virtualisation, elasticity, and scalability which simultaneously activates the operations of the temporal produced virtual guest servers.

The produced virtual guest servers imitate the operations exerted by the main server. In fact the Type 2 Hypervisor creates virtual disks, and operates between the host and guest operating systems. During the operationalisation of the entire 'inthahs', its surrounding technologies such as virtualisation, elasticity and scalability are effectively used to process either the lighter or huge workloads. The collective functionalities of Host Operating System, Type 2 Hypervisor and the Guest Operating System produce five temporal guest servers. These guest servers exactly emulate and operate functions of the host machine. In view of this the produced multiple guest servers execute their respective workloads as though it is coming from the main server. The virtual examination server process the examination data that include production of question papers, marking keys, student list, examination timetables and results. Secondly is the virtual registration server which is used to register all the university students and produce student's acceptance slip. The mail virtual server is used for all internet data accessed by the university community in large quantity. This guest resource deals with large volumes of heterogonous data. The guest web server hosts the university website which has the institutions programmes that puts the visibility of the university. The research server deals with lecturer – student projects, research and consultancy work.

Once the various execution functions are accomplished the guest servers are automatically scaled down back to a single host machine. In that way, the system reduces the overhead costs of operation when fewer resources are only used in the idle workload period demonstrated in Figures 3 and 4. That's for the rest of eight months as shown in these figures, only the single main server will operate to process the salaries, research and teaching workloads. In this way, less resource are used at lower cost of operation.

IMPLEMENTATION OF CRECES

The Copperbelt University has eight schools, one institute and four directorates. Its co-business is teaching, research and community services. The teaching units are schools of: business (SB), the built environment (SBE), engineering (SE), mathematics and natural sciences (SMNS), Michael Chilufya santa school of medicine, graduate studies (SGS) and dag hammarskjold Institute for peace and conflict studies (DHIPS). Whereas, the non-teaching units are the directorates of: information and communications technology (DICT), centre for academic development (CAD), directorate of distance and open learning (DDOL) and external relations. All these listed units have their information processed by the discussed main server. It is worthy important to highlight the programmes and data dealt by each unit of the university.

Programmes and Data Processed by Each Unit

The school of business is the largest unit in the university. It has the capacity of two thousand and three hundred (2,300) registered students in the 2016/17 academic year. It has also the largest number of employed academic staff. The school of business has the majority programmes. For the undergraduate they have the following programmes: the Bachelor of Business Administration (BBA); Bachelor of Science in Banking and Finance (BSc.BF); Bachelor of Science in Economics (BSE); Bachelor of Science in Production and Operations Management (BSPOM); Bachelor of Science in Purchasing and Supply (BSc.PS); Bachelor of Accountancy (B.Acc); Bachelor of Science in Public Procurement (BSPP); Bachelor of Science in Marketing (BSM); Bachelor of Science in Business and Project Management (BSBPM); and Bachelor of Science in Transport and Logistics (BSTL). For the postgraduate programmes include: Management in Business Administration (MBA) General, MBA Finance; Masters of Science (M.Sc.) in Project Management; M.Sc. Accounting and Finance; Masters of Art (M.A.) in Human Resource Management; MPhil/PhD Programmes in Business Studies; MPhil/PhD Programme in Mines and Mineral Sciences.

In view of the above, the ten (10) listed undergraduate programmes, at least each one has more than five (5) courses. In each of course there also at least minimum of sixty (60) students. In each of these courses, they run the final year examinations. That's to say the CRECES processes such huge examination data from the month of November to February in every academic year as demonstrated in Figures 3 and 4. Apart from the examination data, in this period, the CRECES also processes the following data: continuous assessment, results, teaching materials, student / lecturer evaluation, time – tabling, staff appraisal, registration, research, and salaries. The other processing data comes from the seven (7) postgraduate programmes. Each programme as at least a minimum of three (3) courses. In addition, much of research work and community service are done in this programme.

The second largest unit of the university is the School of Mathematics and Natural Sciences in terms of student enrolment. Like the other school discussed above, the School of Mathematics and Natural Sciences runs both the undergraduate and postgraduate programmes. The undergraduate programmes includes: Bachelor of Science in Computer Science (BScCS), Bachelor of Information Technology (BIT), Bachelor of Science in Biology Education (BScBE), Bachelor of Science in Chemistry Education (BScCE), Bachelor of Science in Mathematics Education (BScME),

Bachelor of Science in Physics Education (BScPE), Whereas, the postgraduate programmes are: Master of Science (Mathematics & Science Education), MSc (Mathematics Education) and MSc (Science Education). This school also provides teaching services to other units, like School of Engineering, School of Mines and Mineral Sciences and School of Natural Resources. All this discussed data from the various programmes, are processed as explained in earlier Sections.

The third largest is the School Natural Resources (SNR) with high number of admitted students. Like the other two discussed schools, the SNR also runs the undergraduate and postgraduate programmes. The undergraduate programmes include: Bachelor of Science in Fisheries and Aquaculture (BScFA), Bachelor of Science in Agroforestry (BScA), Bachelor of Science in Wood Science and Technology (BScWST) and Bachelor of Science in Forestry (BScF). Though it has fewer academic programmes, it enrolls many students in every academic year. Following the SNR in size, is the School of Mines and Mineral Sciences (SMMS), which also runs the undergraduate programmes. The undergraduate programmes for the SMMS are: Bachelor of Engineering in Chemical Engineering (BECE), Bachelor of Engineering in Environmental Engineering (BEEE), Bachelor of Engineering in Mining Engineering (BEME) and Bachelor of Science Mining & Exploration Geology (BScMEG). The SMMS also runs the diploma programmes that include: Diploma in Surveying (DipS), Diploma in Mine Ventilation (DipMV), Diploma in Small Scale Mining (DipSSM), Diploma in Metallurgy (DipM), Diploma in Mining Engineering (DipME) and Diploma in Chemical Technology (DipCT). All this discussed workloads from the SNR and SMMS are processed by the same CRECES. The same processing explained for the earlier discussed schools applies to these.

The SNR and SMMS are not the last ones, there others such as the School of Engineering (SE) which has a lot of undergraduate programmes and these include: Bachelor of Engineering Degree with Honours (BEng(Hons)) in Aeronautical Engineering, Bachelor of Engineering Degree with Honours (BEng(Hons)) in Civil Engineering with Construction Management, Bachelor of Engineering Degree with Honours (BEng(Hons)) in Civil Engineering, Bachelor of Engineering Degree with Honours (BEng(Hons)) in Mechanical Engineering, Bachelor of Engineering Degree with Honours (BEng(Hons)) in Mechatronics Engineering, Bachelor of Engineering Degree with Honours (BEng(Hons)) in Telecommunication & Electronics Engineering, Bachelor of Engineering in Electrical/Electronics (Power), Bachelor of Engineering in Civil Engineering, Bachelor of Engineering in Electrical Mechanical Engineering, Bachelor of Engineering in Electrical/Electronics (Power), Bachelor of Engineering in Electrical/Electronics (Power), Bachelor of Engineering in Civil Engineering Power), Diploma in Telecommunications, Diploma Electrical Engineering and Diploma in Civil Engineering Technology.

The School of Engineering also runs the postgraduate programmes and these are: Integrated Masters of Engineering Degree with Honours (MEng(Hons)), and Masters of Philosophy Degree (MPhil). Both the undergraduate and postgraduate programmes have many courses that have tests, final examinations and results that are processed by the CRECES.

The other units of the university are: the School of the Built Environment which runs the following programmes: Bachelor of Architecture, Bachelor of Science in Construction Management, Bachelor of Science in Quantity Surveying, Bachelor of Science in Real Estate, Bachelor of Science in Urban and Regional Planning. The other one is Michael Chilufya Sata School of Medicine which runs the following undergraduate programmes: Bachelor of Dental Medicine, Bachelors of Medicine and Surgery, and Bachelors of Science Clinical Medicine. The school also runs a postgraduate programme which is Masters of Medicine.

The last unit but not the least is the Dag Harmmarskjold Institute for Peace and Conflict Studies which runs both the undergraduate and postgraduate programmes. The undergraduate programmes include: Defence and Security Management, Diplomacy and Strategic Studies Environment, Sustainable Development and Peace, Human Rights, Governance and Peace Building and Human Security and Development. Whereas, the postgraduate programmes include: Masters of Art in Peace and Conflict Studies Human Rights, Governance and Peace Building, Masters of Art in Peace and Conflict Studies Human Security and Development, Masters of Art in Peace and Conflict Studies Environment, Sustainability, Development and Peace, Masters of Art in Peace and Conflict Studies in Diplomacy and Strategic Studies and Masters of Art in Peace and Conflict Studies in Defense and Security Management. As discussed earlier on for other units, similarly, the Dag Harmmarskjold Institute for Peace and Conflict Studies each programme has many courses whose examinations, results, registration, and many more are processed by CRECES.

The knowledge of the available units and their amount of workloads helps the system or network administrators to plan for resource utilisation. The units like school of business and school of mathematics and natural sciences have large enrolment of students. In addition, such units have many and large academic programmes. In these academic units have large volume of data in terabytes to be processed. Whilst the non-academic units have very little workloads to be processed. This gives the university planners to allocate resources accordingly. Much of the academic workload is only concentrated and processed for few months in the academic year calendar and the rest of the period the system is idol. Figure 3 demonstrates the peak workload, as indicated in dark colour at an eye-bird catch covering the months of November, December, January and February. Whereas, the idle period starts from March up to October, with lighter workload and these includes only the salaries, teaching and research work. In fact, these lighter workloads, salaries, teaching and research

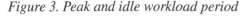

Figure 3. Peak and idle workload period

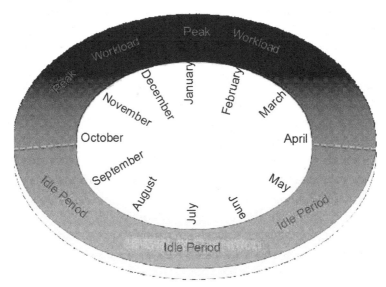

are done throughout the academic calendar from January to December. Whilst the major and compulsory workloads are done in the months of November, December, January and February as illustrated in Figure 3. Some of these key and co-workloads include: tests, continuous assessments (CA), final examinations, student/lecture evaluation, time tabling, staff appraisal, results, and registration. This period also has those workloads that runs throughout the year and these are salaries, teaching and research. At this moment heavy resources are required to process such large workloads. This is the period when the 'inthahs' is virtualised to operate with many guest resources that have been discussed earlier on.

DISCUSSION

In any organisation, the statistical data is useful for day-to-day resource operational planning. It is with this regard that the statistical data given in Figure 4 would assist the Computer Centre System Administrators (SA) or Network Administrators (NA) as to when to scale up and down the hardware and software resources.

Therefore, from the university academic year calendar, sixty percent (60%) to eighty percent (80%) larger portion of the workload occurs within four (4) months that include: November, December, January and February as demonstrated in Figure 4. Whereas, thirty percent (30%) to thirty seven percent (37%) of workload

Figure 4. Resource utilisation

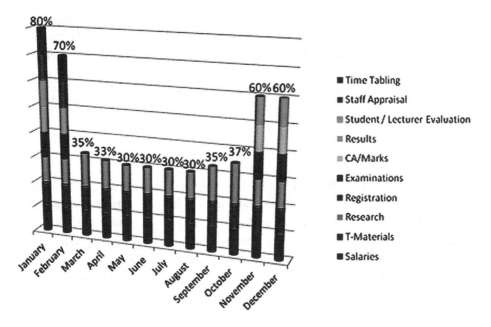

is processed for eight months from March to October, covering almost two thirds of the year. However, this longer period has less workload to be processed, yet the same numbers of servers are used, that's incurring huge cost of production. With the envisaged CRECES, in this period only an average of thirty percent (30%) of resources shall be applied and used. In this way, a huge amount of capital expenditure shall be served.

The larger capital expenditure of the Copperbelt University comes from the running of the Computer Centre, which provides the information communication technology (ICT) or information technology (IT) services to the entire institution community. Currently the Centre has five (5) physical servers that have been consuming a lot of expenditure on electricity which is used to power on the machines 24/7. The electricity is also used to cool the five servers and room ventilation. In addition, the Computer Centre employed a lot of technicians to run, maintain and service the named servers. All the discussed costs are incurred throughout a twelve-month academic year calendar including the idle workload period. All this causes overheard costs even when the same number of machines is running whilst there is less workload being processed. However, the envisaged CRECES will reduce all of the discussed overhead costs. The heavy load resource consumption will be cut down during idle period. For instance, during the idle period that stretches from April to October, the Computer Centre shall only use one server in this case referred to as host server. In this way, fewer resources shall be used, hence very little electricity will be required. During the peak workload period, the host server shall be virtualised, to produce or replicate into five guest servers that will process all the institution work at a low cost of production. The other benefit of the CRECES, is that less manpower shall be maintained and this shall reduce the labour costs. As currently, the university still pays same salaries to the large workforce even during the idle workload period.

CONCLUSION

The CRECES heavily utilises the phenomena and technologies of virtualisation, elasticity, and scaling to automatic re-adjust the hardware and software resources as per workload's size. When the workload is huge, the single host server is automatically built and configured to produce or replicate into several guest servers. These servers each process a particular work as shown in Figure 1. As discussed earlier on, each of the guest servers has the same functional capacity as that of the original and physical host machine. These servers imitate the characteristics of the actual physical servers in terms of application. The envisaged CRECES allows the Copperbelt University Computer Centre to acquire only one good server which is used throughout the whole academic year. Though this machine is switched on throughout the year, the running cost is low and bearable as it is a single one operating. In fact, the peak period lasts only four (4) months as illustrated in Figures 3 and 4, and these are November, December, January and February. It is this period when the System Administrator virtualises the single machine into several virtual servers such as examination, registration, mail, web, and research.

From the university academic calendar, in November and December, the university is processing the examination, results, student's examination slips, student / lecturer evaluation, and continuous assessment. In this period which covers January and February, the university is still busy working on other heavy loads such as registration of returning and new students, timetabling, staff appraisal and student / lecturer evaluation continues. All this work is done by one single machine which has been virtualised into five (5) servers doing multitasking work at the same time. Whereas the idle period which covers almost two thirds of the academic year process very little workload as demonstrated in Figures 3 and 4. At this point in time the network or system administrator configures or scale down the system from the five virtualised servers back to a single main physical server. Hence at this level a single machine will only process thirty percent of the workload making a cost saving of at least 50 percent as compared to that of peak load. It is at such periods when the Computer

Centre carries a rapid elasticity to scale down on the huge server resources. In that way, the Centre manages to run the hardware and software resources at a low cost.

The acquisition of CRECES as given the university a potential to administer the planning of resource utilisation. In that way, it gives the university an edge to appropriately budget according to the idle and peak workload periods. Similarly, CRECES has allowed the university to run the hardware and software resources at a lower cost of production especially during the idle periods which covers two thirds of the academic year as explained above. The ability to use only one single physical machine has cut down the cost of the heavy electricity consumption to power the five machines, cool them as well as reduction of human resources. In this way, the computer centre will run the hardware and software services at a minimal cost. As such the services of the Computer Center are no longer demand huge university budget expenditure. As the Center is running at a low cost more money will be saved to buy the most efficient equipment used to upgrade the existing infrastructure and to train the available personnel. Hence the acquisition of the state-of-art equipment, training of the IT personnel, all will improve the services rendered by the Center. Such benefits justifies the importance of establishing the CRECES which has yielded the best performance management system which will increase the standard of education, administering examination, human resource, payroll, appraisal and many other operational functions.

REFERENCES

Agrawal, D., El Abbadi, A., Das, S., & Elmore, A. J. (2011, April). Database scalability, elasticity, and autonomy in the cloud. In *Proceedings of the 16th Intl. conference on Database systems for advanced applications*. Springer-Verlag. doi:10.1007/978-3-642-20149-3_2

Aljawarneh, S., Aldwairi, M., & Yassein, M. B. (2017). Anomaly-based intrusion detection system through feature selection analysis and building hybrid efficient model. *Journal of Computational Science*. doi:10.1016/j.jocs.2017.03.006

Aljawarneh, S., Yassein, M.B., & Talafha, W.A. (2017). A multithreaded programming approach for multimedia big data: encryption system. *Multimed Tools Appl.* <ALIGNMENT.qj></ALIGNMENT>10.1007/s11042-017-4873-9

Aljawarneh, S. A., Alawneh, A., & Jaradat, R. (2017). Cloud security engineering: Early stages of SDLC. *Future Generation Computer Systems*, *74*, 385–392. doi:10.1016/j.future.2016.10.005

Aljawarneh, S. A., Moftah, R. A., & Maatuk, A. M. (2016). Investigations of automatic methods for detecting the polymorphic worms signatures. *Future Generation Computer Systems, 60*, 67–77. doi:10.1016/j.future.2016.01.020

Aljawarneh, S. A., Vangipuram, R., Puligadda, V. K., & Vinjamuri, J. (2017). G-SPAMINE: An approach to discover temporal association patterns and trends in internet of things. *Future Generation Computer Systems, 74*, 430–443. doi:10.1016/j.future.2017.01.013

Badger, L., Patt-Corner, R., & Voas, J. (2012). Draft cloud computing synopsis and recommendations of the national institute of standards and technology. *Nist Special Publication*, 146. Available at http://csrc.nist.gov/publications/drafts/ 800-146/Draft-NIST-SP800-146.pdf

Bauman, E., Ayoade, G, & Lin, Z. (2015). A survey on hypervisor-based monitoring: Approaches, applications, and evolutions. *ACM Comput. Surv., 48*(1). DOI: 10.1145/2775111

Eisen, M. (2011). *Introduction to Virtualization*. The Long Island Chapter of the IEEE Circuits and Systems (CAS) *Society*.

Fayyad-Kazan, H., Perneel, L., & Timmerman, M. (2013). Full and Para-Virtualization with Xen: A Performance Comparison. *Journal of Emerging Trends in Computing and Information Sciences, 4*, 719–727.

Galante, G., & Luis Carlos, E. de Bona (2012). A Survey on Cloud Computing Elasticity. *IEEE/ACM Fifth International Conference on Utility and Cloud Computing*. doi:10.1109/UCC.2012.30

Gouda, K. G., Patro, A., Dwivedi, D., & Bhat, N. (2014). Virtualization Approaches in Cloud Computing. *International Journal of Computer Trends and Technology, 12*(4), 161–166. doi:10.14445/22312803/IJCTT-V12P132

Grimes, J., Jaeger, P. J., & Lin, J. (2009). Weathering the storm: The policy implications of cloud computing. In *Proceedings of Conference*. University of North Carolina.

Gu, Z. H., & Zhao, Q. L. (2012). A State-of-the-Art Survey on Real-Time Issues in Embedded Systems Virtualization. *Journal of Software Engineering and Applications, 5*(4), 277–290. doi:10.4236/jsea.2012.54033

Herbst, N. R., Kounev, S., & Reussner, R. (2013). Elasticity in Cloud Computing: What It Is, and What It Is Not? *ICAC*, 23 – 27. Retrieved from https://sdqweb.ipd.kit.edu/publications/pdfs/HeKoRe2013-ICAC-Elasticity.pdf

Jan Kremer Consulting Services (JKCS). (2015). *Cloud Computing & Virtualization.* White Paper. Author.

Kalpana, G., Kumar, P. V., Aljawarneh, S., & Krishnaiah, R. V. (2017). Shifted Adaption Homomorphism Encryption for Mobile and Cloud Learning. *Computers & Electrical Engineering.* doi:10.1016/j.compeleceng.2017.05.022

Krishnatej, K., Patnala, E., Narasingu, S. S., & Chaitanya, J. N. (2013). Virtualization Technology in Cloud Computing Environment. *International Journal of Emerging Technology and Advanced Engineering*, 3.

Lakshminarayanan, Kumar, & Raju. (2014). *Cloud Computing Benefits for Educational Institutions.* Higher College of Technology. Retrieved from https://ai2-s2-pdfs.s3.amazonaws.com/d3dc/566db2811b61776d0216ccf9c55d55c0101c.pdf

Malhotra, L., Agarwal, D., & Jaiswal, A. (2014). Virtualization in Cloud Computing. *Journal Information Technology & Software Engineering*, 4(2), 136. doi:10.4172/2165-7866.1000136

Mell, P., & Grance, T. (2011). *The NIST Definition of Cloud Computing.* Tech. rep., U.S. National Institute of Standards and Technology (NIST), Special Publication 800-145. Retrieved from http://csrc.nist.gov/publications/nistpubs/800-145/SP800-145.pdf

Mogul, J. C., Mudigonda, J., Renato Santos, J., & Yoshio Turner, Y. (2012). *The NIC is the Hypervisor: Bare-Metal Guests in IaaS Clouds.* HP Labs.

Mohammed Falatah, M., & Batarfi, O. (2014). Cloud scalability considerations, Saud Arabia. *International Journal of Computer Science & Engineering Survey*, 5(4).

Obasuyi, G. C., & Sari, A. (2015). Security Challenges of Virtualization Hypervisors in Virtualized Hardware Environment. *International Journal Communications. Network and System Sciences*, 8, 260–273. doi:10.4236/ijcns.2015.87026

OCDA. (2012). *Master Usage Model: Compute Infratructure-as-a-Service.* Tech. rep., Open Data Center Alliance. Retrieved from http://www.opendatacenteralliance.org/docs/ODCA_Compute_IaaS_MasterUM_v1.0_Nov2012.pdf

Paper, W. (2012). Cloud 101: Developing a cloud-computing strategy for higher education. *Proceedings of the International Conference on Transformations in Engineering Education.* Retrieved from www.cisco.com/c/dam/en/us/solutions/.../cloud.../cloud_101_higher_education_wp.p

Popek, G. J., & Goldberg, R. P. (1974). Formal requirements for virtualizable third generation architectures. *Communications of the ACM, 17*(7), 412–421. doi:10.1145/361011.361073

Shawish, A., & Salama, M. (2013). Cloud computing: Paradigms and technologies. *Studies in Computational Intelligence, 495*, 39–67. doi:10.1007/978-3-642-35016-0_2

Shawish & Salama. (2014). *Cloud Computing: Paradigms and Technologies*. Academic Press.

Singh, A., Juneja, D., & Malhotra, M. (2015). A Novel Agent Based Autonomous Service Composition Framework for Cost Optimization of Resource Provisioning in Cloud Computing. In JKSU-CIS. Elsevier.

Singh, A., & Malhotra, M. (2015). Evaluation of a Secure Agent based optimized Resource Scheduling Framework in Cloud Environment. IJCAR, 188-198.

Singh, A., & Malhotra, M. (2016). Hybrid Two Tier Framework for Improved Security in Cloud Environment. India-Com, 1601-1606.

Singh, A., & Malhotra, M. (n.d.). A Novel Agent Based Framework for Cost Optimization in Cloud Computing Environment. *International Journal of Cloud Applications*, 53–61.

UNESCO Institute for Information Technologies in Education (IITE) Report. (2010). *Cloud Computing in Education*. Author.

Virtualization Special Interest Group PCI Security Standards Council Report. (2011). *Information Supplement*. PCI DSS Virtualization Guidelines.

VMWare. (2007). *Understanding Full Virtualization, Paravirtualization and Hardware Assist*. Retrieved from http://www.vmware.com/files/pdf/VMware_paravirtualization.pdf

Wolski, R. (2011). *Cloud Computing and Open Source: Watching Hype Meet Reality*. Retrieved from http://www.ics.uci.edu/~ccgrid11/files/ccgrid-11_Rich_Wolsky.pdf

Section 2
Security and Trust Issues of Cloud Paradigm

Chapter 4

Information Dispersal Algorithms and Their Applications in Cloud Computing

Makhan Singh
Panjab University, India

Sarbjeet Singh
Panjab University, India

ABSTRACT

Information dispersal is a technique in which pieces of data are distributed among various nodes such that the data can be reconstituted from any threshold number of these pieces. Information dispersal algorithms employ a method in which a file F needs to be dispersed among n nodes such that any m pieces will be sufficient to reconstruct the whole file F. The size of each piece is |F/m|. We must also ensure that the complete knowledge of any m-1 pieces is insufficient to reconstruct the complete file F. The ideas for accomplishing this have been given in many literatures in the past. A discussion and comparison of some of these is covered in this chapter.

INTRODUCTION

Information storage and its transmission in a network environment cause many problems like security issues, availability problems, compromised reliability of the whole network, confidentiality problems etc. The encryption of the data can remove

DOI: 10.4018/978-1-5225-3029-9.ch004

some of these problems but most of them still remain. One method to remove some of these problems can be replicating the data or file at multiple locations. But this gives rise to new problems like storage and network overload. Two problems where Information Dispersal is used mostly are in the storage of data on various systems or the transmission of data on a computer network. Thus, creating multiple copies of the data only increases overhead of the system. This is why the Information Dispersal Scheme was proposed as it deals with the distribution of n pieces of the file/data F such that the file can be reconstructed from any m parts of the file. In this manner, we can provide efficient solution to most of the above mentioned problems without actually having to increase the system overhead.

The general idea of how Information Dispersal Algorithms work is shown in the diagrams of Figure 1 and Figure 2.

The data/file F is distributed among n parts among various systems. Each part is of the size |F/m| and the sum of the lengths of all these parts is (n/m). F. To make Information Dispersal space efficient we can choose m and n such that the ratio of n/m is as close to 1 as possible. The reconstruction of the file F is similar to the distribution but here we only need any m available parts of the file F. But we must also ensure that no m-1 parts of the file F would give away any information about

Figure 1. Distribution of file F using information dispersal algorithms

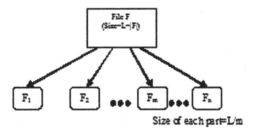

Figure 2. Recombination of file F using information dispersal algorithms

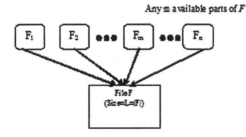

it. This ensures that even if a malicious user gets m-1 parts of the file the security of the file will not be compromised.

The information dispersal scheme is not only explainable using dispersal and recombination of data but also using secret key sharing, transmission problem, storage problem and parallel computing problem as well. This is what makes this scheme so popular because it can be used in a variety of contexts in many different fields.

The Information Dispersal scheme provides many advantages over the conventional method of replicating the file because it is space efficient, secure, provides higher reliability and availability. The reconstruction process is shown in the diagram given below.

These diagrams show the basic procedure for splitting and reconstituting the file F but various authors have used many different techniques to actually split and recombine the file F which we shall discuss and compare in this chapter.

BACKGROUND

Information storage and its transmission in a network environment cause many problems like security issues, availability problems, compromised reliability of the whole network, confidentiality problems etc. In this literature various mechanisms have been proposed that deals with these issues. In this chapter information dispersal schemes proposed by some researchers have been reviewed and thus can deals with above issues.

1. Blakley (1979)

The author discusses the concept of Information Dispersal by considering the safeguarding of cryptographic keys. The keys are distributed among various guards, a threshold number of which is necessary to retrieve the secret that has been encrypted by this key.

The authors consider three types of events concerning the security of any data namely the abnegation incidents, betrayal incidents and combination incidents. They have been referred to as the A, B and C types of incidents. The number of each type of these events is a, b and c respectively. The total number of incidents d is given by d=a+b-c because each of the combination type of events has been counted twice. The abnegation incidents are where a file or data is in an incident that leaves it non-recoverable like destruction, degradation or defection. The betrayal incidents are, as the name suggests, incidents involving the betrayal of one of the guards of the information to the opponent where the information is no longer available to us or is not correctly returned by the guard. Combination type of incidents are where the above two type of incidents are combined.

The author uses the above conditions to disperse a set of K keys among G guards. We choose b+2 dimensional vectors. For every member g of the set G of a + b + 1 guards the author defines a corresponding b+1 dimensional vector subspace V(g) of the b+2 Information of the b+2 dimensional vector space V. For each key k in the set K, there is a set of various lines with the center in V. A set of these guards will choose, at random, one of these lines and call it L(k) of these lines. When b+1 of the guards send their information, i.e. b+1 of their subspaces will intersect into L(k) irrespective of what guards are chosen. For any L(k) only b+2 keys will be corresponded. Thus we can have the set of keys back.

We choose a number z, a & b positive integers that are less than z. Then we choose a small number Q and a number p. Now we create a matrix M which has a+b+2 rows and b+2 columns. All the other entries in M are from the finite vector subspace Z. This matrix must follow the following conditions:

- Each row must contain only one 1 in each row, no 0s should be there in each row and no two elements of the row should be equal unless they are equal to 1.
- Each b+1 by b+1 submatrix must have a non-zero and non equal determinant.

The probability of each of these conditions being satisfied individually is 1-2Q. Thus combined probability is 1-4Q. It is shown that we can form a+b+1 submatrices of b+1 rows and b+2 columns from M. Each of these matrices contains the first row of M. We append a last row to these matrices to form matrices Y(j, x) for each x ϵ V as follows:

$$x = (x(1), x(2), ..., x(b+1), x(b+2))$$

$$= (Y(j, x) [b+2,1], Y(j, x) [b+2,2], ...,$$

$$Y(j, x) [b+2,b+1], Y(j, x) [b+2,b+2]) \tag{1}$$

Now if we interpolate n+1 of these rows each of which represents a vector, we get the line that goes through the origin and thus, effectively the set of keys. This whole process is shown with the diagram given in Figure 3.

Figure 3. Procedure for Blakley scheme

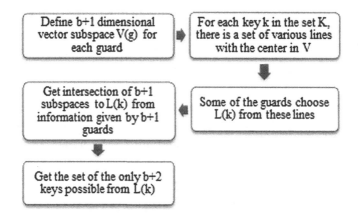

Advantages

The advantages of the scheme discussed above are listed below:

- The secret keys are safe even in any of the three kinds of incidents involving the loss of one or more keys from the guards occurs due to the distribution of the secret among all the guards and requiring only a few of these to reconstitute the secret.
- The secret is safe even if n-m of the keys are somehow compromised because of any kind of attack on the secret, theft of the shares or loss of data in general.

Disadvantages

This technique has certain disadvantages that have been listed below:

- Size of each share or key is less than or equal to the original key which may pose a problem when implementing this technique over some network because it causes storage and transmission overheads.
- The implementation is complex and involves a lot of variables and vector calculations.

2. Shamir (1979)

The author discusses the scheme of Information Dispersal keeping secret sharing in mind. The idea is to distribute a secret into multiple parts, a threshold number of which must be sufficient to reconstitute the secret and shares less than this number must reveal no information about the secret.

The scheme developed by Adi Shamir is based on polynomial interpolation. It assumes that there are k numbers of distinct points (x_i, y_i) in a 2-D plane. This scheme is based on the fact that there is only one k-1th degree polynomial for every i. Thus keeping in mind the Information Dispersal problem, if we have to distribute a file F into n pieces F_i $1 \leq i \leq k$, we take k-1 degree polynomial $p(x)=a_0+a_1x+....+a_{k-1}x^{k-1}$ in which $a_0=F$ and thus we evaluate:

$$F_1= p(1),....F_i = p(i),....F_n = p(n) \tag{2}$$

Thus if we have any k of these values F1 to Fn we can calculate all the coefficients of the P(x) by interpolation of all the k equations and thus find the value of F. However this also ensures that any k-1 of these values will not give away any information about F. The complete procedure is shown in Figure 4.

To prove this fact, the author takes the help of modular arithmetic. We choose a prime number y which is greater than both F and n. the field of interpolation is defined by the set I of all integers mod y. The coefficients of the polynomial q(x) are chosen from the range [0, y) randomly and he calculates the value of F1,....,Fn modulo y. Now if k-1 of these were revealed to a malicious user then for each value F' in the range [0,y) then only one k-1 the degree polynomial can be constructed such that p' (0)=F' and p' (i)=Fi for all k-1 arguments. Thus there are y number of

Figure 4. Procedure for Adi Shamir's scheme

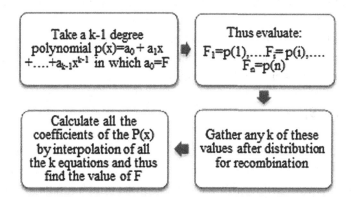

77

polynomials of degree k that can be possible from this k-1 th polynomial, so thus our data F cannot be deduced. The security that this scheme provides to the shares is considerable because the file is distributed among n shares, any m of which would be sufficient to reconstruct the file. However no information about the file or secret is given if any less than these m shares are compromised. A few features of this scheme as observed by the author are as follows:

- The size of each share is always smaller or equal to the size of the original data.
- The changes required in any Fi parts can be made easily by just changing the polynomial.
- We can change or delete the pieces Fi dynamically at any point.

Advantages

The advantages of this scheme are as mentioned bellow:

- The secret can be reconstituted from any threshold number of the shares that are available at that particular time and this threshold can be carefully chosen.
- No significant information about the secret is revealed if less than the threshold number of shares are available.
- The calculations involve only interpolation of polynomials so the scheme is easy to understand and implement, even for beginners.

Disadvantages

The disadvantages of the scheme discussed above are as follows:

- The size of each share is equal to the size of the original share so it may add to storage overhead for storing multiple shares.
- The transmission of each share over the network may add to extra transmission overhead for a network and thus scheme must be used only where the security requirement outweighs other overheads.

3. Rabin (1989)

This paper takes the example of storage and transmission of data files to explain the problem of Information Dispersal. Also the author discusses the use of Information Dispersal on communications between processors in parallel computers in Santis and

Masucci (2002). In the storage problem, we have a file F that needs to be stored on a workstation that is also used by other users. So, to ensure the security of the file the user encrypts this file using some appropriate encryption technique. But, this still does not solve the problem when the file is physically destroyed and cannot be recovered. In the transmission problem, we have a network where a node A needs to send a file F to another node B via a path π. The file is encrypted and sent using some error correction mechanisms as well. But there is possibility that the some node on the path π may go down and thus the data file is lost. As a solution we may store n different copies of the data file and re send it but that only increases the storage overhead n times. Thus we need to find a solution that efficiently distributes file over a network so that they can be reconstructed for either storage or transmission.

Thus the information dispersal algorithm was proposed where a file F of size |F| can be distributed in n pieces and can be reconstructed by using any m of these pieces. The size of each piece will therefore be |F|/m and the total size of all the pieces will be |F|*(n/m). His method can be viewed as belonging to the field of error correction codes Berlekamp (1968), in which extra bits are added to a message creating a block, so that after occurrence of any k errors within the block, the message can still be reconstructed.

The author considers the file F as a series of integers b1,....,bN all of which are within the range [0,B]. The author also assumes that no more than k pieces will be lost at time. He also assumes a number m such that n=m+k. He chooses a number p where B<p. F is thus considered as a set of residues mod p in the field Zp. We then choose a set of vectors ai=(ai1,...,aim) ε Zpm such that each subset of these are linearly independent.

The file is then segmented into parts of length m F=S1, S2,..Sm where S1= (b1,..., bm), S2 = (bm+1,...,b2m).

Thus each piece Fi = ci1, ci2,..ciN/m, Where,

$$cik = ai.Sk = ai1.b(k-1)m+1+...+aim.bkm \tag{3}$$

We consider (aij) $1 \leq i$ $j \leq m$ to be an m × m matrix. Then we get

$$A \cdot \begin{bmatrix} b_1 \\ \vdots \\ b_m \end{bmatrix} = \begin{bmatrix} c_{i1} \\ \vdots \\ c_{m1} \end{bmatrix}$$

We can get the File F reversing the above equation to the equation given below

$$\begin{bmatrix} b_1 \\ \vdots \\ b_m \end{bmatrix} = A^{-1} \begin{bmatrix} c_{i1} \\ \vdots \\ c_{m1} \end{bmatrix}$$

If we denote the ith row of A-1 by ($\alpha 1i,\ldots,\alpha im$), then

bj = $\alpha i1c1k + \ldots + \alpha imcmk$ (4)

Thus we can split the file F using equation (3) and then recombine it using the equation (4) which basically defines the whole Information Dispersal Scheme.

The concept of fingerprints is also discussed by the author, which provides an additional advantage from the security perspective of the secret. A possible attack on the system could be the replacement of the share with some incorrect or malicious content that could be used in the recombination and thus result in the scheme to generate incorrect secrets. Thus, we choose a random k degree polynomial f(x) and calculate the residue

Pi = res (Fi(x), f(x))   (5)

where Fi(x) is share in polynomial form. We send encryption of Pi with Encryption function E, along with the share Fi over the network to the respective node. This can be represented by (E(Pi),Fi). During recombination of the file F, the same package is received and we check if the decryption of the first part that is, E-1(E(Pi), is equal to res(Fi(x),f(x)). We repeat this process till we correctly obtain all the m parts and can reconstitute the file correctly.

This procedure is represented diagrammatically as shown in Figure 5. This diagram covers all the steps that are sequentially followed in our scheme to distribute and reconstitute the file F.

The concept of fingerprints, that the author uses in this manuscript had never been used by any other authors so it provides an edge to the whole algorithm and also ensures the security of each share of the file F from any loss and malicious attack. Beguin and Cresti (1998) analyzed the distribution a file among a set of users such that a threshold number of these users can reconstruct the file. Their scheme is an extension of scheme proposed by M.O. Rabin and it determines a bound on the amount of information made available to a user and the application of this scheme is in cryptography of secret files. This scheme is discussed later in this manuscript in detail.

Figure 5. Procedure for Michael O. Rabin's scheme

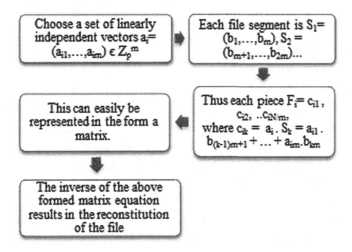

Advantages

The advantages of the above Information Dispersal Scheme are given below:

- The size of each share in this scheme is |F|/m which is much less as compared to the previous schemes and thus makes the Information Dispersal more space efficient.
- Since the size of share is small, the transmission overhead of the system when this scheme is applied on the network is much less as compared to any previous scheme.
- The author pays lot of attention to the security of each share and thus the system as a whole. An example of the same is the discussion involving the use of fingerprints that are attached to the share and thus adds to the security of the file.
- The application of the scheme in various problems has been discussed in the manuscript such as the storage problem, transmission problem, and parallel computing environment problem.

Disadvantages

The disadvantages of the above Information Dispersal Scheme are as follows:

- The solution involves a lot of variables and calculations thus making it tedious to implement, not just locally but also over a network environment that offers multiple nodes as share keepers and the network connections as the mode to transfer the shares to distribute and reconstitute the file.

4. Krawczyk (1993)

In this manuscript, the author discusses a scheme to combine Encryption and Information Dispersal under one scheme. For this, he uses Michael O. Rabin's Information Dispersal scheme (IDA) and Adi Shamir's Secret key sharing scheme (PSS). The IDA is used to distribute the secret and the PSS is used to distribute the encryption key that encrypts the secret. Thus in this way, the author provides a double security Information Distribution Scheme in which the secret as well as the encryption key are both distributed over the network using different mechanisms and thus the distribution is more secure and the secret is safe from malicious users.

The author proposes that we first encrypt the data D using an encryption function ENC using a random secret key K and then distribute the encrypted file using the IDA and distribute the key K using PSS. We thus send each participant the share

$Si=(Ei, Ki)$

where

$Ei = IDA(ENCK(D))$ and $Ki=PSS(K)$.

This is the basic concept that is followed in this scheme showing the technique for splitting and recombining the files. The pseudo code for this technique is as given below:

Distribution

1. Encrypt the secret S using an encryption key K and encryption function ENC. The resultant is E which is equal to ENCK(S).
2. Partition the encrypted file E into n fragments (E1, E2, .., En) using IDA.
3. Distribute the key K into n pieces (k1, k2, .., kn) using PSS.
4. Distribute a pair of (Ek, kk) to each participant in the distribution process.

Recombination

1. Collect m available shares from the participants.
2. Reconstruct E from these m shares using IDA.

3. Reconstruct the Key K from the m shares using PSS.
4. Using decryption scheme ENC, decrypt E using the key obtaines K to get the share S.

This process is shown in diagram given in Figure 6.

To reconstruct the given data D we receive m shares S1,S2,...,Sm from any m participants and reconstruct E using IDA and K using PSS. Then we decrypt E using K to finally reconstruct D. the author further goes on to prove how this scheme is computationally secure and efficient. The author also states that by using the concept of fingerprints as discussed by Rabin (1989) we can achieve a robust secret sharing scheme. There are a few disadvantages with public-key signatures that can be overcome using a scheme of distributed fingerprints in Krawczyk (1993). Alfredo De Santis and Barbara Masucci use Information-theoretics to provide the same in Santis and Masucci (2002).

Advantages

The scheme discussed above has the following advantages:

- The security and reliability provided by this scheme are double than the rest of the Information Dispersal Schemes due to its encryption of the secret and then distribution of the secret and the encryption key using two different mechanisms.
- Since this is a very secure and reliable method of distribution, it is applicable in many areas.

Figure 6. Procedure for Hugo Krawczyk's scheme

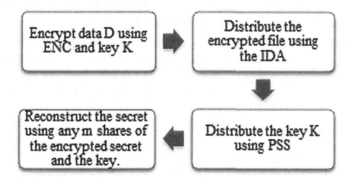

- This scheme is very robust which preserves the space efficiency of the system.
- The scheme provides a way of combing encryption and Information Dispersal in a very efficient manner.

Disadvantages

There are a few disadvantages of the above scheme and these are as follows:

- Since this scheme involves the distribution of both, the secret and the key, the transmission overhead of the scheme can increase.
- The implementation of this scheme involves the implementation of both the distributions schemes and the encryption mechanism which can be a tedious process.

5. Beguin and Cresti (1998)

The authors provide a general Information Dispersal Algorithm or scheme that can be used in any access environment to distribute a piece of information among various users. This scheme however is applicable and more efficient for larger files. In this scheme, the authors describe the lower boundary on the size of each share that a user must have and then propose a scheme that matches this lower boundary value and thus providing us with an optimal solution for Information Dispersal keeping in mind the average size of each share.

The authors use a information theoretic approach to formulate the Information Dispersal scheme. The authors define a term access structure as the set of the participants that are required to reconstruct the file. This set is a subset of the set P={P1,P2,...,Pn} of all participants. The authors also describe the distribution function $\sum$(n,m) used to distribute the piece of information according to the probability distribution function {pF(f)}. Here n is the total number of participants and m is the participants needed to reconstruct the information.

The authors define the information reduction of the information dispersal scheme $\sum$ for the access structure A, when the probability distribution on the set of files F is $\prod$F, as

$$e\left(A,\Pi_{F},\Sigma\right) = H\left(F\right) / \left(\max\left\{H\left(G_{i}\right) : 1 \leq i \leq n\right\}\right)$$

and the average information reduction scheme is given by

$$e'\left(A,\Pi_F,\Sigma\right)=nH\left(F\right)/\sum_{i=1}^{n}H\left(G_i\right)$$

where,

$$H\left(X\right)=-\sum_{x\in X}p\left(x\right)\log\left(x\right)$$

and Gi = set of all possible shares given to a Participant Pi

Now the authors consider the following Information Dispersal Scheme:

Distribution

1. $\sum$ (n, m) is used to distribute the file F into n parts F1,..Fn.
2. We distribute m.xi distinct fragments Fxi,…,Fm.xi in the n participants, such that no two participants get the same fragments.

Recombination

1. Each participant in an access structure contributes its fragments in the recombination.
2. We use $\sum$(n,m) to recombine the file F.

The author then discusses three techniques to optimize the Information reduction of the scheme. The first technique is to assume xi=pi/qi, where pi=1 and qi=emax= min {|A|,A ∈ access structure}. In the second technique, we assume that some participants in P get fragments that are shorter than log|F| / emax. For this we assume that pi = 1 and qi = min{|A|,A ∈ access structure and Pi ∈ Participants}. In the third technique, we give each participant a share that is no longer than necessary. This technique is used to optimize the average information reduction of the scheme.

The process discussed above is shown Figure 7.

The author provides proofs of all the techniques and theorems used above so as to show that the scheme used is actually effective. Also, the authors provide a comparative study of all the techniques discussed in the manuscript, thus going on to modify the Information dispersal and recombination scheme.

Figure 7. Procedure for Philippe Beguim and Antonella Cresti's scheme

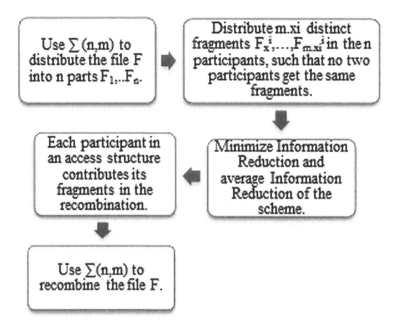

Advantages

- The whole scheme is based on optimizing the information reduction of Information Dispersal Algorithms.
- The scheme provides a lot of applications where this scheme can be used and be applied with existing algorithms to improve their performance and information reduction.
- The scheme provides multiple techniques and then compares these schemes of information reduction to create a modified, optimized scheme for information dispersal.
- The size of each share in this scheme is optimized and each participant gets variable number of shares and thus makes it more efficient.

Disadvantages

- The scheme is difficult to implement on a system because it requires a lot of variables and a lot of calculations need to be made.
- The scheme is focused on optimizing information reduction and neglects important concepts like load balancing and transmission overheads.

- No additional features for the security of the shares or fragments or the secret itself is provided in the manuscript. The whole concern has solely been focused on information reduction and its optimization.

Many other Information Dispersal Algorithms had been developed but each of them lacked some basic conceptual integrity or some basic efficiency and reliability constraints. One such example is the Information Dispersal Algorithm given by Asmuth and Blakley (1982) in which use of number theoretic lacked basic clarity of space optimization and efficiency and is also very complicated. Another example of such a scheme is that proposed by Ogata et al. (1993) in which was also not very popular due to the fact that it had some major optimization and efficiency issues. Many other local Information Dispersal schemes, that were only applicable in various specific types of networks, were also developed but they failed to become global techniques used for Information Dispersal.

COMPARISON

The various Information Dispersal Schemes can be compared on the basis of many parameters like their basic technique used, the size of each share in the distribution and recombination procedure, the security features provided by the scheme and the usage of the scheme that has been shown in the manuscript discussing the scheme. The basic technique involves the comparison of the technique that the author uses to split and recombine the file into various shares and the mathematics involved with this feature. The technique and heuristics taken up by various authors vary from polynomial interpolation and hyperplane intersection to vector subspaces and probability distribution. The comparison of these techniques is shown in the Table 1.

The size of each share is also described by the technique used to distribute the secret and thus may vary from strategy to strategy. This plays a very critical role when comparing Information Dispersal Algorithms because the network or system on which the scheme needs to be applied generally has strict storage constraints and thus need to choose the Information Dispersal scheme carefully. The security that each technique provides is contributed by its basic technique and also any special features added for the sole purpose of adding more security to the system. The network over which the share needs to be distributed or recollected may or may not be secure and thus the loss of important information can take place. It is therefore important that the security the scheme provide can either avoid security breakthrough or can nullify its effects so as not to let the share be completely lost during recollection. The Information Dispersal scheme can be used in various spheres of computing and many authors have discussed the multiple possibilities that their technique can

Table 1. Comparison of various information dispersal schemes

Factors for Comparison	G. R. Blakley	Adi Shamir	Michael O. Rabin	Hugo Krawczyk	Philippe Beguim, Antonella Cresti
Basic Technique used for dispersal	Uses the concept of vector subspaces and the concept of hyperplane intersections are used to form shares.	Polynomial interpolation and modular arithmetic.	Concept of vectors and vector subspaces along with matrices to represent the vector coefficients.	Combined scheme that uses encryption using public key and then distribution of encrypted data as well as the key.	The concept of entropy calculation on the basis of probability distribution is used to provide Information reduction of the system.
Size of each share	The size of each share in this scheme is the same as the size of the secret/ file.	The size of each share in this case is almost equal to the size of the original data.	The size of each share is equal to F.(n/m) where F is the original file or data.	The size of the share is combined size of the Rabin's IDA share of the data and Shamir's IDA share of the key.	Information reduction is used in order to provide optimized share sizes. The size of each share is e'(A, $\prod_F$, $\sum$) = nH(F)/$\sum_{i=1}^{n}$H(Gi).
Security features	By using the concept of hyperplane intersection the security of the shares is ensured. No separate mechanism for share security has been introduced.	There is a simple method to keep changing the polynomial and thus the shares frequently thus increasing the security of the scheme.	The author uses the mechanism of fingerprints to ensure the security of the shares. The concept is to encrypt the share after merging it with a polynomial and reversing the process on the opposite side.	The whole scheme has been developed keeping the security of the secret shares in mind. The encryption of the data using a secret key and distribution of the data and the key ensures safety to a great extent.	No additional security features have been provided other than that of the security provided by the distribution of the secret.
Usage shown	The author only discusses the concept of IDA with respect to securing the keys for various encryptions.	The author considers only the aspects of secret sharing with respect to Information dispersal	The author discusses the concept of storage and transmission problems along with parallel computing and discusses the usage of IDA in all of these	The author combines the usage of secret sharing and IDA and uses them to ensure the safety and security of the secret as well as its encryption keys.	The scheme has been shown to have many applications where it can be used in place of any other Information Dispersal Algorithm and is also shown to be replacing the IDA in Hugo Krawczyk's scheme.

provide in these various areas. Many authors have included a discussion various fields where their technique is used or the fields where the application of their technique can significantly improve the performance of the system.

APPLICATION OF INFORMATION DISPERSAL ALGORITHMS

There are a lot of fields in which we can use Information dispersal algorithms. We shall discuss a few of them below:

Reliable Communication in Computer Networks

Communication in computer networks refers to the transfer of some data or files over a computer network from one node to the other. Reliable computer networks refers to making this transfer of files on the network more secure, available and reliable so that the overall performance of the system can be increased thereby providing us with a more efficient way of communicating among network nodes. Information Dispersal can provide an advantage in this context because it provides mechanisms to distribute the file among various nodes of the network, that can be reconstructed even when a few of the distributed shares are not found, effectively increasing the reliability of the system.

In this type of application, we use Information Dispersal Algorithms to distribute a message M into n various parts over a network such that we can use any n parts to reconstitute the message. Thus we have a benefit that even if n-m parts of the message M are lost we can still reconstitute the message. There is however a probability that the reconstituted message is not the same as the one actually transmitted. Thus, efforts have been made to calculate and maximize the actual probability of the recombined message to be correct message. Sun and Shieh (1994, December) have devised some mechanisms for relating the probability of the message being correct and the complete communication reliability of the network and thus forth the optimality of the IDA.

Any of the above described Information Distribution mechanisms can be used to distribute the file among various nodes of a network. All of them provide for improving the reliability of the system. But the mechanism devised by Sun and Shieh (1994, December) can be used to prove that the scheme has the desired effects.

Security of Data or Secrets

Security of a data file or a secret on a network is one of the most challenging features encountered by most networks. Many threats to the file or secret prevail at every instant on time when in a networked environment like virus, malicious intent, theft, and many others. Many different techniques have been proposed in the past over this type of problem. Most of these include encrypting the secret with some key. But then this key needs to be transmitted over the network which is again risky. Thus, some different approach for the solution to this problem was required.

Most of the research done on Information Dispersal Algorithms was done keeping in mind the security of some data. Blakley (1979) uses dispersal of information to safeguard the cryptographic keys. Adi Shamir also uses Information Dispersal Algorithms to 'share a secret' in Shamir (1979). Then Hugo Krawczyk also uses the concept for secret sharing by integrating Shamir (1979) and Rabin (1989) techniques in Krawczyk (1993). For secret or data security we encrypt the data using n encryption keys which need to be transmitted over the network for decryption. Thus, we use Information Dispersal to distribute these keys and decryption is successful only if any m of these keys is correctly received. Krawczyk (1993) has combined the two techniques of encryption and Information Dispersal to be used as one to help provide better results and a more secure and reliable network.

Dispersal of Probabilistic Latency Targets

Here authors use Information Dispersal Algorithms to create a certain redundancy in a network which is necessary to ensure that we can reconstitute the file F from the dispersed parts. Thus, the data is dispersed using IDA and the (n, m) threshold scheme. The aim here is to add a limit to the time of reconstruction of the file F and determine the value of n and m so as to optimize the delay for reconstruction. The latency can be bound by delay which defines the maximum amount of time it can take to reconstruct the file F. The values of n and m in the (n, m) threshold scheme Rabin (1989) need to be optimally chosen so as to maximize the probability of reconstructing the file successfully and to minimize the delay in reconstructing the file. Nakayama and Yener (2001) also discuss the various parameters such as file size, delay bound, loss rate, distance from destination and their effect on the QoS of the scheme.

Distributed Backup of Files

Backup of files in a distributed network is a necessity because each information or data present on the system is under multiple security threats such as theft, malicious usage, tampering etc.. So to reduce the amount of risk of the loss of a data file, the network keeps a backup of the file in some form within the network. The most popular scheme for the backup of files is to replicate the entire file on multiple locations within the network.

The backup of files in any distributed environment can be made efficient by the use of Information Dispersal Algorithms. The backup of a file can be made distributed with each share of file F, obtained from the Information Dispersal Algorithm, be sent to a different node on the network and the recombination of any threshold number of these shares can correctly provide the original file. This not only makes the backup efficient but also makes the backup scheme more secure and reliable due to the fact that the file can be reconstituted and restored even when a few of the nodes are not available or have their share of the file F due to any reason. This scheme provides significant advantage over the existing replication schemes for backup in terms of their storage and load requirements. Giampaolo Bella, Costantino Pistagna and Salvatore Riccobene discuss the application of Information Dispersal Algorithms in the backup of data on a distributed network called Chord in Bella et al. (2006). This scheme is presented a lot of advantages over the existing replication scheme such as availability, security, optimal redundancy and efficient resource management. The authors use M.O. Rabin's Information Dispersal Algorithm to distribute the backup file in their distributed network. This scheme can be applied in multiple distributed network scenarios such as cloud architecture, private distributed networks etc.

Time-Critical Reliable Communication

In some computational environments, time constraints are levied on the system. This makes the system require some mechanism to optimize the schemes applied on the system such that they can conform to these constraints. Thus, the researchers realized a need to optimize Information Dispersal Algorithms in the same way as well.

Bestavros (1994) compares the probabilistic Information Dispersal schemes discussed in the past with the Adaptive IDA that they developed for time critical communication. Unlike original Information Dispersal Algorithms that just provide a lower limit on the hard time constraints, this adaptive IDA however provides a scheme for bandwidth allocation on various time-critical networks.

Parallel-Computers Processor Communication

As described by Rabin (1989), Information dispersal algorithms can be used to provide optimal routing in an architecture that employs parallel computers. The parallel computing network has 2n processors placed on the vertices of an n-dimensional Boolean cube represented by $Cn = \{0,1\}n$, such that each processor has n processors as its neighbors. Thus, we distribute the file F among its n neighbors by using Information Dispersal Algorithms and recombine it at the destination using any m of these shares. This scheme provides an advantage that even if n-m of the shares are lost due to any reason, we can still reconstitute the file at the receiving node.

The security feature added by the distribution of file to various nodes and never actually existing on one particular node, makes it an additional advantage in this system. Also, it provides the benefits of improving the reliability of the system and the availability of the file on any given instant of time.

The applications discussed above are some of the basic spheres where Information Dispersal Algorithms (IDA) find their usage. Information Dispersal Algorithms can however be used in any system or environment that can be set in such a way that the data is required to be distributed over some network or over some set of participants. With the development of the latest technology and the usage of many kinds of networks in every field, the implementation of this technique can find its way in many prospects.

Many other applications of Information Dispersal Algorithms have also been discussed in the past some of which were not explored to the maximum and thus lacked basic content. A Few of these applications have been discussed in Rabin (1990) as well. We do not discuss these applications in detail because they require further exploration and substantial research to be done on them before they become useful and discussion worthy.

CONCLUSION

The schemes discussed above are simple mathematical techniques that disperse and reconstitute the data or file, when provided with some pre-requisites. They each have their own benefits and drawbacks but all of them consistently show the benefits provided by Information Dispersal such as security, reliability, availability of resource, etc. They have a similar basic strategy but different particulars that make them unique in their own way. These schemes have evolved over time and are very widely used in various fields like security, backup of data, probabilistic latency targets and many others.

REFERENCES

Aljawarneh, S., Aldwairi, M., & Yassein, M. B. (2017). Anomaly-based intrusion detection system through feature selection analysis and building hybrid efficient model. *Journal of Computational Science*. doi:10.1016/j.jocs.2017.03.006

Aljawarneh, S., Yassein, M.B., & Talafha, W.A. (2017). A multithreaded programming approach for multimedia big data: encryption system. *Multimed Tools Appl.* <ALIGNMENT.qj></ALIGNMENT>10.1007/s11042-017-4873-9

Aljawarneh, S. A., Alawneh, A., & Jaradat, R. (2017). Cloud security engineering: Early stages of SDLC. *Future Generation Computer Systems*, *74*, 385–392. doi:10.1016/j.future.2016.10.005

Aljawarneh, S. A., Moftah, R. A., & Maatuk, A. M. (2016). Investigations of automatic methods for detecting the polymorphic worms signatures. *Future Generation Computer Systems*, *60*, 67–77. doi:10.1016/j.future.2016.01.020

Aljawarneh, S. A., Vangipuram, R., Puligadda, V. K., & Vinjamuri, J. (2017). G-SPAMINE: An approach to discover temporal association patterns and trends in internet of things. *Future Generation Computer Systems*, *74*, 430–443. doi:10.1016/j.future.2017.01.013

Asmuth, C. A., & Blakley, G. R. (1982, April). Pooling, splitting, and restituting information to overcome total failure of some channels of communication. In *Security and Privacy, 1982 IEEE Symposium on* (pp. 156-156). IEEE. doi:10.1109/SP.1982.10019

Béguin, P., & Cresti, A. (1998). General information dispersal algorithms. *Theoretical Computer Science*, *209*(1-2), 87–105. doi:10.1016/S0304-3975(97)00098-4

Bella, G., Pistagna, C., & Riccobene, S. (2006). Distributed backup through information dispersal. *Electronic Notes in Theoretical Computer Science*, *142*, 63–77. doi:10.1016/j.entcs.2004.11.046

Berlekamp, E. R. (1968). *Algebraic coding theory*. Academic Press.

Bestavros, A. (1994). An adaptive information dispersal algorithm for time-critical reliable communication. In Network Management and Control (pp. 423-438). Springer US. doi:10.1007/978-1-4899-1298-5_37

Blakley, G. R. (1979). Safeguarding cryptographic keys. *Proc. of the National Computer Conference*, *48*, 313-317.

De Santis, A., & Masucci, B. (2002). On information dispersal algorithms. In *Information Theory, 2002. Proceedings. 2002 IEEE International Symposium on* (p. 410). IEEE. doi:10.1109/ISIT.2002.1023682

Kalpana, G., Kumar, P. V., Aljawarneh, S., & Krishnaiah, R. V. (2017). Shifted Adaption Homomorphism Encryption for Mobile and Cloud Learning. *Computers & Electrical Engineering*. doi:10.1016/j.compeleceng.2017.05.022

Krawczyk, H. (1993a, August). Secret sharing made short. In *Annual International Cryptology Conference* (pp. 136-146). Springer Berlin Heidelberg.

Krawczyk, H. (1993b, September). Distributed fingerprints and secure information dispersal. In *Proceedings of the twelfth annual ACM symposium on Principles of distributed computing* (pp. 207-218). ACM. doi:10.1145/164051.164075

Nakayama, M. K., & Yener, B. (2001). Optimal information dispersal for probabilistic latency targets. *Computer Networks*, *36*(5), 695–707. doi:10.1016/S1389-1286(01)00184-0

Ogata, W., Kurosawa, K., & Tsujii, S. (1993). Nonperfect secret sharing schemes. In Advances in Cryptology—AUSCRYPT'92 (pp. 56-66). Springer Berlin/Heidelberg. doi:10.1007/3-540-57220-1_52

Rabin, M. O. (1989). Efficient dispersal of information for security, load balancing, and fault tolerance. *Journal of the Association for Computing Machinery*, *36*(2), 335–348. doi:10.1145/62044.62050

Rabin, M. O. (1990). The information dispersal algorithm and its applications. In *Sequences* (pp. 406–419). Springer New York. doi:10.1007/978-1-4612-3352-7_32

Shamir, A. (1979). How to share a secret. *Communications of the ACM*, *22*(11), 612–613. doi:10.1145/359168.359176

Singh, A., Juneja, D., & Malhotra, M. (2015). A Novel Agent Based Autonomous Service Composition Framework for Cost Optimization of Resource Provisioning in Cloud Computing. In JKSU-CIS. Elsevier.

Singh, A., & Malhotra, M. (2015). Evaluation of a Secure Agent based optimized Resource Scheduling Framework in Cloud Environment. IJCAR, 188-198.

Singh, A., & Malhotra, M. (2016). Hybrid Two Tier Framework for Improved Security in Cloud Environment. India-Com, 1601-1606.

Singh, A., & Malhotra, M. (n.d.). A Novel Agent Based Framework for Cost Optimization in Cloud Computing Environment. *International Journal of Cloud Applications*, 53–61.

Sun, H. M., & Shieh, S. P. (1994, December). Optimal information dispersal for reliable communication in computer networks. In *Parallel and Distributed Systems, 1994. International Conference on* (pp. 460-464). IEEE.

Chapter 5

Identification of Various Privacy and Trust Issues in Cloud Computing Environment

Shivani Jaswal
Chandigarh University, India

Manisha Malhotra
Chandigarh University, India

ABSTRACT

Cloud computing is a rising paradigm in today's world. In this, users can send his or her request to any CSP, i.e., cloud service provider, of their choice. In return, the CSP reverts him back with that particular service. Now, while communicating from various two locations, the data transferred is not passed through that much amount of security and privacy as expected. So, there are lots of parameters in the environment that are taken care of while sending, receiving or just passing data over the network. This chapter presents various security issues that are underlying in cloud computing. This chapter has illustrated various issues such as Trust, Encryption, Authenticity, Confidentiality and Multi Tenancy. Also, some of the proposed solutions have also been discussed later in the chapter.

INTRODUCTION

Cloud Computing has emerged as a latest domain in terms of technology as well as research. It works basically on the principle of 'pay as per the use model". Cloud computing is a fifth generation computing truly based on service provisioning based

DOI: 10.4018/978-1-5225-3029-9.ch005

on virtualization. This model believes in providing various benefits like speedy deployment, pay as per the usage, economical in costs, scalable, rapid in approving requests, long lasting network access, greater resiliency, hypervisor security against system assaults, lower in cost in context of disaster recovery on-request security controls, continuous recognition of framework altering and quick re-constitution of administrations (Armbrust, et al, 2010).

Cloud computing services can be categorized into three categories: Software as a Service (SaaS), Platform as a Service (PaaS) and infrastructure as a Service (IaaS).

Here, SaaS facilitates to the clients that wants to access provider's software applications which is going to run on a cloud infrastructure (Aljawarneh,et al, 2016). Applications are managed and controlled by cloud service provider. Customersneed not to buy the software but instead they can use those services by using web API. For example, Google Docs purely relies its working on JAVA Script, which further runs in the Web browser (Bonatti et al, 2000).

One of thecategories of cloud service is Platform-as-a-service (PaaS). It is a service that delivers application.In this, the client can utilize the cloud specialist co-op's applications to send their applications by utilizing different programming dialects and devices bolstered by the supplier. The service provider does not need to deal with the basic cloud framework but rather shows the control over the sent application (Aberer, et al., 2001). A common example of PaaS is Google App Engine that facilitates the developer to run program on Google's Infrastructure.

Another type of cloud service model is known as Infrastructure-as-a-service (IaaS). In this, virtual machine images are provided as a service and machines generally contains what developers actually want. Rather than acquiring servers, programming, server farm assets, arrange hardware, and the skill to work them, clients can purchase these assets as an outsourced benefit conveyed through the system cloud. Also, the user can increase or decrease the quantity of virtual machines as per their increasing or decreasing requirements. For example, host firewalls.

CLOUD COMPUTING ARCHITECTURE

The working of Cloud computing is generally divided into two parts: backend and frontend (Armbrust, et al., 2009). Here, Frontend is basically a "user section" and backend is a "cloud section".Also, there is a server which works in centralized manner which is further helpful in administering the system and checks whether the system is running smoothly or not, by fulfilling the client's demands. The proper functioning of the environment is taken under some set of rules and protocols that uses special software known as middleware (Singh et al, 2014).

Figure 1. Architecture of high-level cloud middleware

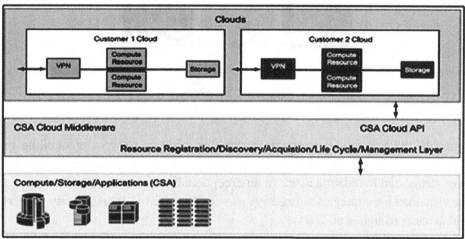

Cloud middleware is also known as Cloud OS, which helps in controlling the services. Networked computers can communicate with each other with the help of middleware. For example: Google App Engine and Amazon EC2/S3.

In an improved vision of the cloud computing, Client sends benefit solicitations to the server. Then system management finds appropriate resources. After the computing resources are found, then the request which was made by client is executed. Finally, the found results are forwarded to clients as a service (Zhang et al, 2010).

INTRODUCTION TO CLOUD COMPUTING CHALLENGES

Over the most recent couple of years, the engaging elements of cloud computing have been filling the incorporation of cloud conditions in the business, which has been therefore inspiring scholarly community and enterprises to proceed onward the way of research (Beth, et al., 1994). Notwithstanding its focal points, the move to this registering worldview raises security concerns, which are the subject of a few reviews. Other than of the issues gotten from Web advancements and the Internet, mists present new issues that ought to be gotten out first keeping in mind the end goal to additionally enable the quantity of cloud arrangements to increment.

The new worldview of Cloud Computing has extreme security dangers to its adopters because of the circulated way of Cloud Computing situations which make them a rich focus for vindictive people. Cloud lives with a completely virtual framework which is, undetectable to the client. This characteristic deliberation guarantees that an application or business administration is not straightforwardly

Figure 2. Security challenges under the services of cloud computing

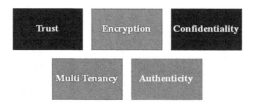

fixing to the basic equipment framework, for example, servers, stockpiling or systems. This permits business administration's to move progressively crosswise over virtualized foundation assets in an exceptionally productive way. In any case, the virtualization strategies utilized as a part of Cloud have various security dangers and assaults (Singh et al, 2015).

As compared to dedicated resource, a Cloud environment which is fully on partially shared, faces a greater risk of attack as compared to dedicated resource environment. Cloud Instances (CIs) are more likely to be got attacked as their task is to move between public and private cloud. Moreover, the easiness of cloning a virtual machine instance leads to propagation of security vulnerabilities and configuration errors. Cloud Consumers run numerous applications/scripts in order to complete their computing tasks. Most of them are too complex and complicated to trust. Even while accessing the source code, it is quite difficult to look after the security of these applications (Rizwana et al, 2012). They might generate codes such as viruses, worms, Trojan horses, bugs that are exploitable to the input generated. It is essential that instead of just relying on conventional defense techniques, the next generation of system software must be designed from the ground up to provide stronger isolation of services running on computer systems.

The users and cloud stores sensitive as well as confidential information on to the cloud service provider to reduce cost financially by giving up the control of data of unnecessary data. Therefore, data over the network can be leaked or attacked by the hacker those results in loss of confidential data (Staab et al, (2004).

TRUST

Cloud computing has turned into a conspicuous worldview of registering and IT benefit conveyance. A user can often ask, "Can this model be trusted?" Furthermore, what exactly is the meaning of "trust" in the area or field of cloud computing? What is the ground nature of that trust? (Beth et al, 2004). On this basis of what attributes a client should trust? Who will be the assigned authorities to check, verify, validate

Figure 3. Broader sections of trust

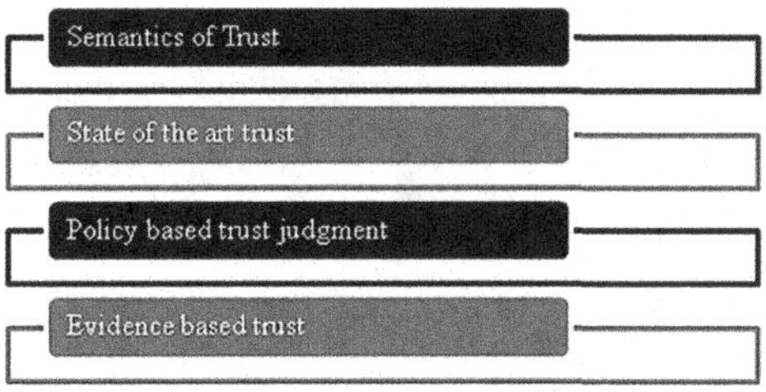

or assess cloud attributes? The answers to all the trust based questions are mandatory to be answered so that cloud computing can be adopted widely and finally be helpful in trustworthy computing paradigm (Singh et al, (2016).

Also, instead of informal trust mechanisms, decisions needs to be based on formal trust mechanisms which further helps in making the "official" type of assessment in the society.

Advancement of trust between any cloud specialist co-op and a client goes about as a most compelling motivation of concern now a days. It generally remains an issue of test for a client which cloud specialist co-op he ought to trust upon and whether his information over the system will stay free from gatecrashers or not.To solve this problem, a type of agreement is signed between the cloud service provider and the user. This agreement is known as Service Level Agreement i.e. SLA. It is a legal contract signed among the client (who will be suing the services of cloud) and the CSP (who will be providing services to the user) (Vaquero et al, 2011).

Basically we can divide the challenge of "Trust" into four broader sections i.e.

- Semantics of Trust
- State of the art trust
- Policy based trust judgment
- Evidence based trust

SEMANTICS OF TRUST

Broadly two types of trust can be identified, based on the expectancy of the trustor: *trust in performance*which purely depends upon the performance of the trustee whereas *trust in belief* depends upon the kind of belief a trustee holds. The trustee's execution could be reality of what the trustee says or the accomplishment of what the trustee does (Shaikh et al, 2012).

A trust in performance relationship,

t r u s t _p(d,e, x,k),

Here, trustor = d

trustee = e

performance = x

Above written relationship shows that if e believes x then d also believes x.

trust_b(d,e,x,k)≡believe(e,k⊃ x)⊃believe(d,k⊃)trust_b(d,e,x,k)≡believe(e,k⊃x)⊃ believe(d,k⊃x).

Therefore, we can say that "Trust in belief" is transitive whereas trust in performance is not. Also, trust in performance can move through trust in belief. From the definition above, the trustor's mental condition of faith in his hope on the trustee is subject to the confirmation about the trustee's competency, trustworthiness, and goodwill. This prompts sensible structures of thinking from confidence in proof to faith in hope (Jingwei et al, 2013).

STATE OF THE ART TRUST

It can be studied under as:

- Reputation based trust
- SLA verification based trust.

REPUTATION BASED TRUST

Trust and reputation are interrelated, but different in some context. Basically, trust is between two substances; whereas reputation is the compiled opinion of a community towards that substance. We can say that, a community having higher level of reputation is trusted by another number of entities. Also, one who wants to make judgment can make use of calculation and estimation analysis. Here, reputation plays a vital role in choosing any service in some manner. In particular, by the time, a user becomes successful in gaining experience with service.

These sorts of frameworks are broadly utilized as a part of online business and P2P systems. The notoriety of cloud administrations or cloud specialist co-ops will without a doubt affect cloud clients' decision of cloud administrations; thus, cloud suppliers attempt to construct and keep up higher notoriety. Actually, notoriety based trust goes into the vision of making trust judgment in distributed computing (Bonatti et al, 2005).

Reputation plays a key role while choosing a service for the first time. Particularly, while using a service, a user gains experience afterwards, new trust is built regarding service service based on performance or reliability requirements. A specific use cannot trust 100% on any CSP but just taking reputation factor into an account.

SLA VERIFICATION BASED TRUST

"Trust, however confirm" is a solid counsel for managing the connections between cloud clients and cloud specialist co-ops. In the wake of building up the underlying trust and utilizing a cloud administration, the cloud client needs to confirm and reconsider the trust. A service level agreement (SLA) is a legal agreement which is signed between a cloud client and a cloud service provider (Aberer, Ket al, 2001). Therefore, quality of service (QoS) monitors and verification of SLA are an important basis of trust management for cloud computing. A number of models have been proposed that derive trust from SLA verification.

Now, arises the major issues. Sometimes, SLA just focuses on "visible" elements of the service and neglects the "invisible" elements of the services. Also, sometimes, many users do not have capability as well as knowledge regarding monitoring of Quality of Service and SLA verification.

In this way, an expert outsider is expected to give these administrations. In a private cloud, there might be a cloud representative or a trust specialist that is confided in the trust space of the private cloud; so the trusted dealer or trust expert can give the clients in the private cloud the administrations of QoS checking and SLA confirmation. In hybrid clouds, a client inside a private cloud may in any case depend on the private cloud trust expert to lead QoS checking and SLA confirmation; be that as it may, in an open cloud, singular clients and some little associations without specialized ability may utilize a business proficient cloud substance as trust dealer.

POLICY BASED TRUST

This type of trust plays a key role in architecture of open and distributed services as it act as a solution to the problem of authorizing access of control in an open system. The main focus lies on the trust management mechanisms which employ various languages based on policies and various engines that specify reasoning on rules for trust establishment. Here the goal is to think whether an unknown user can be trusted fully or partially, specifically based on credentials and policies (Grandison et al, 2002).

Presently, policy based trust involves various access control decisions. For specifying access control conditions, declarative policies are very well suited that further generates a Boolean decision (in which resources are either granted or denied). Various systems that enforces policy based trust use languages with well defined semantics and further make decisions based on "non subjective" attributes (e.g. address, age etc) which are certified by certification authorities (e.g. digital signatures etc). Generally, policy based trust is developed for the system having strong requirements for protection, for systems having complex rules or for the systems having exact authorization process.

EVIDENCE BASED TRUST

From the meaning of trust given in § 'Semantics of trust', a trustor's faith in the normal conduct of trustee depends on the proof about the trustee's traits of competency, goodwill, and trustworthiness, as for that desire. Formally, we could express a general type of proof based trust as takes after:

believe(u,attr1(s,v1))∧...∧believe(u,attrn(s,vn))→trust_*(u,s,x,c)

which expresses that if an individual u trusts a subject s has property a t r1 with esteem v1,..., trait a t r n with esteem v n, then u trusts (either confide in conviction or trust in execution) s as for x, the execution of s or data made or accepted by s, in a particular setting.

TRUST MODEL

Numerous endeavors have been done in setting of creating trust. A trust model is displayed into upgrade the security and interoperability of distributed computing condition. Imposing Healthcare Social Cloud introduces a trust rating instrument to secure the cloud condition in a joint effort with web-based social networking. SLA Framework is utilized as a part of to propose a trust administration display for security in cloud condition (Edna et al, 2012).

Assessing a cloud benefit security is the need for any association moving towards the cloud. We have distinguished a far reaching rundown of security parameters that are vital and adequate to quantify security as for distributed computing condition.

These parameters are consolidated in our trust show and trust esteem is the result. Trust esteem can be a solitary esteem giving the idea of general security of a cloud benefit. It can likewise be separated to different parts of security in light of the parameters and spoken to as a vector. A client can choose a cloud benefit in light of its necessity and requests either for character, information security or whatever other measure recorded in the trust esteem vector (Hamid et al, 2013). Trust demonstrate comprises of different parameters that rely on upon sub parameters and capacities. Capacities are non-flimsy and can be utilized for estimation of quality. Figure 1 shows the theoretical structure of the trust display with the individual parameters expounded with their sub parameters and capacities.

IDENTITY MANAGEMENT-IDM-A

IDM is a key component of the security eco-framework for cloud, and when all is said in done for any web applications. Each cloud benefit has a procedure of creating characters for the cloud clients. This procedure can be inspected to decide security quality related with it. It frames one of the trust segments as IDM quality. Different parameters pertinent to the IDM procedure incorporate personality creation, stockpiling and the life cycle administration of the character. These procedures can be measured against the IDM quality segment of the trust demonstrate.

Figure 4. Parameters of trust model

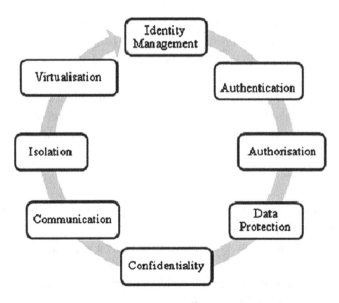

Authentication-B

To expand client certainty at the season of login and character confirmation handle, validation check is required. It is a two sided handle, for client getting to an administration from credible supplier and for supplier to offer administrations to the authentic client. Consequently, genuine utilization of cloud administration by a honest to goodness supplier can be dictated by the quality of verification that structures one of the segments of the trust demonstrate. It quantifies the procedure given by a cloud administration to validation check for client and also benefit (Muchahari et al, 2012).

Authorization-C

A client ought not to have the capacity to utilize any activities not approved for. This property can be checked against the approval quality. An activity including administration get to, playing out any operations, and all information/yield related exercises requires approving clients at these stages. A cloud benefit gives approval by utilizing different strategies. The viability of the strategy is measured regarding the approval quality. It is measured as for the put away ACL (Access Control Strength) trustworthiness, Presence of PMI (Privilege Management Information) and the way toward performing approval check of client.

Data Protection-D

The significant resource of a client and also any association proceeding onward to the cloud is information. Information security issues are at awesome concerns while moving information to and from cloud condition. An information insurance component show by different administrations has qualities that should be measured while assessing the information assurance quality. These can be measured by the information insurance trust esteem part of the model. Information Confidentiality, Integrity and Availability can be measured as for the information assurance quality.

Confidentiality-E

A cloud administration ought to ensure the mystery of the correspondence between a cloud client and supplier and every single other activity performed in different exercises. This property can be measured by privacy parameter. Methods for accomplishing protection of the information, message, Identity era and every other correspondence amongst supplier and client can be measured concerning the classification quality given by the administration.

Communication-F

Information or messages gone in the distributed computing condition inclined to listening in or spillage. The correspondence quality measures the arrangement given by the cloud benefit at the season of information or message transmission. Along these lines the correspondence quality measures quality of norms utilized for message transmission and correspondence.

Isolation-G

Multitenant highlights of distributed computing framework prompts the issue of confinement of assets among numerous clients. Security breaks and infringement are the key variables that are brought on basically because of disengagement. Cloud benefit detachment quality decides the level of assurance given to wipe out the security breaks and limit client get to ranges. The separation quality measured by the trust display, decides the level of security at asset, application and information that is given by the cloud benefit (Shekarpour et al, 2010).

Virtualization-H

The idea of cloud computing is deficient without the virtualization included. A virtualized framework is more inclined to assaults then the physical one. Procedures ought to be given to secure the virtualized condition. The parameter that measures the viability of the security connected to ensure the virtualized condition is virtualization. It decides the security thought at virtualization layer of a distributed computing engineering. It incorporates quality of VM (Virtual Machine), VMM (VM Monitor), Guest VM insurance quality and other checking apparatuses.

Compliance-I

In this, the security can be determined by getting various certifications from various communities and standards.

All the above parameters cover almost all the aspects of cloud security. These parameters are measured individually and the overall sum generates the strength of a service offered by cloud computing

For example

S1(Any cloud service) can have A(Strength value) = 0.8

S2(Any cloud service) can have B(Strength value) = 0.7

Note: The values of Trust evaluated so far just gives an idea of static trust. If a user wants to keep dynamic trust into consideration then it should be made more realistic.

The parameter is shown by the tree structure dictated by the root name. Level alongside root demonstrates sub parameters and leaf hub shows capacities. Hubs speak to parent-tyke relationship. Parent hub can be the weighted whole of its kid hubs. The weights are distinctive for various levels and are talked about in each of the parameters depictions. These weights are chosen in light of the kind of capacity utilized and time to break the accomplished security utilizing them. The genuine parameters are depicted as a gathering of weighted aggregate of its relating sub parameters and capacities. At long last the root hub which demonstrates trust esteem is the vector entirety of the considerable number of parameters.

ARCHITECTURE OF CLOUD USING TRUST MODEL

Various components are required to prepare trust calculation environment. A structure is designed so that trust can be calculated with multiple services provided by cloud service provider. The architecture in figure shows the various components of trust evaluation in cloud environment.

Major components are:

CLOUD SERVICE MANAGER

It plays a vital role in trust model. It provides various specific details such as type of service. It provides details about a specific cloud service like type of service. It also contains information about the specific users associated with that particular

Figure 5. Tree structure of parameters of trust model

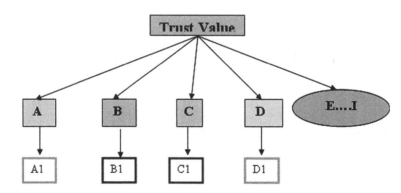

service. Also, this kind of information is present remains present with Cloud Service Manager in an updated format. Now, particularly, Cloud Service Manager further contains two types of trust value i.e. Static trust value and dynamic trust value. Here, static trust value is a value which is associated with cloud service which is going to be in use for the first time. Dynamic trust value is calculated with the help of parameters (Pearson et al, 2010).

TRUST EVALUATOR

It is an evaluator that calculates static or dynamic trust values on the basis of various service details available. It also makes use of service log and web for its calculation.

SERVICE LOG

It is a kind of database or log book that contains various information about any service provided by a cloud. It contains information such as number of successful and unsuccessful transactions, response time, waiting time, throughput time and so on. These details are then transferred to the trust model to calculate trust value.

WEB RESEARCH

It helps in drawing conclusions about dynamic trust values of cloud services by collecting various user feedback and comment. Now, if a cloud user want ot utilise one of the service, then he will contact with cloud service manager. Before providing the service, a cloud service manager will take all the possible details into consideration.

CONFIDENTIALITY

It means to prevent the disclosure of private and confidential information. As it is already known that information on any cloud is stored on dispersed locations, so confidentiality becomes an area of concern.

It assures that the consent is given to authorise users for it access. Here, data confidentiality refers to keep data secure from unauthorized access when it is in safe state as well as when the data is in transit state. While ensuring the confidentiality, some additional dimensions are need to be considered viz. user privacy and access privacy. Privacy is considered as one of the primary requirements for achieving security. User privacy is ensuring when he tries to fetch or manipulate data.

Data confidentiality is considered as one of the arising challenge in the ongoing research in Cloud computing. To ensure confidentiality, data is first encrypted and then transferred to the service provider. To continue with this process, external service provider is taken into account. In this, control is outsourced from the third service provider to ensure the maintainability of the confidentiality. Various cryptographic techniques are considered as an existing solution. Also, Storage as a service is generally used by small scale business which is unable to take overheads of capital budget. Many commercial and legal regulations are demanding the need to develop trustworthy solutions for protecting confidential as well as sensitive data whenever it is saved, processed or communicated among the external parties.

Cryptography algorithms are the most efficient tool to ensure the security of data storage in the cloud. Indeed, there are many encryption algorithms that can encrypt the data and convert them into incomprehensible format, in order to ensure their confidentiality (Kalpana et al, 2017).

In an insecure environment like the public cloud, sensitive data must be secured. Regarding the storage service, data must be encrypted before sending them to the cloud server, using the symmetric key cryptosystems such as: Blowfish, etc. But, to ensure the confidentiality of data storage and their treatments, the cloud providers must adopt techniques that can ensure the confidentiality of this type of service. Indeed, researchers stressed a useful encryption technique in this type of environment: Homomorphic Encryption (HE). This technique is able to ensure the confidentiality of data storage and their treatments, located in cloud servers (Yuefa et al, 2009).

The Homomorphic Encryption cryptosystems are asymmetric key, which use different keys for data encryption and decryption.

These algorithms are divided into two categories: symmetric and asymmetric key. The asymmetric key techniques performance is very slower than the symmetric key techniques, and used in general to exchange the keys of symmetric key algorithms. The symmetric key algorithms are a form of encryption that use same key to encrypt and decrypt the data, and are divided into block ciphers and steam ciphers. The input of block cipher when the data is encrypted or decrypted is in block of the fixed data size. This size is depending on the encryption algorithm used. But, in the case of stream cipher the data are encrypted/ decrypted one bit or one byte of data at that's why this cipher type is more efficient for real time processing. In this section, we focus on symmetric key algorithms which can be adopted by cloud providers to ensure the confidentiality of the data storage.

PRINCIPLES OF SYMMETRIC KEY CRYPTOSYSTEMS OPERATION

The philosophy of symmetric key cryptosystems when adopted to encrypt data in the cloud environment is somewhat different to other use cases. Generally, symmetric key techniques were created to encrypt messages, to ensure confidentiality of communication between the sender and the recipient over internet and network applications. The secret key is shared between them to encrypt and decrypt these messages. In cloud case these cryptosystems are used to ensure confidentiality of data, when transferred and when stored in cloud servers. Only the client can have the key. Thus, the data remains confidential and unreadable even to the cloud provider. The principles of operation of the symmetric key cryptosystems in cloud are as follows, and as shown in Figure3. Key Generation: The client generates private− key (PK). Encryption: The client encrypts data with− PK and sends the encrypted data to the Cloud server. Storage: The encrypted data are stored in the− cloud database. Decryption: The client decrypts data after− retrieve them from the cloud, using PK.

MULTI TENANCY

In a cloud environment, various resources and services re shred by various applications at various geographic locations. This is being carried out to resolve the issue of resource insufficiency and to eliminate the cost which is main purpose of cloud. Data and applications are stored on virtual servers as well as on actual hardware.

If these are stored on virtual servers, then their chances that a single virtual machine can have a malicious application which further affects the performance of their machines.

If these are stored on actual hardware, then there can be issues of multi-core processing. The typical solution to this kind to problem is employment of Intrusion Detection Systems to keep their customers and their information safe in cloud environment. Another method being used is Trusted Cloud Computing Platform i.e. TCCP which is designed to provide better security of the virtual machines.

To create secure and exclusive virtual computing environment, a tenant is considered as an application either inside or outside and enterprise. Basically, this environment works on all or some of the selected layers of the an architecture of enterprise i.e. from user interface to storage. All these applications must be multi-user in nature (Gonzalez et al, 2012).

Multi tenancy is considered as a common key attribute which is applicable to all types of the cloud i.e. public, private or hybrid. It is also applicable to the service models i.e. SaaS, PaaS or IaaS. Multi tenancy is also applies to a new service model i.e. ITaaS.

In general terms, the term "software multitenancy" is considered as an architecture in which a single instance of software runs on a single server which further helps in serving multiple tenants. A tenant is referred as a group of several users who shares some common access to a software with specific privileges. In case of multi tenant architecture, an application of software is designed so that a dedicated instance among some users is shared. Along with this instance, its data, user management information, its properties (functional or non functional) are also shared. Here, it is also known that multi instance is totally different from multi tenancy.

Multi tenancy can further be divided into two levels i.e.

- Hypervisor level isolation.
- DB level isolation.

HYPERVISOR LEVEL ISOLATION

It is applicable to low level layer of any software which maps a physical machine with virtual machine on which a particular operating system is run. When this operating system send request to the virtual machine, it is firstly accepted by the hypervisor. Here, this hypervisor isolation also provides the some operating functions such as process scheduling to know which kind of virtual machine is to be run.

An extra layer of indirection is introduced by hypervisor. If a virtual machine is required than a lesser capacity then a hardware partitioning is done to improve the efficiency of the service. This helps in lessen of security concerns.

DB LEVEL ISOLATION

In this isolation, various applications are run by tenant, only difference is the type of data stored by each tenant. So to make this bifurcated, a special id i.e. "t_id" is associated with the each table. Each and every query is executed with the help of this "t_id".

In this approach, rewritten query is done to make degree of isolation more efficient. This is much easier way than hypervisor level.

One of the advantage of DB level isolation is that there is no use of virtual machine overheads which further compiles to lesser economic value to tenant.

SELECTING OUT OF HYPERVISOR AND DB LEVEL ISOLATION

In hypervisor isolation, tenant is given a choice of selecting a service that will serve to its applications and other IT skills. But, to apply this, efficient system administrators are required to be hired for the maintenance of technology stack.

- In DB level isolation, a tight coupling is created between tenant and Cloud service provider. Also, in this the degree of freedom is also limited.
- In case of hypervisor isolation, no reuse of application is allowed. Tenants are required to create their technology stack and further write their own application logic.
- In case of DB level approach, a set of templates is pre defined by the cloud service provider. It purely focuses on operation of a business.

For example, Amazon AWS lies in the category of hardware level in which many users share a physical machine. On another, Force.com lies in the category of DB level in which many users share common database and tables (Subashini et al, 2011).

Therefore, we can say that hypervisor and DB isolation are valid in different context and is applicable to different set of users.

DEGREE OF MULTI TENANCY

It is commonly defined as the tendency of SaaS layer which is to be designed which is too shared among the various tenants.

The degree of multi tenancy is followed in the below written way:

ADVANTAGES OF MULTI TENANCY OVER SINGLE TENANT APPLICATION

- **Lower Cost:** In case of multi tenant environment, new users as well as old users get access to basic (same) software so in that case scaling requires lesser infrastructure.
- **Sharing:** Medium sized business don't need data centers if they are using Software as a Service. Also, SaaS allows organizations to share all facilities at operational costs.

Table 1. Degree of multi tenancy

S. No.	Level	Applicable to Multi Tenancy
1.	Highest degree	IaaS, PaaS and SaaS are fully supportive.
2.	Middle degree	IaaS, PaaS and small SaaS are fully supportive.
3.	Lowest degree	IaaS, PaaS fully supportive.

- **Maintenance and Updates:** While using cloud services, end users are not required to pay maintenance as well as updation fees. Updates and new features are automatically updated by subscription and are paid to the vendors by the users.
- **Configurable:** As we know that services provided by cloud highly configurable that supports multi tenancy. It is so that users can make their application perform as they want, without making any change in underlying code on backend data structure. As the code will remain unchanged, so they can be updated easily.

AUTHENTICATION

Authentication is the demonstration of affirming reality of a quality of a solitary bit of information (a datum) asserted valid by a substance. Conversely with distinguishing proof, which alludes to the demonstration of expressing or generally showing a claim purportedly validating a man or thing's personality, verification is the procedure of really affirming that character. It may include affirming the character of a man by approving their personality records, checking the credibility of a site with a computerized endorsement, deciding the age of a curio via cell based dating, or guaranteeing that an item is the thing that its bundling and naming case to be. At the end of the day, verification frequently includes confirming the legitimacy of no less than one type of recognizable proof (Puttaswamy et al, 2011).

In private as well as public networking environments, authentication is basically done through the use of username and password. Authentication part is cleared when the user inputs the correct username and password.

In the beginning, a user is required to make him registered with some initial stage password. But the biggest disadvantage is that, these passwords can be easily stolen, can be revealed or can be forgotten. To change password of authentication, previously declared must be remembered (Aljawarneh et al, 2017).

These systems and techniques are not optimized enough to make any authentication secure enough to withstand every type of security breach, which points towards the necessity of more secured and fool proof authentication technique.

There are various ways out of which authentication can be categorized:

On the Basis of Factors of Authentication

- Something that user knows.
- Something that user has.
- Something that covers range of elements to verify user's identity.

On the Basis of Ownership

Something that user possess (like ID cards, wrist band, security tokens, software tokens, phone tokens etc)

On the Basis of Factors of Knowledge

Something user knows i.e. passwords, PIN, challenge response etc.) (Aljawarneh et al, 2016).

On the Basis of Factors of Inherence

Something that user does (renal pattern, finger print, face recognition, voice recognition, bio meteric etc.)

Even these represent general scenario of authentication covering basic definition. Over the years many different methods have been proposed to solve this problem or to reduce it to a considerable extent, but still some flaws always occur in each one of them. So to provide a better insight into this problem of secured authentication, we propose a technique which might put an enormous hold over the topic of secured user authentication and access control. Basically user authentication is not the only step or process, it incorporates three A's i.e.

- Authentication
- Authorization
- Auditing.

In this work our main stress is toward these three A's and towards the security of critical data associated with CSP (like password storing files or access control files etc).

- Methods Providing Secured Access Control
- Message Authentication and one time password generation
- Authentication using Private-key Ciphers
- Hashing Functions
- Digital Signature Scheme

Important points to be stressed upon in this research is related to secured user authentication and making sure that the intended hacker or cryptanalyst acting as intended/genuine customer is not able to access any of critical data/information belonging to CSP (such as passwords file or access control related information). And approach used to make it happen is elaborated in proposed schemata.

DIGITAL SIGNATURE AND RSA ENCRYPTION ALGORITHM FOR ENHANCED DATA SECURITY IN CLOUD

In cloud computing platform there are many problems of security like host security, network traffic, backups and critical user data security. A digital signature is a scheme based on mathematical model which demonstrates the authenticity of message or document encrypted with either RSA algorithm or any other algorithm like MD5/SHA etc. If a digital signature is valid it gives an impression to the recipient that message or document was created by a known and legitimate sender and was not altered in between the process of transferring. One can use digital signature and RSA scheme combined together to ensure the data security over cloud. RSA is the most recognizable asymmetric (i.e. requiring two different keys) algorithm. RSA was created by Ron Rivest, Adi Shamir, and Leonard Adleman in 1978 . In digital signature technique the process is that the data is crunched down in few lines using some kind of hashing algorithm which is a called as message digest. Then message digest is encrypted with private key and decrypted using pair of recipient's private key and public key of sender. Digital signature scheme can be used for distributing data over a network just like cloud where it is compulsory to detect forgery and tampering as cloud provides services like pay per use basis and on demand access to services of CSP. So it might prove to be an asset to implementing better security methods over a cloud.

KEY MANAGEMENT

The technique of managing cryptographic keys in a cryptosystem is known as key management. It includes various functions such as generating keys, storing them, using and replacing them. Whole functions are performed on the basis of protocols only.

This technique concerns with the keys at user level either among users or systems.

Successful key management is often critical for the security of a cryptosystem. Practically, it is the most difficult to implement cryptography because it involves training of users, organizational and departmental interactions and coordination among all of the elements (Singh e al, 2015).

Cryptographic is one of the security mechanisms that protect information from unauthorized confession. It can be used to provide security for data storage to protect its integrity while storing data on Cloud paradigm. Cryptographic key management is the most important element of cryptographic system as effective use of cryptographic system requires proper management of cryptographic key. To date, cryptographic key security has been ensured to protect it from vulnerability and security breaches. However, the use of cryptographic key in online or Cloud based applications has prompted large fraction of information security attacks since the consumer of Cloud does not have access to the physical storage servers. Cloud Security Alliance (CSA), the global leaders in Cloud security, has identified that the cryptographic key management at Cloud is a challenge (Gavriloaie et al, 2004).

They recommended that cryptographic keys should be stored on enterprise domain due to their sensitive nature. However, searching of encrypted data from a large data set is problematic on Cloud storage while cryptographic keys are stored at enterprise premises. Furthermore, these limitations of encrypted data restrict Cloud users and they cannot utilize all benefits of Cloud paradigm. All these concerns require a strong cryptographic key management system that can reduce the intricacy of operation on Cloud stored data by processing them on same platform. This research provides an effective and robust security protocol for symmetric cryptographic key management in Cloud that attempts to resolve the above mentioned issues. This thesis contributes in following aspects; Secure Data Storage on Cloud: This part of research offers a mechanism for secure storage of sensitive data on Cloud. This storage scheme can be further utilized in any type of data storage. Using secure protocol user can share cryptographic key with Cloud to manipulate encrypted data. Symmetric Cryptographic Key as a Service: Our second part of research provides Symmetric Cryptographic Key as a service and user may embed this service in other utilities such as mobile/PDAs digital signature utilities etc. Secure Data Access: On the fly computation of cryptographic key will ensure key access security. Proposed protocol is based on secret splitting and use enhanced Shamir's algorithm for cryptographic key splitting. Furthermore, this protocol distributes cryptographic key components to various Cloud servers. That ensures cryptographic key protection, even if the security on one of the Cloud server is compromised. All data transfer between Clouds is done through pkcs#7 protocols that provides data enveloping and de-enveloping during data travelling in insecure environment. In addition to this, SSL protocol is also used which connect end user browser to an application server securely.

As security is delicate issue in distributed computing .the information are originating from cloud utilizing open system (web) there are opportunities to hack the information (Armbrust et al, 2009). There have been parcel of work done on security issues and difficulties yet at the same time there is not 100% full confirmation arrangement. There are numerous physical and some other assault on information that decimate information on server. one answer for that is scattered the information on more than one server rather than one server .yet this not take care of issue totally in light of the fact that information put away in encoded mode utilizing encryption scratch .the aggressors assault on key and might be hack the information.

Attackers attack on data which is placed on same server. So presently ongoing solution is creating multiple copies of same data and that data is to be placed on multiple servers. But again, data is encrypted by an encrypted key. Further, attackers may attack on that encrypted key which further reveals date to the attackers. The solution of this problem is instead of keeping multiple copies of data on various serverson which we can apply Shamir's secret sharing on key. The encrypted key is divided into number of modules and to store them on different server. But again, if any of the attacker attacks on one of the server then that module or part of key is lost but still they can be reconstructed using Shamir's threshold scheme.

Secret Sharing Scheme

The most famous and perfect secret sharing scheme is (k,n)- threshold scheme which was proposed by Shamir in 1979. In this, a key can be reconstructed again and again with minimum number of secrets that are kept on various servers, even if attacked by an attacker. This scheme also overcomes the problem of key exchange. Division of keys is done with the range of polynomial (Aberer 2001).

Also, in this method secret is distributed among all the participants of the group. This secret can only be reconstructed or restructured when a number of shares are combined together. Individual secrets with a single sharing scheme, there are number of players associated with a single dealer. This dealer allocates a secret to a player after the completion of some conditions. In this, it is kept in mind that group of 't' (threshold) can together reconstruct a secret but no group of members less than 't' can reconstruct it. This system is sometimes known as (k-n) threshold scheme).

CONCLUSION

This chapter explains the concept of cloud and various other security issues related to cloud. This chapter has helped in throwing light on some of the major concerns of security i.e. Trust, multitenancy etc. Also, it has explained various solutions that are available till date in the market. As, we know, data security is one of the important issue in cloud computing. In any case, cloud specialist organizations are as yet utilizing customary symmetric key calculations for information security and not giving much straightforwardness on the security calculations being sent. It has also explained the concept of trust with the help of various parameters which are implemented in the trust model. Various key management mechanisms, authentication techniques have been explained in detail. This chapter has illustrates various cryptographic key management schemes (like Shamir secret sharing) used for sending data from one server to another. Also, the future work is concentrating on providing more and more solutions to the cloud computing security issues.

REFERENCES

Abdul-Rahman, A., & Hailes, S. (2000). Supporting trust in virtual communities. *Proceedings of 33rd Hawaii International Conference on System Sciences*, 777-780.

Aberer, K. (2001). P-grid: A self-organizing access structure for p2p information systems. *Proceedings of Ninth International Conference on Cooperative Information Systems*, 179-194.

Aberer, K., & Despotovic, Z. (2001). Managing trust in a peer-2-peer information system. *Proc. of 10th International Conference on Information and Knowledge Management*, 310-317. doi:10.1145/502585.502638

Aljawarneh, S., Aldwairi, M., & Yassein, M. B. (2017). Anomaly-based intrusion detection system through feature selection analysis and building hybrid efficient model. *Journal of Computational Science*. doi:10.1016/j.jocs.2017.03.006

Aljawarneh, S., Yassein, M.B., & Talafha, W.A. (2017). A multithreaded programming approach for multimedia big data: encryption system. *Multimed Tools Appl.* <ALIGNMENT.qj></ALIGNMENT>10.1007/s11042-017-4873-9

Aljawarneh, S. A., Alawneh, A., & Jaradat, R. (2017). Cloud security engineering: Early stages of SDLC. *Future Generation Computer Systems*, *74*, 385–392. doi:10.1016/j.future.2016.10.005

Aljawarneh, S. A., Moftah, R. A., & Maatuk, A. M. (2016). Investigations of automatic methods for detecting the polymorphic worms signatures. *Future Generation Computer Systems*, *60*, 67–7. doi:10.1016/j.future.2016.01.020

Aljawarneh, S. A., Vangipuram, R., Puligadda, V. K., & Vinjamuri, J. (2017). G-SPAMINE: An approach to discover temporal association patterns and trends in internet of things. *Future Generation Computer Systems*, *74*, 430–443. doi:10.1016/j.future.2017.01.013

Armbrust, M., Fox, A., Griffith, R., Joseph, A., Katz, R., Konwinski, A., . . . Stoica, M. (2009). Above The Clouds: A Berkeley View of Cloud Computing. UC Berkeley Reliable Adaptive Distributed Systems Laboratory, 1-23.

Armbrust, M., Fox, A., Griffith, R., Joseph, A. D., Katz, R. H., & Konwinski, A. (2010). A view of cloud computing. ACM Communication, 53(4), 50–58. doi:10.1145/1721654.1721672

Atallah, M., Frikken, K., & Blanton, M. (2005). Dynamic and Efficient Key Management for Access Hierarchies. *Proceedings of ACM Conference Computer Communication Security*, 190–202. doi:10.1145/1102120.1102147

Banirostam, H., Hedayati, A., Zadeh, A. K., & Shamsinezhad, E. (2013). A Trust Based Approach for Increasing Security in Cloud Computing Infrastructure. *15th International Conference on Computer Modelling and Simulation*, 717-721. doi:10.1109/UKSim.2013.39

Beth, T., Borcherding, M., & Klein, B. (1994). Valuation of trust in open networks. In *Proc. of the 3rd European Symposium on Research in Computer Security*. Springer-Verlag.

Bonatti, P., & Samarati, P. (2000). Regulating service access and information release on the web. *Proc. of the 7th ACM conference on computer and communications security*, 134-143. doi:10.1145/352600.352620

Bonatti, P. A., & Olmedilla, D. (2005). Driving and monitoring provisional trust negotiation with metapolicies. In *IEEE 6th International Workshop on Policies for Distributed Systems and Networks (POLICY)*. Stockholm, Sweden: IEEE Computer Society. doi:10.1109/POLICY.2005.13

Bonatti, P. A., Shahmehri, N., Duma, C., Olmedilla, D., Nejdl, W., Baldoni, M., . . . Fuchs, N. E. (2004). Rule-based policy specification: State of the art and future work. *Report I2:D1, EU NoE REWERSE, 2*(14), 10.

Canedo, E. D. (2012). Trust Model for Private Cloud. *IEEE International Conference on Cyber Security, Cyber Warfare and Digital Forensic (CyberSec)*, 380-389.

Caronni, G. (2000). Walking the web of trust. *Proceedings of 9th IEEE International Workshops on Enabling Technologies (WETICE)*, 153-158.

Duma, C., Shahmehri, N., & Caronni, G. (2005). Dynamic trust metrics for peer-to-peer systems. *Proc. of 2nd IEEE Workshop on P2P Data Management, Security and Trust*, 776-781.

Gavriloaie, R., Nejdl, W., Olmedilla, D., Seamons, K. E., & Winslett, M. (2004). No registration needed: How to use declarative policies and negotiation to access sensitive resources on the semantic web. In *1st European Semantic Web Symposium (ESWS 2004)*. Springer. doi:10.1007/978-3-540-25956-5_24

Gonzalez N, Miers C, Redigolo F, Jr M, Carvalho T, Naslund M & Pourzandi M (2012). A quantitative analysis of current security concerns and solutions for cloud computing. *Journal of Cloud Computing: Advances, System and Applications*, 1-11.

Goyal, O., & Pandey, A. (2006). Attribute-based encryption for fine-grained access control of encrypted data. *ACM Conference Computer Communication Security*, 89–98.

Grandison, T., & Sloman, M. (2002). Specifying and analysing trust for internet applications. In Towards The Knowledge Society: eCommerce, eBusiness, and eGovernment. In *The Second IFIP Conference on E-Commerce, E-Business, E-Government (I3E 2002), IFIP Conference Proceedings*. Lisbon, Portugal: Kluwer.

Hossein, R., Elankovan, S., Zulkarnain, M. A., & Abdullah, M. Z. (2013). Encryption as a service as a solution for cryptography in cloud. *International Conference on Electrical Engineering and Informatics indexed in Science Direct*, 1202-1210.

Huang, J., & Nicol. (2013). *Trust mechanisms for cloud computing*. Retrieved from http://www.journalofcloudcomputing.com/content/2/1/9

Jungwoo, R., Syed, R., William, A., & John, K. (2013). *Cloud Security Auditing: Challenges and Emerging Approaches*. IEEE Security and Privacy.

Kalpana, G., Kumar, P. V., Aljawarneh, S., & Krishnaiah, R. V. (2017). Shifted Adaption Homomorphism Encryption for Mobile and Cloud Learning. *Computers & Electrical Engineering*. doi:10.1016/j.compeleceng.2017.05.022

Krumm, J. (2009). A survey of computational location privacy. *Personal and Ubiquitous Computing*, *13*(6), 291–399. doi:10.1007/s00779-008-0212-5

Li, Chinneck, Wodside, & Litoiu. (2009). Fast scalable optimization to configure service system having cost and quality of service constraints. *IEEE International Conference on Autonomic System Barcelona,* 159-168. doi:10.1145/1555228.1555268

Li, N., Mitchell, J. C., & Winsborough, W. H. (2002). Design of a role-based trust-management framework. In *Security and Privacy, 2002. Proceedings. 2002 IEEE Symposium on*. IEEE.

Muchahari, M. K., & Sinha, S. K. (2012). A New Trust Management Architecture for Cloud Computing Environment. *IEEE International Symposium on Cloud and Services Computing (ISCOS)*, 136-140. doi:10.1109/ISCOS.2012.30

Paper, W. (2010). *Introduction to Cloud Computing*. Retrieved from http://www.thinkgrid.com/docs/computing-whitepaper.pdf

Pearson, S., & Benameur, A. (2010). Privacy, security and trust issues arising from cloud computing. *Proceedings of the 2nd IEEE International Conference on Cloud Computing Technology and Science,* 693-702. doi:10.1109/CloudCom.2010.66

Putri & Mganga. (2011). *Enhancing Information Security in Cloud Computing Services using SLA Based Metrics*. School of Computing, Blekinge Institute of Technology.

Puttaswamy, K. P. N., Kruegel, C., & Zhao, B. Y. (2011). Silverline: Toward Data Confidentiality in Storage-Intensive Cloud Applications. *Proc. Second ACM Symp. Cloud Computing (SOCC '11)*, 10:1-10:13. doi:10.1145/2038916.2038926

Rizwana Shaikh, M. (2012, April). Cloud Security issues: A Survey. *International Journal of Computers and Applications*.

Sapuntzakis, C., Brumley, D., Chandra, R., Zeldovich, N., Chow, J., Lam, M., & Rosenblum, M. (2008). Virtual appliances for deploying and maintaining software. *17th USENIX Conference on System Administration*, 181–194.

Shaikh, & Sasikumar. (2012). Trust Framework for Calculating Security Strength of a Cloud Service. *IEEE International Conference on Communication, Information & Computing Technology (ICCICT)*, 1-6.

Shekarpour, S., & Katebi, S. D. (2010). Modeling and evaluation of trust with an extension in semantic web. *Journal of Web Semantics*, 8(1), 26–36. doi:10.1016/j.websem.2009.11.003

Singh, A., Juneja, D., & Malhotra, M. (2015). A Novel Agent Based Autonomous Service Composition Framework for Cost Optimization of Resource Provisioning in Cloud Computing. In JKSU-CIS. Elsevier.

Singh, A., & Malhotra, M. (2015). Analysis of security issues at different levels in cloud computing paradigm: A review. *Journal of Computer Networks and Applications*, *2*(2), 41–45.

Singh, A., & Malhotra, M. (2015). Evaluation of a Secure Agent based optimized Resource Scheduling Framework in Cloud Environment. IJCAR, 188-198.

Singh, A., & Malhotra, M. (2016). Hybrid Two Tier Framework for Improved Security in Cloud Environment. India-Com., 1601-1606.

Singh, A., & Malhotra, M. (n.d.). A Novel Agent Based Framework for Cost Optimization in Cloud Computing Environment. *International Journal of Cloud Applications*, 53–61.

Staab, Bhargava, Lilien, Rosenthal, Winslett, Sloman, … Kashyap. (2004). The pudding of trust. *IEEE Intelligent Systems, 19*(5), 74–88.

Staab, S., Bhargava, B. K., Lilien, L., Rosenthal, A., Winslett, M., Sloman, M., & Kashyap, V. et al. (2004). The pudding of trust. *IEEE Intelligent Systems*, *19*(5), 74–88. doi:10.1109/MIS.2004.52

Subashini, S., & Kavitha, V. (2011). A survey on security issues in service delivery models of cloud computing. *Journal of Network and Computer Applications*, *34*(1), 1–11. doi:10.1016/j.jnca.2010.07.006

Vaquero, L. M., Rodero-Merino, L., & Morán, D. (2011). Locking the sky: A survey on IaaS cloud security. *Computing*, *91*(1), 93–118. doi:10.1007/s00607-010-0140-x

Yang, Jia, Ren, Zhang, & Xie. (2013). DAC-MACS: Effective Data Access Control for Multiauthority Cloud Storage Systems. *IEEE Transaction on Information Forensics and Security*, 1790-1801.

Yang, H., & Tate, M. (2009). Where are we at with Cloud Computing?: A Descriptive Literarure Review. *Proceedings of 20th Australasian Conference on Information Systems*, 807-819.

Yuefa, D., Bo, W., Yaqiang, G., Quan, Z., & Chaojing, T. (2009). Data security model for cloud computing. *International Workshop on Information Security and Application*, 141-144.

Zhang, Q., & Cheng, L. (2010). Cloud computing: state-of-the-art and research challenge. *Raouf Boutaba J Internet Serv Appl*, 7-18.

Chapter 6
Sniffers Over Cloud Environment:
A Literature Survey

Thangavel M
Thiagarajar College of Engineering, India

Narmadha N
Thiagarajar College of Engineering, India

Deepika B
Thiagarajar College of Engineering, India

ABSTRACT

Cloud computing is a technology for complex computing, it eliminates the need to have computing hardware, storage space and software. Multi tenancy is considered as important element in which same resources will be shared by multiple users. The users are named as tenants in the cloud environment. The tenants may run their applications in their own cloud environment which will have some vulnerability. These vulnerabilities will cause some attacks to the tenant virtual machine. In general, the cloud providers will not provide that much security to the cloud tenants. So, it is the duty of the tenant to make some countermeasures to avoid these attacks. In a cloud environment, there may be multiple tenants in that there is a possible of malicious tenant also present in the cloud environment. The attacker will do sniffing attack by monitoring all the user traffic. In the cloud, it is a fact that all the user data will resides in same hardware so the attacker monitor the activities of all the user and observes the type of traffic.

DOI: 10.4018/978-1-5225-3029-9.ch006

INTRODUCTION

Cloud computing is a technology for complex computing, it eliminates the need to have computing hardware, storage space and software. For scientific applications, it requires computing requirements like local servers, less reduced capital costs and increased volume of data produced and consumed by the experiments.

In Platform as a service model the users are provided with a scalable and elastic runtime environment for deploy their applications. These services are offered by a core middleware platform which provides a abstract environment for the where applications are deployed and executed. The middleware is software that sits between the application and another application. It makes connection between two clients, servers, databases and applications. It can't be directly used by the end users. Cloud middleware, however, is always accessible to the user in the form of remote software platform for communication or management of data. The service provider is responsible for providing scalable and manageable services to the users.

In Software as a service providers able to provide applications and services to the users based on the user demand. The common applications such as office automation, photo editing, document management and some other user applications. These services will be replicated in the cloud service providers place for the purpose of scalability and accessibility based on demand users. These may be shared by the multiple users whose process will be isolated by other users. Cloud is based on sharing the resources with multiple users. Virtualization plays an important role in cloud computing, it provides an abstract layer environment in that cloud user can have their operating systems or virtual hardware to implement their applications to run. In Infrastructure as a service deployment model hardware virtualization plays a fundamental role. In older days virtualization is meant for the operating system level, the programming language level and the application level. Now it provides virtual environment for the hardware, software, platform and networking (Buyya, 2013).

The virtualization provides some key advantages as well underutilized hardware and software, in this it is occurred due to increased performance and the computing capacity for all the hardware, the need of limited resources. Lack of space, since virtualization technique is used, the users don't want to have their own space. The advantage is green initiatives nowadays companies are promoting green initiatives for reducing the amount of energy they consume and to reduce their carbon footprint. The more power will be consumed by the data centers and the organization needs a cooling system to keep them cool. Hence by virtualization we can reduce the number of servers by server consolidation here there will be no need of any cooling system.

BACKGROUND

The resources of the cloud are provided by the basis of pay as you go. The users are charged for the service they are to be provisioned. Some important characteristics of cloud computing are on demand service; the services are provided to the user whenever they request it. The Cloud is a type of parallel and distributed system contains a collection of interconnected and virtualized computers that are dynamically provisioned and presented as one or more unified computing resources (Yash, 2016).

DEPLOYMENT MODELS

The cloud computing involves three deployment models as:

- Infrastructure as a service
- Platform as a service
- Software as a service

Infrastructure as a Service

In Infrastructure as a service the cloud user will buy an entire infrastructure to run their applications. The infrastructure will be in the form of virtual things as hardware, storage, and network. This will be created on service provider side based on user request. The users are provided with a tool and interface to configure their applications. The virtual space can be delivered by the form of disk space or any object storage. The technology used is the hardware virtualization. The users are provided with an environment in which more number of virtual machines is interconnected to form a distributed system on the top of which applications are deployed.

This reduced the maintenance and performance cost for the underlying hardware. The users are provided with a full customization in the virtualization to deploy the infrastructure in the cloud. The users can configure their packages and the applications. For the use of web servers, data centers, database servers, the user can use the prepackaged system images that containing the software stack for required the applications.

Platform as a Service

The next service is a Platform as a service, where the user can deploy their platform for running their application in the cloud. It provides a development and deployment for the user to run their application. It mainly runs in the middleware on the top the applications are executed. These services are offered by a core middleware platform which provides an abstract environment for the where applications are deployed and executed. The middleware is software that sits between the application and another application. It makes connection between two clients, servers, databases and applications. It can't be directly used by the end users. Cloud middleware, however, is always accessible to the user in the form of remote software platform for communication or management of data. The service provider is responsible for providing scalable and manageable services to the users.

In the PaaS environment the users are not allowed to manage the underlying hardware. The cloud service providers will automate the process of deploying applications to the infrastructure based on the policies set by the user. The core middleware provides an interface that allows programming and deploying applications in the cloud. These can be in the form of programming APIs, web-based interface and libraries. Some implementation of the PaaS provides the object based model for representing an application with programming language based methods (Buyya, 2013).

Software as a Service

In the software as a service model users are provided with a service delivery model to access the application via the web based interface. This eliminates the need for underlying hardware, implementing the software; these services are offered to the multiple users through the web browser. The user can access the application website with their credentials and can use the application and customizable according to their needs. In the software delivery model where and application can be shared by the multiple users. This comes under the concept of multi tenancy. Multi tenancy is considered as important element in which same resources will be shared by multiple users. The users are named as tenants in the cloud environment. The tenants may run their applications in their own cloud environment. From the multi tenancy the cloud service providers can manage the resource utilization effectively. It is an important key factor that can be offered in both public and private clouds. Some clouds use virtualization-based architectures to isolate tenants, others use custom software architectures to get the job done. The Application service providers who will offer packaged application which is shared by multiple users.

The SaaS introduces a flexible model in which user can able to customize their services, integrate new services, incorporating new components etc. based on service level agreements the SaaS provides a more robust infrastructure and application platform. Some benefits of software as a service model is software reduction cost, the user no need to have a software or any hardware to run their application, they simply invoke this with as a delivery model with the help of the web based interface.

In the SaaS model user can monitor the services offered to them with service level improvements. The SaaS delivery model is standalone and configurable the users need not to have additional components.

TYPES OF CLOUD

Based the three deployment models cloud is of four types:

- Public cloud
- Private cloud
- Hybrid cloud
- Community cloud

Public Cloud

In the public cloud, the services are made available to all. It offers solution for the IT infrastructure cost, provides an efficient place for the small enterprises. In the small enterprise, they need not invest more money on the infrastructure. Here the multi tenancy is the important characteristics of public cloud. A public cloud will serve for multiple users not for a single user. With the help of isolation, the cloud customers are separated with other users who are all sharing the same cloud. The cloud service provider need to ensure that the QoS is well managed and keeps on monitoring the cloud user behavior. A public cloud can offer all kind of services infrastructure, platform, or applications. The public cloud is inexpensive and scalability (Rouse, 2009).

Private Cloud

To store the sensitive information most organization are willing to take the private cloud. The private cloud is same as the public cloud but it is proprietary. The private cloud will applicable for single organization rather than multiple organizations as in the public cloud. The direct control and privacy is provided to the organization in the private cloud and provides secure environment (Rouse, 2015). It provides a virtual unit in which hardware and computing resources are combined (Maguir, 2013).

Hybrid Cloud

The usage of public cloud and private cloud will be provided in the hybrid cloud. The services and data will be combined from variety of cloud models. The public and private cloud operates independently. It creates an isolated environment. This will help the organization to store the sensitive data in the private cloud and to run the application the computational resources are relying on the public cloud. The benefit of hybrid cloud, it is on-premise and provides private infrastructure which is directly accessible (Sanders, 2014). It reduces the work load, it is scalable and improves resource allocation.

Community Cloud

In community cloud a group of people will share the computing resource in a multi-tenant infrastructure. The community cloud may be on-premise or off-premise (Rouse, 2012). The community cloud will be provided to the limited number of people and will be governed, secured by the organization. This is mainly designed for organization which will undergo joint products (Community Cloud, 2016). The deployment cost of the community cloud is cheaper than private cloud (Goyal, 2014).

VIRTUALIZATION

Cloud is based on sharing the resources with multiple users. Virtualization plays an important role in cloud computing, it provides an abstract layer environment in that cloud user can have their operating systems or virtual hardware to implement their applications to run. By dividing the resources of the computer in a usable execution framework it provides a framework by applying the concept of the hardware and software partitioning. In Infrastructure as a service deployment model hardware virtualization plays a fundamental role. In older days virtualization is meant for the operating system level, the programming language level and the application level. Now it provides virtual environment for the hardware, software, platform and networking.

The virtualization provides some key advantages as well underutilized hardware and software, in this it is occurred due to increased performance and the computing capacity for all the hardware, the need of limited resources. Lack of space, since virtualization technique is used the user are don't want have their own space. The advantage is green initiatives nowadays companies are promoting green initiatives for reducing the amount of energy they consume and to reduce their carbon footprint. The more power will be consumed by the data centers and the organization needs a cooling system to keep them cool. Hence by virtualization we can reduce the number of servers by server consolidation here there will be no need of any cooling system. The virtual machine provides a real machine representation with the help of the software and can able to run the host or guest operating system. The guest operating system will run on the virtual machine (Yash, 2016). Virtualization provides server consolidation in which workloads are consolidated into multiple underutilized machines to save hardware management and infrastructure administration. Virtual machines provide secure environment with the help of the sandboxes. The sandboxes are isolated environment which is used to run the less trusted applications. Virtual machine manager enables us to configure virtual machine, networking and storage resources (Virtual Machine Manager, 2012).

COMMON ATTACKS IN CLOUD COMPUTING

Following are the common attacks in cloud environment (Kumar, 2014).

Denial of Service Attacks

In this attack the intruders overload the server with more requests so that it cannot be respond to the requests from legitimate user and hence resources will be made unavailable (Vidhya, 2014). The DOS attack originates from the single device where distributed denial of service gives malicious request from various machines. For example, an attacker can send large number of connection requests to overload a server using the botnets. A botnet is an interconnected network of computers infected with malware without the user's knowledge and controlled by an attacker (Botnet, 2016). They are mainly used to send spam emails, transmit viruses and malicious request to the server. It is known as a zombie army. In dos attacks the sends a synchronization packets (SYN) to the server, in which the server will reply with SYN/ACK. The server then waits for the response from the source system that never arrives. The bogus connection request will eventually time out, in this meantime the legitimate user cannot get the service. The specific DOS attacks are SYN flood, UDP flood, ICMP flood, Ping of Death, Smurf attack, HTTP based DOS attack. In cloud Environment, out of 14% attacks are DOS attacks, when the workload increases on a service; it provides more computational power to maintain the additional load. For some extents it allows the attacker to do damage on the Quality of services (Deshmukh, 2015).

Malware Injection Attack

Malware injection is a web based attack. In this attack attacker creates an own malicious service implementation module or virtual machine instance and deploy it into the cloud. Then, the attacker need to pretend as to be the Cloud system that it is some the new service implementation instance and among the valid instances for some particular service attacked by the attacker. If a user request for services, the Cloud automatically redirects the requests of valid user to the malicious service implementation and the attacker code is executed (Singh, 2014). Now the attacker gets the full control of the user and steals the sensitive information. The SQL and Cross site scripting are the two important forms of attack in malware injection attacks. The SQL injection attack is that the vulnerable database applications are exploited by the attacker by injecting the malicious code to bypass the login, once the attacker gets the access then he gains unauthorized access to the backend database. In cross site scripting attack the attacker injects malicious scripts, such as VBScript, JavaScript, HTML, ActiveX, and Flash, into a vulnerable webpage. The attacker executes the scripts on victim's web browser. From this the attacker gets the session cookie and uses it for authorization and gain the credential information.

Wrapping Attack

When a user requests a service to a web server through a web browser, it is interacted Simple Object Access Protocol (SOAP) messages transmitted through HTTP protocol with the Extensible Markup Language (XML) format. In wrapping attack, the attacker injects a malicious element in the SOAP message structure in Transport Layer Service (TLS) and after inserting the malicious code, malicious content of the message is copied into the server and while executing it, the working of the cloud server is interrupted by the attacker. This is done during the transmission of SOAP messages between a valid user and the web server. By duplicating the user's account and password in the login period, the attacker embeds a bogus element (the wrapper) into the message structure, moves the original message body under the wrapper, replaces the content of the message with malicious code, and then sends the message to the server. The server will authorize the message and the attacker is able to gain unauthorized access to protected resources and perform the intended operations (Chou, 2013).

Authentication Attack

In hosted and virtual services authentication is the weak issue and it occurs frequently. The user can be authenticated what a user knows, what he has or is. In the cloud computing architecture, it includes SaaS, IaaS, and PaaS. Among these IaaS is able to offer authentication for information protection and data encryption. If user wants to transmit sensitive data the cloud computing service based on IaaS architecture is suitable for securing the data in communication. In addition, the data are management and processed by that enterprise but it will be stored on the cloud service provider place that must be authorized by the user. The attacker tries to compromise the authentication token of the user and gets access to the system. By using the authentication information attacker can do a man in the middle attack, this attack commonly occurs in the SaaS environment. The attacker intercepts the communication channel established between legitimate users and the server, modifies the communication between client and server without their knowledge. The attacker uses the authentication information and impersonates as the valid user (Sumitra, 2014).

Insider Attack

A malicious insider is an employee of the Cloud Service Provider who abuses the position to gain information. The extent of access granted could enable such an attacker to steal confidential data or gain complete control over the cloud services. The CERT defines malicious insider as a "current or former employee, contractor, or other business partner who has or had authorized access to an organizations network, system or data and intentionally exceeded or misused that access in a manner that negatively affected the confidentiality, integrity, or availability of the organizations information or information systems" (Claycomb, 2013). The insider uses the cloud to damage the brand, monetary impact, and productivity losses are just some of the ways a malicious insider can affect an operation in the cloud. The very effective insider attack is Rogue administrator who is employed by the cloud provider. The insider will steal the sensitive information which results in loss of integrity and confidentiality. To do this the insider will be financially motivated.

All the Network applications communicate by exchanging the network packets. Attackers can build a code and let their machine to examine the content of each packet that are transmitted. He can able to monitor the airways to intercept packets in a wireless network. The wireless traffic is being monitored when users are connected to an insecure network (Kris, 2009).

SNIFFING

The sniffing can be achieved in cloud using placing the sniffers in the cloud environment and an attacker can capture the traffic of all the users. The sniffers are used to analyze the network traffic and bandwidth utilization. The sniffers will work in the Network Interface Card and it analyzes all the data packets (CEH, 2012). The sniffer decodes the information that passes through the NIC. It may be software or hardware that works only in TCP/IP protocol and some sophisticated tools will works on all protocol (Mitchell, 2014). The sniffers are of two types passive sniffing and active sniffing. In passive sniffing, the attacker observes and monitors the packet sent by the victim. The active sniffing is performed by injecting the ARP packet into network. Protocols vulnerable to sniffing attacks are Telnet and Rlogin it is vulnerable to keystrokes which includes username and passwords other protocols like HTTTP, SMTP, NNTP, POP, FTP the passwords are sent in clear texts (Kancharla, 2012). It is shown in Figure 1.

WIRETAPPING

Wiretapping involves intercepting the telephone transmission by monitoring the telephone signals (Wiretapping, 2016). In wiretapping all the conversation will be monitored by a third party with covert inventions. To wiretap we need to select target or host on the network and need to connect a listening device to the channel that carries information in the internet. It is achieved through placing a monitoring device informally known as a bug on the wire The information is tapped with the help of the electrical signal generated from the telephone wires, with this we can able to monitor, record and access the information in the communication system.

METHODS IN WIRETAPPING

- The official tapping of telephone lines
- The unofficial tapping of telephone lines
- Recording the conversation
- Direct line wiretap
- Radio wiretap

Figure 1. Sniffing

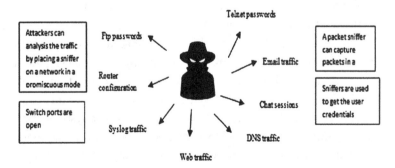

TYPES OF WIRETAPPING

- Active wiretapping
- Passive wiretapping

Active Wiretapping

This is also known as man in the middle attack. In which we can able to record and monitor the flow of information the communication and we can also alter or inject data into the communication.

Passive Wiretapping

This is also called as eavesdropping. In this we can able to monitor and record the traffic in the communication. From this we can observes the pattern of the communication and we can also get knowledge of the data.

LAWFUL INTERCEPT

It is a form of obtaining information in the communication network with lawful authority for evidence. This is moreover used in cyber security related activities like protection, investigation. The network operator need to provide legally sanctioned to access the private network data like call information, email messages. Law enforcement agencies will perform these activities. The interception is only upon the monitoring the messages in the communication. This lawful intercept is more useful in identifying the terrorist activities (CEH, 2012).

PACKET SNIFFING

The wiretapping technique is applicable in the telephone communication, and also in analyzing the traffic the computer networks. This can be achieved with packet sniffing. The packet sniffing can be achieved in shared Ethernet and switched Ethernet. In a network packet sniffing is achieved by monitoring and capturing the data packets that goes through the network with the help of any hardware or software devices. The filters employed by the Ethernet cards are turned off by the sniffing program to avoid the system to monitoring the other system's traffic, now the sniffing program can see the traffic of all the systems in the network. Now a days switch technology is used in all the network topology. Switch is a device that is used to channel the incoming data from the input port the intended output port. In an Ethernet local area network a switch is identified by a physical device address such as Media Access Control (MAC) (Rouse, 2007). To analyze the traffic we need to install the remote sniffing program into the servers or routers to get the traffic information. From this we can observe and monitor the total network traffic. With the help of the packet sniffers we can gather the sensitive information such as passwords, credit card information. This information is in the clear text format. The packet sniffers also sniff the protocol traffic such as POP, IMAP, HTTP traffic's, Telnet authentication, Sql database and FTP traffic. The attackers will launch an effective attack when they get this information.

How a Sniffer Works

1.   Sniffer turns the NIC of a system to the promiscuous mode so that it listens to all the data transmitted on its segment.
2.   A sniffer can constantly monitor all the network traffic to a computer through the NIC by decoding the information encapsulated in the data packet. It is shown in Figure 2.

Uses of Packet Sniffers (Thakur, 2010)

1.   To capture the username and passwords which are in cleartext.

Figure 2. Working of sniffers
CEH, 2012.

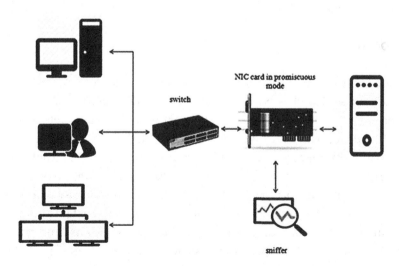

2.   To map the network.
3.   To convert the network traffic into readable format.
4.   To find the bottlenecks in the network.
5.   To redirect the communication to the attacker's computer.

SNIFFING THREATS

1.   Email traffic
2.   DNS traffic
3.   Web traffic
4.   Chat traffic
5.   Ftp passwords
6.   Router configuration
7.   Telnet password
8.   System log traffic
9.   Http password

TYPES OF SNIFFING ATTACK

1.   MAC flooding
2.   DHCP attacks
3.   Password sniffing
4.   Spoofing attack
5.   DNS poisoning
6.   ARP poisoning

Mac Flooding

In computer networking, MAC flooding is a technique employed to compromise the security of network switches. Switches maintain a CAM Table that maps individual MAC addresses on the network to the physical ports on the switch. This allows the switch to direct data out of the physical port where the recipient is located, as opposed to indiscriminately broadcasting the data out of all ports as a hub does. The advantage of this method is that data is bridged exclusively to the network segment containing the computer that the data is specifically destined for. Switch is a device which identifies a system by its Mac address. The switch contains ports by this means it maps all the Mac address to the physical ports with its limited memory. The attacker will send the request to the switch, the switch will act as a hub and broadcast packets to all the machines on the network and he can analyze the traffic of the entire machine. The switch maintains a table called CAM table i.e. Content Addressable Memory which has fixed size to store the available Mac address with their appropriate VLAN parameters.

The Mac address is of 48 bits in length the first twenty-four is for manufacturer code the second twenty four is for specific interface. To avoid flooding attack the switch needs to convert into hub. It will broadcast the packets and the attacker can sniff it easily.

MAC flooding is a method that can be used to impact the security protocols of different types of network switches. Essentially, MAC flooding inundates the network switch with data packets that disrupt the usual sender to recipient flow of data that is common with MAC addresses. The end result is that rather than data passing from a specific port or sender to a specific recipient, the data is blasted out across all ports.

The basics of MAC flooding begin with a corruption of the translation table that is part of the function of the network switch. When functioning properly, the table will map each individual MAC address that is found on the network. Each MAC address is associated with a physical port on the network switch. This approach makes it possible to designate a specific and single point of termination for data sent across the network.

By flooding the switch with data packets, the translation table is thrown out of kilter and the connection between the ports and specific MAC addresses is destroyed. Instead, any data that is intended for a single MAC address is now sent out on all ports associated with the network. This means that any type of data that was intended for a single address is received by multiple addresses (Mac Flooding, 2016).

To Defend Against the MAC Flooding

By using port security we can restrict the inbound traffic from a selective set of MAC address and can restrict the MAC spoofing attack.

DHCP Attack

The DHCP server is a network protocol, the server automatically assign IP address for a computer. It maintains a database for with TCP/IP parameters, valid IP address. It provides address configuration in the basis of DHCP- enabled clients based on the lease offer.

The following are the messages involved in the DHCP Request/Reply messages

- DHCPDISCOVER – to locate the available servers the client will broadcast the message.
- DHCP RELAY agent it captures the client request.
- DHCPOFFER/ADVERTISE- it contains the client and server's MAC address.

Steps Involved in the DHCP Client Configuration

Step 1: To get the DHCP configuration information the client will broadcast the DHCP DISCOVER message.

Step 2: the DHCP relay agent capture the client message and send it to the DHCP server in the network.

Step 3: The DHCP server unicasts the DHCP OFFER message.

Step 4: Now the Relay agent broadcast the same message in the client network.

Step 5: The client will ask the server to provide the DHCP configuration information by broadcasting the DHCPREQUEST message.

Step 6: Finally the DHCP server will send the DHCPACK message to the client which contains IP config information (CEH, 2012).

DHCP Request/Replay Messages

To get the other configuration information from the DHCP server, a device which has an IP address can use the DHCP request/replay messages. This DHCP offer is received by aDHCP client, it immediately responds with DHCP request packet. The other capabilities are used by the devices which are not using the DHCP. To get information about the how the network is used the client need to broadcast the DHCPINFORM message to the available server, and then the server will send the available parameters to the client.

DHCP Starvation Attack

In this attack the attacker tries to send a large number of requests to the DHCP server to flood the server. The attacker does this attack to get all the IP address that DHCP will issue to the clients. This may lead to the dos attack the server cannot provide services to the client. The legitimate user cannot get or renew their IP address to access the network.

To Defend Against DHCP Starvation Attack

Limit the maximum number of MAC address on the switch port with the help of port security, it will prevent the DHCP starvation attacks.

ROGUE DHCP SERVER ATTACK

The attacker will introduce a rogue server into the network. The rogue server will work as original server and respond to the client requests as DHCP discovery requests. When a client provides a request to the server both the original and rogue server will respond to the request, the client will get the request of server which comes first. If it is a request of the rogue server the client is denied to access the network which causes DOS attack, other attacks such as Man in the middle attack and Reconnaissance attacks. The rogue device may be a modem or wireless router with DHCP capabilities attached to the network without the knowledge of the user, and it will not be in the control of the network administrator. The rogue server provides a duplicate IP address which may be of an attacker's IP address to access the network. This may also lead to an attacker will the change the attacker's IP address the default gateway of the client, so all the information will passes through the attacker's machine. This cannot be identified earlier by the client, they will think everything goes right (DHCP Attacks, 2016).

TO DEFEND AGAINST ROGUE SERVERS

- Enable DHCP snooping that allows switch to accept DHCP transaction coming only from a trusted port.
- In order to defend against rogue DHCP servers, configure DHCP snooping on the port on which the valid DHCP server is connected.
- Once you configure DHCP snooping, it does not allow other ports on the switch to respond to DHCP discover packets sent by clients.
- Thus, even if an attacker manages to build a rogue DHCP server and connects to the switch, he or she cannot respond to DHCP discover packets.

ARP POISONING

Address resolution protocol is a stateless protocol used to map the IP address with the MAC address with the help of data link layer protocol. With this protocol we can get a MAC address of any machine in the network. To send a packet in the network the source host machine need to mention the MAC address of the destination. So this protocol is used by the host machine to get a MAC addresses.

The operating system will also maintain the MAC address table. When one machine needs to communicate with another, it looks up its ARP table. If the MAC address is not found in the table, the ARP_REQUEST is broadcasted over the network.

All machines on the network will compare this IP address to their MAC address. If one of the machines in the network identifies with this address, it will respond to ARP_REQUEST with its IP and MAC address. The requesting machine will store the address pair in the ARP table and communication will take place (CEH, 2012).

ARP SPOOFING ATTACK

1. The attackers will create a forged ARP packets can be able to send data to the attacker's machine.
2. To overload a switch ARP Spoofing involves constructing a large number forged ARP request and reply packets to.
3. The forwarding mode will be set when the ARP table is flooded with forged ARP requests and can sniff all the packets in the network.
4. Poisoning is method that an attacker floods the victim computer's ARP cache with forged packet entries.
5. The ARP does not provide authentication to the requesting machine.
6. The ARP spoofing is, when a valid user creates a session to communicate with other user and waits for the MAC address of the recipient. Now the attacker will get the MAC address and impersonate as the original recipient.
7. It is a method of attacking the Ethernet LAN.
8. The attacker uses the forged ARP packet and updates the victim's ARP cache and tries to changes of his MAC address with the victim's MAC address.
9. The attacker perform man in the middle attack as the ARP reply has been forged, whenever a victim sends a frame it will directed to the attacker's machine. Now the attackers modify the frames and send it to the destination (ARP Poisoning, 2016).

Threats to ARP Poisoning

The attacker uses the fake ARP messages to divert the communication between two machines.

The threats includes:

1. Packet sniffing
2. Session hijacking
3. VoIP call tapping
4. Manipulating data
5. Man in the middle attack
6. Data interception

7.   Connection hijacking
8.   Stealing passwords
9.   Denial of service attack

To Defend Against ARP Poisoning

Dynamic ARP inspection is implemented in order to prevent the ARP poisoning attack. In a network we can analyze the ARP packet with the help of the Dynamic ARP inspection. When it is enabled the DAI validates the entire ARP packets with DHCP snooping binding table. The DAI validates the ARP packet with performing IP to MAC address binding inspection that is stored in the DHCP snooping table. It discards the packet when there is an invalid mapping between IP to MAC address is found. It ensures only the valid requests and avoids the man in the middle attack.

Spoofing Attack Threats

In spoofing attack, the attacker impersonates as the legitimate user and accesses the resources.
   Threats:

1.   MAC Spoofing
2.   ICMP Routing Discovery Protocol (IRDP) Spoofing

MAC Spoofing

The attacker changes the information in the header of a packet and forging the source MAC address. The MAC address is generally used by the Intrusion Detection system for providing authorization. These MAC addresses are cannot be changed but in some most hardware it can be changed. An attacker uses this and changes the MAC address and legitimately obtain the connection after some hardware failure which causes a severe security risk. With this threat an attacker can get the MAC address of the legitimate user and gain access to the network and impersonate as the valid user.

ICMP Routing Discovery Protocol (IRDP) Spoofing

It is an extension of the ICMP protocol. The router will broadcast the router advertisement to all the hosts to discover the router in the network. The host machine listens the router messages. If a host receives this message it changes the value in its routing table. The attacker will send the same message to the router because IRDP doesn't provide authentication for router messages. The attacker tries to do denial of service and man in the middle attack (CEH, 2012).

DNS POISONING TECHNIQUE

DNS is Domain Name Server used to convert the domain name into the IP address. It maintains a large database to store the domain name and its relevant IP address. The DNS attack is, the legitimate user redirected to a malicious server instead of an intended server. The attacker gets an access to the DNS table and changes the entries in the DNS system, by this the attacker will redirected to the malicious server. The attacker changes the IP address of the original serve to malicious server and redirects the victim. Now the attacker gets access to the victim's system and gains all information.

DNS Poisoning Steps

1. Create a fake website.
2. Change the IP address of the server to your website's IP address in the readme. txt by installing treewalk.
3. Modify the dns-spoofing.bat file and change the IP address.
4. Create trojans in the dns-spoofing.bat and send it to the victim.
5. When the victim clicks the file, it will change the properties of TCP/IP.
6. Now the entire request will pass through the attacker system.
7. If victim needs access the original website it will be redirect to the attacker's website.

TYPES OF DNS POISONING

1. Intranet DNS Poisoning
2. Internet DNS Poisoning
3. Proxy server DNS Poisoning
4. DNS cache poisoning

Intranet DNS Poisoning

The Intranet DNS Poisoning is the attacker will performs DNS poisoning in the local area network. Attacker uses the ARP poisoning technique to do the intranet

DNS Poisoning in the switch of local area network. All the traffics are monitored by the attacker to perform the attack. The attacker uses the ARP Spoof to poison the router and if a client sends a DNS request it will be redirect to the attacker's machine. For the DNS request sent by the client the attacker provides a malicious DNS response and redirect it. The client will not know the redirection hence he may give the credential information in the website which will be accessed by the attacker.

Internet DNS Poisoning

It is also known as remote DNS poisoning. The attacker will do the Internet DNS Poisoning by compromising the one or more victim's machine. Attacker uses the rouge DNS server which will in static IP address. The victim's system must be connected to an internet to do this attack. The attacker the changes DNS of the victim's system into his DNS entry, in which all request will redirect to the attacker's machine. Then attacker sniffs the confidential information of the victim.

Proxy Server DNS Poisoning

In this type of attack the attacker changes the proxy server settings to his proxy settings by using the trojans. The attacker infects the victim's system by changing the proxy address. The victim sends a request it will goes through the attacker's machine and now attacker send it the fake website and sniff all the information.

DNS Cache Poisoning

The recently requested domain names are stored in the cache memory of the DNS system as IP address with relevant domain names. If a user request the domain names the DNS system will checks for the request that is cached. The attacker changes the domain names as his malicious domain name's IP address whenever a user request for the original website the DNS system checks the cache and will redirects the victim to the attacker's malicious website.

To Defend Against DNS Spoofing

1. Implement DNSSEC
2. Configure firewall
3. Secure the internal machines
4. Always use SSH encryption
5. Use static IP table
6. Use trusted proxy sites

7.   Monitor the DNS server regularly

SNIFFING IN CLOUD COMPUTING

Attacker uses sniffers to attack the system by sniffs the packet and monitor the traffic in the network. The attacker first fixes the target network and finds the switch and connects his machine to that port. Then he will be the one of the person in the network and tries to find the topology of the network using tools. Now the attacker finds the target machine in the network and uses the ARP spoofing technique. The attacker gets the entire traffic of the victim's machine from his machine and gets the sensitive information of the victim.

The attacker can get the system log of the other tenants in the system. If an attacker spoofed a tenant machine he may able to create attack traffic. Packet sniffing is possible in cloud environment whenever a data moves from client to server machine packet sniffing is achieved. There are two types of passive sniffing and active sniffing. The cloud service provider will maintain a hub in that the traffic is sent through all ports. It just involves monitoring the packet sent by others, in cloud we can say that when a user request for the cloud service provider for any service the attacker in the same environment will analyze the traffic.

The cloud service providers will also use sniffers to analyze the behavior of the tenants. The cloud service provider will install the sniffing tool analyze the pattern first of all the cloud service provider will have a attack signature, now the cloud service provider will analyze the traffic of all the tenants in their environment if any suspicious activity is matched with the observed pattern the service provider will immediately take action against the malicious tenants. The tenant will also have multiple customers to serve their service. If any suspicious activity is found in the tenant machine by the cloud customer, the cloud provider immediately will alert the responsible customer.

In this paper author defines a security model as one that contains two components called Service Provider Attack Detection (SPAD) and Tenant Specific Attack Detection (TSAD). The Service Provider Attack Detection receives the traffic from the tenant machine and enforces the baseline security, if any tenant virtual machine violates the security policies an alert will send to the tenant administrator. The SPAD component enforces the security policy that includes detection of spoofed address and related attacks. The Tenant Specific Attack Detection enforces tenant specific policies on the tenant machine. The tenant specific policies are developed by the tenant at the time of registration. If the traffic violates the TSAD then it is dropped. The TSAD contains policies based on predefined signatures. It discards the packet, if it matches the pattern defined. The tenant traffics are monitored using the sniffers.

SNIFFING TOOLS

The various tools available to perform sniffing are shown in Table 1.

Table 1. Sniffing tools

Tools	Description
Wireshark	Wireshark is a network packet analyzer. It will capture the live packet data from a network with a detailed information of used in the packet. This tool is available for UNIX and Windows (Wireshark, 2016).
Tcpdump/Windump	It is an open source command line tool for analyzing the network traffic by capturing the packet and displays its header (Rouse, 2008).
Capsa Network Analyzer	The Capsa Network Analyzer is used for Ethernet Monitoring and troubleshooting. It provides the Email monitoring (Capsa, 2016).
Omni Peek Analyzer	It provides an interface that includes Ethernet, VoIP, Gigabit. It gives a visibility of the network condition to the organization (Omni Peek, 2016).
Sniff-O-Matic	It is a network protocol analyzer with an intuitive interface and captures all the traffic and enables us to analyze it with detailed information of the packet (Sniff-O-Matic, 2016).
JitBit Network Sniffer	It is a network sniffer tool monitors the network traffic and shows the captured packets in text or HEX view and it can be filtered using many parameters (JitBit, 2016).
MSN Sniffer 2	It is used to capture all the MSN chat in all the computers that are connected to the LAN and store it in a database to analyze it (MSN Sniffer 2, 2016).
Cola Soft Packet Builder	It enables to create custom network packets, it checks for protection against attacks and intruders. It provides Decoding Editor allows user to edit protocol fields (Cola Soft, 2016).
Ace Password Sniffer	It provides effective password recovery utility. The network administrator can use this tool to capture the passwords for user who forgot the passwords. It supports password monitoring through FTP, POP3, HTTP, and Telnet (Ace Password Sniffer, 2016).
RSA NetWitness Investigator	RSA Security Analytics is a security monitoring platform that extends the architecture and analytics of RSA NetWitness (RSA Net Witness, 2016)
EtherDetect Packet Sniffer	It passively monitors the network and we can view it in Hex format. It captures IP packets in the LAN with no packet losing and it parses and decodes a variety of network protocol (EtherDetect Packet Sniffer, 2016).
Dsniff	It provides ability to access the raw data packets in the network interface and for debugging it clearly looks up the network traffic and provides detailed information (Dsniff, 2016).
Effe Tech HTTP Sniffer	It enables us to capture the full TCP/IP packet and organize it by the TCP connections or UDP threads. Using the filters we can filter the capture packets that we need (Effe Tech HTTP Sniffer, 2016).
Ntop	It shows the network usage and it is based on libpcap, we can run it in UNIX platform, Mac OS and on Windows virtually. It provides a web interface, limited configuration with reduced CPU and memory usage (Ntop, 2016).

continued on following page

Table 1. Continued

Tools	Description
Ettercap	It is a comprehensive suite for man in the middle attacks. It provides sniffing of live connections, content filtering and it supports active and passive dissection of protocols (Ettercap, 2016).
SmartSniff	It is a network monitoring utility that allows capturing of TCP/IP packets that pass through the network adapter, and view the captured data as sequence of conversations between clients and servers (SmartSniff, 2016).
EtherApe	EtherApe is a graphical network monitor for UNIX. Featuring link layer, IP and TCP modes, provides network activity in graphical visualization. It supports Ethernet, FDDI, Token Ring, ISDN, PPP, SLIP and WLAN devices (EtherApe, 2016).
NetworkMiner	NetworkMiner is a Network Forensic Analysis Tool for windows and also works in Linux, Mac OS X. It is used as a passive network sniffer in order to find the operating systems, open ports (NetworkMiner, 2016).
PacketMon	The PacketMon tool can capture the IP packets that pass through the network interface and we can examine the packet headers (Packetmon, 2016).
NADetector	NADetector tool is used to monitor and analyze the traffic from the network and provides detailed information of the traffic and provides different types of statistics for each IP address and protocols (NADetector, 2016).
Ethereal	It is a protocol analyzer used to examine the granular details of network traffic at the packet level. It detects the intrusion attempts, collect statistics, filter content from network traffic (Ethereal, 2016).
KSniffer	It is a network statistics collector, allows a user to monitor all network traffic over any network interfaces connected to the host machine. It supports most TCP/IP protocols (KSniffer, 2016).
WebCookieSniffer	It is a packet sniffer tool that captures all Web site cookies sent between the Web browser and the Web server and displays them in a simple cookies table (WebCookieSniffer, 2016).
IP Traffic Spy	By using the IP Traffic Spy we can monitor the traffic that is transmitted over the network. It reads the TCP/IP packets from the network adapter and displays it (IP Traffic Spy, 2016).
VxSniffer	It is a complete network monitoring tool for Windows CE-based devices. It provides User defined filtering capability and save the trace packets for future analysis (VxSniffer, 2016).

SNIFFING DETECTION

Sniffing let the attacker to steal the confidential information. An attacker can download a sniffer program and run it in the Ethernet, and then the sniffers can capture sensitive information. If the NIC is set to promiscuous mode, packets that are needed to be filtered by the NIC are now passed to the system kernel. Therefore, if we create an ARP packet such that it does not have broadcast address as the destination address, send it to every machine on the network and discover that some hosts reply to it, then that hosts are set to the promiscuous mode. *Packet sniffing* includes a network attack strategy, captures network traffic in the Ethernet frame level. After capturing, all the data can be analyzed and sensitive information will be retrieved. The sniffing can be detected using software filtering based detection, this software will block the ARP packet with MAC address that do not exists. The hardware does not filter the ARP packets. Another method is RTT (Round Trip Time) Detection. The RTT is the time of the round trip of a packet sent to a destination. The RTT detection technique involves, at first to collect a training data. This is done by first sending to a host set to the normal mode and with a particular OS, a number of packet requests is sent, and wait for the response packets, then we need to take the RTT measurements. The host then is set to the promiscuous mode, the same request packets are sent again to the host, and the corresponding RTT measurements are collected. The averages of the RTT, the standard deviations, and the percentage of changes of the gathered RTT measurements are computed. The RTT averages, standard deviations, percentage of changes are called the training data. From these analysis the system administrator can able to identify that the host is running in promiscuous mode or normal mode. The RTT detection is based on statistical model (Trabelsi, 2004).

The sniffers will always run in the promiscuous mode, it is difficult to identify it. In promiscuous mode all the packets are allowed to pass without validating its destination address. The non-standalone sniffers are detected by the reverse DNS lookup method. IDS is an Intrusion Detection System used to detect the sniffing activities in the network. It will notify if there is any abnormal activity in the network. Ping method is also used to detect that any sniffers are installed in the system. By sending the Ping request to the suspect system with correct IP address and incorrect MAC address. If it is rejected by the Ethernet adapter as incorrect MAC address and if it is accepted then the sniffers are installed in the system. The one another method is ARP method if we send a non-broadcast to all nodes in the network, the ARP address is cached if it is in the promiscuous mode. When we a send ping message to all the nodes the response will come only from the cached the ARP address. The organization's DNS server needs to be monitored and identify the reverse DNS lookups. The sniffers will always use reverse DNS lookups. The reverse DNS lookup is done by sending ICMP request to non-existing IP address, the system that respond to ping will perform the reverse DNS lookup. To avoid sniffing in cloud computing the sender and receiver need to use strong encryption methods.

COUNTERMEASURES

- Ensure that the packet sniffer is not installed by restricting the access to the network media.

- Provide Encryption
- Use static IP addresses and static ARP table
- Use IPv6 protocol
- Use SSH Encryption
- Use HTTPS to protect user name and passwords
- Use Switch instead of hubs
- Encrypt the communication
- Use AntiSniff tools
- Use IP Security
- Use SSL/TLS protocol
- Use Virtual Private Network
- Add the Mac address of the gateway to the ARP cache.
- Use one time passwords
- Use PGP and S/MIME
- Retrieve MAC directly from NIC instead of the OS; this prevents MAC address spoofing.
- Always encrypt the communication between the wireless PC and access point to prevent MAC spoofing.
- Use crossover cables as they restrict unauthorized hosts from being accidentally or intentionally plugged into hubs and switches

PENETRATION TESTING

It simulates all the methods that an attacker tries to penetrate and gain unauthorized access to the system. The Pen testing plays an important role in assessing and maintaining the security of the organization's network (CEH, 2012).

In sniffing pen test we need to check for the transmission of data is secure and to identify any sniffers or interception attack is launched in the organization. It helps the administrator to, check for malicious content in the traffic, implementation of secure mechanism such as SSL and VPN to ensure security in the network traffic, to identify the rogue sniffing, rogue DHCP and DNS servers in the network, to discover the unauthorized networking devices is present in the network.

STEPS

Step 1: Perform a MAC flooding attack

Using different source MAC address in the Ethernet frames and floods the switch. The switch will move to failopen mode, in which broadcasts the data to all the ports. If this happens attackers may try to sniff it. We can do this by using tools such as Yersinia and macof.

Step 2: Perform a DHCP starvation attack

By broadcasting the DHCP request with spoofed MAC address may exhaust the DHCP server address space for some period of time. If this occurs then attacker has the chance to sniff the network traffic.We can test for DHCP starvation attacks using tools such as Dhcpstarv and Gobbler

Step 3: Perform a rogue server attack

The rogue server attack is achieved by using the rogue server running the network.

Step 4: Perform ARP poisoning attack

The pen tester need to compromise the ARP table and change the MAC addresses, this cause the IP address to point to the another machine. Then the attacker has the ability to steal the sensitive information by changing the MAC address. This can be done by using tools such as Cain & Abel, WinArpAttacker, and Ufasoftsnif.

Step 5: Perform MAC spoofing

In MAC spoofing the pen tester need to spoof the MAC address in the network. If this happens then the attacker has the possibility to bypass the access control lists on the routers by impersonating as legitimate device and steals the information.

Step 6: Perform IRDP spoofing

This can be performed by sending spoofed IRDP router advertisement messages to the machines in the network. The pen tester has to check for whether the router changes to malicious router suggested by the advertisement. If it changes then it is vulnerable to Dos attacks and Man in the middle attack.

Step 7: Perform DNS spoofing

The pen testers use the Arp snoof or dns spoof to perform DNS spoofing. The DNS spoofing attack is redirecting the victim to the malicious website which is controlled by the attacker. The attacker tries to intercepts the DNS request of victim to spoofed site. To avoid this kind of attack, proper IDS/IPS should be maintained.

Step 8: Perform cache poisoning

Using Trojan we can change the proxy server settings in the victim's machine, it will redirect the victim to a fake website.

Step 9: Perform proxy server dns poisoning

The attacker sets up a proxy server sets a rogue DNS as the primary DNS entry in the proxy server system. If the victim uses the attacker's proxy server, the attacker will sniff all the traffic between victim and the website.

Step 10: Document all findings

Once we perform all tests, document all the findings and the tests conducted. This helps you to analyze the target's security and plan respective countermeasures to cover the security gaps, if any.

CONCLUSION

The cloud is the shared environment attacker will impersonate as the legitimate tenants and do the all the type of attacks, here the attacker need not to use any sniffing tool to because he is also the one of the shared tenant user in the cloud environment, the attacker will monitor the system log of the tenant user and he can get the traffic of any user from the traffic he can gather the type of communication is performed. By this way the attacker can gather the information of the legitimate tenant in the cloud by using sniffing attacks. The sniffing can also be used by the tenant machine for monitoring the network activities like bandwidth range, delay, jitter, latency services provided by the clod service provider. The cloud users use the sniffers to monitor their tenant traffic to detect any attack patterns in it. If the tenants send a spoofed traffic then it will be identified by the detection technique which contains a predefined signature stored in a database and the spoofed traffic will be monitored and an alert will be sent to the administrator. We can use sniffers program for positive use like to identify the spoofed packet requests from the malicious host.

REFERENCES

Aljawarneh, S., Aldwairi, M., & Yassein, M. B. (2017). Anomaly-based intrusion detection system through feature selection analysis and building hybrid efficient model. *Journal of Computational Science*. doi:10.1016/j.jocs.2017.03.006

Aljawarneh, S., Yassein, M.B., & Talafha, W.A. (2017). A multithreaded programming approach for multimedia big data: encryption system. *Multimed Tools Appl.* <ALIGNMENT.qj></ALIGNMENT>10.1007/s11042-017-4873-9

Aljawarneh, S. A., Alawneh, A., & Jaradat, R. (2017). Cloud security engineering: Early stages of SDLC. *Future Generation Computer Systems*, *74*, 385–392. doi:10.1016/j.future.2016.10.005

Aljawarneh, S. A., Moftah, R. A., & Maatuk, A. M. (2016). Investigations of automatic methods for detecting the polymorphic worms signatures. *Future Generation Computer Systems*, *60*, 67–77. doi:10.1016/j.future.2016.01.020

Aljawarneh, S. A., Vangipuram, R., Puligadda, V. K., & Vinjamuri, J. (2017). G-SPAMINE: An approach to discover temporal association patterns and trends in internet of things. *Future Generation Computer Systems*, *74*, 430–443. doi:10.1016/j.future.2017.01.013

Kalpana, G., Kumar, P. V., Aljawarneh, S., & Krishnaiah, R. V. (2017). Shifted Adaption Homomorphism Encryption for Mobile and Cloud Learning. *Computers & Electrical Engineering*. doi:10.1016/j.compeleceng.2017.05.022

Singh, A., Juneja, D., & Malhotra, M. (2015). A Novel Agent Based Autonomous Service Composition Framework for Cost Optimization of Resource Provisioning in Cloud Computing. In JKSU-CIS. Elsevier.

Singh, A., & Malhotra, M. (2015). Evaluation of a Secure Agent based optimized Resource Scheduling Framework in Cloud Environment. IJCAR, 188-198.

Singh, A., & Malhotra, M. (2016). Hybrid Two Tier Framework for Improved Security in Cloud Environment. India-Com, 1601-1606.

Singh, A., & Malhotra, M. (2016). A Novel Agent Based Framework for Cost Optimization in Cloud Computing Environment. *International Journal of Cloud Applications*, 53–61.

Chapter 7

A Comprehensive Survey on Trust Issue and Its Deployed Models in Computing Environment

Shivani Jaswal
Chandigarh University, India

Gurpreet Singh
Chandigarh University, India

ABSTRACT

Cloud computing is growing with a giant pace in today's world. The speed with which it is growing, the same speed is taken over by the insecure data transfer over the cloud. There are many security issues that are underlying in cloud computing. This chapter presents how a trust is built between any user and a cloud service provider. Various techniques have been adopted to calculate the value of trust and further how it can be strength. This chapter has also explained various trust models based on the necessities of a user. This chapter has also thrown some light over the concept of TTP, i.e., Trusted Third Party which further helps in maintaining trust over the cloud environment.

INTRODUCTION

By the growing era of various computing techniques, resources have become cheaper in cost, powerful and available more than required without any hindrance or disturbance. This computing technology has enabled the world of realization that denotes a Cloud Computing model.

DOI: 10.4018/978-1-5225-3029-9.ch007

In Cloud Computing environment, resources are provided that can be leased on demand and then can be released by the users when their need is over. This Cloud Computing has made an impact on the IT industry over the past few years. Some of the examples of cloud services are Google, Amazon and Microsoft that provide the most powerful, trustworthy and cost efficient services.

The cloud works on the "Pay-as-you-go" model that supports storage and network bandwidth services, whereas computation slightly depends on virtualisation level. While talking about Google AppEngine, it automatically scales in or scales out their services as required by the user. Amazon Web Services (AWS) charges the by number of instances that a user occupy per hour (even if the user's machine is idle) (Mell at al, 2009).

Cloud Computing providers provide various techniques for optimum use of resources. By imposing technique of per-hour or per-byte costing, a user can pay attention to his/her efficiency i.e. they need to release and acquire resources only when highly required by them.

VARIOUS DEFINITIONS OF CLOUD COMPUTING

A style of figuring where greatly versatile IT-related abilities are given as an administration over the Internet to different outside clients (Zissis et al, 2012).

A pool of disconnected, exceedingly versatile, and oversaw framework fit for facilitating end-client applications and charged by utilization.

The fantasy of vast processing assets accessible on request, the disposal of in advance responsibilities by cloud clients, and the capacity to pay for utilization of figuring assets on a fleeting premise as required.

Distributed computing grasps digital foundation, and expands on virtualisation, dispersed figuring, framework registering, utility processing, systems administration, and Web and programming administrations (Singh et al, 2015).

A kind of parallel and disseminated framework comprising of an accumulation of interconnected and virtualised PCs that are progressively provisioned and exhibited as at least one bound together figuring assets in light of administration level assentions built up through transaction between the specialist co-op and customers.

An expansive pool of effectively usable and available virtualised assets, (for example, equipment, improvement stages as well as administrations). These assets can be progressively reconfigured to acclimate to a variable load (scale), permitting additionally for an ideal asset use. This pool of assets is normally misused by a compensation for every utilization display in which ensures are offered by the framework supplier by methods for tweaked SLAs (Singh et al, 2016).

A model for empowering advantageous, on-request organize access to a mutual pool of configurable figuring assets (e.g. systems, servers, stockpiling, applications, and administrations) that can be quickly provisioned and discharged with negligible administration exertion or specialist co-op collaboration (Subashini et al, 2011).

TRUST IN CLOUD COMPUTING

Security is considered as one of the most important field that needs to be handled in the emerging area of cloud computing. If security is not handled as per requirement, then there are high chances of failing of cloud computing environment as it involves management of personal sensitive information in a public network.The security which is provided by service a provider becomes an important factor to protect the network and its resources so as to fulfil the feature of vigorous and trustworthiness.

For the proper administration of cloud system and its services to take place, trust management models the trust based on various elements and entities.Several leading research groups both in academia and the industry are working in the area of trust management in cloud computing (Kumar et al, 2012).

Many researchers have studied the issue of trust from user's perspective.Also, some of them have analysed various other issues related to trust from what an expectation is expected by the user in terms of privacy and security. Many techniques have been undertaken by the service providers to enhance the trust of the user in cloud and its services. Particularly, in this context, many parameters have been identified such as control, ownership, prevention and security etc. Decreasing control and absence of straightforwardness have distinguished as the issue that lessens the client trust on cloud frameworks. The creators have anticipated that remote get to control offices for assets of the clients, straightforwardness concerning cloud suppliers activities as programmed traceability offices, affirmation of cloud security properties and abilities through an autonomous confirmation expert and giving security enclave to clients could be utilized to improve the trust of clients in the administrations and specialist organizations (Shaikh et al, 2012).

A mechanism has been proposed separate software which can further create a trust binding between them. This mechanism introduces an involvement of four parties, namely those shown in Figure 1.

Here, the resource provider helps in hosting data and software both which further provides platform to execute that software on data. The software providers are the respective owners of software and data. The coordinator helps in coordinating all the resources in a better away. It also provides some of the important services such as searching for a specific resource or providing an interface to execute some applications.

Figure 1. Components of trust software proposed

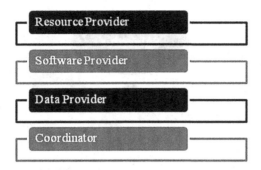

The operation of the model is as follows:

The software provider and data provider can save their resources to the specific resource provider. Now, the uploaded resources can go through the encryption technique before they are used for the communication by various users. A coordinator i used by the data provider for a searching of a specific software. After the execution, an ID is generated for a individual requests which is forwarded to the data provider. After the usage is over, results are displayed on the data provider's interface which can be further printed or viewed anytime. In this due course, a log of operation is also prepared for the future reference. This is done so that it can be known that the product has been used and for the amount of time it was used (Huan et al, 2013).

Despite the fact that the creators guarantee that this model isolates the product and information, there is no affirmation that the product can't make a duplicate while the information is being prepared as just the calculation or depiction of the product is given to the information proprietor. Without the source code, there is no confirmation that the code won't contain any malevolent code covered up inside. Additionally, since the product keeps running on information proprietor's rights and benefits, the product would have finish control over information. This is a security danger and the review trail regardless of the possibility that it is accessible, won't identify any security breaks.

TRUST ISSUE

At the time of origin, trust was usually used in the subjects of social science in constructing relationships and now its is considered as one of the important entity to make decisions.

Figure 2 interprets various features of developing a trust on an individual entity.

Figure 2. Parameters (benefits) of trust

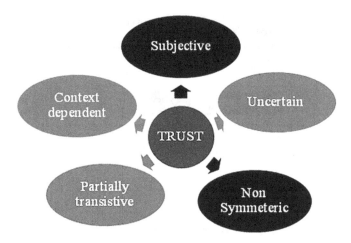

Basically, evaluation of trust includes the answering of a question, "That while interacting in a system, which nodes a user should interact and which should not?

Suppose there are two parties A & B.

B is using a service X.

Then A will trust on party B by the honesty of service X being used by the party B.

Traditionally, encryption and authorization plays a vital role in providing a strong foundation but now they are failing in case of cloud system as it provides scalability feature with it. Now, here trust acts as a security barrier and can fight against threats by limiting their interactions in a cloud computing environment.

Broadly, trust issues can be divided into three sections:

1. How to evaluate trust and which parameters to be taken into an account.
2. How to handle with fake information provided to generate a good value of trust.
3. How different level of security to be provided when a relationship based on trust in always dynamic in nature.

TRUST THIRD PARTY

We guarantee that utilizing Trusted Third Party benefits inside the cloud, prompts the foundation of the vital Trust level and gives perfect answers for safeguard the classification, honesty and credibility of information and correspondence. In cryptography, a Trusted Third Party (TTP) is a substance which encourages secure connections between two gatherings who both put stock in this outsider. The extent of a TTP inside an Information System is to give end-to-end security administrations, which are adaptable, in light of norms and valuable crosswise over various spaces, land zones and specialization divisions. The foundation and the affirmation of a trust connection between two executing parties might be finished up because of particular acknowledgments, systems and components. The Third Party surveys all basic exchange interchanges between the gatherings, in view of the simplicity of making false computerized content. Presenting a Trusted Third Party can particularly address the loss of the customary security limit by creating confided in security spaces (Srujan, 2012).

''A Trusted Third Party is a fair association conveying business certainty, through business and specialized security highlights, to an electronic exchange. It supplies in fact and lawfully solid methods for completing, encouraging, creating autonomous proof about and additionally mediating on an electronic exchange. Its administrations are given and guaranteed by specialized, lawful, budgetary or potentially basic means''. This framework use an arrangement of advanced testament dissemination and a component for partner these authentications with known source and target destinations at each taking an interest server. TTP administrations are given and guaranteed by specialized, as well as by legitimate, money related, and auxiliary means. TTPs are operationally associated through chains of put stock in (more often than not called declaration ways) with a specific end goal to give a web of trust framing the idea of a Public Key Infrastructure (PKI). Open Key Infrastructure gives actually stable and lawfully adequate intends to actualize (Figure 3).

Figure 3. Public key infrastructure (PKI)

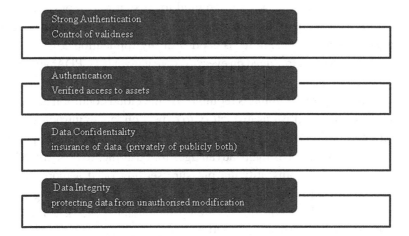

The trusted third party can be relied upon for:

- Low and High level confidentiality.
- Server and Client Authentication.
- Creation of Security Domains.
- Cryptographic Separation of Data.
- Certificate-Based Authorization.

LOW AND HIGH LEVEL CONFIDENTIALITY

The technique of securing information going over the system is a hard and a complex issue, while the danger of information adjustment and information intrusion is ceaselessly rising. A cloud situation expands this unpredictability as it doesn't just require security of activity towards the cloud yet also between cloud has, as they do not have a customary physical association. PKI empowers executing IPSec or SSL for secure interchanges. IPSec is an IP layer convention that empowers the sending and getting of cryptographically secured bundles of any sort (TCP, UDP, ICMP, and so forth.) with no change. IPSec gives two sorts of cryptographic administrations. In view of need, IPSec can give privacy and realness, or it can give credibility as it were. IPsec clients can confirm themselves to the companion substance, utilizing PKI authentications in a way that upgrades versatility, on the grounds that exclusive the trusted CA certificate(s) should be transmitted in advance. SSL convention creates end-toend encryption by interfacing amongst applications and the TCPIP conventions to give client–server verification and a scrambled correspondences channel between client–server. Because of the cloud conditions interesting qualities, interchanges are required to be secured amongst clients and has yet in addition from have to-have. Picking IPSec or SSL relies upon the various needs and security necessities. IPSec is good with any application however requires an IPSec customer to be introduced on every remote gadget (PC, PDA, and so forth.) to include the encryption. Conversely, SSL is incorporated with each program, so no unique customer programming is required. As the cloud condition advances use by heterogeneous stages it is unsatisfactory to expect clients to introduce an IPSec customer for encryption. Also as cloud administrations are for the most part gotten to through programs, SSL has many advantages for customer to have interchanges. Then again, IPSec underpins utilizing pressure settling on it a more productive decision for have to-have interchanges. This paper proposes actualizing IPSec for scrambling correspondences for have to-have interchanges and SSL for Client-to Cloud interchanges (Aljawarneh et al, 2017).

SERVER AND CLIENT AUTHENTICATION

In a cloud situation a Certification expert is required to ensure elements associated with cooperations, these incorporate confirming physical foundation servers, virtual servers, conditions clients and the systems gadgets. The PKI accreditation specialist is in charge of creating these required endorsements while enrolling these inside the put stock in work. At the end of the day, a Certification Authority constructs the important solid qualifications for all the physical or virtual elements associated with a cloud and it along these lines assembles a security space with particular limits inside the generally fluffy arrangement of elements of a cloud. Advanced marks in mix with SSO and Ldap, execute the

most grounded accessible confirmation process in appropriated conditions while ensuring client versatility and adaptability. The marking private key can be utilized to validate the client naturally and straightforwardly to different servers and gadgets around the system at whatever point he/she needs to build up an association with them. While the cloud is turning into the normal working stage, each administration will require a protected confirmation and approval process. As the calculated limit between an associations claim administration's and outsourced administrations moves toward becoming "fluffy", the need to embrace Single-Sign-On arrangement is basic. Clients require to make utilization of uses sent on their virtual ""office"" without repeating the confirmation procedure on each administration (application) supplier or keep up various passwords, yet make utilization of a solitary solid validation process that approves them to utilize benefits crosswise over confided in parties. "Eight years back, it was tied in with securing applications inside the venture through character administration (Kalpana et al, 2017). Today we discuss securing applications in the cloud with characters beginning inside the endeavor". Shibboleth is benchmarks based, open source middleware programming which gives Web Single Sign On (SSO) crosswise over or inside authoritative limits. It enables locales to settle on educated approval choices for singular access of ensured online assets in a security protecting way. Shibboleth innovation depends on an outsider to give the data about a client, named properties. In the proposed framework design, this is performed by the TTP LDAP archive. It is basic to recognize the verification procedure from the approval procedure. Amid the confirmation procedure a client is required to explore to his home association and validate himself. Amid this stage data is traded between the client and his home association as it were. After the fruitful validation of a client, as indicated by the client traits/qualifications, authorization to get to assets is either allowed or dismissed. The procedure in which the client trades his properties with the asset server is the approval procedure amid which no individual data is released and must be performed after fruitful confirmation. To boost interoperability between conveying parties, it is a need to receive broadly utilized benchmarks (Aljawarneh et al, 2016).

CREATION OF SECURITY DOMAINS

Presenting alliances, in relationship with PKI and Ldap innovation, will prompts proficient confide seeing someone between included substances. An organization is a gathering of lawful substances that offer an arrangement of concurred approaches and leads for access to online assets. An alliance gives a structure and a legitimate system that empowers validation and approval crosswise over various associations. Cloud frameworks can be sorted out in particular security areas (an application or gathering of utilizations that all trust a typical security token for validation, approval or session administration) empowering ''Federated mists''. Combined Clouds are a gathering of single Clouds that can interoperate, i.e. trade information and processing assets through characterized interfaces. As indicated by fundamental organization standards, in a Federation of Clouds each single Cloud stays autonomous, yet can interoperate with different Clouds in the league through institutionalized interfaces. A league gives a structure and a lawful system that empowers verification and approval crosswise over various associations (Armbrust et al, 2010).

CRYPTOGRAPHIC SEPARATION OF DATA

The assurance of individual data or/and delicate information, inside the structure of a cloud domain, constitutes a urgent factor for the effective arrangement of SaS and AaS models. Cryptographic Separation in which procedures, calculations and information are hidden such that they seem impalpable to pariahs (Aljawarneh et al, 2017). Classification and trustworthiness, yet additionally security of information can be ensured through encryption. Utilizing a mix of deviated and symmetric cryptographic (frequently alluded to as crossover cryptography) can offer the productivity of symmetric cryptography while keeping up the security of hilter kilter cryptography.

CERTIFICATE-BASED AUTHORIZATION

A cloud situation is a virtual net of a few free areas. In a cloud situation, the connection amongst assets and clients is all the more specially appointed and dynamic, asset suppliers and clients are not in a similar security area, and clients are typically recognized by their qualities or properties instead of predefined personalities. Along these lines, the conventional personality based get to control models are not powerful, and get to choices should be made in view of properties. An illustration is the utilization of an expanded X.509 authentication that conveys part data about a client. These endorsements are issued by a confirmation specialist that goes about as a put stock in focus in the worldwide Web condition. Characteristic authentications contain an attribute–value combine and the essential to whom it applies (Aljawarneh et al, 2017). They are marked by quality experts that have been determined in an utilization condition testament. Characteristic based get to control, settling on get to choices in light of the qualities of requestors, assets, and nature, gives the adaptability and versatility that are fundamental to huge scale conveyed frameworks, for example, the cloud.

A trusted declaration fills in as a solid electronic ""international ID"" that builds up an element's personality, accreditations and duties. Trust can be seen as a chain from the end client, to the application proprietor, who thusly puts stock in the foundation supplier (either at a virtual or equipment level as indicated by the chose benefit demonstrate). A Trusted Third Party can give the required trust by ensuring that imparting parties are who they claim to be and have been examined to hold fast to strict prerequisites. This procedure is performed through the affirmation procedure, amid which an element requiring accreditation is required to accommodate with an arrangement of approaches and necessities.

Some of the key factors that are common in front of various disciplines and researchers in field of trust are:

- Trust plays a role only when the environment is uncertain and risky.
- Trust is the basis based on which certain decisions are made.
- Trust is built using prior knowledge and experience.
- Trust is a subjective notion based on opinion and values of an individual.
- Trust changes with time and new knowledge while experience will have overriding influence over the old ones.
- Trust is context-dependent.
- Trust is multi-faceted.

VARIOUS TRUST MODELS

Cuboid Trust

CuboidTrust is a worldwide notoriety based trust display for distributed systems. It takes three factors in particular, commitment of the companion to the framework, associate's reliability in giving input and nature of assets to assemble four relations. At that point it makes a cuboid utilizing little solid shapes whose directions (x,y,z) where z – nature of asset, y – peer that stores the esteem and x – the associate which appraised the asset and indicated by Px,y,z. The rating is parallel, 1 showing credible and (–1) demonstrating inauthentic or no evaluating. Worldwide trust for each associate has been figured utilizing power emphasis of the considerable number of qualities put away by the companions.

Eigen Trust

EigenTrust relegates each associate a one of a kind worldwide trust an incentive in a P2P document sharing system, in light of the companion's history of transfers. This reduces the downloading of inauthentic records. Nearby trust esteem Sij has been characterized

$$Sij = sat\left(i, j\right) - unsat\left(i, j\right)$$

where sat(i,j) indicates the tasteful downloads by i from j and unsat(i,j) is the inadmissible downloads by i from j. Power cycle is utilized to process the worldwide trust for each associate.

AntRep

AntRep calculation depends on swarm insight. In this calculation, each companion keeps up a notoriety table like separation vector steering table. The notoriety table somewhat varies from the directing table as in

Figure 4. Cuboid trust i.e. associatively P(x,y,z)

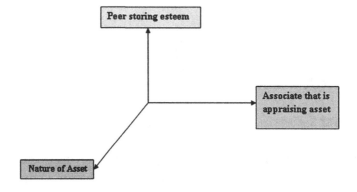

1. Each associate in the notoriety table compares to one notoriety content;
2. The metric is the likelihood of picking each neighbour as the following jump while in the steering table it is the bounce tally to goals. Both forward ants and in reverse ants are utilized for discovering notoriety esteems and proliferating them.

In the event that the notoriety table has a neighbour with the most astounding notoriety, a unicast subterranean insect is sent toward that path. On the off chance that no inclination exists, communicate ants are sent along every one of the ways.

Once the required notoriety data is discovered, a retrogressive subterranean insect is produced. At the point when this subterranean insect goes back, it refreshes all the notoriety tables in every hub on its way.

Peer Trust

This is notoriety based put stock in supporting structure. This incorporates a rational versatile put stock in display for measuring and looking at the reliability of associates in light of an exchange based input framework. It presents three fundamental trust parameters to be specific input an associate gets from different companions, the aggregate number of exchanges a companion plays out, the believability of the criticism sources and two versatile components that are exchange setting factor and the group setting factor in processing dependability of associates, at that point it consolidates these elements to figure a general trust metric.

TRUST EVOLUTION

Also, trust advancement display for Peer to Peer Systems have been introduced. This model uses two basic measurements, experience and setting to assemble confide seeing someone among peers. It fabricates two sorts of trust: coordinate trust and suggestion trust measures trust inside the interim.

Coordinate trust (CT) between two companions is processed utilizing the keep going n associations between those substances. Prescribed trust is ascertained utilizing proposals from different associates and the past collaborations with the suggesting peers.

TRUST ANT COLONY SYSTEM (TACS)

TACS depends on the bio-enlivened calculation of insect settlement framework. In this model pheromone follows are related to the measure of trust a companion has on its neighbours when providing a particular administration. It processes and chooses both the most dependable hub to associate and the most reliable way prompting that companion. Each associate needs to monitor the present topology of the system as each companion has its own particular pheromone follows for each connection. Ants go along each way looking building the most reliable way prompting the most trustworthy server.

Ants stop the hunt once they discover a hub that offers the administration asked for by the customer and the pheromone follows having a place with the present way prompting it are over the preset limit, else they would take after on additionally choosing a neighbor that has not been gone to yet.

CONCLUSION

Nowadays, lots of security issues are arising while using any service of Cloud. Similarly, the issue of trust is the biggest issue which is hindering user ot use various services of cloud required as per their needs. This chapter has thrown light that why trust is considered as threat in communicating over the cloud. Also, this Chapter has elaborated the issue of trust in detail by taking various perspectives in detail. Also, some of the various trust models have been explained which are used for calculating trust strength and other parameters.In the end, various other trust models have been discussed in detail that takes various parameters of security into an account.

Figure 5. Interface between substances via coordinate trust

REFERENCES

Aberer, K., & Despotovic, Z. (2001). Managing trust in a peer-2-peer information system. *Proc. of 10th International Conference on Information and Knowledge Management*, 310-317. doi:10.1145/502585.502638

Ahmed, Xiang, & Ali. (2010). Above the Trust and Security in Cloud Computing: A Notion towards Innovation. *IEEE/IFIP International Conference on Embedded and Ubiquitous Computing*. doi:10.1109/CSCWD.2010.5471954

Aljawarneh, S., Aldwairi, M., & Yassein, M. B. (2017). Anomaly-based intrusion detection system through feature selection analysis and building hybrid efficient model. *Journal of Computational Science*. doi:10.1016/j.jocs.2017.03.006

Aljawarneh, S., Yassein, M.B. & Talafha, W.A. (2017). A multithreaded programming approach for multimedia big data: encryption system. *Multimed Tools Appl.* <ALIGNMENT.qj></ALIGNMENT>10.1007/s11042-017-4873-9

Aljawarneh, S. A., Alawneh, A., & Jaradat, R. (2017). Cloud security engineering: Early stages of SDLC. *Future Generation Computer Systems, 74*, 385–392. doi:10.1016/j.future.2016.10.005

Aljawarneh, S. A., Moftah, R. A., & Maatuk, A. M. (2016). Investigations of automatic methods for detecting the polymorphic worms signatures. *Future Generation Computer Systems, 60*, 67–77. doi:10.1016/j.future.2016.01.020

Aljawarneh, S. A., Vangipuram, R., Puligadda, V. K., & Vinjamuri, J. (2017). G-SPAMINE: An approach to discover temporal association patterns and trends in internet of things. *Future Generation Computer Systems, 74*, 430–443. doi:10.1016/j.future.2017.01.013

Armbrust, M., Stoica, I., Zaharia, M., Fox, A., Griffith, R., Joseph, A. D., & Rabkin, A. et al. (2010). A view of cloud computing. *Communications of the ACM, 53*(4), 50–58. doi:10.1145/1721654.1721672

Barsoum & Hasan. (2012). Enabling Dynamic Data and Indirect Mutual Trust for Cloud Computing Storage Systems. *IEEE Transactions on Parallel and Distributed Systems*.

Beth, T., Borcherding, M., & Klein, B. (1994). Valuation of trust in open networks. In *Proc. of the 3rd European Symposium on Research in Computer Security*. Springer-Verlag.

Bonatti, P. A., & Olmedilla, D. (2005). Driving and monitoring provisional trust negotiation with metapolicies. In *IEEE 6th International Workshop on Policies for Distributed Systems and Networks (POLICY)*. Stockholm, Sweden: IEEE Computer Society. doi:10.1109/POLICY.2005.13

Boukerche & Ren. (2008). A trust-based security system for ubiquitous and pervasive computing environments. *Computer Communications*.

Buyya, R., Yeo, C. S., Venugopal, S., Broberg, J., & Brandic, I. (2009). Cloud computing and emerging IT platforms: Vision, hype, and reality for delivering computing as the 5th utility. *Future Generation Computer Systems*, *25*(6), 599–616. doi:10.1016/j.future.2008.12.001

Canedo. (2012). Trust Model for Private Cloud. *IEEE International Conference on Cyber Security, Cyber Warfare and Digital Forensic (CyberSec)*.

Grandison, T., & Sloman, M. (2002). Specifying and analysing trust for internet applications. In *Towards the Knowledge Society: eCommerce, eBusiness, and eGovernment, The Second IFIP Conference on E-Commerce, E-Business, E-Government (I3E 2002), IFIP Conference Proceedings*. Lisbon, Portugal: Kluwer.

Huang, J., & Nicol, D. M. (2013). *Trust mechanisms for cloud computing*. Retrieved from http://www.journalofcloudcomputing.com/content/2/1/9

Kalpana, G., Kumar, P. V., Aljawarneh, S., & Krishnaiah, R. V. (2017). Shifted Adaption Homomorphism Encryption for Mobile and Cloud Learning. *Computers & Electrical Engineering*. doi:10.1016/j.compeleceng.2017.05.022

Kotikela & Gomathisankaran. (2012). CTrust: A framework for Secure and Trustworthy application execution in Cloud computing. *International Conference on Cyber Security*.

Li, N., Mitchell, J. C., & Winsborough, W. H. (2002). Design of a role-based trust-management framework. *Security and Privacy, 2002. Proceedings. 2002 IEEE Symposium on*.

Li, T., Lin, C., & Ni, Y. (2010). Evaluation of User Behavior Trust in Cloud Computing. *International Conference on Computer Application and System Modeling*.

Mell, P., & Grace, T. (2009). *The NIST Definition of Cloud Computing*. National Institute of Standards and Technology.

Microsystems, S. (2009). *Introduction to Cloud Computing Architecture*. White paper.

Muchahari & Sinha. (2012). A New Trust Management Architecture for Cloud Computing Environment. *IEEE International Symposium on Cloud and Services Computing (ISCOS)*.

Pearson, S., & Benameur, A. (2010). Privacy, security and trust issues arising from cloud computing. *Proceedings of the 2nd IEEE International Conference on Cloud Computing Technology and Science*, 693-702. doi:10.1109/CloudCom.2010.66

Putri & Mganga. (2011). *Enhancing Information Security in Cloud Computing Services using SLA Based Metrics*. School of Computing, Blekinge Institute of Technology.

Shaikh, R., & Sasikumar, M. (2012). Trust Framework for Calculating Security Strength of a Cloud Service. *IEEE International Conference on Communication, Information & Computing Technology (ICCICT)*, 1-6. doi:10.1109/ICCICT.2012.6398163

Shaikh & Sasikumar. (2012). Cloud Security issues: A Survey. *International Journal of Computers and Applications*.

Shekarpour, S., & Katebi, S. D. (2010). Modeling and evaluation of trust with an extension in semantic web. *Journal of Web Semantics*, *8*(1), 26–36. doi:10.1016/j.websem.2009.11.003

Singh, A., Juneja, D., & Malhotra, M. (2015). A Novel Agent Based Autonomous Service Composition Framework for Cost Optimization of Resource Provisioning in Cloud Computing. In JKSU-CIS. Elsevier.

Singh, A., & Malhotra, M. (2015). Evaluation of a Secure Agent based optimized Resource Scheduling Framework in Cloud Environment. IJCAR, 188-198.

Singh, A., & Malhotra, M. (2016). Hybrid Two Tier Framework for Improved Security in Cloud Environment. India-Com., 1601-1606.

Singh, A., & Malhotra, M. (n.d.). A Novel Agent Based Framework for Cost Optimization in Cloud Computing Environment. *International Journal of Cloud Applications*, 53–61.

Subashini, S., & Kavitha, V. (2011). A survey on security issues in service delivery models of cloud computing. *Journal of Network and Computer Applications*, *34*(1), 1–11. doi:10.1016/j.jnca.2010.07.006

Takabi, H., Joshi, J. B. D., & Ahn, G.-J. (2010). Security and privacy challenges in cloud computing environments. *IEEE Security and Privacy*, *8*(6), 24–31. doi:10.1109/MSP.2010.186

Yang, Jia, Ren, Zhang, & Xie. (2013). DAC-MACS: Effective Data Access Control for Multiauthority Cloud Storage Systems. *IEEE Transaction on Information Forensics and Security*.

Yang, Z., Qiao, L., Liu, C., Yang, C., & Guangming, W. (2010). A Collaborative Trust Model of Firewall-through based on Cloud Computing. *14th International Conference on Computer Supported Cooperative Work in Design*.

Zhang, Q., Cheng, L., & Boutaba, R. (2010). *Cloud computing: state-of-the-art and research challenges* (Vol. 7). Springer.

Zissis, D., & Lekkas, D. (2012). Addressing cloud computing security issues. *Future Generation Computer Systems*, *28*(3), 583–592. doi:10.1016/j.future.2010.12.006

Chapter 8
DOS Attacks on Cloud Platform:
Their Solutions and Implications

Rohit Kumar
Chandigarh University, India

ABSTRACT

IaaS, PaaS, and SaaS models collectively form the Cloud Computing Infrastructure. The complexity of interrelationship of service models is very high and so security issue becomes essentials and must be developed with utmost care. Distributed DOS attacks are a major concern for different organization engaged in using cloud based services. The denial of service attack and distributed denial of service attacks in particular in cloud paradigms are big threat on a cloud network or platform. These attacks operate by rendering the server and network useless by sending unnecessary service and resource requests. The victims host or network isn't aware of such attacks and keeps providing recourses until they get exhausted. Due to resource exhaustions, the resources requests of genuine users doesn't get fulfilled. Severity of these attacks can lead to huge financial losses if, they are able to bring down servers executing financial services. This chapter presents DOS threats and methods to mitigate them in varied dimensions.

INTRODUCTION

Cloud computing has gained significant importance and has become obvious part of our day to day computation and communication needs. The cloud provides a platform for computation in terms of both hardware and software. The IaaS, PaaS and SaaS

DOI: 10.4018/978-1-5225-3029-9.ch008

are cloud based services and provide online storage spaces, computational platform, customized software's etc. With more and more dependence on cloud computing, the issue of security becomes very important and is critical to the success of cloud based services. Many type of threats exists in cloud domain but, in this chapter we particularly focuses on Denial of Service attacks and methods to control them.

Denial of service attacks (DoS) are well known attacks and poses a serious problem in internet and other types of networks. The goal of DoS is to disturb the services and making them inaccessible to the user. In this kind of attack the network is rendered useless by attacking vehemently on the bandwidth and connectivity. In these attacks the attacker sends a large stream of packets which causes huge congestion on the victims network. Due to this high congestion, the network cease to works and even a single request doesn't get served. In past there have been numerous attacks of these kind which targeted many famous internet sites and exposed their vulnerabilities. The distributed DOS called DDOS has been a complex and powerful technique to attack internet and its resources. As multiple machine or attackers can target a single machine; to identifying the real attackers for such attacks and to mitigate their effect is very difficult to achieve. The internet protocols like TCP/IP are well studied and some of them provides open resources access model which makes them easily targetable by the attackers. The attackers targets the some key loopholes in the internet system architecture to carry out such attacks. The DDOS attacks are called many to one attack as multiple sources attacks a single machine in well planned and synchronized way. These multiple attacker machines strangulates the target machine by huge data i.e. large volume of data or packet steams are sent to target machine to swamp it and efforts are made to make these packets genuine, this process renders the target useless. The traffic or data from multiple machines is transferred in aggregated and intelligent manner so that the target cannot distinguish among them and treat them as genuine and valid packets. The attacker usually knows the traffic handling capacity of the target and generates far more data than its capacity. The DDOS attack can damage the target form moderate to critical level. These attacks can lead the system to get shutdown, to corrupt files and usually results in total or partial loss of services.

The difficult thing about DDOS is that there is no clearly apparent feature which can lead to detection of these attacks. So, clear and direct methods to deal which such attacks aren't easy to devise and implement. The attackers now a days has access to user friendly and easy to use software's which assists in carrying out these attacks and averagely secured machine cannot handle such attacks.

The DoS attacking programs are devised with simple logic and occupy small memory making their handing easier. The attackers are vigilant and keep on devising new methods to carry out such attacks and its reverse is reciprocated by the defenders. The defenders must be pro-actively vigilant to secure their system. The DDOS handling technique are growing at a rapid rate but, a real panacea for such attacks is difficult to achieve. In practice multiple flavours of these attacks exists and providing a safe solution for all of them is very difficult to achieve. The mitigating techniques employed for such attacks tries to stop the attacker by making such attack difficult to carry out and making the attacker accountable for these attacks.

CLASSIFICATION OF DOS ATTACKS:

The DoS attacks can be carried out in different ways. The major distinguishing features has been mentioned here. Figure 1 presents the classification of DoS attacks. Below is a brief introduction to these attacks:

- **Network Device Level Attack:** DoS attacks in network device level can be caused by exhausting hardware resources of network devices (Douligeris, 2004) and by exploiting bugs in software also. One of the most common examples of such attack is buffer overrun attack. Some password checking routines are not well coded and can easily become target of buffer overrun attack by entering long passwords.
- **The OS Level Attacks:** These attacks are carried out by targeting the vulnerabilities in the underlying OS. One such attack Is Ping of death attack (S.F Rouger, 2012). In Ping death attacks large number of ICMP messages with data length larger than the capacity of standard IP packet are sent to target machine. This usually crashes the victims' machine and can incur unrecoverable losses.

Figure 1. Classification of DOS attacks

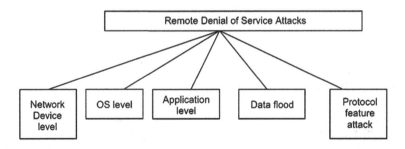

- **Application-Based Attacks:** These attacks are carried out by finding the specific bugs in the application itself. The attacker tries to set the machine and application out of order and or makes it too slow to respond. Finger bomb (W. Paper, 2002) is one such application based attack.

- **Flooding Attacks:** Are very common and tries to choke the network and machine by sending it large voluminous data. Flood pinging is a commonly used attack using flooding method. The flooding attacks usually target the bandwidth of the victim's network by sending more data (meaning less data) than the network capacity. In some instances a server providing some services is overwhelmed with large service requests causing denial of service. The attacker uses a spoofed address to carry out such attacks to avoid detection.

- **Protocol Based Attacks:** The protocol feature based attacks tries to figure out possible loopholes in the protocols used for communication. One such attack is IP spoofing which can be done with moderate efforts. Many other kind of attacks targets DNS cache on name servers changing their configuration and changing the registration details of the web sites and other services. This usually results in wrong routing by the victim and ultimately he lends up at a wrong place.

A Typical DDOS Policy

Figure 2 (a) and 2(b) presents a typical policy for carrying out DDOS attacks. Figure 2(b) is same as Figure 2(a) represents the actual attack environment for better understanding. This strategy consists of following four components:

Figure 2. DDOS attack process

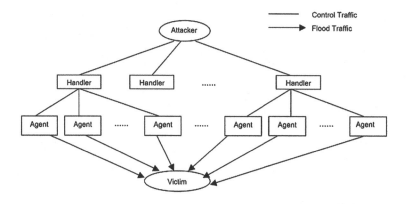

1. The attacker
2. The compromised masters or handlers which can control other machines/agents
3. Compromised hosts which acts as zombie nodes and generates large volume of data.
4. The victim.

The real attacker doesn't carry out attacks directly but, uses handles and agents to carry out the desired attack. The handler nodes are compromised host and execute a specialized code on them. This code or program is capable of governing number of agents. The agents are the nodes which actually generate false requests and are called zombie hosts. These hosts also run a special program to generate large number of false requests.

Different Types of DoS Attacks

Dos attacks can be carried out in number of ways and are evolving continuously. Figure 3 presents all kinds of DDOS attacks which depends upon degree of automation, by exploited vulnerability, attack are dynamics and by impact.

Some of these attacks are general DoS attacks and will not be discussed in detail But, attacks relevant to cloud domain will be discussed.

Cloud and Major DoS Attacks

The cloud provides a platform for computing through the utilization of software and hardware which empowers the users and organizations to perform their tasks efficiently. So, provision of robust security is pivotal to the success of cloud as it's a network based platform. The cloud providing virtualisation introduces vulnerabilities which includes DDOS, spoofing, sniffing and lot more which are obstruction in cloud growth. The main goal of this chapter is to provide comprehensible discussion of DoS attacks in context of cloud and to provide overview of techniques which provides mitigation from DoS attacks. Figure 3 provides a comprehensive list of all types of DoS attacks but, the present chapter focuses on key cloud based DoS attacks and their repercussions.

- **DDOS Attacks Impact on Layer 3 and 4 OSI:** Attack on these two layers are based on jeopardizing the network capacity. In these DDOS attack voluminous data is generated which targets the network infrastructure. High floods of data is sent to slow down the web server and gradually decrease the performance of Layer three, i.e., network layer and layer four i.e. transport

Figure 3. DDOS architecture

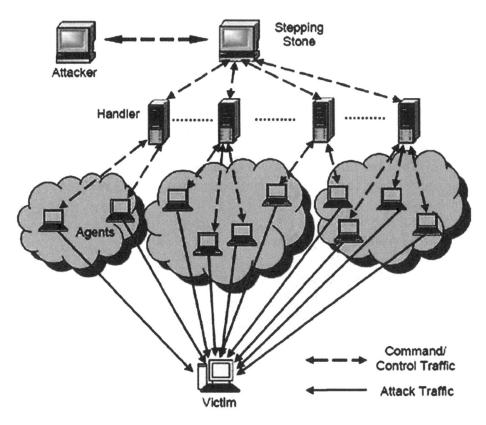

layer. Figure 4 Represents a bandwidth attack where red represents attackers and green represents legitimate users.

- **Flooding Attack:** SYN food attacks are common, simple but yet, powerful kind of DDOS attacks. The SYN attacks are performed by sending stream of packets with spoofed IP address. The recipient treats them as genuine and reserves resources for them. As the requests are so large in number that a given server runs out of its resources. The key to this attack is spoofed IP address for which a client actually doesn't exists. This fictitious client creates number of half connections to rob a server of its resources and renders it useless. Figure 5(a) presents the TCP connection setup process and Figure 5(b) shows how SYN floods affects the receiver and causes half closed connections.

SYN flooding attacks are illustrated with following example:

Figure 4. Classification and types of DDOS attacks

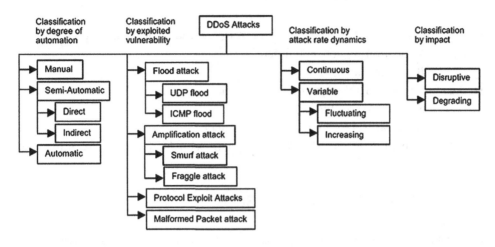

Figure 5. Bandwidth attack

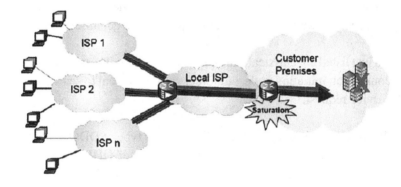

- **TCP Connection Management:** The sender first establishes connection before actual transfer of data

Setup Process

- First set and initialize TCP variables, i.e., sequence number, buffers, flow control information, receiver window, etc.
- Then client initiates a connection
- Server responds to the client

Process of Three-Way Handshake

Step 1: Client sends TCP SYN seg. to server (seg. Stands for segment)
- ○ It mention sequence number
- ○ It contains no data

Step 2: Server gets SYN segment, which replies with SYNACK seg.
- ○ Server reserves buffers
- ○ Mentions server first sequence number

Step 3: The client node gets SYNACK, responds with ACK which may or may not contain data

Process of SYN Flooding and Its Steps

- Attacking computer uses spoofed address and sends multiple (flood) of request
- Victim machine reserves resources for every request
  - ○ The connection state remain maintained until timeout
  - ○ Half connections remains for fixed bound time
- Upon resource exhaustion legitimate requests from genuine users are declined

These steps just listed are classical example of DoS attack. These attacks don't harm the TCP connection initiating node, but forces the respondent to spawn a new thread for each service request.

- **UDP Attacks:** It is a most commonly observed type of DDOS attack in recent past. In UDP flood attack, a very large number of UDP packets are sent to different ports on the victim host by the attacker. Major Drawback in UDP Packets is lack of congestion monitoring and control system. The attacker knowing this vulnerability sends extremely large numbers of packets. Again this attacks are carried out by using IP address spoofing. The IP spoofing makes it difficult to control attack and to track the attacker.
- **Domain Name Server Amplification Attack:** The domain name server can be made to participate in DDOS attacks by wrong configuration. In this attack the victim is overwhelmed by large number of DNS replies which he never initiated. The domain name server is a publically accessible and open system and if programmed wrong can have sever repercussions. In DNS amplification attacks the response to the DNS request is quite large than the request itself. To perform this attack the attacker first creates a reliable domain name server and attaches a large garbage file with it. After this the attacker programs

and commands zombies. These zombies have spoofed IP address of a victim machine and starts sending queries to the server. In response to the query the victim machine starts getting large replies ensuring resource exhaustion.

- **Internet Control Message Protocol (ICMP) Flooding Attacks:** This is a simple DDOS attack in which an attacker sends voluminous ICMP echo requests i.e. ping masseuses to slow done the receiver network and its associated services.

- **Smurf Attacks:** It is a ICMP kind of attack and operates by utilising broadcast IP address of a network. Here again the attacker utilizes the spoofed IP address to make the attack work. Using this spoofed IP it sends volumes of ICMP messages on the network and the victim in turn starts sending the replies. Figure 6 shows how an attacker sends a broadcast message with IP address of the victim host and then all devices are forced to reply to the victim host shown by red lines between the devices and victim.

Method

The attacker, i.e., DoS source sends ICMP message with wrong source address and wrong destination address. In ICMP message source address contains the address of the victim and destination address used is broadcast address. When this request reaches to the gateway (broadcast network) the gateway is not able to comprehend it and sends three ICMP replies to victim. Here three replies are created because gateway consists of three hosts and each host replies to the ICMP request from the attacker. In this process, the victim keep getting unnecessary replies and wastes its resources. In order to carry out these attacks the attacker must know the network topology very well.

Figure 6. TCP connection process

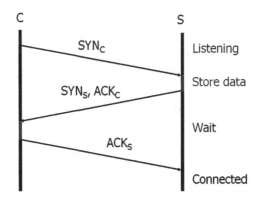

- **Application Layer Attacks:** Application layer threats and attacks are hard to perceive in cloud based services, as they are difficult to be differentiated from authentic traffic, which intends makes the system vulnerable. Figure 7 Depicts Application Layer DDOS attacks which hampers the services of the application zone i.e. Web Server and Database Server.

Application Layer DDOS Attacks

- **Request-Flooding Attacks:** All the major application layer protocols like HHTP GETs, DNS requests, and SIP Invites can participates in DDOS attacks though unwilling fully. All these attacks tries to overwhelm the server with genuine looking large number of requests (Shamsolmoali, 2014).
- **Application Layer Asymmetric Attacks:** Asymmetric Attacks send "high-workload" requests to the server. In these types of attacks the CPU, memory or disk space are completely brought down and their services are severely degraded.
- **Repeated One-Shot Attacks on Application Layer:** Attackers send one heavy request per session and in other words you can say attack load is spread around multiple sessions.
- **Application-Exploit Attacks:** These attacks finds out loopholes in the applications and makes these applications vulnerable. These types of attacks deliberately targets the application software to make them work in inappropriate manner and to take the control over application system. One of its common type of attacks is Structured Query Language (SQL) injection attack (Khajuria, 2013).

Figure 7. SYN floods and half-closed connections

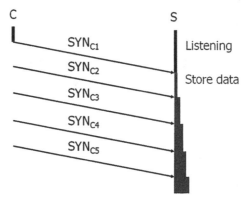

- **DDOS Attacks in Web Services:** Web applications available in cloud servers are hampered by these attacks they include:
- **Attack Using HTTP:** Non-specific request are targeted on the host, i.e., request of ambiguous nature are presented to the system. The web services are outperformed by extensively large process requests. Due to heavy use of resources (consumed/reserved by false requests), denial of services attacks are easily carried out and can result in huge losses in terms of data and functionality.
- **Malfunctioned HTTP:** Invalid packets are sent to the web servers which in-turn consumes server resources. The ZAFI.B is worm attack which best suites as an example for malfunctioned HTTP attack.
- **HTTP Request Attacks:** This type of attacks flood web servers with number of legitimate HTTP requests seeking to consume server resources to carry out DDOS attack.
- **HTTP Idle Attacks:** An attack that opens HTTP connections but then goes idle without actually sending a complete HTTP request but a small number of bytes dribbles out which never completes the request. Figure 8 depicts the "Slowloris" DDOS Attack where a prolonged and low bandwidth incomplete HTTP requests are delivered from a host to the server.
- **XML XXEA Attacks:** XML attacks target web application, which communicate through XML documents. Attackers construct a message which is malformed send it to the web applications. As shown in Figure 9 a message is sent from the client to the Web Application on the Cloud and which in turn gives response with a locally stored file address as ["/etc/hostname"]. If these requests, are made in abundance, can result in different losses.

Figure 8. Smurf attack

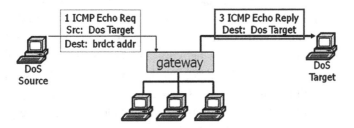

Figure 9. Access zone and application zone

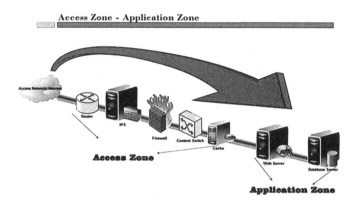

Detection and Mitigation Techniques Against DDOS Attacks

Numerous methods have been invented to tackle DDOS attack. Each of these mechanism tackles different variation of DDOS and cloud based attacks. Figure 10 presents all such possible methods. Among all of them few have been discussed here which are specific about cloud platform.

- **Covariance Matrix Modelling:** Covariance modelling theory tries to find out the differences between normal and abnormal traffic behaviours. If the traffic behaviour is quite abnormal then it can be a possible DoS attack and should get detected. For more accurate predication Multi-variable variance model should be employed to capture multiple adverse factors. Figure 11 illustrates working method of covariance matrix modelling. The traffic is analysed and covariance matrix is used to predict about vulnerable and safe state. This output can be used to initiate and control the subsequent actions for ensuring secure, and smooth working of the system.
- **Cloud Trace Back Method (CTB):** Here major objective is to find out the real source of the attack and to protect a server form directly being attacked. CTB can be thought of as an extra layer of protection to safeguard the cloud network. The CTB is usually deployed at the edge routers of the network to close all source ends of the cloud network. If such systems are not put in place than it can make the network and server extremely vulnerable. In conventional setup the CTB precedes the server and all the server requests passes through it. All the requests first comes the CTB which places a cloud trace back mark (CTM) tag within the CTB header. So, all the requests passes

Figure 10. Idle attacks

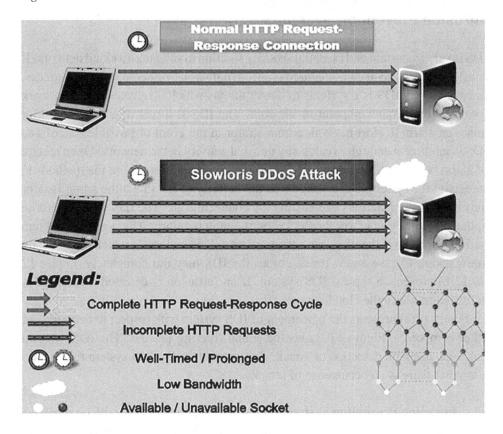

Figure 11. XML attacks

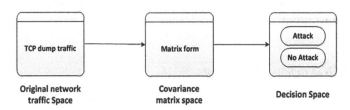

through CTB and are marked properly before leaving. During this marking process the CTB removes the destination server address and itself passes the request to the server and thus ensure elimination of direct attack on the server. Upon discovery of an attack the victim asks for reconstruction by extracting the mark to make them aware of the real origin of the message. After reconstruction the system will start to filter out the attack traffic as well.

Intrusion Detection System (IDS) and Intrusion Prevention System

IDS is very important and essential security solution to safeguard a cloud network. If configured properly it can safeguards us from numerous vulnerabilities and attacks. In easier terms IDS is a systems to detect threats which originates in the network form any malicious computer or network. The IDS is a real time systems and it raises an alarm to alert network administrator in the event of possible threat. The IDS is intelligent enough to catch any unusual activity in the network. Upon receipt of alarm by the IDS the administrator takes the call and figures out the methods to safeguard the system. Depending upon the severity of the threat the administrator may take different actions like closing the connection etc. The IDS system must be updated regularly as newer threats keeps evolving regularly. The possible problem with IDS system is that they can safeguard us only from threats which they already know about. In case a new threat comes the IDS may fail completely. Figure 12 (a),12(b) presents a typical IDS system. If an intrusion is detected a message is delivered to notify the cloud servers.

Figure 12(a) presents the placement of IDS system with respect to network and other componets. Figure 13 shows the actual filtering process. The IDS systesm raises an alarm on detection of attack. But, sometimes the IDS system raises false alarm but there is no occurrence of attack.

- **Intrusion Prevention System:** Intrusion prevention system (IPS) is an active system involved in preventing DoS attacks. This system can work without manual administration and can respond to newer threats easily and can adapt itself as per newer threats. IPS systems requires stricter configuration for effective working.

Figure 12. DDOS defence mechanism

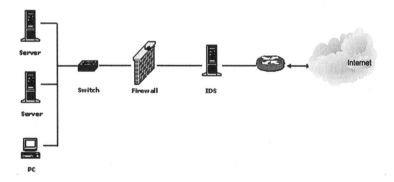

Figure 13. Covariance matrix view

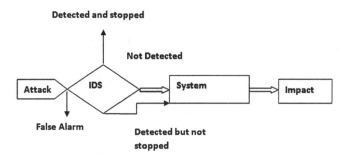

- **Differences Between IDS and IPS Systems:** IPS is bit different in functioning than the IDS system. There are few major difference between them. Table 1 presents the key differences between IDS and IPS Systems.

For optimal and best security both the IDS and IPS must be integrated together. With this integration the systems becomes bit complex but intelligent and secure. This setup is more powerful and can tackle newer kind of threats easily. Figure 14 shows a typical integration of IDS and IPS systems.

Intrusion Detection System Types

- **Signature-Based Detection:** This method is extremely accurate for those attacks which are well known attacks. Using this method, we can handle a broader range of known attacks and capability to figure out attacks remains considerably good. Disadvantage of this type of method is its efficiency which degrades when number of new attacks increases. This happens because it is

Figure 14. Placement of IDS

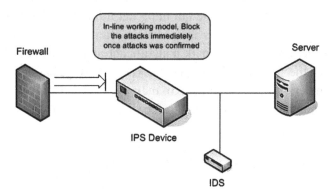

Table 1. Differences between IDS and IPS

IDS	IPS
• Detection Mode Only • Traffic replication required • Decoupling detection and reaction functionalities • IDS as good assistant for network administration • Usually used for testing rules	• Active Traffic Control • Original traffic required • Detection and reaction support • No administration assistance needed • Requires strict configuration • Two network cards bridging required

based on signature and for every new attack it has to create a new signature and store it in its database to thwart future attacks. The big drawback of this approach is that the system is able to detect only those types of intrusion which matches a know predefined pattern. The method of signature based detection will not work properly when the attacker uses advanced technologies like Payload Encoders, NOP Generators and encrypted data channels (Ashwini Khadke, 2016). Other major problem with signature based attacks is that they suffers from the problem of false alarm i.e. the system may show the system in unsafe state though the system is in safe state.

- **Anomaly-Based Detection:** This approach generates a pattern of normal activity and if something deviates from the normal activity or processing patterns to certain different type of data processing/activity then anomaly based detection raises an alarm. The anomaly based system finds out the anomaly in the executing pattern (i.e., current processing) by checking the list of the normal activity processing types. Based on this if, something wrong is observed then the system automatically raises an alarm. Advantage of using this approach we can add new rules without tempering and modifying the existing ones. It is capable to find the new attacks easily. Disadvantage to use this approach is it goes off falsely sometimes which consumes time and processing speed (Shuyuan Jin, 2004).

- **Entropy-Based Method:** It is method to find the advent of DDOS attacks. This method clearly shows the fall in packet traffic or a sharp decrease from regular "fingerprint" profiles immediately after the start of DDOS attack. Severe DDOS attacks will mark a significant and immediate change in the entropy of the packet traffic monitored. These changes are even marked on small number of routers regardless of their position and kind of routing policy or algorithm they use to route the traffic (Raghav, 2013).

Stealthy DDOS Attacks in Cloud

A newer kind of DDOS attack called stealthy DDOS attacks have made their presence known in the security arena. These attacks are different from regular DDOS attacks in the way that their detection is difficult with the regular detection methods. In some of these attacks genuine users participates and try to gain information of the victim's computer and hosts. This involvement of real users makes their detection difficult. To detect these attacks extensive time series analysis needs to performed. In addition multi variance models can be used to detect these attacks (Zargar, 2013).

CONCLUSION

Cloud computing has lots of significance in today's competitive computing world. With the rise of cloud computing and its associated platforms security for these platforms has become vital and essential. In the present chapter denial of service attacks in context of cloud computing has been discussed. Different types of DOS attacks and working methods has been briefly discussed and presented. Different methods to control and mitigate the DOS and DDOS attacks have also been mentioned.

It can be concluded from the chapter that, to control such attacks multiple dimensions needs to be investigated and viable working methods needs to be envisaged. These attacks cannot be controlled by fixed kind of methods and algorithms. Instead some dynamic methods and policy must be implemented to detect and control these attacks like integration of IDS and IPS system.

REFERENCES

Ashwini Khadke, C. (2016). *Review on Mitigation of Distributed Denial of Service (DDOS).* Attacks in Cloud Computing. doi:10.1109/ISCO.2016.7726917

Douligeris, C., & Mitrokotsa, A. (2004). DDoS attacks and defense mechanisms: Classification. *Computer Networks*, *44*(5), 643–666. doi:10.1016/j.comnet.2003.10.003

Khajuria & Srivastava. (2013). Analysis Of The DDOS Defence Strategies In Cloud Computing. *International Journal Of Enhanced Research In Management & Computer Applications*, (2), 1-5.

Raghav, C. I. (2013). Intrusion Detection and Prevention in Cloud Environment. *Systematic Reviews*, (24), 21–30.

RougerS. F. (2012). Retrieved from http://www.akamai.com/dl/akamai/akamai-ebook-guide-to-multilayered-web-security.pdf

Shamsolmoali. (2014). CDF: High rate DDOS filtering method in Cloud Computing. *Computer Network and Information Security*, 43-50.

Shuyuan Jin, C. (2004). A Covariance Analysis Model for DDOS Attack Detection. IEEE.

Zargar, S. T., Joshi, J., & Tipper, D. (2013). A Survey of Defense Mechanisms Against Distributed Denial of Service (DDOS)Flooding. *IEEE Communications Surveys and Tutorials*, 1–24.

Section 3

Approach of Cloud Towards Internet of Things

Chapter 9
Security Issues in the Internet of Things:
A Review

Muneer Bani Yassein
Jordan University of Science and Technology, Jordan

Wail Mardini
Jordan University of Science and Technology, Jordan

Amnah Al-Abdi
Jordan University of Science and Technology, Jordan

ABSTRACT

Internet of Things (IoT) is one of the most active and hot topics these days in which most of our everyday objects are connected with each other over internal and external networks. As in any data communication paradigm there are security aspects that should be taken care of. The traditional security mechanisms are usually not applicable in IoT because there are different standards involved, this make the security preservation is one of the main challenges in IoT. According to previous surveys, there are many of security issues in regards to IoT. In this chapter, five issues from the security issues in IoT are discussed; Access Control, Authentication, Privacy, Policy Enforcement, and Trust. After that, major proposed solutions from the literature is listed and compared according to the strength and weakness points for each of them.

DOI: 10.4018/978-1-5225-3029-9.ch009

INTRODUCTION

Internet of Things (IoT) can be defined as huge network that consist of a massive number of heterogeneous computing systems, sensors, devices, equipment, software and information services, and applications are connecting together (Samani, Ghenniwa, & Wahaishi, 2015). IoT can be divided into three layers: perception, transmission, and application layer. Each layer has its own responsibilities, perception layer is responsible for collecting data from the physical system, transmission layer is responsible for transmitting the collected data, and the application layer is responsible for processing the data and providing the needed services (Aljawarneh et al., 2016; Aljawarneh et al., 2017). In each IoT layers, there are security issues that must be solved.

An object in IoT can be attacked if no secure and reliable communication is developed, so it is important to ensure the security and reliability between IoT objects (devices). The devices in IoT are not homogenous, this property is one of the main challenges when developing security mechanisms, and the other main challenge is the ambiguity of the information which is collected from IoT devices. Figure 1 show the main security issues in IoT (Sicari, Rizzardi, Grieco & Coen-Porisini, 2015). In this chapter five issues from the security issues in IoT will be discussed, these issues are: Access Control, Authentication, Privacy, Policy Enforcement, and Trust.

Figure 1. The main security issues in IoT
Sicari et al., 2015.

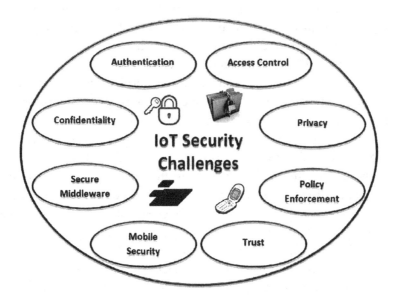

The chapter is organized as follow: section discusses many security issues as mentioned above, section three discuss the solutions for each issue as appeared in the literature and show a classification and a comparison between these solutions. Finally, the last section includes some concluding remarks.

SECURITY ISSUES IN INTERNET OF THINGS

Access Control

Bernabe, Ramos & Gomez, 2016, developed a trust-aware access control system for IoT (TACIOT) which is a trust model based on fuzzy logic. This model uses a multidimensional approach, and also it uses security and social relation to obtaining access control logic.

The integration of the objects on the Internet, and in addition to the traditional consideration such as service feedback and reputation, the demand of new consideration such as security aspects and social relationships between the IoT devices rise the need of developing new security standards which are suitable to use in IoT (Bernabe et al., 2016).

TACIOT use a multidimensional approach to developing the trust model, this means that the user can add new features to the model, so the trust model becomes extendable. There are four main dimensions: Quality of Service, Security, Reputation, and Social relationship dimension, each of these dimensions is explained in details in (Bernabe et al., 2016; Aljawarneh et al., 2015), it is important to know that there are two type of trust properties which will be covered in each dimension, the first property can be measured as a real number between zero and one, and the second property can be measured as Boolean value true or false.

TACIOT is the integration between the trust model and control access technique. Virtually IoT consists of bubbles, each bubble contains set of devices (smart devices) with single Authorization Manager which is in charge to provide an authorization credential for each device, also each device must have Trust Manager which responsible for estimating the trust degree of an object. When an object need to access another object from different bubbles, the requester Trust Manager job is to provide the most trust destination among the set of devices that can provide the services, on another hand, the Trust Manager in the destination job is to obtain the trust value from the requester.

In TACIOT exchanging message is divided into four stages, in the first stage object 1 is discover the most trust object (object 2) which provides a service, this done by accessing the Trust Manger. In the second stage, which is optional, before object 1 requests to access object 2, it needs an authorization credential. In the third stage, the object1 access the service located in the object 2, it uses the authorization credential which was obtained from the previous stage. Finally, in the fourth stage the trust values, which is associated to object 2, is updated.

The Trust Manager was implemented in Android software development kit (SDK) and tested in Android Platform 2.3.3 (API level 10) (Bernabe et al., 2016; Aljawarneh et al., 2016), Constrained Application Protocol (CoAP) is used to obtain the Trust value, the Trust Manager was relied on a jfuzzylite library to deal with the Fuzzy Trust.

To validate the TACIOT, set of different tests are executed on the four stages, and then compute the consumed time, these tests are applied into two types of devices: constraint, and non-constraint devices.

Many operations are performed in each stage. The first stage consists of two operations trust requests, and trust query processing. The second stage consist of four operations: sign message, token generation, validate signature, and Authz request. The third stage consist of three operations: authentication, trust processing, and token validation. Finally, the fourth stage consist of two operations reward Request, fuzzy Trust quantification.

From the result, it was concluded that the first stage is the fastest because there is no need to calculate the trust. The third stage is the heaviest because of the need of encryption operation which is expensive.

In (Saxena, Duraisamy & Kaulgud, 2015, November) focused on developing a scalable access control which is suitably using in IoT. The proposed access control which called Simple Messaging and Access Control (SMAC) is based on Capability Based Messaging (CBM) technique which is allow to send a message based on the capability rather than Access Control List (ACL) because ACL is not suitable for the huge number of devices that are connected in IoT environment and it will face the bottleneck problem. The control access in SMAC is performed in the communication layer, by this approach the access control problem is converted to how to control read and write access to a communication channel. SMAC has some features that make it more suitable to be used in IoT, but the most important feature is SMAC use two port channel that isolates the read and writes capabilities if anyone knows one port (read or write) he cannot know the other unless he has a secret key.

Rivera, Cruz-Piris, Lopez-Civera, de la Hoz, & Marsa-Maestre, 2015, used User-Managed Access (UMA) which is a profile developed on the top of OAuth 2.0 to provide the users with the ability to control and detect which of the third parties can access their resources (Maler, Catalano, Machulak, & Hardjono, 2016). UMA has a set of entities: Recourse Owner, Requesting Party, Client, Resource Set, Resource Server, and Authorization Server, each of these entities has a specific role .This

UMA profile was used to propose a schema that unifies access control between IoT devices, intelligent agents, and hybrid elements. The main challenge is to apply access control rules on the different entities (with different natures) in IoT environment.

Authentication

Wireless Sensor Networks (WSN) is the base stone in IoT, it contains a set of sensors which are dealing with the data that are collected from the physical system. Usually signals sensors and other wireless transmission mediums can interfere and cause a loss of data (Mardini, Khamayseh, Jaradat, & Hijjawi, 2012). The data which is obtained from the sensors is usually sensitive data and it is important to have an effective data protections mechanism in spite of the limitations in WSN environment such as limited computing power, and storage (Ye, Zhu, Wang & Lin, 2014).

The authors in (Ye, Zhu, Wang & Lin, 2014) use a user authentication mechanism to prevent an unauthorized user to access the sensitive recourses and data, at the same time it must enable the authorized user to access it, by this mechanism the malicious attack will be prevented.

The authentication process can be divided into two parts, in the first part the authentication is done between the user and the nodes (this part is used to control the network access), and the second part a session key is created between the node and the user (this part is used to make the communication secure).

Elliptical Curve Cryptography is an encoding system uses elliptic curves over finite fields to send information in public without risking the security of that information (Ye et al., 2014), this encoding system is used to develop mutual authentication model to produce public and private keys.

The authentication model can be performed in two phases, the first phase is the initialization phase, and the second is the mutual authentication and key establishment.

1. **Initialization Phase:** In this phase, the nodes are initialized. The main parameters that should be initialized for each node are private and public keys, identity, hash function, and Elliptical Curve (EC) parameters (Ye et al., 2014).
2. **Mutual Authentication and Key Establishment Phase:** When a user makes a request for information from WSN, the authentication take it process in five steps, these steps are explained in details in (Ye et al., 2014), at the end of this phase the authentication of the user is identified.

The authors in (Lee, Lin & Huang, 2014, May) construct an encryption method based on XOR rather than using other complex methods such as hash function. In IoT, it is important that only the authorized devices are involved and communicate with other authorized devices. RFID is the main technology that it used to identify the devices in IoT, it is important to have strong cryptography for security purpose. Electronic Product Code (EPC) tag is the main scheme that is used to identify the objects in RFID, but the attacker can simply read the EPC and many malicious actions using it, so it is useful to have cryptography method or protocol that prevent these actions. The operation of a lightweight cryptography protocol based on XOR is presented in (Lee, Lin & Huang, 2014, May), then the passwords are used to the mutual authentication purpose.

Privacy

Privacy concern is one of the main security issues in IoT. The nature of IoT environment elevates the privacy concern because the objects (things) in IoT are having the authority to share their capabilities and information to do a certain task (Samani et al., 2015).

There are two main categories of privacy approaches in IoT, the first one is a rule-based approach which it provides privacy model that is suitable for the closed environment, which is definitely can't be used in IoT, The second one is an architectural-based approach which is suitable to IoT environment (open environment) (Samani et al., 2015).

Smart objects uses what is called Wireless Home Automation Networks (WHANs) to connect with each other and exchange information (Yassein, Mardini, & Khalil, 2016, September). This information can be classified as sensitive and non-sensitive information.

The two type of information mentioned above can be expressed mathematically by using boundary for exposure, the information which is within the exposure boundary the information will be considered as not sensitive information (Samani et al., 2015) proposed a framework for Cooperative Distributed Systems (CDS), this framework depends on two type of strategies, detect the non-authorized operations and prevent the execution of them (Samani et al., 2015), however, these two strategies cannot be performed perfectly because of the incomplete nature of the knowledge. Anonymization technique can be used to provide privacy protection with probability or with Privacy Protection Level (PPL).

The goal of the proposed framework is to develop interaction protocol with privacy protection, Contract Net Protocol (CNP) is an interaction protocol that is used to detect the role of every entity in the smart space using brokering architecture.

Alpár et al., 2016, May, focus to develop a framework that it is based on attribute-based (AB) authentication, this framework enable the users communicating in IoT environment to control the data which they shared and prevent the linkability, as result this framework will preserve their privacy.

The privacy problem in IoT found because a large amount of data that belongs to the user are generating without direct control from the users themselves, this will be given the threats a big chance to access the data.

Attributes can be defined as anything that can be described as a bit of string, the attributes used to obtain security level and unlinkability. Attribute-based Credentials (ABC) is a technology that it is used to provide flexible and privacy-preserving authentication(Alpár et al., 2016, May), this technology can be used to prevent privacy threats.

AB authentication take place on four points, sensing: when the sensors are communicating with each other the authentication is based on attributes, collection: the sensors must authenticate when it communicate with data processor, Dissemination: communicate the information after AB authentication take place, and Issuing: authenticate the entity based on attribute and give it a credential (Alpár et al., 2016, May).

The authors in (Ukil, Bandyopadhyay, & Pal, 2014, April) proposed a privacy scheme that provides to the users the ability of estimate the privacy risk before sharing the private data depending on statistical representation of the sensitivity (privacy metric).

Policy Enforcement

Policy enforcement is the mechanisms used to force the application of a set of defined actions in a system (Sicari et al., 2015).

One of the main aspects in IoT is to make the system secure, to obtain this goal, flexible middleware which is able to handle the huge amount of produced data is integrated with flexible policy enforcement framework (Sicari, Rizzardi, Miorandi, Cappiello & Coen-Porisini, 2016).

NetwOrked Smart objects (NOS) is a middleware consist of smart nodes which provide distributed storage to handle the huge amount of data which is produced from IoT devices (Rizzardi, Miorandi, Sicari, Cappiello, & Coen-Porisini, 2015, October) . NOS is not originally designed to control the access of user and data recourses, and not to provide the data to the users, the idea to integrate NOS with enforcement system is established to solve this problem.

By integrating Policy enforcement with NOS, there will be a set of policies and rules which are used to manage the resources and to control the access to IoT and the communication. The enforcement framework is responsible for controlling the access and providing the services with maintaining the quality.

In traditional access control enforcement frameworks, there are three types of policy points: Policy Enforcement Point (PEP), a Policy Decision Point (PDP), and a Policy Administration Point (PAP) (Rizzardi et al., 2015, October) . When a user makes a request for data the PEP is responsible for receiving this request and send a decision request to PDP. PDP will use the authentication policies to detect if the request will be accepted or rejected, this response sends to PEP and it either grant or denies the access to the resources. The previous framework is not used in (Sicari et al., 2016) because the communication is based on the MQTT protocol, and the requests are handled by the MQTT broker.

Sicari et al., 2016, use an approach based on Attribute-Based Access Control (ABAC) model, in this model both the subjects that want to access or grant the resources and the data itself will be represented by attributes, these attributes will be used in the policies definition. The implementation of the policy enforcement in (Sicari et al., 2016) is written used JSON syntax which is chosen because it is flexible to represent the context. The validation of the proposed approach was done by using a simple use case.

Neisse (Neisse, Steri, & Baldini, 2014, October) provides a solution to the lack of policy enforcement, especially in privacy and protection, in MQTT implementation. The solution is to use SecKit (which is a model based security) to address the privacy and data protection problem in IoT. The contribution in the provided solution that develops the existence implementation of MQTT open source broker, and also to enforce the security policies. By the provided solution the policies were applied with a small delay (10 ms).

Trust in IoT

In IoT, a huge amount of data will be produced from the smart objects in IoT environment. The challenge is how to make a balance between the trust in the services and the privacy of the information. Daubert et al. (Daubert, Wiesmaier & Kikiras, 2015, June) aim to establish a model that is trying to make this balance.

There is no agreed definition of the trust term, but in general, it can be defined as "the assurance that Personally Identifiable Information (PII) will be only used as agreed and will be protected against unauthorized access" (Daubert et al., 2015, June). There is a strong relation between the trust, privacy, and sensitivity: to obtain trust this depend to have privacy, to obtain privacy this depend on having sensitivity, and finally the sensitivity depends on the PII. The model that is described in (Daubert et al., 2015, June) may facilitate new application in IoT.

Sato et al. (Sato, Kanai, Tanimoto & Kobayashi, 2016, March) establish a trust framework in IoT environment. This work define the architecture of IoT to consist of four layers: Cyberphysical Layer which is detect where the devices are placed (on a physical or cyberspace), Device Layer which is include the different types of devices, Data Service and Control Service Layer which is responsible to collect the data from the devices and to control the devices, and Bigdata Analysis Cloud layer which is collects and analyses data from the service layer.

Building trust in IoT faced many problems such as the huge number of connected devices in IoT environment, the mobility feature of the control and data services, and lack of security base in IoT. Building a trust on an area and control it depends on four criteria: device identification which will be more complex in IoT because there are a large number of devices, device behavior monitoring which it is important to monitor the devices to protect them from other harmful devices, connection process to devices including key generation and device authentication, and connection protocols in which we need high-security scheme in wireless communication between control services (Sato et al., 2016, March).

In (Chen, Guo, & Bao, 2016), the authors established a trust management protocol for Service-Oriented Architecture (SOA) based IoT system, and developed a filtering technique to obtain the feedback from the owner of the IoT devices who collaborating the same social interests based on three different type of relationship: friendship, social contact, and community of interest.

SOLUTIONS AND DISCUSSIONS

This section discusses the solutions of the issues mentioned in the previous section. In Table 1, we list a summary for the major Strength and Weakness points for each solution. In the following we provide a discussion for the major points.

In (Saxena et al., November 2015) propose a framework that is more suitable in scalable IoT than the framework that is proposed by (Bernabe et al., 2016), however it does not support smart object privacy (Hernández-Ramos, Bernabe, Moreno, & Skarmeta, 2015), also the framework presented in (Saxena et al., 2015, November) use two port channel to prevent sending messages to the channel, which is an overhead. Rivera et al., October 2015, propose a schema to unifies the access control between different entities, this schema make the application of the access control policies easier regardless the nature of the participating entities in IoT environment, also the proposed schema provide an enhancement in the access control management system, however the authors provide only theoretical description and neither formal description nor protocol implementation is provided (Ouaddah, Mousannif, Elkalam, & Ouahman, 2017).

Ye et al. (Ye et al., 2014) build the mutual authentication based on ECC which is based on fuzzy logic, however Provide only theoretical results of the proposed

Table 1. Solutions discussions

Security Issue	Solutions	Strength Points	Weakness Points
Access Control	Bernabe et al., 2015	• Flexible access control • Reliable security • lightweight authorization	Does not support Smart Objects Privacy
	Diego et al., 2015	• Proposing a schema which unifies access control between intelligent agent, IoT devices, and hybrid entities. • Applying the unified access control regardless the nature of the elements in the IoT environment. • Providing solutions to the security issues which occurred as a result of using multi-agent system. • Interconnecting the agents without changing the security level.	• Provide only a theoretical description. • Neither formal description nor protocol implementation is provided
	Amitabh et al., 2015	• Decentralized access control database • Easy-revocation and device discovery • Prevents unauthorized communication. • Saving the bandwidth • suitable for deploying large-scale IoT systems • Use of two port channels which separate read and write capabilities, if only one is given it is hard to compute the other.	Use two port channel to prevent sending messages to the channel, this is an overhead.
Authentication	Ye et al., 2014	• Mutual authentication between user and nodes. • Fine-grained access Control. • Solve the resource-constrained problem of the IoT perception layer • Focused on mutual authentication and secure key establishment based on ECC: lower storage and communication overheads.	Provide only theoretical results of the proposed model.
	Lee et al., 2014	• Provide an encryption method based on XOR manipulation. • The proposed protocol can be used to establish the mutual authentication procedure in RFID system to be used in IOT applications.	Does not guarantees end-to-end security.
Privacy	Afshan et al., 2015	Define the sensitive information clearly to prevent untheorized access and then preserve the privacy.	Does not Supports all privacy principles.
	Arijit et al., 2014	• Providing a privacy management scheme that provides the user with the expected risk before the sharing private data. • Strong sensitivity detection scheme.	The construction of privacy metric depends on the detection of the data type and on the goal of use which is hard to model.
	Gergely et al., 2016	Authorize the user to control the data that he wants to be disclosed	It is not clear how the proposed framework makes the balance between the cost and the protection action.
Policy Enforcement	Sabrina et al., 2016	• Propose a framework that can be reusable in different domains and has an ability to detect attempts. • The presented framework supports security and data quality enforcement policies ; • Integrate distributed IoT middleware, NetwOrked Smart objects NOS enforcement framework.	Complex integration between the enforcement mechanism with NOS without change the current functionality
	Neisse et al., 2014	• Integrate SecKit security toolkit with MQTT to establish a mechanism that enforces the policies. • Apply complex security policies with a small delay.	Additional delay in the process.
Trust	Daubert et al., 2015	• Provide a relation between the PII, information sensitivity, privacy, and trust. • Classify the trust into device trust, entity trust, and data trust.	Does not support all privacy principles.
	Chen et al., 2016	• Establishing an adaptive and scalable trust protocol. • The established protocol overcomes many other protocols in term of accuracy, trust convergence, and the flexibility in facing the malicious nodes.	The assumption of the availability of high-end device for each user cannot be guaranteed.
	Sato et al., 2016	• Establishing a trust framework for IoT. • Defining an IoT architecture and discussing the problem of each layer in building trust. • Discussing the features of the trust framework in the Internet • Existing secure wireless networks play an important role in fast establishing the trust framework of IoT.	The cost of management and operation is high.

model (Hernandez-Ramos, Pawlowski, Jara, Skarmeta & Ladid, 2015), in another hand, Lee et al. (Lee et al., 2014, May) provide an encryption method based on XOR rather than used complex manipulation such as hash function, however it does not guarantees end-to-end security (Singh, Pasquier & Bacon, 2015, April).

Both Afshan et al. and Gergely et al. (Samani et al., 2015), Alpár, Batina, Batten, Moonsamy, Krasnova, Guellier, & Natgunanathan, 2016, May) are trying to preserve the privacy in IoT, However, Afshan et al. (Samani et al., 2015) do not support all privacy principles that are defined in (Organisation for Economic Co-operation and Development, 2002), also it is not clear how Gergely et al. framework makes the balance between the cost and the protection action. On other hand, (Ukil et al., April 2014) define a privacy metric that provide the owner with a vision to the probability of expected privacy attacks, however, the construction of such this metric is complicated because it is depend on the detection of the data type and on the goal of use which is hard to model (Pal, 2015).

Sabrina et al. (Sicari et al., 2016) integrate an IoT middleware with policy enforcement to make the management of interactions between different field and policy conflicts easier, however it provide Complex integration between the enforcement mechanism with NOS without change the current functionality. Neisse et al. (Neisse et al., 2014, October) integrate SecKit security toolkit with MQTT to apply the policy enforcement. Although Neisse et al. perform complex security policies with very small delay but it is still considered as an overhead delay (Mahmoud, Yousuf, Aloul & Zualkernan, 2015, December).

Daubert et al. establish a relation between the PII, sensitivity, privacy, and trust and present this relation mathematically, however, it also not supports all privacy principles which are defined in (Aleisa, & Renaud, 2016) and (Organisation for Economic Co-operation and Development, 2002), in other hand Sato et al. (Sato er al., 2016, March) establish a trust framework but the cost of management and operation for established framework is high (Sato, 2016). Chen et al., 2016, establish an adaptive and scalable trust protocol which is overcome many other trust protocols in term of accuracy, trust convergence, and the flexibility in facing the malicious nodes by using many techniques such as self-promoting and others, however, the authors assume that each user has a high-end device and this assumption does not always true (Ramanathan, 2015).

CONCLUSION

Security is one of the main concern in Internet of Things (IoT), traditional security mechanisms cannot be directly applied in IoT because there are different standards imposed. In this chapter, five main issues from the security issues in IoT was discussed, these issues are Access Control, Authentication, Privacy, Policy Enforcement, and trust. For each issue, the strength and weakness points of the corresponding solutions are discussed.

REFERENCES

Aleisa, N., & Renaud, K. (2016). *Privacy of the Internet of Things: A Systematic Literature Review (Extended Discussion).* arXiv preprint arXiv:1611.03340

Aljawarneh, S., Yassein, M. B., & Telafeh, W. (2017). A resource-efficient encryption algorithm for multimedia big data. *Multimedia Tools and Applications*, 1–22.

Aljawarneh, S. A., Alawneh, A., & Jaradat, R. (2016). Cloud security engineering: Early stages of SDLC. *Future Generation Computer Systems*.

Aljawarneh, S. A., Moftah, R. A., & Maatuk, A. M. (2016). Investigations of automatic methods for detecting the polymorphic worms signatures. *Future Generation Computer Systems*, *60*, 67–77. doi:10.1016/j.future.2016.01.020

Aljawarneh, S. A., & Yassein, M. O. B. (2016). A Conceptual Security Framework for Cloud Computing Issues. *International Journal of Intelligent Information Technologies*, *12*(2), 12–24. doi:10.4018/IJIIT.2016040102

Alpár, G., Batina, L., Batten, L., Moonsamy, V., Krasnova, A., Guellier, A., & Natgunanathan, I. (2016, May). New directions in IoT privacy using attribute-based authentication. In *Proceedings of the ACM International Conference on Computing Frontiers* (pp. 461-466). ACM. doi:10.1145/2903150.2911710

Bernabe, J. B., Ramos, J. L. H., & Gomez, A. F. S. (2016). TACIoT: Multidimensional trust-aware access control system for the Internet of Things. *Soft Computing*, *20*(5), 1763–1779. doi:10.1007/s00500-015-1705-6

Chen, R., Guo, J., & Bao, F. (2016). Trust management for SOA-based IoT and its application to service composition. *IEEE Transactions on Services Computing*, *9*(3), 482–495. doi:10.1109/TSC.2014.2365797

Daubert, J., Wiesmaier, A., & Kikiras, P. (2015, June). A view on privacy & trust in iot. In *2015 IEEE International Conference on Communication Workshop (ICCW)* (pp. 2665-2670). IEEE. doi:10.1109/ICCW.2015.7247581

Hernández-Ramos, J. L., Bernabe, J. B., Moreno, M., & Skarmeta, A. F. (2015). Preserving Smart Objects Privacy through Anonymous and Accountable Access Control for a M2M-Enabled Internet of Things. *Sensors (Basel)*, *15*(7), 15611–15639. doi:10.3390/s150715611 PMID:26140349

Hernandez-Ramos, J. L., Pawlowski, M. P., Jara, A. J., Skarmeta, A. F., & Ladid, L. (2015). Toward a lightweight authentication and authorization framework for smart objects. *IEEE Journal on Selected Areas in Communications*, *33*(4), 690–702. doi:10.1109/JSAC.2015.2393436

Lee, J. Y., Lin, W. C., & Huang, Y. H. (2014, May). A lightweight authentication protocol for internet of things. In *Next-Generation Electronics (ISNE), 2014 International Symposium on* (pp. 1-2). IEEE. doi:10.1109/ISNE.2014.6839375

Mahmoud, R., Yousuf, T., Aloul, F., & Zualkernan, I. (2015, December). Internet of things (IoT) security: Current status, challenges and prospective measures. In *2015 10th International Conference for Internet Technology and Secured Transactions (ICITST)* (pp. 336-341). IEEE.

Maler, E., Catalano, D., Machulak, M., & Hardjono, T. (2016). *User-Managed Access (UMA) Profile of OAuth 2.0*. Academic Press.

Mardini, W., Khamayseh, Y., Jaradatand, R., & Hijjawi, R. (2012). Interference problem between ZigBee and WiFi. *International Proceedings of Computer Science and Information Technology*, 133-138.

Neisse, R., Steri, G., & Baldini, G. (2014, October). Enforcement of security policy rules for the internet of things. In *2014 IEEE 10th International Conference on Wireless and Mobile Computing, Networking and Communications (WiMob)* (pp. 165-172). IEEE. doi:10.1109/WiMOB.2014.6962166

Organisation for Economic Co-operation and Development. (2002). *OECD Guidelines on the Protection of Privacy and Transborder Flows of Personal Data*. OECD Publishing.

Ouaddah, A., Mousannif, H., Elkalam, A. A., & Ouahman, A. A. (2017). Access control in The Internet of Things: Big challenges and new opportunities. *Computer Networks*, *112*, 237–262. doi:10.1016/j.comnet.2016.11.007

Pal, A. (2015). Internet of things: Making the hype a reality. *IT Professional, 17*(3), 2–4. doi:10.1109/MITP.2015.36

Ramanathan, A. (2015). *A Multi-Level Trust Management Scheme for the Internet of Things*. Academic Press.

Rivera, D., Cruz-Piris, L., Lopez-Civera, G., de la Hoz, E., & Marsa-Maestre, I. (2015, October). Applying an unified access control for IoT-based Intelligent Agent Systems. In *Service-Oriented Computing and Applications (SOCA), 2015 IEEE 8th International Conference on* (pp. 247-251). IEEE. doi:10.1109/SOCA.2015.40

Rizzardi, A., Miorandi, D., Sicari, S., Cappiello, C., & Coen-Porisini, A. (2015, October). Networked smart objects: moving data processing closer to the source. *2nd EAI International Conference on IoT as a Service*.

Samani, A., Ghenniwa, H. H., & Wahaishi, A. (2015). Privacy in Internet of Things: A model and protection framework. *Procedia Computer Science, 52*, 606–613. doi:10.1016/j.procs.2015.05.046

Sato, H. (2016). Practical Correctness in ICT Environments. *IT Professional, 18*(6), 4–8. doi:10.1109/MITP.2016.107

Sato, H., Kanai, A., Tanimoto, S., & Kobayashi, T. (2016, March). Establishing Trust in the Emerging Era of IoT. In *2016 IEEE Symposium on Service-Oriented System Engineering (SOSE)* (pp. 398-406). IEEE. doi:10.1109/SOSE.2016.50

Saxena, A., Duraisamy, P., & Kaulgud, V. (2015, November). SMAC: Scalable Access Control in IoT. In *Cloud Computing in Emerging Markets (CCEM), 2015 IEEE International Conference on* (pp. 169-176). IEEE.

Sicari, S., Rizzardi, A., Grieco, L. A., & Coen-Porisini, A. (2015). Security, privacy and trust in Internet of Things: The road ahead. *Computer Networks, 76*, 146–164. doi:10.1016/j.comnet.2014.11.008

Sicari, S., Rizzardi, A., Miorandi, D., Cappiello, C., & Coen-Porisini, A. (2016). Security policy enforcement for networked smart objects. *Computer Networks, 108*, 133–147. doi:10.1016/j.comnet.2016.08.014

Singh, J., Pasquier, T. F. M., & Bacon, J. (2015, April). Securing tags to control information flows within the Internet of Things. In *Recent Advances in Internet of Things (RIoT), 2015 International Conference on* (pp.1-6). IEEE. doi:10.1109/RIOT.2015.7104903

Ukil, A., Bandyopadhyay, S., & Pal, A. (2014, April). IoT-privacy: To be private or not to be private. In *Computer Communications Workshops (INFOCOM WKSHPS), 2014 IEEE Conference on* (pp. 123-124). IEEE.

Yassein, M. B., Mardini, W., & Khalil, A. (2016, September). Smart homes automation using Z-wave protocol. In *Engineering & MIS (ICEMIS), International Conference on* (pp. 1-6). IEEE.

Ye, N., Zhu, Y., Wang, R. C., & Lin, Q. M. (2014). *An efficient authentication and access control scheme for perception layer of internet of things*. Academic Press.

Chapter 10
The Rise of Big Data, Cloud, and Internet of Things:
Three Trends to Watch

Reema Abdulraziq
Jordan University of Science and Technology, Jordan

Muneer Bani Yassein
Jordan University of Science and Technology, Jordan

Shadi Aljawarneh
Jordan University of Science and Technology, Jordan

ABSTRACT

Big data refers to the huge amount of data that is being used in commercial, industrial and economic environments. There are three types of big data; structured, unstructured and semi-structured data. When it comes to discussions on big data, three major aspects that can be considered as its main dimensions are the volume, velocity, and variety of the data. This data is collected, analysed and checked for use by the end users. Cloud computing and the Internet of Things (IoT) are used to enable this huge amount of collected data to be stored and connected to the Internet. The time and the cost are reduced by means of these technologies, and in addition, they are able to accommodate this large amount of data regardless of its size. This chapter focuses on how big data, with the emergence of cloud computing and the Internet of Things (IOT), can be used via several applications and technologies.

DOI: 10.4018/978-1-5225-3029-9.ch010

INTRODUCTION

Big data is defined as a large amount of data with three dimensions of volume, velocity, and variety. It is brought about by the collecting and analysing of different applications and acquisitions. This has motivated the use of complicated tools to store and deal with these data (Science Definition Team Report, 2016).

The focus of big data is not on how much data are collected or produced, but on how the important data can be extracted, and the benefits that can be derived from these data. For instance, when the Hemagglutinin Type 1 and Neuraminidase Type 1 (H1N1) diseases appeared, researchers collected all the Google search queries from users to limit, from their questions, where this disease was populated. All the data were obtained from a search of about 20-100 queries. When the entire data was filtered, they found about 45 queries that were able to help them achieve their goal. This is the purpose of the use of big data, and this is what motivates the search for techniques that can deal with this large amount of data to minimize it and achieve the goals of researchers (Anwaar Ali et al., 2016).

There are a lot of techniques that deal with big data (such as cleaning and classification) and on data extraction, data fusion and data mining for data collection, data modelling, and visualization. These techniques focus on how the data is presented for use in several applications and technologies (Corporate Partnership Board Report., 2015). It is necessary to manage these big data techniques and to store the data in a faster and cheaper way for its users. Cloud computing enables users to connect to the Internet for several applications and to solve most of the big data problems caused by the huge amount of used data that has to be dealt with. Cloud computing is associated with the Internet of Things (IoT), which allows different types of data from different domains to be connected via the Internet. It can be inferred that the IoT is the whole concept of this connection, while cloud computing, which uses the open-source software, the Hadoop, is the model that is used to store and analyse the data via the Internet (Ibrahim Abaker Targio Hashem et al., Moeen Hassanalieragh et al., 2015; Jeong-Tae Kim and Sung-Han-sim et al., 2016; Al-Ali et al., 2015; Anvari-Moghaddam et al., 2015; Huang et al., 2015; Gonnot & Saniie, 2014; Zafari & Christidis, 2015; Aegis, 2015).

Big data and IoT using cloud computing play a significant role in various important applications that are classified as smart city for healthcare, smart transport and smart grids, telecom in terms of both the user and the company, and how they can communicate using big data. The food industry can use big data in a significant way in terms of the storage of its products and how the customer can be serviced in a better way. One of the important big data applications has to do with education due to the huge amount of data that can be created in several domains. There is no limit to the above applications. However, they exceed some technologies such as RFID, that uses a small wireless card for reading several information types; Wi-Fi, that focuses on how a huge amount of data can be scalable and accommodate several user needs; Zigbee, which is a wireless technology that has some features in terms of the big data era; and Ultra-wideband, that plays a significant role in the collection of information in hidden objects (Ibrahim Abaker Targio Hashem et al.; Heba Aly et al., 2015; Robinson et al., 2016; Madakam et al., 2015; Wi-Fi Alliance, 2014), as will be discussed in the next section.

This chapter can be completed as follows, section 2 shows what the big data with its main dimensions are and what are the roles of cloud computing and the Internet of Things in this domain. The big data resources in section 3, with its techniques in section 4. The big data challenges in section 5. The role of cloud computing is shown in section 6, with the cloud characteristics are shown in section 7. Section 8 shows the cloud service brokerage. Some of the cloud computing considerations are shown in section 9. Finally, big data and the Internet of Thing applications and technologies will be shown in both sections 10 and 11, respectively and it is concluded with the future work in section 12.

MAIN FOCUS OF THE CHAPTER

Big Data

As different technologies develop, the amount of data has been gradually increasing over time such that it has become impossible to store or deal with such a huge amount of data. This is known as the big data concept. When it comes to big data, researchers are not concerned about how much data are produced or collected, but rather, how to store, analyse and extract the important data (Min Chen et al., 2014; Samiddha Mukherjee et al., 2016; Amir Gandomi et al., 2015).

The increasing use of the Internet, such as for Google search queries, Facebook, and YouTube downloading and others, plays a significant role in the increasing amount of data collected from these resources (Min Chen et al., 2014).

The big data has three main different types such as structured data like tables with rows and columns, semi-structured like XML and HTML tags that takes different types of data like names, numbers, etc while the third type is unstructured data, which is the biggest data becomes from this type and it is the most difficult to deals with like word, pdf and text files.

Figure 1 shows the dimensions for big data, which are:

Figure 1. Features of big data
Amir Gandomi et al., 2015.

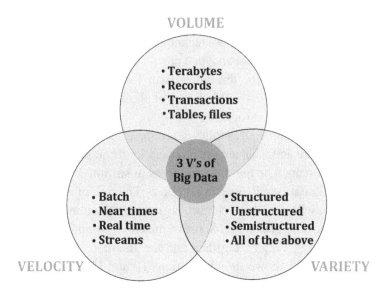

- **Volume:** Which indicates the increased data size;
- **Velocity:** The speed of increased data over time due to its increased usage;
- **Variety:** The different data types that are produced from different applications such as texts, videos, audios and others (Min Chen et al., 2014; Samiddha Mukherjee et al., 2016; Amir Gandomi et al., 2015).

The value of big data is that it focuses on what researchers want from this huge amount of data when it is pre-processed to extract the important data that will achieve their goal. For instance, in terms of healthcare, researchers collected all the Google search queries about questions from people concerning the H1N1 disease to know where this disease was populated. The total collected data was about 20-100 queries. After it had been pre-processed, it was discovered that there were 45 queries that contained the most important data to identify the specific locations populated by the disease.

Several studies were conducted from 2000 to 2013 to determine the statistics for big data during this period and how these data have been gradually increasing, as shown in Figure 2.

Figure 2. Distribution of big data distribution from 2000 to 2013
Amir Gandomi, 2015.

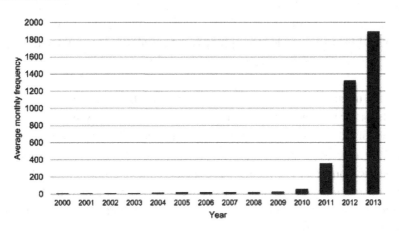

Big Data Resources

The big data becomes from different devices like the sensor network when reading a specific data in specific place (i.e. military, weather predictions as temperatures and others) and different application like the social media devices (i.e. Facebook, twitter, etc). Other big data resources like the black box in airlines based on the number of travels and their problems, transport term, the search engine like the Google queries by multiple users (Sofia Majawar, 2015).

Big Data Techniques

There are a number of big data techniques that can be used as follows:

1.   **Extraction and Cleaning:** When dealing with a large amount of data, it is necessary to extract the most important data that will be of benefit to researchers in different applications. Data extraction allows four data techniques to be used, namely:
     a.   **Data Fusion:** Focuses on how data can be collected from different resources into one resource;
     b.   **Data Mining:** Analyses the data to get the most significant ones;
     c.   **Optimization:** Similar to the data classification process; and
     d.   **Visualization:** How these data can be presented as images, graphs or tables to facilitate understanding (Corporate Partnership Board Report, 2015).

The huge amount of collected data may include the incorrect ones as well, especially in the case where two types of data are merged, namely the common structured data and the unstructured data such as images, videos and audios. This has motivated the use of a cleaning process, where all the incorrect and misspelled data are dropped (Corporate Partnership Board Report, 2015).

2. **Data Fusion:** A huge amount of data must be collected for storage and analysis for the benefit of end users and to enable many big data challenges to be solved, the most important ones being collision and redundancy, which will be discussed in the next sections. Data fusion is similar to the data collection process. However, it is considered as a combination of structured and unstructured data types. This process is complemented by the next step, which is data integration or aggregation (Corporate Partnership Board Report, 2015).

3. **Data Integration or Aggregation:** This is similar to data fusion in terms of the data collection, but it varies with regard to how the data collection is performed. In this step, the data are collected as groups of data based on the common criteria between them. Therefore, this is a classification process instead of just being a collection process, and it will be of great help in the data analysing step (Corporate Partnership Board Report, 2015; Samiddha Mukherjee et al., 2016; Amir Gandomi et al., 2015).

4. **Data Mining:** After the data have been collected based on some common criteria in terms of data fusion and aggregation, these data must be analysed according to certain algorithms and steps as follows:
   a. **Classification:** Collect the data based on some common features;
   b. **Clustering:** Place each of the similar data that relates to the same feature in one group;
   c. **Association:** Detect the relationships between these data;
   d. **Regression:** Separate the data that contain any numbers that are far from the textual ones.
   e. **Anomaly Detection:** Detect the data that are not related to any of the data groups in the clustering step.
   f. **Summarization:** Make a summary of the most important data features (Corporate Partnership Board Report., 2015).

5. **Data Modelling:** This technique can help, provided there is better understanding of the data in a complex system which contains a huge amount of collected and analysed data by building data models and detecting the data relationship between them in a better way than the traditional classification, clustering, and other data mining steps. (Corporate Partnership Board Report, 2015) Data modeling can result in three types of data models as follows:

a. **Conceptual Data Models:** These are used to identify the main data concepts and determine the relationships at an abstract level for each application that the data are used for (Corporate Partnership Board Report., 2015).

b. **Logical Data Models:** These give more details than the previous models for these concepts to be ready for the physical data models (Corporate Partnership Board Report, 2015).

c. **Physical Data Models:** These models focus on how the data are implemented as tables, and determine the data types of each data concept based on the database management system that supports these features (Corporate Partnership Board Report, 2015).

6. **Visualization:** Visualization complements the modelling techniques in terms of data representation but differs in how these data are presented. In the modelling step, the data, with their attributes and relationships, are presented as tables, while in the visualization step; the data are presented as pictures and maps for better human understanding. This technique has tools with different features that must be included to achieve their purpose, such as geospatial, time resolution, 3D data presentation and free data animation, and easier data control in terms of data pan and zoom (Corporate Partnership Board Report, 2015).

Recently, many studies have been carried out with regard to the combination of big data with the Internet of Things as follows:

- At the beginning, the studies were focused on how the data could be obtained from small devices like Smartphones, and the big challenge at that time was how the data could be analysed and stored (Ron Bisio, 2016).
- Next, studies were carried out to investigate how the most important learning approaches, such as neural networks and natural language processing, could be used, especially between two companies sharing similar works and goals, where these approaches could facilitate their work in dealing with the data and reducing the cost and time (Sathish Sashadri, 2016).
- Following this, the studies then focused on how the best printers that were relevant to and associated with the amount of big data could be used. The new printers were able to merge with the Internet of Things concept as their equipment was comprised of sensors that were able to control its properties in a high-speed, low-cost printing process (Scott Steele, 2016).
- The remaining studies focused on how this big data with the IoT could be used in several applications such as in healthcare, transportation, telecom

and others (Paul Santili, 2016; Sibanjan Das, 2016; Gianni Giacomelli and Prashant Shukla, 2016)

Big Data Challenges

The big data has different challenges that motivate to use different tools and technologies to solve them such as how to collect the huge amount of data, how it is analyzed, searched, stored and presented as results for the end users.

Big Data Tools and Software

1. **Map Reduce:** This is a technique that is similar to the divide and conquer process; which takes a large problem, divides it into small subsections, and solves them in a combined, reduced version. This technique, in terms of big data, focuses on how this large amount of data can be reduced and solved in a faster way. Its main advantage is the extraction of redundant data before pre-processing commences (Amtikamar Manekar et al., 2015).
2. **Hadoop:** This is an open source that contains a file called a Hadoop Distributed File System (HDFS) for facilitating the Map Reduce function in terms of the storage and retrieval of data. Its main advantages are the scalability of the data and its fault tolerance property, since it is used for the frequent saving of data results after each Map Reduce step (Amtikamar Manekar et al., 2015).
3. **Yarn:** It is the modified version of the MapReduce technique; it is especially used for data scheduling and management, it uses the next tool(i.e. Spark) without requiring to be installed before with some of its features, it is a scalable tool and available anytime with reliable features (Sudhakar Singh et al., 2015).
4. **Spark:** It is an Apache open source that uses Hadoop platform to compute the huge amount of data. It is faster than Hadoop from 10-100 times since it has a distributed memory that stores the data temporarily during the processing step before it is stored finally to the HDFS file to view the results (Yuzhong Yan et al., 2015).

Cloud Computing

Cloud is used for the most common big data challenges with regard to how to select, classify, store and analyse this huge amount of data. It offers ready servers and storage that is scalable and can be adapted whenever there in an increase in the data and when any data type is used or received (Intel IT Centre, 2015)

Cloud provides a service which is known as Analytics as a Service (AaaS). This service focuses on how to deal with and handle this amount of data when it is received by the servers. It has three processes for selecting different types of data, and certain rules to classify them and to facilitate big data techniques (i.e. integrate, analyse, transform and visualize) as follows:

- Infrastructure as a Service (IaaS) provides the cloud tools that will deal with the data for selection and classification processes such as Hadoop.
- Platform as a Service (PaaS) provides tools for enhancing Hadoop to run several applications at reduced time and cost.
- Software as a Service (SaaS), its most popular feature, makes it scalable to adapt whatever the amount of data that is received by extending the tool size so as to be flexible for users to transmit and receive data (EMC, 2014; Neves et al., 2016).

There are different types of cloud computing depending on when this data is used as follows:

- Private cloud is used by a specific company or organization, and this data cannot be accessed by others (Intel IT Centre, 2015; Alessico Botta et al.).
- Community cloud is used between two common communities for sharing their common issues (e-skills UK, 2013).
- Public cloud, which allows the data to be shared as public data without any conditions or limitation rules (Intel IT Centre, 2015; e-skills UK, 2013).
- Hybrid cloud, which is a combination of three different types (i.e. public, private and community clouds) (EMC,2014) (Intel IT Centre, 2015; Alessico Botta et al.).
- Virtual private cloud uses a virtual private network that focuses on most data challenges in terms of how it can be made more secure (Alessico Botta et al.).

As mentioned before, the Internet of Things (IoT) plays a significant role in bringing this huge amount of data to users. In order to allow users to deal with flexibility and scalable probabilities, more techniques are needed to extend its range when this data increases in the future. The cloud can be integrated with the IoT to build a new concept known as CloudIoT, which offers new computing properties of low cost and greater scalability in terms of gathering, storing and computing the data (e-skills UK, 2013). CloudIoT is an improvement over the traditional cloud types in that it focuses more on the interconnections to the Internet such as Sensor Event as a Service (SEaaS), Sensor as a Service (SenaaS), Database as a Service (DBaaS), Ethernet as a Service (EaaS), Identity and Policy Management as a Service (IPMaaS), and Video Surveillance as a Service (VSaaS) (Alessico Botta et al.).

Over the years, several published articles, shown in the table below, have focused on how to improve the cloud to make it flexible, easy to use and scalable, and also on how to make it more secure.

Cloud Characteristics

The cloud computing has different characteristics to outperform the IoT in term of solving the big data challenges such as:

- On demand, i.e. the services are available whenever the user needs.
- Broad access network, according to receive and use huge of data the cloud has a perfect access network via the Internet that accommodate this data amount.
- Resource pooling, this data via the cloud is stored in a place called the pool can be accessed by the users anytime they want.
- Rapid elasticity, the user can request whatever he wants of service that the cloud has more scalability than IoT.
- Measured service, the cloud can compute how much of service the user consume to get at the end the bill of consumption (EMC, 2014)(Pedro Caldeira Neves et al., 2016)

Cloud Service Brokerage

When the user uses the cloud via the Gmail, Drop Box, Google drive companies, the main question is who the main direct use of this service, the user or these companies?

The companies of course, they are considered as a brokers term between the user and the cloud itself for providing the user these services (EMC, 2014)(Liaison) (Center for Digital government).

Table 1. Comparison of cloud computing studies in terms of the emergence of the IoT

Study	Goal
IEEE Standards Association	How the cloud can be scalable in order to reduce the cost
Cloud portability and interoperability	How data can be dealt with in the cloud whenever it is increased every year
Intercloud Interoperability and Federation	A flexible space for the user to use the data in the cloud for several applications
Adaptive management of cloud computing environments	Data management in the cloud
Architectural framework for the Internet of Things (IoT)	A combination of IoT with cloud computing to better serve the needs of users

Consideration When Building Cloud Computing

There are different factors must be taken into account when dealing with the cloud computing like:

- The finance factor (i.e. how much the user will pay for the needed service).
- The tools that the cloud provides to the user (like the integration, Application Programming Interface (API), specialized connection and transformation and business logic programs).
- The service level agreement or contract, i.e. a contract between the user and the cloud service provider describes how the user will get the service with its cost (if it has).
- Avoiding vendor lock-in, most of the company can control the user with specific constraints when using the cloud like the IBM company, the user when uses the cloud should avoid these constraints by building its own cloud from the existing basic hardware by renting some servers and other cloud computing components from another company for period time then it can be released rather than be as a controlled by this company continuously for this service.
- Software licensing concerns for the cloud technologies (i.e. IaaS, PaaS, and SaaS).
- Migration, i.e. how the cloud can be moved from one place to another.
- Testing (EMC, 2014).

Applications

1. **Smart City:** The smart city focuses on how small wireless sensor nodes can be used in different applications such as health, transport and grids that collect a large amount of data at reduced time and cost (Ibrahim Abaker Targio Hashem et al, 2014)
    a. **Healthcare:** The IoT can provide a remote health monitor with the ability to monitor a patient's health using a wireless body sensor node (WBAN) (Ibrahim Abaker Targio Hashem et al., 2014; Moeen Hassanalieragh et al., 2015; Jeong-Tae Kim et al., 2016). A WBAN is a set of sensor nodes that can be allocated inside the human body to monitor the pressure, temperature and other health measurements. The process is carried out when these sensors send the health information to a server known as the gateway server. This server stores this information in a file to be

reviewed later by the doctor, Cloud computing can play a role in terms of allowing an online service to read and control the patient's health (Moeen Hassanalieragh et al., 2015; Jeong-Tae Kim et al., 2016). The remote healthcare application via IoT can be categorized into three phases:

i.   Data acquisition sensing transmission
ii.   Data concentration cloud processing
iii. Cloud processing, analytics and visualization (Moeen Hassanalieragh et al., 2015).

The body sensor nodes can monitor the health of a body and send this information via a ZigBee or Bluetooth connection to a data concentration. This concentration can connect to a new service, called the cloudlet, which allows access to the Internet rather than storing on a mobile device and having to deal with the challenge of memory space. Finally, the cloud will play an important role in analysing and visualizing this information before it is sent to the doctor, as shown in Figure 3 (Moeen Hassanalieragh et al., 2015).

b.   **Smart Transport:** The IoT can play a significant role in the monitoring and management of transportation in terms of tracking and controlling the movement of vehicles. This process is performed by allowing vehicles to

Figure 3. Healthcare monitoring component based on IoT-cloud architecture
Moeen Hassanalieragh et al., 2015.

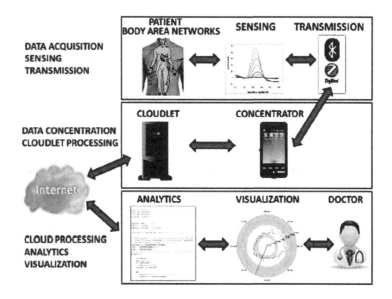

communicate with each other through wireless links. These vehicles include wireless sensor networks that are controlled to provide several services (Moeen Hassanalieragh et al., 2015; Jeong-Tae Kim et al., 2016). The vehicles are controlled to maintain a wide distance between them and other vehicles. The sensors can detect parking spaces and monitor the road and traffic (Moeen Hassanalieragh et al., 2015; Jeong-Tae Kim et al., 2016).

c.   **Smart Grids:** This refers to smart homes that have smart devices based on a wireless sensor network to provide their service. For instance, a sensor enables the doors to open and close by themselves when someone comes or leaves, the windows can open in the morning and close by themselves, and there are other devices that can work as a remote service controlled by a sensor (A. R. Al-Ali et al., 2015; Anvari-Moghaddam et al., 2015; Huang, Z.C. and Yuan, F. 2015; Gonnot, T. et al., 2014; Faheem Zafari et al., 2015).

The emergence of the Internet of Things (IoT) allows these devices to contain an IP address connection, store the data from the devices, and upload this data via the Internet (A. R. Al-Ali et al., 2015; Anvari-Moghaddam et al., 2015; Huang, Z.C. and Yuan, F. 2015; Gonnot, T. et al., 2014; Faheem Zafari et al., 2015). These devices can also work based on 6LowPAN as a personal area network associated with a cloud service to receive the users, who may be the homeowners, consumers or server providers (A. R. Al-Ali et al., 2015).

2.   **Telecom:** Telecom can be categorized into different types of mobile devices and social media such as Facebook, Twitter and others. Due to the continuous development of mobile technologies and the increasing use of these communication media, the transmitted data will be increasing continuously at all times. These data must be collected, stored and analysed to be protected from any attacks and changes (Samiddha Mukherjee et al., 2016; Aegis, 2015).

Telecom can be considered as a communication between the telecommunication company and the customer in terms of tracking and solving their call problems, records of call details, emails and short messages from the telecom companies to the customers at different times and different social occasions (Samiddha Mukherjee et al., 2016; Aegis, 2015). With the use of big data analytics over the Internet, these data can be stored and accommodated to be flexible, satisfying and scalable for the customer and its end users. The big data analytics can manage the different types of data as structured, semi-structured and unstructured data, while avoiding collisions between them and congestion (Aegis, 2015).

3. **Food Industry:** This application can be considered as one of the important benefits where big data is concerned due to the increased data that emerge in different places like markets, food stores, and restaurants. In marketing, the data can be product information, numbers, and costs (Samiddha Mukherjee et al., 2016).

A customer can request for a meal via a screen without having to communicate with any staff in the restaurant. The meal information can be collected, analysed and related to the appropriate customer in a faster manner that will allow a huge amount of data to be collected (Samiddha Mukherjee et al., 2016; Aegis, 2015).

As big data can affect the industry, restaurants should consider this idea of changing their service to the customers. This can be done by a three-step strategy. The first step is to develop an online survey for the customer to select a set of choice of food to be included in the dessert menu. The data is then collected and a comparison is made between this data and the current dessert menu to add in new selections based on the customer's demand. These three steps will increase the data gradually over time, and several strategies will be required to analyse the data. From this it can be inferred that big data has different advantages in terms of the food industry such as tracking the quality of food and detecting bad restaurant food and dropping them before their information is analysed, determining exactly what the customer wants from their demands, and reducing the waiting time for meals. In addition, this will motivate restaurants to provide better products with higher profits for them (Aegis, 2015).

4. **Education:** One of the important big data applications has to do with its association with different domains such as teachers and students. The E-learning online service can be considered as one of the remote education tools used between students and their teachers. This tool allows teachers to install the courses, grades, and surveys for improving the education process. At the same time, it allows the students to download these courses, submit their assignments, and go through the course registration process. The use of E-learning for two terms can result in a huge amount of data that must be collected and analysed in a better way to achieve the main goals of education.

Technologies

1. **RFID:** Radio Frequency Identification technology focuses on how a large amount of data can be read in different applications in a better way than the barcode in the market. It contains tags, readers, antennae, batteries or radio energy based on the type of tag. RFID tags, as shown in the following figure,

can be allocated to any object such as humans, animals, cars and others to track any developments and movements, and to store their information, which can be read and transmitted by the RFID reader using the antenna (Ibrahim Abaker Targio Hashem et al., 2014; Christoph Jechlitschek, 2015; Heba Aly et al., 2015; John Robinston et al., 2016; Somayya Madakam et al., 2015). There are three types of RFID tags, as follows:

a.   **Passive Type:** Based on the reader energy for the information transmission. It contains a condenser for protecting the tag from any interruption. Its advantages are that it is small in size and inexpensive, and it can transmit for a long period since it does not use any type of battery. However, it lacks a wide transmitting range, as its transmission is between 2 mm and a few meters (Ibrahim Abaker Targio Hashem et al., 2014; Christoph Jechlitschek, 2015; Heba Aly et al., 2015; John Robinston et al., 2016; Somayya Madakam et al., 2015).

b.   **Semi-Passive Type:** Uses a form of energy to keep the RFID microchip active over a period but without the use of an RFID antenna. This will encourage faster usage in several applications and allows the transmission range to be wider than that of the passive tag (Ibrahim Abaker Targio Hashem et al., 2014; Christoph Jechlitschek, 2015; Heba Aly et al., 2015; John Robinston et al., 2016; Somayya Madakam et al., 2015).

c.   **Active Type:** Similar to the previous types, except that it focuses on keeping the tags active and building the signals from the antenna. It outperforms the other types in terms of its wide range and long lifetime (Ibrahim Abaker Targio Hashem et al., 2014; Christoph Jechlitschek, 2015; Heba Aly et al., 2015; John Robinston et al., 2016; Somayya Madakam et al., 2015).

2.   **Wi-Fi:** Wireless Fidelity is one of the important big data and IoT technologies since it allows objects to be connected through the wireless Internet without the need for network cables or links. This allows it to have low-cost features and a wide transmitting and receiving range. Due to the increased use of Smartphones and tablets, and the need for Internet connections for emails and social media websites with low-cost capability, Wi-Fi has been increasing gradually and continuously over time. This, in turn, has motivated an increase in the amount of transmitted data to be collected and analysed through big data analytics techniques (Ibrahim Abaker Targio Hashem et al., 2014; Wi-Fi Alliance, 2014).

3.   **Zigbee:** This is a wireless technology that consists of a transceiver, that transmits the data as packets using a radio frequency band, and a receiver, that receives these packets (Ibrahim Abaker Targio Hashem et al, 2014). The

Figure 4. RFID tag
Christoph Jechlitschek, 2015.

main advantages of Zigbee are its low transmitted data rate, cost, and power consumption (Professor Dhotre and Rupesh Chaudhari).

4. **Ultra-Wideband:** This technology can also be considered as a wireless technology that allows a large amount of data to be transmitted. With its wide transmission range, it can also outperform complex objects unlike other wireless technologies like Wi-Fi and Zigbee. It consists of a transmitter and receiver that must be able to communicate with each other in order to transmit and receive the data at low cost, power and without interruption using digital pulses (Ibrahim Abaker Targio Hashem et al.). Therefore, it can be inferred that the main advantages of the Ultra-wideband are that it is able to transmit the largest data among all the big data technologies, and that it is inexpensive and can detect hidden objects behind doors and walls. It can be used for USB and entertainment clusters that wirelessly transmit data of different types, as shown in the following figures (Intel, 2015).

DISCUSSION

Big data is the large amount of data that is caused by several applications and technologies; it has both advantages and disadvantages. It offers a lot of services to users, especially in the industry domains, and it increases their work by giving them more information than they want due to the large amount of data that appears. At the same time, it is considered as a challenge to main users when it increases over time in terms of how it will be collected and analysed. Although several big data techniques are being used and, with the emergence of the Internet of Things, a lot of problems are being solved in terms of Internet connections, however, this still remains a challenge. Cloud computing is more scalable in terms of accommodating a large amount of data that cannot be predicted by the user. The main issue that can be inferred is that as the problem increases, there are a lot of solutions that can be used and that improve the big data concept. From the several studies of big data and cloud computing, this study chose to focus on cloud computing, and it should be added that every technique, especially when it creates more benefits, is prone to attacks to the domains, thereby reducing its ability. From this point on, the focus will be on what the main cloud computing challenges are and how they can be solved.

The rise of big data, Cloud and IoT have a significant effect on academia and industries. For example, the multimedia big data is incorporated into smart cities, smart devices and smart environments. To handle the multimedia big data correctly, it is necessary to utilize Cloud centres for storage. Aljawarneh (Aljawarneh, 2011_a, Aljawarneh, 2011_b) mentioned that there is a new direction which is being used, known as Fog Computing, which results from the use of the Cloud in the SDLC (Services Development Life Cycle), IDLC (Infrastructure Development Life Cycle) or PDLC (Platform Development Life Cycle). However, there are many issues to be considered in this kind of emergence between IoT and Cloud, such as security and scalability. Some good progress is being made to enforce a number of security and scalability policies. However, they still need to be enhanced to cover security vulnerabilities such as Cloud DoS and metamorphic viruses.

CONCLUSION AND FUTURE WORK

Big data is one of the important topics that is being discussed and that will be taken into consideration for future domains. It focuses on how a huge amount of data can be dealt with to fulfil the needs of researchers and users. It consists of several structured, semi-structured and unstructured data types. The Internet of Things plays a significant role due to the huge amount of data that can be generated. Big data has several techniques for dealing with these data such as extraction and classification, data fusion, data mining, data modelling and visualization. Cloud computing is used for dealing with the huge amount of big data and also the Internet of Things due to its scalability. Finally, big data and the Internet of Things have several applications and technologies that have become the focus of most people and that have changed their lives.

There are many big data techniques for dealing with the increasing data, and the emergence of cloud computing has solved competing trends in terms of the scalability and accommodation of these analysed data in addition to the Internet of Things. However, from the big data and cloud computing studies discussed that focused on several goals and domains to make the data even better, these technologies are still lacking from the perspective of security since cloud computing is prone to several

Table 2. Comparison of big data techniques

	Extraction	Cleaning	Data Fusion	Data Aggregation	Data Mining	Data Modeling	Data Visualization
Collect data	Focuses on to get the data to get the important one		It is similar to the extraction, however it deals with collecting different types of data like structure and unstructured data rather than just getting the important one				
Analyze and classification		Analyze the data to remove the incorrect results of the data	It is the data fusion 's next step that classify the data as a group based on common characteristics between them	It focuses on more analyzing and frittering the data than the data aggregation step.			
Presentation						It focuses on how the data Is presented in several models in active and passive mode to ensure the data security	It is similar to the data modeling, however, the data is presented as pictured and maps for more understanding for the end users.

Table 3. The big data tools and software comparison

	MapReduce	Hadoop	Yarn	Spark
Definition	It is a technique that divide the problems to small subsets (using map process) to get the result then combine the results again (by reduce process).	It is a Google platform that uses Map Reduce to store the result using the Hadoop Distributed File System (HDFS)file	It is the modifies version of the MapReduce techniques, it is used for data scheduling and management	It is an Apache open source for solving more the big data challenges; it is the latest update for this solving.
Advantages	To reduce th amount of the processing data when it is divided into smaller parts	It is more scalable than MapReduce due to HDFS file and more secure since the data is stored frequently in different steps in this file, thus the data is not lost.	By using the Spark it benefits from its features that outperform the Hadoop features	It is faster than Hadoop from 10-100 times because it uses a distributed memory for storing temporarily the results during the data processing step
Challenges	It is not scalable for large amount of data that is increased by the time	It has a delay problem when the data is increased since it writes the results frequently each part of the results in HDFS in spite it give the data a security property.	It doesn't add any additional process on the MapReduce; it is only used for the data management not for solving the large amount of data.	It is the latest updates and It doesn't have any challenge right now.

Table 4. Comparison of cloud type's

Private Cloud	Public Cloud	Hybrid Cloud	Virtual Private Cloud
It is accessed by only specific organization	It is accessed by all the cloud's users	It is mixed between all the types	It is similar to private cloud, however with more security of data due to the use of the virtual network to protect the data.

Table 5. Comparison of cloud computing technologies

Infrastructure as a Service (IaaS)	Platform as a Service(PaaS)	Software as a Service(SaaS)
It provides only the hardware for the user	The hardware + application are provided	It is similar to PaaS, however with more flexibility and scalability of provided applications in term of increasing the data over the time.

Table 6. The comparison between the big data, IoT and the cloud computing as three trends to watch

	Big Data	Internet of Thing(IoT)	Cloud Computing
Definition	It is a collection of large data	Technique for connect this data via the Internet	It is a technique that communicate with IoT via the Hadoop open source to solve the big data challenge
Types	Structured, semi-structured and unstructured data		Private, public, hybrid and virtual private cloud
Advantages	It is used in different applications and technologies	It is used in more scale for the big data applications	It reduces the cost and increase more the range for the data to be transmitted via the Internet
Technologies	RFID, Wi-Fi, Zigbee and Ultra wideband	Wi-Fi	Infrastructure as a Service(PaaS), Platform as a Service(PaaS), Software as a Service(SaaS)
Challenges	The huge amount of data that can't be stored and analyzed by normal devices	It is not more scalable as the data increased over the time	It is usually pay per use for the services and it sometimes deals with the scalabilty term
Solutions	IoT and the cloud computing	The cloud computing	The CloudIoT

attacks such as denial of service and end user attacks. This is one of the important points that are still begging for a solution, and one of the big data solutions that are being considered for a start is the Cloud and the important role that it plays. However, future studies should focus on developing new approaches to deal with such attacks.

REFERENCES

Aegis. (2015). *Opportunities in Telecom Sector: Arising from Big Data*. School of Business and Data Science and Telecommunications

Al-Ali & Aburukba. (2015). Role of the Internet of Things in the smart Grid. *Journal of Computer and Communications, 3*, 229-233.

Ali, Qadir, Rasool, Sathiaseelan, & Zwitter. (2016). *Big Data for Development: Applications and Techniques*. National University of Sciences and Technology (NUST).

Aljawarneh, S. (2011a). Cloud Security Engineering: Avoiding Security Threats the Right Way. *International Journal of Cloud Applications and Computing, 1*(2), 64-70. doi:10.4018/ijcac.2011040105

Aljawarneh, S. (2011b). _A web engineering security methodology for e-learning systems. *Network Security, 3*(3), 12–15. doi:10.1016/S1353-4858(11)70026-5

Wi-Fi Alliance. (2014). Connect your life: Wi-Fi and the Internet of Everything. *International Journal on Recent Innovation Trends in Computing and Communication, 4*(1), 86-189.

Alonso, V., & Arranz, O. (2016). *Big Data and e- Learning: A Binomial to the Future of the Knowledge Society*. Special Issue on Big Data and AI.

Aly, , Elmogy, & Barkat. (2015). Mansoura university, Egypt, Big data on Internet of Things: Application Architecture, Technologies, Techniques and future directions. *International Journal on Computer Science and Engineering*.

Anvari-Moghaddam, A., Monsef, H., & Rahimi-Kian, A. (2015). Optimal Smart Home Energy Management Considering Energy Saving and a Comfortable Lifestyle. *IEEE Transactions on Smart Grid, 6*(1), 324–332. doi:10.1109/TSG.2014.2349352

Hashem, Chang, Anuar, Adewole, Yaqoob, Gani, & Ahmed. (2014). *The role of big data in smart city*. University of Malaya.

Chen, Mao, & Liu. (2014). *Big Data: A Survey*. Springer.

Corporate Partnership Board Report. (2015). *Big Data and Transport Understanding and assessing options*. OEC.

eSkills UK. (2013). *Big Data Analytics Adoption and Employment Trends, 2012-2017*. Author.

Gandomi, A., & Haider, M. (2015). Beyond the hype: Big data concepts, metho- ds, and analytics. *International Journal of Information Management.* doi:10.1016/j. ijinfomgt.2014.10.007

Gonnot, T., & Saniie, J. (2014). User Defined Interactions between Devices on a 6L- OWPAN Network for Home Automation. *IEEE International of Technology Management Conference,* 1-4.

Hassanalieragh, M., Page, A., Soyata, T., Sharma, G., Aktas, M., & Mateos, G. (2015). Health Monitoring and Management Using Iternet-of- Things (IoT) Sensing with Cloud-based Processing: Opportunities challenges. *IEEE International Conference on Service Computing.*

Herrera, F.Research Group on Soft Computing and Information Intelligent Systems. (2015). *Data Mining Methods for Big Data Preprocessing.* INIT/AERFAI Summer School on Machine Learning.

Huang, Z. C., & Yuan, F. (2015). Implementation of 6LoWPAN and Its Application in Smart Lighting. *Journal of Computer and Communication., 3*(03), 80–85. doi:10.4236/jcc.2015.33014

Intel. (2015). *Ultra-Wideband (UWB) Technology Enabling high-speed wireless personal area networks.* Intel.

Intel IT Center (2015). *Big data in the cloud convergenging technologies, big data in the cloud.* Unpublished.

Jechlitschek. (2015). *A survey paper on Radio Frequency Identification.* Academic Press.

Kim,Sung-Han-sim, Cho, Yun, & Min. (2016).*Recent Rand D activities on structural health monitoring in Korea.* Pukyoung National University.

Madakam, , Ramaswamy, & Tripathi. (2015). Internet of Things (IoT): A Literature Review. *Journal of Computer and Communications., 3,* 164–173. doi:10.4236/ jcc.2015.35021

Manekar & Pradeepin. (2015). A review on cloud Based Big data analytics. *Journal on Computer Networks and communications, 1.*

Mukherjee, S., & Shaw, R. (2016). *Big Data Concepts, Applications, Challenges and Future Scope. International Journal of Advanced Research in Computer and Communication Engineering.*

Neves, Schmerl, Bernardino, & Cámara. (2016). *Big Data in Cloud Computing: features and issues*. Academic Press.

Ribeiro, Silva, & Rodrigues da Silva. (2015). Data Modeling and Data Analytics: A Survey from a Big Data Perspective. *Journal of Software Engineering and Applications*, 617-634.

Robinston, Starr, & Vass. (2016). *Implementation of Radio Frequency Identification in hospitals*. Academic Press.

Science Definition Team Report. (2016). *Enhancing STScls astronomical data science capabilities over the next five years*. Academic Press.

Singh, Singh, Garg, & Mishra. (n.d.). Big Data: Technologies, Trends and Applications. *International Journal of Computer Science and Information Technologies, 6*, 4633-4639.

Yan, Huang, & Yi. (2015). *Is Apache Spark Scalable to Seismic Data Analytics and Computations?* Academic Press.

Zafari & Christidis. (2015). *Micro-location for Internet of Things equipped Smart Buildings*. IEEE.

Chapter 11

Roof to Technology Implementation:
The Adoption of Cloud Concept in Various Areas

Inderbir Kaur
Khalsa College, India

ABSTRACT

Cloud computing is an upcoming IT approach that presents various new economic benefits, effective rapid deployment of services to achieve ultimate benefits and goals. Cloud computing reveals an effective connection of internet and computing technologies with personal or business computing that is changing the environment of computing process by providing solutions which are designed, delivered and managed. This model is a remarkable shift from the traditional model of computing. The cloud is an attractive technology solution as it enables to reduce the total cost of ownership and giving "green computing" environment by energy saving concept. Use of Cloud computing technology in different areas provides greater opportunities in the overall development of world, especially India. This chapter throw lights on various dimensions in which cloud computing concept is used . This paper also reviews the potential and opportunities for cloud computing in the healthcare industry, tourism, defence and military applications and various another aspects.

INTRODUCTION

"Cloud" term is defined as the combination of the infrastructure of a data centre with the ability to provide facility of hardware and software.

Cloud computing refers to applications and services that run on a network which is distributed using the concept of virtualized resources and accessed by the common

DOI: 10.4018/978-1-5225-3029-9.ch011

internet protocols and various networking standards. Cloud computing depicts the real paradigm shift/move in the way in which systems are deployed.

The massive scale of cloud computing (Singh et al., 2015) systems is enabled due to the large popularization of Internet and growth of large and small service companies. Cloud computing concept made a utility platform of providing various services and application in different arenas.

The cloud mainly works on two essential concepts:

1. **Abstraction:** Cloud computing abstracts the details of system implementation from developer and user. Also, data is stored in unknown location, applications run on unspecified physical systems; and access by user is ubiquitous.
2. **Virtualization:** Pooling and sharing of resources is done to implement the subject of virtualization in cloud computing. In this, infrastructure is centralized, costs are accessed on the metered basis, resources are scalable and multi-tenancy is enabled.

Cloud computing subject of abstraction is based on the concept of pooling the different physical resources and presenting them as virtual resources.

It is a new model which provides an efficient platform for provisioning resources for staging application and for platform independent user access to services. Cloud computing is a valuable concept as it helps to shift capital expenditures into operating expenditures. It also shifts the risk to cloud provider rather than to organization (Kalpana et al., 2017). This concept depicts the latest opportunities to users and developers as it is based on the footstep of a shared multi-tenant utility.

Applications implemented by cloud computing can be categorized into two ways:

1. **"Low Touch Applications":** These have low margins and normally low risks.
2. **"High Touch Application":** These have high margins which require committed resources and pose more risks.

The service/application that concentrates on the hardware follows the Infrastructure as a service (IaaS) e.g. Amazon Web services, the service/application concentrates on software stack(such as o/s) follows the software as a service(SaaS) model, e.g. Microsoft Window Azure, and the service/application concentrates on complete hardware/software/application stack, it follows the most refined and restrictive service (PaaS), e.g. Sales Force.com.

- **Benefits:** Various benefits of cloud computing includes Broad Network access, sharing and pooling of resources, on demand self service, measured and scalable service, rapid elasticity etc. It also helps to reduce the overall costs to enhance quality of service, increased reliability and outsourcing of IT management, to provide ease to utilization, to simplify maintenance and up-gradation.

CLOUD COMPUTING BACKGROUND

Cloud computing is a intelligent move of significant innovations in grid computing, virtualization, abstraction, utility computing process, elasticity, distributed computing . "Clouds, or clusters of distributed computers, provide on-demand resources and services over a network, usually the Internet, with the scale and reliability of a data centre" The U.S. National Institute of Standards and Technology (NIST) includes some other important aspects of cloud computing in its definition: "A model for enabling ubiquitous, convenient, on-demand network access to a shared pool of services (e.g., networks, servers, storage, applications and services) that can be rapidly provisioned and released with minimal management effort or service provider interaction". This definition enhances the availability of cloud and the computing with cloud and defines its essential characteristics in addition to its delivery models and deployment models.

MAIN FOCUS OF THE CHAPTER

This chapter tries to aim at the various application fields of Cloud computing concept as below.

Cloud Computing in Healthcare

Recent technology has seeped in all aspects of human lives, also in healthcare migrating from traditional to new concept. According to Current Market Dynamics, Cloud computing is a latest and fast growing theme and zone of service development in healthcare (Gartner, 2000). Cloud computing is normally used in an "OMICS-context", e.g. for computing in genomics, proteomics and molecular medicine, Diagnosis, and other healthcare concepts. Cloud computing in healthcare provides benefits in various aspects as operational, economical, functional etc.

Various Solutions and services in healthcare, provided by the health and cloud providers and IT companies are:

1. Telemedicine,
2. Telesurgery
3. Audio/video conferencing and teleradiology
4. Electronic medical records
5. Medical imaging
6. Patient management
7. E-doctor
8. Online Diagnosis
9. Storage of personal health information online.

Various medical records services provided are: Microsoft's HealthVault, Oracle's Exalogic Elastic Cloud and Amazon Web Services (AWS) etc.

The cloud based health service model mainly involves:

*   Patient Registration
*   Doctor Selection
*   Data Management and Review
*   Investigation and Analysis
*   Remote Screening

Advantages of Cloud Technology

1. Transformed and efficient Service Delivery model.
2. Provides efficient IT resources to the Healthcare Providers
3. Improves Performance.
4. Improves management of data and Reduces Operating Risks.
5. Reduces Financial and fund issues.
6. Increases Security and privacy concept.
7. Promotes Green computing concept.
8. Enhances Research.

Cloud based Medical information systems is playing an important role in supporting doctors and nurses, enhancing the quality of medical services, reducing the medical expenses, providing security to patient personal data and improving the care of chronic patients (Beyk, 2000).

Figure 1. Cloud in healthcare
Source: Google Images.

Cloud Computing in Hospitality and Tourism

Another ideal candidate for the use of Cloud computing concept is the hospitality and tourism industry. According to Jean-Philippe Courtois, President of Microsoft International, "the tourism sector has undergone a drastic transformation over the past years and has been evolving towards Tourism 3.0, where users connect to travel websites and interact by sharing their experiences, thus directly influencing the perceptions and decisions of other users and potential travelers. Because of this, it is more and more important for tourism sector enterprises to develop their online businesses by looking to the most advanced technology (Hawkins, et al.,1993). In this regard, the adoption of cloud computing is key, as it provides access to a solid web platform that will make it possible to offer more productive, efficient and competitive services. "The tourism sector is considered amongst the top three industries dependent on the internet. In the UK alone, 86% of adults use the internet and tourism related services (e.g. hotel, travel and accommodation) which are the third most purchased service from the internet.

Cloud solution provides facility in three key business technology areas: email storage and services, web conferencing and web portal hosting. The concept of cloud computing is well-suited to meet the needs of a broad set of e-tourism service environment. Timely and Effective communication between tourists, government agencies, people, guides, private agencies and other professionals is vital for the good e-tourism services (Chanwick et al., 2003). Cloud provides the concept of shared infrastructure and services which is the basic foundation for supporting tourism service ecosystems. There is a noticeable rise in the number of tourist using the internet to communicate directly with hotels, tourism suppliers and making reservations. With quick data transmission on the internet, fast response time from tourism firms to customer request is made faster.

The cloud concept is becoming common in tourism because of various characteristics as:

- Scalability
- Quick speedy response time
- Efficient Software Hosting

Cloud computing allows tourist people and the various firms dealing with tourism to keep up with the online travel demands. With the proliferation of cloud computing environment, bring-your-own-device (BOYD) such as laptops, smart mobile phones, tablets etc are becoming more and more popular. The software as a Service (SaaS) or Platform as a Service (PaaS) cloud model provide help to small medium tourism firms to meet the demands by providing or helping tourism firms by hosting a wide range of sophisticated public or private cloud software applications.

Cloud Computing in E-Government

Another application area of Cloud computing is in the zone of the E-governments in providing best possible services to its stockholders as citizens and businesses, and to reduce the costs by reducing repetitive operations and enhance the effective use of resources, in the global arena (Bansal, 2004). In Australia, agencies are seeking for innovative ways to deliver government services and want to rationalize their ICT asset so they announced small pilots to evaluate the potential of application, platforms and infrastructure cloud computing. The UK government also published its ICT strategy which covered the cloud computing and involved reducing ICT costs for governments, optimizing the use of data center infrastructure, and increasing public sector agility using G-Cloud(Government Cloud). The Singapore Government currently working on a whole-of-government infrastructure (SHINE) to provide shared computing resources to government agencies on an "Software-as-a -service" subscription model. Another upcoming new model Central G-Cloud that will replace the previous model SHINE .

In Japan, A nation-wide "Kasumigaseki Cloud" is being developed to enable various ministries to communicate. At the local level, the "Jichitai Cloud" is being developed to provide interoperability among local governments which helps in the efficient working of government. In India, Punjab, is trying for the implementation of cloud in governance. Also, The Jammu & Kashmir state government took the initiative to adopt first for Cloud computing for its e-governance services. The Madhya Pradesh government is also implementing the concepts of State Data Centers, for provisioning e-governance services such as issuing death or birth certificates and trade licenses through the Cloud. It is a concept of Microsoft's solution to implement Cloud computing. The governments of Himachal Pradesh and Uttaranchal are also in tie up with Microsoft to implement e-Government services based on the Cloud concept.

Kuwait cloud computing has achieved several projects involving data infrastructure which are needed to develop E-government that incorporates relevant official bodies comprises of 56 governmental bodies, sharing electronic documents and data at a very high speed where the aim of using cloud computing is for easy data access and storage. Cloud computing technologies have many advantages in different parts of E-government. These are:

- Scalability
- Green technology
- Availability and Accessibility
- Backup and Recovery
- Cost Saving
- Unlimited Storage

The main issues and challenges for adopting cloud computing for the E-government are (Gartner, 2000):

1. Security and privacy
2. Data protection and compliance
3. SLA implementation concept.
4. Quality Assurance.

Cloud Computing in Business

Cloud computing model is also seen as a business delivery model and an infrastructure management methodology. The organization delivery model predicts the experience of user by which platform of hardware, software and network resources are effectively and optimally used to provide new and vital services over the World Wide Web, and the server-client concept issued in accordance with the logical needs of the required business using new techniques, advanced, automated tools. The cloud also enables the users and the technology creators, program administrators and others to implement these services through a Web-based interface that deliver the service and filter the complexity of the implemented dynamic infrastructure. The infrastructure management methodology helps IT industries to manage huge numbers of large virtualized resources as a single large resource. It also enables IT organizations to effectively increase their data centre resources without massively increasing the number of people required to maintain the growth.

For organizations that are currently using traditional infrastructures, a cloud will enable users to consume IT resources in the data centre in ways that is newer concept and were never available before. Companies that employ traditional data centre management practices know that making IT resources available to an end user can be time consuming. It involves many steps to proceed, such as procuring hardware; finding raised and sufficient floor space and accurate power and cooling; allocating resources and allows administrators to install operating systems, middleware and software; provisioning the network; and securing the environment.

Cloud Computing in Agriculture

Now a days, agriculture is embedded with new and advance services like GPS, sensors etc that enable to communicate to each other compute the data and also exchange data. IT innovations help to provides services in the form of cloud to agriculture. Agri-Cloud offers expertise service to farmers regarding cultivation of crops, seeds development, pricing, fertilizers, and disease detail method of cure to be used etc.

One of the framework of application of cloud in agriculture is MAD-Cloud which offers expertise service to farmers for better crops (Kun, 2012).

MAD-Cloud can make use of establish cloud infrastructures, various networks and servers available etc., other than the existing resources. MAD-cloud framework is a layered architecture contains layers like-

- MAD-Data Acquisition Layer (MDAL)
- MAD-Data Processing Layer(MDPL)
- MAD-Data Storage Service Layer(MDSSL)

Cloud Computing Applications in Agriculture

- **High Integration and Sharing of Agriculture Information:** Cloud computing provides a new management method, which can combine information resources in different regions and departments, develop information sharing space and share hardware and software infrastructure. The 'Agriculture Information Resources Cloud (AIRC)' offers the agricultural sector and farmers a real-time access to a full range of agricultural information that is required and greatly reduces operating costs by increasing the efficiency of information sharing with the help of various terminals.
- **Providing Agricultural Science and Technology Service:** As an vital helping technology of digitizing the traditional agriculture, cloud computing technology depicts advanced information technology services, and gives digitizing and visualizing expression, by controlling, by designing and by management of whole agriculture process (Kun, 2012).. Agricultural extension, education and scientific research attain a peak in cloud computing environment. In addition to this, the cloud computing technology can be used to generate advanced agricultural production information and latest geographical information software to gain organic pointers among agricultural production and operating procedures.

Figure 2. Cloud in agriculture
Source: Google Images.

Military Clouds

► **DoD Cloud Computing key objectives:**
  ► Increased mission effectiveness and operational efficiencies

  ► Enable the Department to consolidate and share commodity IT functions resulting in a more efficient use of resources

  ► Cloud services can enhance Warfighter mobility through device and location independence while providing on-demand secure global access to mission data and enterprise services

  ► Cloud platforms and services can provide increased opportunity for rapid application development and reuse of applications

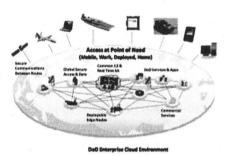

DoD Cloud Computing Goal
"Implement cloud computing as the means to deliver the most innovative, efficient and secure information and IT service in support of the Department's mission, anywhere, anytime, on any authorized device"

- **Real-Time Monitoring and Guidance in Agricultural Production:** In the production of agriculture, the application of cloud computing technology can be reflected in two following aspects:
  - Production process monitoring and controlling, experiment simulation and support.
  - Nowadays, cloud computing technology proceeds in visualizing real-time monitoring of crop growth, such as leaf area and perimeter, stem diameter and height, etc. It also helps to detect the level of water and fertilizer content in the soil. Cloud computing technology also can be applicable to the study of agricultural science.
- **Construction and Improvement of the Agricultural Products Supply Chain:** Agricultural products have strong regional and seasonal features. The cloud platform facilitates the exchange of information and effective communication between farmers and agricultural enterprises which is act as an important bridge in constructing and improving the varieties of agricultural products, the supply chain, ameliorating agricultural products sales, and enhancing profits of farmers.
- **Tracking and Monitoring of the Animal Husbandry Products Quality:** In the cloud computing platform, the animal husbandry can take advantage of advanced computer imaging technology to calculate the estimation of animal meat, choose and cultivate good varieties, establishing the magneto-therapy database and animal good nutrition demand model, optimize real feed formulation, to meet a number of animals nutritional needs indicators etc. The cloud computing technology is used to perform the scientific research, raw materials access, processing, marketing, traceability and information services, inspection, and administration, etc.

Researchers working at Agri-research stations can add their research results, discoveries and suggestions regarding upcoming techniques for cultivation, effective use of fertilizers, cultivation history of the region etc.

Another Help of Cloud Computing in Agriculture

- Data Readiness and data availability any time & any where without delay.
- Local and global communication to enhance the GDP of the nation.
- Improve economic condition of the Nation by motivating the farmers and research scholars.
- Assurance of food security level

- Reduction of technical issue
- Improving Rural-Urban movement
- Improve market price of Food, seeds, other product.

Challenge of Cloud Computing in Agriculture

- Threat to security in case of Maintenance & Supervision by third party.
- Indirect administrator accountability
- Unawareness of Farmer for new technology, tools and cloud computing concept
- Less physical control and poor network connectivity sometimes.
- More prone to hackers
- Requires a constant Internet connection and the hardware and software platform
- Proper Farmers training necessary for this technology.

Cloud Computing in Defence

I don't need a hard disk in my computer if I can get to the server faster...carrying around these non-connected computers is byzantine by comparison. – Steve Jobs (1997)

Technology has also played the vital role in defining the outcome of war. The modern-day military is working upon many aspects of cloud to invest in cutting-edge technologies to leverage their benefits in the evolving nature of warfare, which encompasses every aspect of science. The information and communication technology (ICT), the research and development has unleashed vast potential for civilian and military applications, which can display from simple logic execution to high-end supercomputing. The cloud computing has not only made a roads in the operations of private sectors, but it also slated to perform a central role in the functioning of governments and defense and security agencies in terms of scalability, agility and interoperability.

The main interest of the US Department of Defense (DoD) with respect to cloud computing, is to deploy cloud computing in terms to deliver the most innovative, efficient and secure information and IT services in support of military and defense Departments aim anywhere, any time on any authorized device. Cloud computing implementation proceeds with the aim of efficiency, agility, and innovation and with the concept of security and cost effectiveness. In the present era. the army requires to recrystallize its future IT landscape, with new concepts more secure and safe environment and latest technologies (Aljawarneh, et al., 2016).

Cloud Projects Running in Defence

1. **Garrison Networks:** These networks provide voice, video, and data services over unclassified or classified network United States (CONUS) and abroad (Coursey, et al., 2008). These networks include the technology having backbone of fibre optic cable linking between various servers and networks for army installations.
2. **The Joint Information Environment:** The JIE is the DoD's effort to integrate and consolidate IT infrastructure and to fulfill the goals of more reliable, improved and simplified cyber security, effectiveness, and efficiency.
3. Enterprise Email
4. Global Network Enterprise Construct (GNEC)

Figure 3. Cloud in defense and military
Source: Google Images.

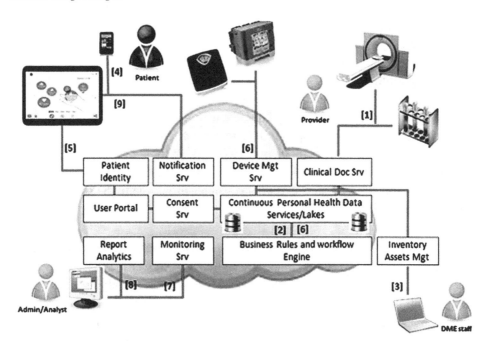

WEAKNESSES

There are many issues that need to be resolved before cloud computing can be accepted as a viable and choice in business computing. Some of them are:

- The content should be checked, verified and justified before putting on to the cloud.
- Locations for storage are not known to identify errors.
- Absence of High Quality of service and availability.
- Cloud providers often fail to live up to uptime standards required for the efficient working of cloud in various fields.

OPPORTUNITIES

- One of the prominent opportunities of cloud computing lies in its potential to help developing countries reap the benefits of information technology without the necessary upfront capital investments.
- Other is to handle the sensitive data to cloud, to provide security and global access.
- Opportunities for small business to exploit high-end applications like ERP software and business analytics.
- Mashups represent another opportunity in cloud computing. In the process of web development, a mashup is a web page or use of cartographic data that relates data or functionality from two or more external sources to create a new service
- In era, where businesses are looking to burnish their 'green' credentials, cloud computing guides large IT infrastructures to reduce their carbon prints.
- Another opportunity is in the area of energy efficiency and equipment recycling .

THREATS

The biggest threat to cloud computing is the possibility of backlash from entrenched incumbents. The threats are in the terms of data security, IT audit policies, Cyber laws etc.

CONCLUSION

Cloud computing concept attracts huge attentions of organizations, countries and enterprises with its marvelous benefits and market potential, the feasibility and applicability in various industries. This technology is bringing greater opportunities to the agricultural development, education, and also be the inevitable choice to achieve modernization and various others fields. Yet the concepts are suffering from various flaws which need to be rectified. Therefore, departments and institutions should pay interest to the implementation of this upcoming technology, raise awareness, and especially provide strong support in platform construction, resource and module integration and service capabilities. Then only one should believe that with the support of modern information technology and cloud concept in various dimensions, the nation can touch the heights of development.

REFERENCES

Aljawarneh, S., Aldwairi, M., & Yassein, M. B. (2017). Anomaly-based intrusion detection system through feature selection analysis and building hybrid efficient model. *Journal of Computational Science*. doi:10.1016/j.jocs.2017.03.006

Aljawarneh, S., Yassein, M.B., & Talafha, W.A. (2017). A multithreaded programming approach for multimedia big data: encryption system. *Multimed Tools Appl*. <ALIGNMENT.qj></ALIGNMENT>10.1007/s11042-017-4873-9

Aljawarneh, S. A., Alawneh, A., & Jaradat, R. (2017). Cloud security engineering: Early stages of SDLC. *Future Generation Computer Systems*, *74*, 385–392. doi:10.1016/j.future.2016.10.005

Aljawarneh, S. A., Moftah, R. A., & Maatuk, A. M. (2016). Investigations of automatic methods for detecting the polymorphic worms signatures. *Future Generation Computer Systems*, *60*, 67–77. doi:10.1016/j.future.2016.01.020

Aljawarneh, S. A., Vangipuram, R., Puligadda, V. K., & Vinjamuri, J. (2017). G-SPAMINE: An approach to discover temporal association patterns and trends in internet of things. *Future Generation Computer Systems*, *74*, 430–443. doi:10.1016/j.future.2017.01.013

Army Battle Command Systems (ABCS). (n.d.). Retrieved from http://www.dote.osd.mil/pub/reports/FY2005/pdf/ army/2005abcs.pdf

Bansal, H. S., McDougall, G. H. G., Dikolli, S. S., & Sedatole, K. L. (2004). Relating e-satisfaction to behavioral outcomes: An emprical study. *Journal of Services Marketing*, *18*(4), 290–302. doi:10.1108/08876040410542281

Beyk Mohammadi, H. (2000). New outlook on the economic effects of tourism development by looking at Iran. Political-Economic Information, 248-253.

Build your business on Google Cloud Platform. (n.d.). Retrieved from https://cloud.google.com

Chanwick, A., & Mary, C. (2003). Interaction between states and citizens in the age of the internet: EGovernment and E-Governance. *An International Journal of Policy, Administration & Institutions*, *16*, 271–300. doi:10.1111/1468-0491.00216

Coursey, D., & Norris, D. (2008). Model of e-Governance: Are they correct? An empirical assessment public administration overview. Academic Press.

Cui, W. (2011). Application and Developing Prospect of Cloud Computation in the Agricultural Informationization. *Agricultural Engineering*, *2*(1), 40–43.

Egger, R., & Buhalis, D. (2008). *E-tourism case studies: Management and marketing issues*. Elsevier Ltd.

Gartner. (2000). *Key issues in E-Government strategy and management*. Research Notes, key issues.

Kalpana, G., Kumar, P. V., Aljawarneh, S., & Krishnaiah, R. V. (2017). Shifted Adaption Homomorphism Encryption for Mobile and Cloud Learning. *Computers & Electrical Engineering*. doi:10.1016/j.compeleceng.2017.05.022

Mohammed, A. B., Altmann, J., & Hwang, J. (2010). *Cloud computing Value: Understanding Businesses and Value Creation in the Cloud*. Economic Models and Algorithms for Distributed Systems.

Qian, K. (2012). The Application of Cloud Computing in Agricultural Management Information System. *Hubei Agricultural Sciences*, *5*(1), 159–162.

Shilendra, Jain, & Sustal. (2007). E-Government and E-Governance: Definition and status around the world. *ICEG*.

Singh, A., Juneja, D., & Malhotra, M. (2015). A Novel Agent Based Autonomous Service Composition Framework for Cost Optimization of Resource Provisioning in Cloud Computing. In JKSU-CIS. Elsevier.

Singh, A., & Malhotra, M. (2015). Evaluation of a Secure Agent based optimized Resource Scheduling Framework in Cloud Environment. IJCAR, 188-198.

Singh, A., & Malhotra, M. (2016). Hybrid Two Tier Framework for Improved Security in Cloud Environment. India-Com., 1601-1606.

Singh, A., & Malhotra, M. (n.d.). A Novel Agent Based Framework for Cost Optimization in Cloud Computing Environment. *International Journal of Cloud Applications*, 53–61.

Williams, P. (1993). Information technology and tourism: a dependent factor for future survival. In World Travel and Tourism Review: Indicators, Trends and Issues (2nd ed.; vol. 3, pp. 200-205). CAB International.

Youseff, L., Botrico, M., & Silva, D. D. (2008). Towards a unified Ontology of Cloud Computing. *Proc. Of Grid Computing Environments Workshop.*

Section 4
Networks and Energy Efficiency in Virtual Cloud

Chapter 12

A Cloud–Based Approach for Cross–Management of Disaster Plans:
Managing Risk in Networked Enterprises

Samia Chehbi Gamoura
Université de Strasbourg, France

ABSTRACT

With the democratization of Data management through Big Data and Cloud Computing, and the proliferation of business lines into complex networks, industries are ever more subject to disasters than ever. It is practically impossible to forecast their happening and degree of damages. Consequently, companies try to collaborate in integrating risk management in their information systems against downtimes. This chapter addresses this problem by outlining and discussing insights from the extensive literature review to produce a generic approach for cross-management. A set of prerequisites of disaster planning is also provided with comparative analysis and arguments. The proposed approach is focused on risk assessment methodology based on Fuzzy Cognitive Map. The method is able to aggregate all assessment variables of the whole stakeholders involved in the business network. The key findings of this study aim to assist enterprises in improving risk readiness capability and disaster recovery. Finally, we indicate the open challenges for further researches and an outlook on our future research.

DOI: 10.4018/978-1-5225-3029-9.ch012

1. INTRODUCTION

In today's massive digital transformation, the way we do business is mutating each day. Indeed, progresses in Big Data and Cloudified environment are affording more information than ever before (Hashem, et al. 2015). In fact, business continuity and risk management topics are propelled at the forefront of interest for both scholars and practitioners (Papadopoulos, et al. 2017).

Companies and especially sensitive industries face continually various disrupting events that could happen separately or simultaneously (Sahebjamnia, Torabi and Mansouri 2015). Each trouble might have different impact on resources, manpower, products, facilities, sites, factories, etc. Usually, two main plans are settled by organizations to prevent and face calamities: the Business Continuity Plan (BCP) (Montshiwa, Nagahira and shida 2016) and the Disaster Recovery Plan (DRP) (Al Hamed and Alenezi 2016). However, these two plans are developed separately in each information system where event happening for a company may impact all businesses of far or near connected companies around the world (Papadopoulos, et al. 2017). Actually, complex and large virtual networks of enterprises confirm today that any disaster may impact all stakeholders of the businesses chain (Noran 2014). For example, a German computer manufacturer should integrate the disaster plan of Japan zone since it subcontracts the manufacture of microprocessors to a Polish constructor who supplies to factories in the Japanese islands of Ryūkyū.

An Interesting recent survey, published by Gartner® (Gartner 2017) in (Witty 2016), revealed that nearly three from every ten companies settled a real Disaster Recovery Plan. The same investigation reported that in the occurrence of an outage; where 67% evaluate their business lose more than 20, 000 USD for every one day of interruption.

To make their energies the most useful, enterprises should consider every potential state when analyzing the possible risks (Kristo and Cingula n.d.). This means that enterprises involved in networks, supply chains, and virtual markets should consider all disaster sources of stakeholders in the entire network (Takakuwa 2013). These risks should be taken into account from somewhat routine vulnerabilities like power failures to extremely dangerous events like acts of war or terrorist attacks (Huatuco, Ullah and Burgess 2017). As the purpose of a Disaster Recovery Plan is to outline what acts will be taken in the event that an organization does experience disaster (Gasbarro, Iraldo and Daddi 2017), recovery management should cover all concepts and events in the entire network (Timperio, et al. 2016). However, the investigation of academic and industrial publications and projects highlights a clear shortage in collaboration practices, cross data management, and governance issues on risks planning from a networked enterprises perspective ((Brindley 2017), (Sarmiento, et al. 2016), (Chatterjee, Ismail and Shaw 2016)).

That is, we propose in this chapter a structured approach based on cross-management of disaster planning. Prior to detailing the solution, an extensive literature review examines and classifies existing research streams focus to different disruption risks and recovery in networked organization context. By the way, we try to identify gaps in current research and outline future research opportunities. The proposed methodology is based on risk assessment by the technique of Fuzzy Cognitive Mapping (FCM) (Papageorgiou and Salmeron 2014) in order to predict causality relationships between disruption patterns and phenomena among the enterprises network.

The chapter is organized as follows: We begin by stating the research concern and introducing sustainability, downtimes challenge and characteristics of Disaster management, with a brief reminder of cloud and Big Data environments. We then advance the proposed methodology that is based on risk assessment by Fuzzy Cognitive Mapping. Finally, we conclude by highlighting the current trends of cross risk management in the context of networked enterprises, the untaken research gaps, and the expected open views in the near future.

2. BACKGROUND AND RESEARCH GAPS

2.1. Sustainability in Cloudified Information Systems

In the following sub-sections, we introduce the IS downtime characterization with regard to the key used measurements. Then, we state the main causes, the effects and the main impacts on enterprises components. Finally, we provide an understating of disaster planning with an extensive literature review and analysis.

2.1.1. Downtime vs. Availability and Reliability Measures

The consequence of natural or man-made disasters to enterprises can cause huge financial damages, as well as all business collapses (Brindley 2017). The outcomes produced cause a loss of function and operational business services (Chang, et al. 2016). Thus, plans and actions regarding downtimes not only affect economic resources, but also all enterprises assets. This legitimizes the need for non-tolerant management and high ability to restoration (Lockamy III 2014). Figure 1 shows a sample of automated decision tree when a downtime occurs.

The downtime term denotes the time that the IS infrastructure provides unsuitable service (Franke, Holm and König, The distribution of time to recovery of enterprise IT services 2014). We talk about system fail when it is not delivering the appropriate expected service. According to literature, there are two aspects for downtime

Figure 1. Sample of automated procedure when downtime event occurs

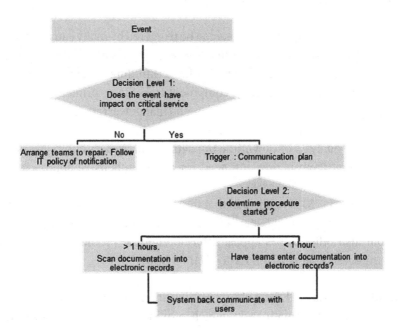

measurement: availability and reliability (Närman, et al. 2014): (1) Reliability in IS is a measure of the uninterrupted delivery of suitable service (Daniel 2014). In cloud computing, demands on large scale tend to be fast and responsive, especially in the field of business. In such system, reliability affects directly the usability of the application service and becomes the key measurement of enterprises sustainability (DiStefano and Hawkins 2016). (2) Availability is an IS measurement of the delivery of the suitable service with considering the alternation with the unsuitable service (Lyu, et al. 2016). This can be performed by stochastic methods for probabilities measurement.

To clarify these measures, their relationship and their usage, let us define the Mean-time To Failure (MTF) as the probability of time given to an operating system to fail, and the Mean-time To Repair (MTR) as the probability of time given to a failed system to be repaired. Then, availability and reliability measurements can be expressed:

$$Reliability = MTF + MTR \tag{1}$$

$$Availability = \frac{MTF}{MTF + MTR} \tag{2}$$

243

2.1.2. Downtimes Causes and Effects

Information Systems (IS) interruptions can be triggered by many causes. Through an extensive review of literature, we synthetize the most common of them with impacts analysis on organizations components: facilities (building, electricity power, water, janitorial services, real estate, etc.), equipment (machines, printers, PC, Monitors, tablets, laptops, projectors, peripherals, etc.), and manpower (administrative, technical and management human resources) (Table 1).

Based on the analysis of downtime impacts on enterprises components in Table 1, we believe that there is pressing need for a comprehensive approach to tackle effects into networked businesses.

Authors in (Q. Li 2016) indicated that the damages of IS downtimes are not only related to the service stoppage period which can be directly evaluated in terms of finance, but also other losses appear after solving the problems. They identified four sorts of seven effects (from E1 to E7):

1. **Breakdown Loss (E1):** Due to service interruptions, staffs and machines cannot accomplish their tasks which provide unexpected productivity loss. Besides, if stoppage extends to customers, the profit loss is added.

Table 1. Literature review of the most common IS downtime causes with analysis of impact on enterprises components

Disaster			Impact in Enterprises			Reference
Category	Cause	Brief Description	Facilities	Equipment	Manpower	
man-made	power outage	All electronic supply needs power. Once a break happens, all electronic devices stop working	✓	✓		(Brazelton et Lyons 2016)
	Human error	All incorrect actions, such as omission may provoke big issues.	✓	✓	✓	(Levy, Yu and Prizzia 2016)
	Cyber attack	Hackers ae considered as a real threat as they may disturb or collapse all the system		✓		(Q. Li 2016)
	Epidemic disease	Serious contagious disease eruption, such as an epidemic flu, enforces employees being inept to report to work. In addition, social officialdoms may be required limiting or stopping public gatherings, needing quarantines, etc.			✓	(Mohan and Bakshi 2017)
	Vandalism	People may damage voluntarily facilities and or components, which is distinguished with the unintentionally human error.	✓	✓		(Tammepuu, Kaart and Sepp 2016)
	Politic crisis & acts of war	War zones and political crisis can make local staff unavailable. In extreme situations, they can generate calamities in buildings and equipment.	✓	✓	✓	(Yeboah, et al. 2014)

continued on following page

Table 1. Continued

Disaster			Impact in Enterprises			Reference
Category	Cause	Brief Description	Facilities	Equipment	Manpower	
Technical and/or environmental	Industrial accidents	Chemical accidents, nuclear explosions and radiation, biological catastrophes are common today, and can seriously impact all facilities, as well as human and financial resources.	✓	✓	✓	(Bohtan, Vrat and Vij 2016)
	Hardware failure	Damaged hardware accounts for 13% of the downtime causes.		✓		(Gupta, Kapur and & Kumar 2016)
	Software failure	Software applications do not performing the required processes, cause 73% of downtime causes.		✓		(Becker, et al. 2015)
	System over-load	When a critical component turns much more than the concrete needs which cannot be instantly shortened, this may lead to waste the available resources and stoppage of all the system.		✓		(Javadi, et al. 2013)
	Traffic accidents	• Transport shut-downs and crashes due to weather, strike, or more serious events could cause serious staffing problems, and in serious case, it can provoke damages in installations, services and components.	✓	✓	✓	(Miller and Engemann 2015)
	Weather	Weather disasters include a wide range of events, such as tornado, severe thunderstorm, and so on. The impact of each incident is various in terms of impact, and restoration time.	✓	✓	✓	(Sullivan 2017)
Natural	Flood	With climate changes, floods are becoming more frequent and devastations could occur in an unpredictable zones and periods.	✓	✓	✓	(Chang, et al. 2016)
	Earthquake	The effects of an earth trembling might contain a considerable blow in constructions, possible loss of life, interrupted transportation and the probability of recurrent disruption in the near future due to aftershocks. In IT recovery planning, the arrangements for an earthquake require out-of-zone incomes for retrieval purposes.	✓	✓	✓	(Li, et al. 2016)
	Fire	Fire can be one of the most destructive forces that IT systems confront. In data centers, machines shouldn't even get too warm. The slightest problem in the cooling system could be devastating. In addition, firefighting services don't care about data systems when they're trying to save lives.	✓	✓	✓	(Hiller, Bone and Timmins 2015)

2. **Disaster Recovery (E2):** This comprises the spent time on operations of recovery from the disaster

3. **Liability (E3):** This is typically related to customers' service and engagements of Service Level Agreements (SLA), where customers usually claim for a reimbursement payments.

4.   **Productivity Decreasing (E4):** When an outage occurs, the information transfer time increases or stop. In some critical businesses enterprises use workaround procedures to insure continuity, such as use of paper as an alternative way to transfer information, which needs longer time to reintegrate this manual support to the digital system.

5.   **Customer Loss (E5):** This is the case of shortened service which leads to terminating customers contracts and fewer new clients arrive because of bad repute.

6.   **Idle Staff and Equipment (E6):** The Possibility of idle staff and equipment is fairly short today but it still occurs in the some critical businesses like banking. For instance, server stoppage in production environment at centralized level. This case is uncommon but stills possible and the recovery in such situation can take many hours and in sometime many days

7.   **Damaged Reputation (E7):** It might be quite difficult to estimate the value of the enterprise's reputation, while the value can replicate on the profits and cost-effectiveness. The reputation loss does not arise nearly during or after the interruption but it affects the long-term performance.

In order to clarify measurement of negative impacts, costs of downtime are usually integrated in disaster management: The first consequence of stoppage is the inactivity of employees and machines. In term of time wasting, employees report the cessation and then wait for repairing. In addition, repairing incurs repairing cost, such as recruiting a specialized expert in reparation of a damaged machine.

Research works of academics and industrials linked to disaster costs and downtime negative effects are amply. Agostinho et al. in (Agostinho, et al. n.d.) supposed that the downtime affects the complete productivity and it is complex to model it at long-time period. Similarly, authors in (Saltoglu, Humaira and Inalhan 2016) reported that downtime costs shouldn't be neglected and have to integrated part in maintenance management. The main costs due to IS breakdowns can be categorized into the following table (Table 2, Figure 2).

2.2. Disaster Recovery Planning

According to (Levy, Yu and Prizzia 2016), a disaster recovery plan outlines with documentation support the set of procedures for preventing, stating, replying to, and recovering from a disaster event. The plan identifies and defines the responsibility and scope of each team in each division in situation of a disaster. It also enables control of communications among managers, employees, and external units, law institutions, emergency units, and media (Wang, et al. 2015).

Table 2. List of costs categories related to downtime effects (synthesized from literature review)

Cost Category	Description	Samples	Reference	Related Effect
Cost of equipment idleness	All equipment in activity are expected to working fully and productively until the end of the service life.	Broken equipment, Incident in building.	(Q. Li 2016)	*Disaster recovery (E2), Idle staff and equipment (E6).*
Costs of employees idleness	This cost is related to the lazy or stopping time of human resources	Epidemic episode, Terrorist attack, Crash in transports.	(Tabikh 2014)	*Disaster recovery (E2), Idle staff and equipment (E6), Productivity decreasing (E4).*
Costs of revenue losses	It denotes the loss of customer satisfaction due to the failure of the company to achieve customer demand	Inaccessibility to online stores,	(Agostinho, et al. n.d.)	*Customer loss (E5), Damaged reputation (E7), Productivity decreasing (E4).*
Costs of repairing	This denotes to the costs that apply on fixing broken gears, such as procurement of substituted machineries. Besides, enterprises may rent equipment to face the interruption if affecting critical activities	Floods in factories, Earthquake in building and offices, Power-off in datacenter.	(Saltoglu, Humaira and Inalhan 2016)	*Disaster recovery (E2).*
Liability costs	It defines the financial loss of equipment that are involved in agreed contractual obligations.	Damages of loaned cars,	(Q. Li 2016)	*Liability (E3), Damaged reputation (E7).*
Disaster recovery costs	This mentions to the financial spent on time, physical and human resources in recovering from the unforeseen disaster.	Storm damages, Seismic damages in offices.	(Tabikh 2014)	*Disaster recovery (E2).*
Customers and partners losses	All businesses are built on customers revenues. When these customers change to concurrent service provider, all business losses occurred. In addition, compensation costs may be added to partners if existed under contractual clauses.	Close stores, Inaccessibility to online purchasing.	(Agostinho, et al. n.d.)	*Liability (E3), Customer loss (E5), Damaged reputation (E7).*

A disaster is defined as a disordering event associated to a social alteration (Montshiwa, Nagahira and shida 2016) that needs communication among stakeholders to manage a set of raised interdisciplinary challenges (Bohtan, Vrat and Vij 2016) (Li, et al. 2016).

Figure 2. Relationship between effects and costs of downtime
Synthesized from literature review.

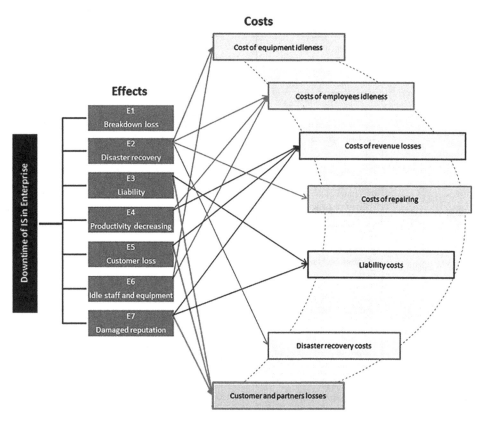

2.2.1. Processes and Sub-Processes in Disaster Planning

The primary vital role of Disaster Recovery Planning is the sustenance and partaking in upper-level management of business units (Al Hamed and Alenezi 2016). Authors in (Brazelton et Lyons 2016) stated that Disaster Recovery Planning can be divided into six key processes. Each process comprises a set of sub-processes, is turn, where each one figures upon the others (Figure 3). These processes are: (1) consolidating

Figure 3. Main processes of a disaster recovery plan

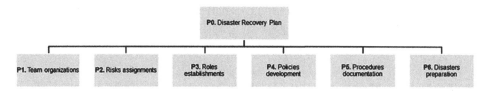

the team, (2) evaluating risks in the organization, (3) instituting roles in divisions, (4) developing rules, strategies, and actions to perform, (5) documenting rescue procedures, (6) formulating the way to handle disasters in preparation instructions.

P1: Team Organization Sub-Process

This first stage consists of defining teams and organizing their planning in situation of disaster recovery. The team has to comprise representors from all the functions in the organization (Bohtan, Vrat and Vij 2016). During this stage, the selected teams attend professional training sessions in order to be prepared in case of disaster recovery situation (Brindley 2017). This process includes five other sub-processes (Figure 4): (1) P11. Training disaster recovery team, (2) P12. Making the planning schedules, (3) P13. Preparing and setting the awareness promotional campaigns, (4) P14. Costing budgets for disaster recovery management, (5) P15. Handling standards and directing figures.

P2: Risks assignments Sub-Process

This step is concerned by the measurement of all risks and threats that the company faces in situation disaster. It can be the inventory of all involved causes and effects of probable disasters (Gbadeyan, Butakov and Aghili 2017). This stage may be long and complex to run, as it consists of listing and evaluation all business impacts and associated assesses of risks (DiStefano and Hawkins 2016).

The set of sub-processes involved in this stage includes (Figure 5): (1) P21. Data collection related to risks, (2) P22. Listing of all business processes in a documented inventory, (3) P23. Detecting and classifying weaknesses and vulnerabilities, (4) P24. Quantifying treats, (5) P25. Gathering risk charges reports.

Figure 4. Main sub-processes team organization process (P1)

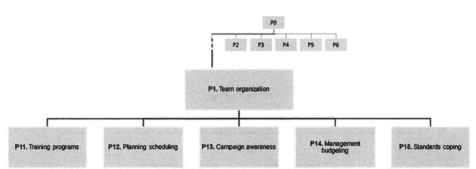

Figure 5. Main sub-processes risks assignment process (P2)

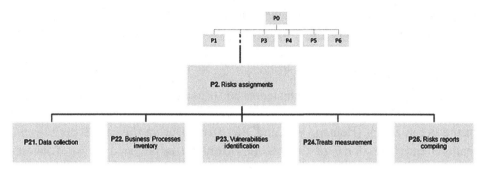

P3: Roles Establishment Sub-Process

This phase involves institution of the roles that each division, branch, and business partner plays in disaster recovery (Huatuco, Ullah and Burgess 2017). It may be broken down into the following sub-processes (Figure 6): (1) P31. Identification of critical business activities, (2) P32. Ordering and categorizing Functions for recovery priority fulfillment, (3) P33. Developing maps (charts) of duties, (4) P34. Evaluating protection by insurance and coverage requirements.

P4: Policies Development Sub-Process

The settlement of guidelines of policies step-by-step constitutes this process to repair the functions of business activities (Gasbarro, Iraldo and Daddi 2017). It is imperative that all divisions, institutions, services, and staff to be involved in development of these procedures guidelines (Gupta, Kapur and & Kumar 2016). It includes (Figure 7): (1) P41. Defining what disaster recovery instructions are required

Figure 6. Main sub-processes role establishment process (P3)

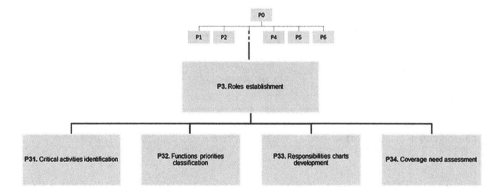

Figure 7. Main sub-processes role establishment process (P4)

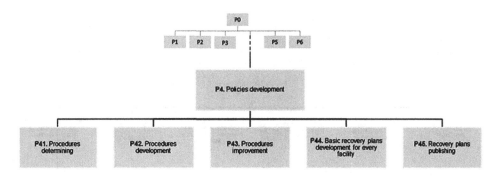

to be developed, (2) P42. Implementing and documenting recovery procedures, (3) P43. Revising and validating recovery guidelines, (4) P44. Developing elementary plans for facilities, (5) P45. publishing the disaster recovery procedures.

P5: Procedures Documentation Sub-Process

The fifth process is the documentation of policies developed in the previous process (P4). The produced reports need to be revised and updated recurrently (Nagurney, Masoumi and Yu 2015). It may be broken down into five sub-processes (Figure 8): (1) P51. Documenting recovery plan following the P4 procedures, (2) P52. Revising the recovery procedures, (3) P.53.Implementing basic plans for all identified facilities, (4) P55. Publication of the recovery plan.

P6: Disasters Preparation Sub-Processes

In this step, the recovery plan is distributed to entire services, sub-organizations, divisions, and staff involved in the disaster recovery (Sahebjamnia, Torabi and Mansouri 2015). The step includes six sub-processes (Figure 9): (1) P61. Dispatching

Figure 8. Main sub-processes role establishment process (P5)

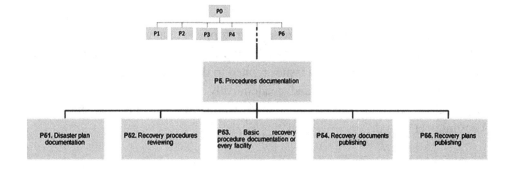

Figure 9. Main sub-processes role establishment process (P6)

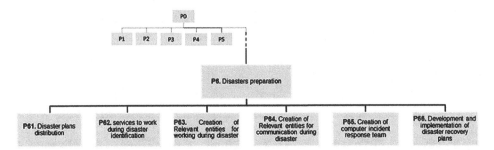

the recovery plan to divisions, and staff, (2) P62. Finding teams and staff to work with during a disaster, (3) P63. Making procedures dedicated to working with public providers (i.e. media, emergency office), private providers (i.e. phone/internet providers), insurance companies, (4) P64. Making communication protocols with media and the other stakeholders (i.e. employees families), law supports, (5) P65. Creating instructions for IT recovery and handling of incidents, (6) P66. Implementing the disaster scheduling.

2.2.2. Challenge of Disaster Planning in Context of Networked Enterprises

Today, no organization remains isolated and businesses implies multitude channels of partners, which can be contractors, suppliers, mediators, third-party services providers, and customers. This constitute volatile or permanent networks that are organized in forms such as supply chains (Brindley 2017), supply chain networks (Yu, Li and Yang 2017), extended enterprises (Wang, et al. 2015), and so forth. In such networked businesses, each two-way edge integrates the movement of products; the information streams; the transmission of titles; and many other flows (Witty 2016) in addition to business activities that comprise human resources, IT systems, real estate, facilities, equipment, carriage, finance, etc. (Murnane, et al. 206). Supposing all of these flows and gears are functioning routinely, so what happens if something interrupts an activity?

Companies are aware that any unexpected stoppage of any of these parts can put end to the activity or companies involved (Yu, Li and Yang 2017). But in reality of literature review, several critical issues related to this challenging question remain disconcerted, fewer explored, and academically underdeveloped (Bohtan, Vrat and Vij 2016, Al Hamed and Alenezi 2016, Montshiwa, Nagahira and shida 2016, Agostinho, et al. n.d.).

In situations of crisis, the coordination between enterprises belonging to the same business line is extremely challenging. The challenge is mainly due to two factors: (1) the inconsistencies in IT infrastructures of different stakeholders (Epstein and Khan 2014), and (2) the difficulties in validation of overflows of information generated during disaster (Al Hamed and Alenezi 2016). For example, the conflict in alert warning format may suspend interventions and encumber the situation where the population may be flooded with confusing or irrelevant alerts (Brindley 2017).

The literature review offers two ways to face this problem: the first way is by standardizing the communication channels in situations of crisis. Unfortunately, efforts to standardize warning protocols are stagnant and very restricted (Klafft and Ziegler 2014, Rieser, et al. 2015). The second approach is the cross-management of disaster plans by converge procedures upstream at the early step of design. It seems to be the best way for enterprises to contribute and master the risk management overall the business line (Lam 2014). However, it is necessary to point out that the collaboration know-how is somehow daring (Wang, et al. 2015) because of the following hurdles: (1) Fluctuation is closed to the life-cycle phase proper to each enterprise. For instance, the collaborative potential may decline during the reengineering step, which may comprise simultaneous operation, investigation and design phases (Noran 2014), (2) Due to the situation of urgency, enterprises may be tempted to supersede, eliminate or substitute dedicated teams, assuming a central control approach instead of cooperative plan (Nagurney, Masoumi and Yu 2015), (3) Interdisciplinary of disaster crisis management depends on on a widespread range of communities from healthcare, economic, public institutions, social, and political assets (Ojha, Salimath and D'Souza 2014).

To diagnose the growth of research works dealt with sustainability of networked enterprises, we reviewed extensively the literature of industrials and academics. The synthesis is illustrated in figure 10.

2.3. Big Data and Cloud Computing to Support Disaster Planning

In contemporary epoch, mainly due to the expansions in the use of large-scaled technologies of Cloud Computing and Big Data, large volumes of data, have been accumulated and processed (Hashem, et al. 2015). These technologies have the potential to transform business processes as it does not only concern economics or industry, but extents all aspects of enterprises in their internal organization and in their entire chains and business networks (Daniel 2014). Within operations of networked enterprises, cloudified environments and Big Data systems have the potential to bring upgraded productivity, as well as to contribute in risk reduction (Chang, et al. 2016).

Figure 10. Relevant literature review by disaster stages (with network c and publication type)

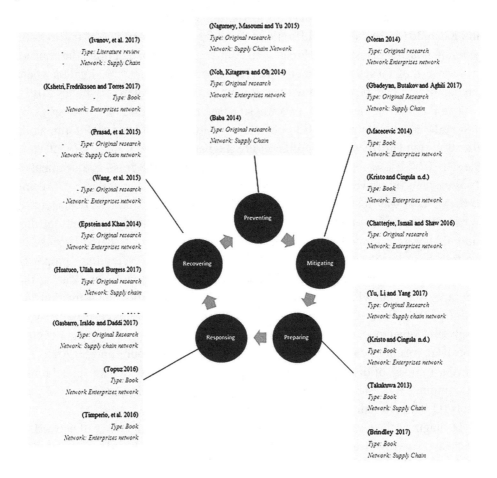

In refining sustainable development based on resilient disaster infrastructure, Big Data environment can help in policy making, and risk strategies development by internalizing currently externalized environmental and societal circumstances (Kshetri, Fredriksson and Torres 2017). Big data can therefore help data scientists and risk strategy makers in: (1) developing and executing guidelines that manage man-made and natural threats (Papadopoulos, et al. 2017); (2) avoiding excess in resources and deprivation of capabilities that can offer sufficient services in situation of crisis (Kshetri, Fredriksson and Torres 2017), (3) watching into disaster analyzing how people and companies respond to downtimes in order to take the right policy that will allow recovery and reestablishing back to regularity (Hashem, et al. 2015), (4)

Big Data can be a good support of valuable information needed to improve prediction and then help in acting proactively to face disasters (Papadopoulos, et al. 2017).

However, academic works has been limited in giving future profits of the role of Big Data in sustainability and more prominently (Hashem, et al. 2015). Although there are works regarding Big Data and disaster management, there have been no publications that use Big Data value-added to elucidate disaster recovery and preparation in enterprises networks (Papadopoulos, et al. 2017). Our work in the present chapter aims to clarify some aspects related to Big Data that could facilitate deployment of our solution, but the approach is not directly based on unstructured data features. More clarifications regarding the proposed approach will be provided in section 3.

Today, Cloud Computing can be perceived as one of the modern dynamic services in the IT for business activities, because of its flexibility (Chang, et al. 2016). However, the problem of disaster planning is more critical in cloud computing, since Cloud Service Providers (CSPs) have to deliver the contracted services to customers even if the system is down (Hashem, et al. 2015).

In the past years, academic works have focused on disaster recovery in cloudified environment, and a substantial amount of literature has been issued; such as (Chang, et al. 2016, Daniel 2014, Hashem, et al. 2015, Kshetri, Fredriksson and Torres 2017). However, these publications reveal a lack in a consensus and detailed analysis of cloud-based disaster recovery plan. To fill this gap, this chapter provides an approach of disaster recovery concepts in the cloudified environments of businesses. We present step-by-step the approach of cross-management of disaster recovery for networked enterprises, in the next section.

3. RESEARCH METHODOLOGY

3.1. Risk Assessment in Networked Context

In the development of Disaster Recovery Plan, the primary function of risk valuation is to encode as many types of disasters as conceivable that a firm may occur, and then to figure out the plan of it will deal with each emergency if it arises (L'Hermitte, et al. 2016). Unfortunately, risk assessments are usually very complex to develop in advance, and very expensive in terms of tests, impact analysis and preparation (Murnane, et al. 206). In addition, the complexity of the collaborative aspect in the network can make the task more tedious (Papadopoulos, et al. 2017).

State-of-the-art regarding risk assessment is plenty: In (Yu, Li and Yang 2017), authors propose a stochastic optimization model that emphasizes the ambiguity in risk preference and probability distribution through supply chain networks. The model is interesting but lacks in applicability and is much closed to the presented case study. Authors in (Noran 2014) proposed a new holistic model for responsivity of recovery teams in collaborative way within networks of enterprises. In (Nagurney, Masoumi and Yu 2015), authors proposed a costs model minimization in recovering process for supply chain networks. In (Epstein and Khan 2014), Authors presented a risk-based approach named Application Impact Analysis (AIA) that is able to consider business key attributes and then provides a model for viewing data, assessing impact, and carrying out key results.

In order to create the most operative plan after a disruption, an enterprise must first study what the would-be disasters are that they could practicably meet, and how each of these might affect their business continuity (Epstein and Khan 2014). This could be settled through Risk Assessment Management (Macecevic 2014). To alleviate this task, we propose a solution to guide in risk assessment integrating prediction method. This approach could be used taken into consideration when preparing a disaster recovery plan.

3.2. Fuzzy Cognitive Maps for Cross-Management

3.2.1. Paradigm of Fuzzy Cognitive Mapping

With the advent of Big Data Analytics (BDA), application of Fuzzy Cognitive Mapping (FCM) is increasing and comes to be useful in the search for the causality between patterns and phenomena (Feyzioglu, Buyukozkan and Ersoy 2017). In modelling, FCM is graph representation of likelihood relationships between concepts (Papageorgiou and Salmeron 2014).

FCM provides an understanding of complex relationships between concepts (also called nodes or events) and represent the components behaviors in the model. Connections weighted by likelihood coefficients on directed arrows represent causal relations between concepts (nodes). The weight value reflects the degree to which the concept is the strength of impact in the system at a specific lap of time. This value is a function of the sum of all upcoming weights multiplied and the value of the original concept at the directly previous state. A threshold function is also introduced to regulate the weighted sums. Weights have values in the interval *[-1, 1]* and increasing values describe the strong likelihood of another concept (strength of causality) where decreasing values indicate weak causality relationship. Figure 11 illustrates an example of some concepts with weighted relationships.

Prediction by FCM can be made through the assessment of the likelihoods between concepts (nodes) (Salmeron and Lopez 2012). The model is derived by labelling the components of the systems that are causalities values in relationships between its components (Papageorgiou and Salmeron 2014).

Figure 11. Example of FCM

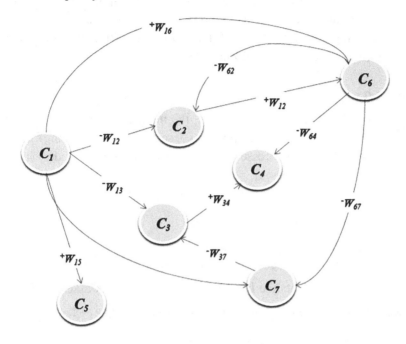

As proposed in modeling process in some research works such as (Salmeron and Lopez 2012), (Wei, Lu and Yanchun 2008), (Salmeron and Lopez 2012), (Zhang, Zhu and Zhao 2016), and so forth, we opt to use FCM in analysis of causality likelihood to the context of enterprises.

3.2.2. Fuzzy Cognitive Map for Risk Assessment

An FCM model can help in identifying and access risks that may occur due to several shortcomings that impact a given enterprise (Zhang, Zhu and Zhao 2016). Furthermore, it can also be generalized to help in complex assessment of risks in the entire network of a given enterprise.

The Disaster Recovery Plan process-based model, as described above (section 3.1.1), can be transcoded into a FCM model. In such modeling task, processes and sub-processes are represented by concepts (nodes), where likelihood relationships between them may be weighted. Administrators, and staff involved in disaster procedures can help in assessing weights of the different causal-links for each concept. In this study, we carefully considered the disaster recovery plan processes/ sub-processes to prepare integrating weights in the FCM.

When applying FCM in the context of processes/sub-processes of the Disaster plan; the weights and the activation function value (threshold function) vary for each enterprise with regards to the nature of the business, the strategic aims, the budget, and the priorities (Zhang, Zhu and Zhao 2016).

Formulation

Behind the graphical schema of the FCM, the mathematical model in context of processes/ sub-processes of Disaster plan is as described in the following formulation:

Suppose the set P of N processes/sub-processes (concepts or nodes) (number of all processes and sub-processes).

$$P = \left\{ P_i \right\}_{1 \leq i \leq N} \tag{3}$$

For each process/sub-process p_i, there is a state vector V of N weights w_{ij}. A weight value w_{ij} represents the likelihood relationship (risk assessment) between the processes/sub-processes p_i and p_j in the interval rang e$\left[-1, +1\right]$.

$$\forall p_i \in P, \exists V = \left\{ w_{ij} \right\}_{1 \leq j \leq N} \tag{4}$$

with

$$w_{ij} \in \left[-1, +1\right], w_{ii} = 0 \tag{5}$$

This model state can be presented using a what-if matrix W of $N \times N$ weights w_{ij}.

$$W = \begin{bmatrix} w_{11} & w_{12} & \cdots & w_{1n} \\ w_{21} & w_{22} & \cdots & w_{2n} \\ \cdots & \cdots & \cdots & \cdots \\ w_{n1} & w_{n1} & \cdots & w_{nn} \end{bmatrix} = \begin{bmatrix} 0 & w_{12} & \cdots & w_{1n} \\ w_{21} & 0 & \cdots & w_{2n} \\ \cdots & \cdots & \cdots & \cdots \\ w_{n1} & w_{n1} & \cdots & 0 \end{bmatrix} \tag{6}$$

Applicative Example of P1-P3 Processes

To illustrate the approach and formulation of FCM, we model the risk assessment in the restricted model of both processes *{P1, P3}*, and their respective sub-processes *{P11, P12, P13, P14, P15, P31, P32, P33, P34}*. Figure 12 shows the schema of FCM.

The what-if matrix *W* is *11 X 11* and should be as following:

$$
W = \begin{bmatrix}
W_{1-1} & W_{1-11} & W_{1-12} & W_{1-13} & W_{1-14} & W_{1-15} & W_{1-3} & W_{1-31} & W_{1-32} & W_{1-33} & W_{1-34} \\
W_{11-1} & W_{11-11} & W_{11-12} & W_{11-13} & W_{11-14} & W_{11-15} & W_{11-3} & W_{11-31} & W_{11-32} & W_{11-33} & W_{11-34} \\
W_{12-1} & W_{12-11} & W_{12-12} & W_{12-13} & W_{12-14} & W_{12-15} & W_{12-3} & W_{12-31} & W_{12-32} & W_{12-33} & W_{12-34} \\
W_{13-1} & W_{13-11} & W_{13-12} & W_{13-13} & W_{13-14} & W_{13-15} & W_{13-3} & W_{13-31} & W_{13-32} & W_{13-33} & W_{13-34} \\
W_{14-1} & W_{14-11} & W_{14-12} & W_{14-13} & W_{14-14} & W_{14-15} & W_{14-3} & W_{14-31} & W_{14-32} & W_{14-33} & W_{14-34} \\
W_{15-1} & W_{15-11} & W_{15-12} & W_{15-13} & W_{15-14} & W_{15-15} & W_{15-3} & W_{15-31} & W_{15-32} & W_{15-33} & W_{15-34} \\
W_{3-1} & W_{3-11} & W_{3-12} & W_{3-13} & W_{3-14} & W_{3-15} & W_{3-3} & W_{3-31} & W_{3-32} & W_{3-33} & W_{3-34} \\
W_{31-1} & W_{31-11} & W_{31-12} & W_{31-13} & W_{31-14} & W_{31-15} & W_{31-3} & W_{31-31} & W_{31-32} & W_{31-33} & W_{31-34} \\
W_{32-1} & W_{32-11} & W_{32-12} & W_{32-13} & W_{32-14} & W_{32-15} & W_{32-3} & W_{32-31} & W_{32-32} & W_{32-33} & W_{32-34} \\
W_{33-1} & W_{33-11} & W_{33-12} & W_{33-13} & W_{33-14} & W_{33-15} & W_{33-3} & W_{33-31} & W_{33-32} & W_{33-33} & W_{33-34} \\
W_{34-1} & W_{34-11} & W_{34-12} & W_{34-13} & W_{34-14} & W_{34-15} & W_{34-3} & W_{34-31} & W_{34-32} & W_{34-33} & W_{34-34}
\end{bmatrix}
$$

$$(7)$$

Figure 12. Example of FCM applied to disaster recovery plan; the processes and sub-processes: {P1, P3, P11, P12, P13, P14, P15, P31, P32, P33, P34}

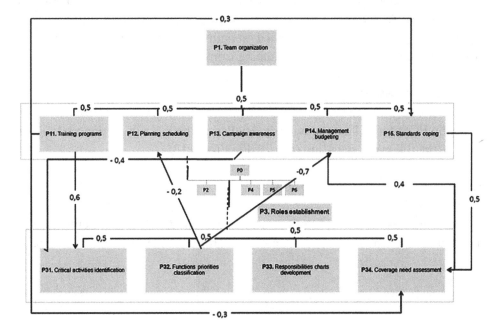

$$W = \begin{bmatrix} 0 & 0 & 0 & & 0 & 0 & 0 & 0 & 0 & 0 & 0 & 0 \\ 0,5 & 0 & 0 & 0 & -0,3 & 0 & 0,6 & 0 & 0 & 0 & -0,2 \\ 0,5 & 0 & 0 & & 0 & 0 & 0 & 0 & 0 & 0 & 0 & 0 \\ 0,5 & 0 & 0 & 0 & 0 & 0 & 0 & -0,3 & 0 & 0 & 0 \\ 0,5 & 0 & 0 & 0 & 0 & 0 & 0 & 0 & 0 & 0 & 0,4 \\ 0,5 & 0 & 0 & 0 & 0 & 0 & 0 & 0 & 0 & 0 & 0,5 \\ 0 & 0 & 0 & 0 & 0 & 0 & 0 & 0 & 0 & 0 & 0 \\ 0 & 0 & 0 & 0 & 0 & 0 & 0,5 & 0 & 0 & 0 & 0 \\ 0 & 0 & -0,2 & 0 & -0,7 & 0 & 0,5 & 0 & 0 & 0 & 0 \\ 0 & 0 & 0 & 0 & 0 & 0 & 0,5 & 0 & 0 & 0 & 0 \\ 0 & 0 & 0 & 0 & 0 & 0 & 0,5 & 0 & 0 & 0 & 0 \end{bmatrix} \tag{8}$$

3.3. Aggregated Fuzzy Cognitive Maps for Risk Cross-Management

Applying FCM to face the issue of risk management is not new. Many other research works attempted to introduce the approach to understand and model disaster management, such as: (Singh and Chudasama 2017), and (Szwed, Skrzynski and Chmiel 2016). However, as far as we know, no one tried to generalize the concept of FCM to the context of cross-management and collaboration aspect in networks of enterprises. As these research studies, we propose a method of generalization (aggregation) of the FCM to be applied on entire network of enterprises. Thus, a cross-management of the Disaster planning is insured.

3.3.1. Formulation

Based on FCM formulation previously detailed in the last sub-section (3.2.2), we propose the following steps, also clarified in Figure 13:

Step 1: Extraction of individual FCMs.

Once the stakeholders of the business line in the network are identified, the individual FCM of processes and sub-processes are extracted from each Disaster Plan.

Figure 13. Steps of FCM aggregation in the proposed approach

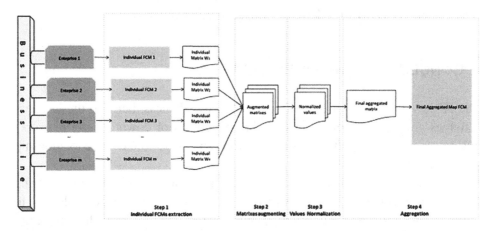

Step 2: Augmenting what-if matrixes.

The individual maps extracted in step 1 are gathered, combined and augmented by auditioning them in superposed manner producing a single matrix.

Step 3: Normalization of values.

Weights of the single matrix obtained in step 2 have to be normalized according to the number of stakeholders who supported it (suppose k stakeholders), then normalized weights (Suppose a_{ij}) is computed in the formula:

$$a_{ij} = \sum_{i=0}^{k} p_i \cdot a_i / k \qquad (9)$$

with

$$\sum_{i=0}^{k} p_i = 1 \qquad (10)$$

Step 4: Aggregation into one what-if matrix.

The normalized values constitute a single normalized matrix (suppose A) which has to be published to all stakeholders and updated regularly.

4. CONCLUSION AND OPEN VIEWS

The IT downtimes do not only affect employees' idleness, but also the business activities are impacted on it. In this chapter, effects of downtimes in networks businesses are depicted. Based on these effects and the related costs, a relationship is built in generic model.

In large-scaled environments of Big Data and Cloud Computing, recovering Information Technology (IT) infrastructure after an outage becomes complex due to the large demand of information and the high scalability, in addition to the complexity of relationships between enterprises themselves. This also challenges enterprises the ability to manage disasters. Therefore, this chapter proposed an interdependency risk assessment method that is based on a semi-quantitative approach; the Fuzzy Cognitive Map (FCM). The FCM is an adequate method that can be used to provide promises for what-if investigation scenarios of risks analysis. In addition to be a conventional predictive method, it can help in understanding the vulnerability in each part, and each division of enterprises in the network.

The key finding of this chapter is a cross-management model able to predict causality relationships between disruption patterns and risk phenomena among the enterprises network. On the other hand, outcome of this study may help in preventing enterprises that are involved in business linkages, from massive financial damages.

In the continuation of this work, the proposed approach can be applied on a real-world industrial case, although the collection of data seems to be a tedious and time-consuming task. Thus, a confirmatory analysis may reinforce the hypothesis of our approach.

In the future open studies, the researchers can explore in the way that enterprises do to keep the system safe from downtimes. Further, to make the assessment model more accurate, researchers can apply the approach in a network of enterprises, gathering more details of downtime outcomes and the cost issues. An industrial case-study would be suitable in this situation. Additional research perspective can be to what scope does the organization profits from the disaster management program. Despite preventing for the potential downtimes can considerably reduce or avoid the harms, the investments in the planning programs can be colossal.

REFERENCES

Agostinho, C., et al. (n.d.). Towards a sustainable interoperability in networked enterprise information systems: Trends of knowledge and model-driven technology. *Computers in Industry*, *79*, 64-76.

Al Hamed, T., & Alenezi, M. (2016). Business Continuity Management & Disaster Recovery Capabilities in Saudi Arabia ICT Businesses. *International Journal of Hybrid Information Technology*, *9*(11), 99–126. doi:10.14257/ijhit.2016.9.11.10

Baba, H., Adachi, I., Takabayashi, H., Nagatomo, N., Nakasone, S., Matsumoto, H., & Shimano, T. (2014). Introductory study on Disaster Risk Assessment and Area Business Continuity Planning in industry agglomerated areas in the ASEAN. *IDRiM Journal*, *3*(2), 184–195. doi:10.5595/idrim.2013.0069

Becker, M., Goldszal, A., Detal, J., Gronlund-Jacob, J., & Epstein, R. (2015). Managing a Multisite Academic–Private Radiology Practice Reading Environment: Impact of IT Downtimes on Enterprise Efficiency. *Journal of the American College of Radiology*, *12*(6), 630–637. doi:10.1016/j.jacr.2014.11.002 PMID:25686641

Bohtan, A., Vrat, P., & Vij, A. K. (2016). *Peculiarities of Disaster Management in a High-Altitude Area*. Managing Humanitarian Logistics. doi:10.1007/978-81-322-2416-7_19

Brazelton, N. C., & Lyons, A. M. (2016). Downtime and Disaster Recovery for Health Information Systems. In *Health Informatics-E-Book: An Interprofessional Approach*. Elsevier.

Brindley, C. (2017). *Supply chain risk*. Ashgate Publishing.

Chang, V., Ramachandran, M., Yao, Y., Kuo, Y. H., & Li, C. S. (2016). A resiliency framework for an enterprise cloud. *International Journal of Information Management*, *36*(1), 155–166. doi:10.1016/j.ijinfomgt.2015.09.008

Chatterjee, R., Ismail, N., & Shaw, R. (2016). *Identifying Priorities of Asian Small- and Medium-Scale Enterprises for Building Disaster Resilience*. Urban Disasters and Resilience in Asia. doi:10.1016/B978-0-12-802169-9.00012-4

Daniel, W. K. (2014). Challenges on privacy and reliability in cloud computing security. *Information Science, Electronics and Electrical Engineering (ISEEE), 2014 International Conference*, 1181-1187. doi:10.1109/InfoSEEE.2014.6947857

DiStefano, B., & Hawkins, B. (2016). Achieving top-quartile reliability returns. *Asset Management & Maintenance Journal*, *29*(2), 18.

Epstein, B., & Khan, D. C. (2014). Application impact analysis: A risk-based approach to business continuity and disaster recovery. *Journal of Business Continuity & Emergency Planning*, *7*(3), 230–237. PMID:24578024

Feyzioglu, O., Buyukozkan, G., & Ersoy, M. S. (2017). Supply chain risk analysis with fuzzy cognitive maps. *Industrial Engineering and Engineering Management, 2007 IEEE International Conference*, 1447-1451.

Franke, U., Holm, H., & König, J. (2014). The distribution of time to recovery of enterprise IT services. *IEEE Transactions on Reliability*, *63*(4), 858–867. doi:10.1109/TR.2014.2336051

Franke, U., Johnson, P., & König, J. (2014). An architecture framework for enterprise IT service availability analysis. *Software & Systems Modeling*, *13*(4), 1417–1445. doi:10.1007/s10270-012-0307-3

Gartner. (2017). Retrieved from www.gartner.com

Gasbarro, F., Iraldo, F., & Daddi, T. (2017). The drivers of multinational enterprises' climate change strategies: A quantitative study on climate-related risks and opportunities. *Journal of Cleaner Production*, *160*, 8–26. doi:10.1016/j.jclepro.2017.03.018

Gbadeyan, A., Butakov, S., & Aghili, S. (2017). IT governance and risk mitigation approach for private cloud adoption: Case study of provincial healthcare provider. *Annales des Télécommunications*, *72*(5-6), 347–357. doi:10.1007/s12243-017-0568-5

Gupta, Kapur, & Kumar. (2016). Exploring disaster recovery parameters in an enterprise application. In *International Conference of Innovation and Challenges in Cyber Security (ICICCS-INBUSH)*. Greater Noida, India: IEEE.

Hashem, I. A. T., Yaqoob, I., Anuar, N. B., Mokhtar, S., Khan, A., & Gani, S. U. (2015). The rise of "big data" on cloud computing: Review and open research issues. *Information Systems*, *47*, 98–115. doi:10.1016/j.is.2014.07.006

Hiller, M., Bone, E. A., & Timmins, M. L. (2015). Healthcare system resiliency: The case for taking disaster plans further—Part 2. *Journal of Business Continuity & Emergency Planning*, *8*(4), 356–375. PMID:25990980

Huatuco, L. H., Ullah, G. S., & Burgess, T. F. (2017). Supply Chain Major Disruptions and Sustainability Metrics: A Case Study. *International Conference on Sustainable Design and Manufacturing*, 185-192. doi:10.1007/978-3-319-57078-5_18

Ivanov, D., Dolgui, A., Sokolov, B., & Ivanova, M. (2017). Literature review on disruption recovery in the supply chain. *International Journal of Production Research*, 1–17. doi:10.1080/00207543.2017.1343507

Javadi, B., Kondo, D., Iosup, A., & Epema, D. (2013). The Failure Trace Archive: Enabling the comparison of failure measurements and models of distributed systems. *Journal of Parallel and Distributed Computing*, *73*(8), 1208–1223. doi:10.1016/j.jpdc.2013.04.002

Klafft, M., & Ziegler, H. G. (2014). A concept and prototype for the integration of multi-channel disaster alert systems. *Proceedings of the 7th Euro American Conference on Telematics and Information Systems*, 20. doi:10.1145/2590651.2590669

Kristo, Filipovic, & Cingula. (n.d.). Methodological aspects of measuring business resilience. *Economic and Social Development Proceedings*.

Kshetri, N., Fredriksson, T., & Torres, D. C. R. (2017). *Big Data and Cloud Computing for Development: Lessons from Key Industries and Economies in the Global South*. Taylor & Francis.

L'Hermitte, C., Tatham, P., Brooks, B., & Bowles, M. (2016). Supply chain agility in humanitarian protracted operations. *Journal of Humanitarian Logistics and Supply Chain Management*, *6*(2), 173–201. doi:10.1108/JHLSCM-09-2015-0037

Lam, J. (2014). *Enterprise risk management: from incentives to controls*. John Wiley & Sons. doi:10.1002/9781118836477

Levy, J., Yu, P., & Prizzia, R. (2016). Economic Disruptions, Business Continuity Planning and Disaster Forensic Analysis: The Hawaii Business Recovery Center (HIBRC) Project. Disaster Forensics, 315-334. doi:10.1007/978-3-319-41849-0_13

Li, G., Zhang, Q., Feng, Z., & Wang, W. (2016). A disaster recovery solution based on heterogeneous storage. *Journal of Intelligent & Fuzzy Systems*, *31*(4), 2249–2256. doi:10.3233/JIFS-169065

Li, Q. (2016). *Estimation of the costs of information system downtime in organisations: underlying threats, effects and cost factors* (Master's thesis). University of Twente.

Lockamy, A. III. (2014). Assessing disaster risks in supply chains. *Industrial Management & Data Systems*, *114*(5), 755–777. doi:10.1108/IMDS-11-2013-0477

Lyu, H., Li, P., Yan, R., Qian, H., & Sheng, B. (2016). High-availability deployment for large enterprises. *Progress in Informatics and Computing (PIC), 2016 International Conference,* 503-507.

Macecevic, D. (2014). Enterprise risk management-priority of export-oriented firm in emerging economy. *Economic and Social DevelopmentProceedings*.

Miller, H. E., & Engemann, K. J. (2015). Threats to the electric grid and the impact on organisational resilience. *International Journal of Business Continuity and Risk Management*, *6*(1), 1–16. doi:10.1504/IJBCRM.2015.070348

Mohan, S., & Bakshi, N. (2017). Supply Chain Resilience-Epidemiological Characterization. *History (London)*.

Montshiwa, A. L., Nagahira, A., & Ishida, S. (2016). Modifying Business Continuity Plan (BCP) Towards an Effective Auto-Mobile Business Continuity Management (BCM): A Quantitative Approach. *Journal of Disaster Research*, *11*(4), 691–698. doi:10.20965/jdr.2016.p0691

Murnane, Simpson, & Jongman. (n.d.). Understanding risk: what makes a risk assessment successful? *International Journal of Disaster Resilience in the Built Environment*, *7*(2), 186-200.

Nagurney, A., Masoumi, A. H., & Yu, M. (2015). *An integrated disaster relief supply chain network model with time targets and demand uncertainty* (pp. 287–318). Regional Science Matters. doi:10.1007/978-3-319-07305-7_15

Närman, P., Franke, U., König, J., Buschle, M., & Ekstedt, M. (2014). Enterprise architecture availability analysis using fault trees and stakeholder interviews. *Enterprise Information Systems*, *8*(1), 1–25. doi:10.1080/17517575.2011.647092

Noh, H. W., Kitagawa, K., & Oh, Y. S. (2014). Concepts of Disaster Prevention Design for Safety in the Future Society. *International Journal of Contents*, *10*(1), 54–61. doi:10.5392/IJoC.2014.10.1.054

Noran, O. (2014). Collaborative disaster management: An interdisciplinary approach. *Computers in Industry*, *65*(6), 1032–1040. doi:10.1016/j.compind.2014.04.003

Ojha, D., Salimath, M., & D'Souza, D. (2014). Disaster immunity and performance of service firms: The influence of market acuity and supply network partnering. *International Journal of Production Economics*, *147*, 385–397. doi:10.1016/j.ijpe.2013.02.029

Papadopoulos, T., Gunasekaran, A., Dubey, R., Altay, N., Childe, S. J., & Fosso-Wamba, S. (2017). The role of Big Data in explaining disaster resilience in supply chains for sustainability. *Journal of Cleaner Production*, *142*, 1108–1118. doi:10.1016/j.jclepro.2016.03.059

Papageorgiou & Salmeron. (2014). Methods and algorithms for fuzzy cognitive map-based modeling. *Fuzzy Cognitive Maps for Applied Sciences and Engineering*, 1-28.

Prasad, S., Su, H. C., Altay, N., & Tata, J. (2015). Building disaster-resilient micro enterprises in the developing world. *International Journal of Production Economics*, *39*(3), 447–466. PMID:25546436

Rieser, H., Dorfinger, P., Nomikos, V., & Papataxiarhis, V. (2015). Sensor interoperability for disaster management. *Sensors Applications Symposium (SAS)*, 1-6.

Sahebjamnia, N., Torabi, S. A., & Mansouri, S. A. (2015). Integrated business continuity and disaster recovery planning: Towards organizational resilience. *European Journal of Operational Research*, *242*(1), 261–273. doi:10.1016/j.ejor.2014.09.055

Salmeron, J. L., & Lopez, C. (2012). Forecasting risk impact on ERP maintenance with augmented fuzzy cognitive maps. *IEEE Transactions on Software Engineering*, *38*(2), 439–452. doi:10.1109/TSE.2011.8

Saltoglu, R., Humaira, N., & Inalhan, G. (2016). Scheduled maintenance and downtime cost in aircraft maintenance management. *International Journal of Mechanical, Aerospace, Industrial, Mechatronic and Manufacturing Engineering*, *10*(3), 580–585.

Sarmiento, J. P., Hoberman, G., Jerath, M., & Jordao, G. F. (2016). Enterprise engineering and management at the crossroads. *Computers in Industry*, *79*, 87–102. doi:10.1016/j.compind.2015.07.010

Singh, P. K., & Chudasama, H. (2017). Assessing impacts and community preparedness to cyclones: A fuzzy cognitive mapping approach. *Climatic Change*, 1–18.

Sullivan, J. (2017). Considering employee needs during a catastrophe requires innovative recovery plans: Why traditional workplace recovery solutions are outdated. *Journal of Business Continuity & Emergency Planning*, *10*(3), 259–267. PMID:28222849

Szwed, P., Skrzynski, P., & Chmiel, W. (2016). Risk assessment for a video surveillance system based on Fuzzy Cognitive Maps. *Multimedia Tools and Applications*, *75*(17), 10667–10690. doi:10.1007/s11042-014-2047-6

Tabikh, M. (2014). *Downtime cost and Reduction analysis: Survey results* (Thesis of Master degree). Mälardalen University, School of Innovation, Design and Engineering, Innovation and Product Realisation.

Takakuwa, S. (2013). *A perspective on manufacturing and environmental management*. Daaam International Scientific.

Tammepuu, A., Kaart, T., & Sepp, K. (2016). Emergency preparedness and response in ISO 14001 enterprises: An Estonian case study. *International Journal of Emergency Management*, *12*(1), 55–69. doi:10.1504/IJEM.2016.074879

Timperio, G., Panchal, G. B., De Souza, R., Goh, M., & Samvedi, A. (2016). Decision making framework for emergency response preparedness: A supply chain resilience approach. *Management of Innovation and Technology (ICMIT), 2016 IEEE International Conference,* 78-82. doi:10.1109/ICMIT.2016.7605011

Topuz, Ç. (2016). Crisis management and strategies in tourism industry. *Proceedings Book.*

Wang, Ramasamy, Harper, Plattier, & Viswanathan. (2015). Experiences with Building Disaster Recovery for Enterprise-Class Clouds. In *Dependable Systems and Networks (DSN), 45th Annual IEEE/IFIP International Conference.* Rio de Janeiro, Brazil: IEEE.

Wei, Z., Lu, L., & Yanchun, Z. (2008). Using fuzzy cognitive time maps for modeling and evaluating trust dynamics in the virtual enterprises. *Expert Systems with Applications*, *35*(4), 1583–1592. doi:10.1016/j.eswa.2007.08.071

Witty, R. J. (2016). *Cool Vendors in Business Continuity Management and IT Resilience, 2016. IT Regular Report.* Gartner.

Yeboah, Feng, Daniel, & Joseph. (2014). Agricultural Supply Chain Risk Identification-A Case Finding from Ghana. *Journal of Management and Strategy*, *5*(2), 31.

Yu, G., Li, F., & Yang, Y. (2017). Robust supply chain networks design and ambiguous risk preferences. *International Journal of Production Research*, *55*(4), 1168–1182. doi:10.1080/00207543.2016.1232499

Zhang, W., Zhu, Y., & Zhao, Y. (2016). Fuzzy Cognitive Map Approach for Trust-Based Partner Selection in Virtual Enterprise. *Journal of Computational and Theoretical Nanoscience*, *13*(1), 349–360. doi:10.1166/jctn.2016.4812

Chapter 13

A Survey of Probabilistic Broadcast Schemes in Mobile Ad Hoc Networks

Muneer Bani Yassein
Jordan University of Science and Technology, Jordan

Mohammed Shatnawi
Jordan University of Science and Technology, Jordan

Nesreen l-Qasem
Jordan University of Science and Technology, Jordan

ABSTRACT

Mobile ad hoc networks (MANETs) is a collection of wireless mobile devices that dynamically communicates with each other as a self-configuration without the need of centralized administration or fixed infrastructure. In this paper, we interested to introduce the different broadcast methods based on the probabilistic scheme which is simple implement code with speed broadcast and to reduce a storm broadcast problem effects and to alleviate redundancy through rebroadcast by using different routing protocols such as (AODV, DSR, LAR, PAR) that we interested in MANETs.

INTRODUCTION

MANETs occupies the large importance of different applications such as emergency operations, military, disaster recovery and other applications (Bani Yassein & Khaoua, 2007); which supports infrastructure-less network, mobility, dynamically topology feature, and also rapid communication with high performance (Bani

DOI: 10.4018/978-1-5225-3029-9.ch013

Yassein, Masadeh, Nimer, & Al-Dubai, 2010). Broadcast is the main operation in MANETs which keeps a track of connectivity and stability and also helps management procedures used to support updating of control information and exchanging of control information by using schemes of routing protocol such as proactive (table-driven), reactive (on-demand) and hybrid in MANETs (Ade, & Tijare, 2010; Manickam, Baskar, Girija, & Manimegalai, 2011; Gill, Anju, & Diwaker, 2012)]; because it's important operation we interest to search broadcast methods based on probabilistic scheme help us to reduce a storm broadcast problem which causes many of problems such as contention, collision, duplicate messages (Bani Yassein, Ould-Khaoua, & Papanastasiou, 2005; Bani Yassein, Khalaf, & Al-Dubai, 2010) causes waste of resources and more of the traffic load. Each method based on probabilistic scheme has advantages and disadvantages.

The rest of the survey is organized as follows. Section 2 gives a review about probabilistic broadcast schemes, in section 3 given Comparison between Probabilistic Broadcast Schemes, in section 4 given a conclusion.

PROBABILISTIC BROADCAST SCHEMES

This algorithm proposed a novel density depends on a flooding scheme that a source sends a packet to all nodes in MANETs; it mainly based on the area density(dense, low), if the average of neighbors for the node x is larger than the threshold as a standard value, x takes "β type" and gets a high probability that rebroadcast without delay; if the average of neighbors for x is smaller than the threshold, x takes "α type" and gets a small probability that waits a time duration before rebroadcast; this approach interested in broadcast with less routing overhead and collision but the bandwidth may be lost if the intensity is limited in two levels (dense, low).

This approach proposed new route discovery algorithm named Efficient and Dynamic Probabilistic Broadcasting (EDPB) concerns to solve the Broadcast Storm problem AODV, it is implementing simulation on Global Mobile Simulator GPS; this algorithm depends on the knowledge and probabilistic that dynamically adjusted based on both local neighbors and changing the neighbors of node; initially the node x is hearing a message then getting number of neighbors (n) for x to compare with average node (n bar) typically in general network, the result either it implies the probability is higher (n < n bar) in low density or it implies the probability is lower (n > n bar) in high density; it supports main performance evaluation metrics such as reducing end-to-end delay, but it can't cover type of zones such as the density of medium zone Reference.

This algorithm depends on getting the information that is collecting by broadcasting "Hello" packet every second for only one hop to calculate the number of the nodes N in the networks, and the minimum average (avg min) of neighbors and also maximum average of neighbors (avg max); then it compares N with avg min, if (N < avg min) this implies N in low sparse region and the probability is higher if (avgmax $\leq$n<avg) this implies N in medium sparse ; if (avg$\leq$n<avgmax) this implies medium density; if (n$\geq$avgmax) this implies N in high density. This algorithm decreased of a huge amount of flooding packets and delay of RREQ packets, so it consequently keeps the time and cost, however can't support all Routing protocol and HELLO packets do not provide accurate information about the number of neighbors can pray to my god to marry, maybe happen impossible.

This paper proposed probability approaches such as (fixed, adjusted, smart) probabilistic with Dynamic Source Routing (DSR) algorithm to solve a broadcast storm problem. this approach using neighbor's information and the current state of the node and also general network's information to take more accuracy of routing decision, this method take into account four degrees of density: sparse area with high probability, medium sparse area with a medium high probability, medium dense area with medium low probability, high dense area with low probability. Which reduces of contention, broadcast storm problem and it develops on the performance of network at higher network area (e.g., 1000×1000) and can't use location service such as GPS design; however, it needs to calculate additional information which constitutes an extra burden on MANET.

Efficient Power Aware broadcasts (EPAB) that combined between power aware based and dynamic probability-based approaches based on Power Aware Routing (PAR) Protocol, it works when it receives the message; which calculates the degree of n node x and gets power field for each node as an immediate neighbor then it calculates the average both nodes and powers for x, finally it compares average nodes and average powers with both typically average node and typically average power field, if the result is less, it shows x in a low degree, so the probability of rebroadcast will be high; otherwise it shows x in a high degree, so the probability of rebroadcast will be low; this approach keeps both the battery capacity and bandwidth.

This paper collected advantages both probabilistic and packet energy, it employs threshold random delay and node's current remaining energy strength using AODV protocol which is broadcast Route Request REEQ to combine packet energy information and add its additional information to REEQ format(such as a number of received packet), then it uses modified REEQ packet to take of decision the probability depends on broadcasting mechanisms, simulation results show technique improves the performance broadcasting and reduces of overhead in network control.

This article proposes the modified Bayesian probability approach based on extended AODV (AODV EXT_BP) to transfer RREQ message to reduce routing overhead with better energy efficiency by calculating a probability according to the neighbor's density as the posterior probability which has two majors: firstly, when we have 5 nodes or less, the forward probability is 100%; secondly the forward probability depends on both the number of neighbors and the minimum expected neighbors. However, it needs to calculate additional information that supposes all nodes have a location service as GPS.

A novel adaptive scheme named Fuzzy Logic Probabilistic FLoP and FLOPs schemes depend on Fuzzy logic to alter hello time interval with frequency adaptivity according to the network conditions and fuzzy approach to achieve optimum results for this algorithm that chooses its rebroadcast decision based on a probability model; simulation results shows whenever the density of region increases, performance will be degradation in FLOP but it contributed to improve control overhead and delay and also speed.

A dynamic probabilistic broadcasting scheme cross-layer design for MANETs (DPBSC) to solve a storm broadcast problem, by using cross layer design which allows isolation routing layers to participate received signal power information at MAC layer with conservation on separation between layers for calculating additional information and then to adjust probability of rebroadcast packets (flooding routing layer), the simulation results prove reduction of: the redundant retransmission, contention, collision in the networks.

This approach concerned to study both network mobility and the effect of the network density on probabilistic methods(fixed (p1), multiple thresholds (p2, p3, p4)) with the Pessimistic Linear Exponential Backoff (PLEB) algorithm to compare with MAC standard, this algorithm depends on the assumption that congestion lead to the failure in transmission process, before the next transmission PLEP increments the contention window size (CW) exponentially to avoid redundant increasing on the back off and to reduce waiting time, after a number of exponential increments PLEP begin increasing linearly, by ns-2 network simulator the result shows the PLEP overcome standard MAC highly (in dense networks the normalized routing load, routing packets, delay).

Adaptive Broadcasting Scheme (ABS) as a method concerned to solve BSP, it collects benefits of both counter and probabilistic scheme, this method using one-to-all model to rebroadcast a RREQ packet based on flooding technique, when a node receives a RREQ packet then it gets both local information by a broadcasting HELLO packet for one hope and global information through transmission range, through this information it adjusts the forwarding probability that sets by run time code, according to results of evaluation performance by NS-2 .34 under different operating conditions shows this algorithm reduced of collision rate and routing overhead.

A novel broadcasting counter-based algorithm (Inspired Counter-Based Broadcasting) (DSRICB) that suggests a dynamic counter-based threshold using within (DSR) instead of using fixed counter that causes blind-flooding, initially it works re-broadcast "Hello" packets to get information secondly it calculates the counter(threshold) to count the received packets number and counts another threshold depending on the status of neighbors, which dividing density of zones to five degrees (sparse, medium, dense, extra, ultra-degree) and also getting the degree n of node x then it compares the degree n with zones to get a value of threshold; which aims to increase the reachability hits with reducing of delay and routing overhead, on the other hand it doesn't include broad range of routing protocols and different mobility mode.

A new dynamic counter-based algorithm with AODV protocol using a threshold dynamic by a simple flooding to solve the broadcast storm problem, it rebroadcast a message when the number of duplicated packet is less than threshold, which depends on three dynamic thresholds to determine density of area (dense, medium distribution or sparse regions) using information neighbors, and then it compares the total number of neighbors with the average number of neighbors to define a threshold to take a decision of rebroadcast, according the ns-2 network simulator to evaluate performance of this approach, it develops on delivery ratio and enhance the throughput of network but it needs additional information about neighbors of node to take a decision .

This paper suggests Position-aware Counter based Broadcast PCB, which combines pros both position-based and counter-based; PCB approach using information location of destination by a source node can be calculated Expected Additional coverage EAC, this Mechanism has two-tier threshold values of counters of nodes are putting in EAC, then The source node compares between EAC and the first tier threshold, if EAC is less than first tier threshold, the node doesn't rebroadcast packet and also for all next reception it will be discard; otherwise it compares between EAC and the second tier threshold to put an suitable RAD to the node and to set a counter C to one before delivery; this approach improved saved rebroadcast and reachability but it didn't take more than two threshold values.

This paper proposes an angle-aware broadcasting algorithm as a solution for storm problem, it mainly depends on angle covered between a node and its neighbors (as a distance between receiver and sender) so it gets information from both the sender by own position and position information and the receiver by the global positional system(GPS) or any other localization techniques; all this information used dynamically to adjust a probability value to take decision rebroadcast for node based on the cover angle, if it is small, the probability is high; otherwise it is low; this algorithm reduced from number of transmissions and improved reliability, but delivery ratios are higher in dynamic networks and the power consumption along the cost of using GPS and also may increase latency.

A Directive Location Aided Routing (DLAR) protocol which is to promote the Location-Aided Routing (LAR) protocol used to get location information, by GPS DLAR can get node position, then it calculates its moving direction to select the relay node, DLAR Protocol depends on four principles: the first principle shows all nodes uses the same routing path that have the same moving Direction and the speed difference to protect the route more steady, the second principle it uses AODV (route discovery) on above LAR protocol, then it chooses the next relay node, the third principle which uses AODV local repair mechanism for finding the destination node in the disconnect site, the fourth principle that restricts the range of RREQ broadcast area to avoid the storm problem, this approach needs more bandwidth to increase packet delivery, on other hand it reduces storm problem largely.

This approach suggests a reliable broadcasting algorithm depends on mainly efficient forward node selection mechanism which is a sender-based algorithm, in this algorithm a sender used a greedy approach to broadcast packets, as example the node x chooses a subset of neighbors and calculates its weights (the summation of its distance and neighbor's battery lifetime) to forward the packets according of probability from top to low, and using Mac layer to schedule a broadcast to cover 2-hop neighbors, The other hand used Negative Acknowledgement (NACK) mechanism for knowing reliability for each non forwarding nodes and as a method to decrease: a storm problem, ACK implosion, forwarding, control overhead.

COMPARISON BETWEEN PROBABILISTIC BROADCAST SCHEMES

Reactive protocols (known as On-demand driven). These Protocols initiate route discovery when a source node request to find a route; this supports: little maintenance, smaller routing overhead, easy of mobility, on demand with the lowest communication overhead but it needs a higher latency such as AODV is characterizing: low connection setup, fast discovery, free loop and it quickly gets routes for new destination and support the best performance with communication but needs many of control overheads cause of many route reply message.

Another reactive protocol (DSR) that reduces route discovery, control overheads and don't need periodic routing messages so it keeps battery power and less network bandwidth and also avoiding routing updates; but needs a longer size of packet header with route length.

Location-Aided Routing (LAR) uses location information for route discovery to reduce the number of routing messages but it is costly because it needs location service such as GPS.

On the other hand, flooding broadcast which is an easy code and includes reachability highly but this is the waste of resources. Efficient Energy such as Power Aware Routing using to reduce minimizing mobile nodes' energy when they are inactive communication.

CONCLUSION

This paper introduces many of broadcast methods based on probabilistic scheme in MANET as an important type supports many of application such as recovery disaster; which is useful for mobility and dynamic topology but has limited resources. so,

Table 1. Comparison between probabilistic methods

Name Research	Characteristics		
	Advantages	Disadvantages	Algorithm
(Natesapillai, Karthikeyan, Palanisamy, & Duraiswamy, 2010)	it helps to reduce collision, power consumption, MAC load and routing load	it can't considerate all degrees of density such as medium	a novel density based flooding scheme
(Dembla, & Chaba, 2010)	1- it reduces the overall routing overhead with improved end-to-end delay 2- it reduces packet collisions and contention in the network	1-It was not a comprehensive as solution for a broadcast storm to all routing protocol such as DSR, only abbreviated on AODV.	Efficient and Dynamic Probabilistic Broadcasting (EDPB)
(Bani Yassein, Khalaf, & Al-Dubai, 2010)	1-it generates much lower routing overhead and end-to-end delay 2-it reduces of the packet collisions and contention in the network 3- it improves the performance of AODV	1-it isn't feasible for all routing protocols 2-it mainly depends on global density measures such as Navg 3- it needs the hello packets for modification of neighborhood information	Smart Probabilistic Broadcasting (SPB)
(Bani Yassein, l-Rushdan, Mardini, & Khamayseh, 2011)	1-It reduces average end-to-end delay and overhead at low speed of nodes (1m/s) 2-it improves performance of higher network 3- it enhances the accuracy of the routing decisions	1-it depends on collecting information so it Consumes Bandwidth and energy	probability with Dynamic Source Routing Protocol (DSR) algorithm
(Vijayakumar, & Poongkuzhali, 2012)	1-it selects an optimal path with suitable bandwidth and battery capacity 2- it doesn't need the use of any additional hardware devices 3- increasing the throughput by decreasing the packet loss	1-It needs additional information about its degree power of neighbors and degree of neighbors	Efficient Power Aware broadcasts (EPAB)
(Nand, Parma, & Sharma, 2011)	1-it enhances broadcasting performance 2-it reduces of overhead, end-to-end delays 3-It is more adaptive to the MANET environment and more reachability and better throughput.	1- it needs to gather energy information of nodes	Probability based Broadcasting Technique
(Kanakaris, Venetis, Ndzi, Ovaliadis, & Yang, 2012)	1- reducing of both routing overhead and the number of rebroadcasts 2-it decreases the power consumption	1- it assumes all nodes have service location such as GPS to collect information, so it is additional cost	AODV_EXT_BP

continued on following page

Table 1. Continued

Name Research	Characteristics		
	Advantages	**Disadvantages**	**Algorithm**
(Liarokapis, Dimitrios, & Shahrabi, 2011)	1- the superiority of FLoPS in terms of control overhead, adaptation capabilities, delay, reachability, speed	1-when increasing the total number of nodes (70 to 90), will there be degradation of FLoP's performance 2- The need for a safety mechanism to be triggered by FLoP in case the network	Fuzzy Logic Probabilistic (FLoP)
(Wang, Shi, Qi, 2010)	1-saved-rebroadcast, it reduces the average packet drop fraction 2-it decreases number of collisions and average end-to-end delay	The probability dynamically in different traffic situations is hard task	A Dynamic Probabilistic Broadcasting Scheme based on Cross-Layer design
(Bani Yassein, Manaseer, Al-hassan, Taye, and A. Y. Al-Dubai, 2010)	1- using the exponential increment improves network throughput 2- to avoid the redundant increasing on the back off 3- PLEP overcome the standard MAC in delay	1-routing packets are high so it is costly 2- In dense networks the result latency is increased with 3P, 2P and Fixed P	the Pessimistic Linear Exponential Backoff (PLEB)
(Bani Yassein, Al-Dubai, & Buchanan, 2010)	1- it is easy to implement as a simple code to design 2- there is no need for additional hardware such as GPS. 3- it reduces network overhead and packets collision	it needs collecting additional information about global and local neighborhood information	Adaptive Broadcasting Scheme (ABS)
(Yassein, & Al-Dubai, 2016)	1- it reduces the broadcast storm problem, redundant packets transmission, collision, and contention 2-it achieves high packets delivery ratio with a reduced level of delay while keeping the routing overhead to a minimum 3- enhance the route discovery operation within reactive routing Protocols	1-it isn't included broad range of routing protocols and different mobility models such as Manhattan Model 2- it needs to wait a random delay time such as RAD in counter based scheme	a novel broadcasting counter-based algorithm, namely Inspired Counter-Based Broadcasting (DSRICB)or DSR-5C
(Wu et., 2010)	1-reducing overhead by 28% for low speed of nodes (1 m/s) 2-reducing average end-to-end delay 3-it achieves substantial improvement of the NRL by 23%	1-it doesn't include ad hoc and vehicular networks 2-in dynamic networks, it is difficult to determine a priori various threshold parameters	a new counter-based broadcasting scheme
(Khan, Ali, Madani, Anwar, & Hayat, 2011)	1-it has improved performance by saved broadcast(SRB) and reachability 2-it reduces of collision problem	1-it needs tools to get location as a major information about nodes 2-just it used two threshold values as region (density, sparse), it didn't take a medium density	Position-aware Counter based Broadcast(PCB)
(Jang, Hung-Chin, &Hung, 2010)	1-. The distance-based scheme may cover a large part of the network 2- it minimizes the number of transmissions 3-improve reliability and packet deliver 3-it doesn't use knowledge information or any complex calculations thereof.	1-it is costly because it may cover a large part of the network so it needs many number of broadcast 2- delivery ratios are higher in dynamic networks 3- it doesn't evaluate the performance algorithm on AODV and DSR algorithms as a routing protocols.	an angle-aware broadcasting algorithm
(Kalpana, Govindaswamy, & Punithavalli, 2012)	1-it reduces the average retransmission redundancy 2-it solves both the broadcast storm problem and the ACK implosion problem 3-it recovers the transmission error locally 4-it increases the broadcast delivery ratio.	1-the receiver-initiated approach which needs a longer delay for detection of a lost packets	A Reliable Broadcasting Algorithm

Table 2. Comparison between methods based on probabilistic scheme

Paper	Probabilistic Scheme				
	Distance	Location	Density	Counter-Based	Energy
(Natesapillai, Karthikeyan, Palanisamy, & Duraiswamy, 2010)			YES		YES
(Dembla, & Chaba, 2010)		YES	YES		
(Bani Yassein, Khalaf, & Al-Dubai, 2010)			YES		
(Bani Yassein, l-Rushdan, Mardini, & Khamayseh, 2011)			YES		
(Vijayakumar, & Poongkuzhali, 2012)			YES		YES
(Nand, Parma, & Sharma, 2011)			YES		YES
(Kanakaris, Venetis, Ndzi, Ovaliadis, & Yang, 2012)[		YES	YES		YES
(Liarokapis, Dimitrios, & Shahrabi, 2011)			YES		
(Wang, Shi, Qi, 2010)			YES		YES
(Bani Yassein, Manaseer, Al-hassan, Taye, and A. Y. Al-Dubai, 2010)			YES	YES	
(Bani Yassein, Al-Dubai, & Buchanan, 2010)			YES	YES	
(Yassein, & Al-Dubai, 2016)			YES	YES	
(Bani Yassein, Nimer, & Al-Dubai, 2011)			YES		YES
(Wu et., 2010)		YES		YES	
(Khan, Ali, Madani, Anwar, & Hayat, 2011)		YES			
(Jang, Hung-Chin, &Hung, 2010)		YES			
(Kalpana, Govindaswamy, & Punithavalli, 2012)	YES				YES

this paper interested in showing methods (such as density, counter-based, location, energy Efficient) help to reduce a storm broadcast problem and trade-offs between metrics of methods according to Requirements of networks.

REFERENCES

Ade S. A., & Tijare P.A. (2010). Performance comparison of AODV, DSDV, OLSR and DSR routing protocols in mobile ad hoc networks. *International Journal of Information Technology and Knowledge Management, 2*, 545-548.

Aljawarneh, S., Aldwairi, M., & Yassein, M. B. (2017). Anomaly-based intrusion detection system through feature selection analysis and building hybrid efficient model. *Journal of Computational Science*. doi:10.1016/j.jocs.2017.03.006

Aljawarneh, S., Yassein, M.B., & Talafha, W.A. (2017). A multithreaded programming approach for multimedia big data: encryption system. *Multimed Tools Appl*. 10.1007/s11042-017-4873-9

Aljawarneh, S. A., Alawneh, A., & Jaradat, R. (2017). Cloud security engineering: Early stages of SDLC. *Future Generation Computer Systems*, *74*, 385–392. doi:10.1016/j.future.2016.10.005

Aljawarneh, S. A., Moftah, R. A., & Maatuk, A. M. (2016). Investigations of automatic methods for detecting the polymorphic worms signatures. *Future Generation Computer Systems*, *60*, 67–77. doi:10.1016/j.future.2016.01.020

Aljawarneh, S. A., Vangipuram, R., Puligadda, V. K., & Vinjamuri, J. (2017). G-SPAMINE: An approach to discover temporal association patterns and trends in internet of things. *Future Generation Computer Systems*, *74*, 430–443. doi:10.1016/j.future.2017.01.013

Bani Yassein, M., Al-Dubai, A. Y., & Buchanan, W. (2010). A new adaptive broadcasting approach for mobile ad hoc networks. In *Proceeding of the Sixth Conference on Wireless Advanced (WiAD)*. London: IEEE.

Bani Yassein, M., Al-Dubai, A. Y., Khaoua, M., & Al-jarrah, O. (2009). New adaptive counter based broadcast using neighborhood information in manets. *Proceeding of the IEEE International Symposium on Parallel & Distributed Processing*.

Bani Yassein M., Al-Humoud S., Khaoua, & Mackenzie, L. (2007). *New counter based broadcast scheme using local neighborhood information in manets*. Academic Press.

Bani Yassein, M., Al-Rushdan, S., Mardini, W., & Khamayseh, Y. (2011). Performance of Probabilistic Broadcasting of Dynamic Source Routing Protocol. In *Proceeding of The Fourth International Conference on Communication Theory, Reliability, and Quality of Service*. Budapest, Hungary: IARIA.

Bani Yassein, M., Khalaf, M., & Al-Dubai, A. (2010). A new probabilistic broadcasting scheme for mobile ad hoc on-demand distance vector (AODV) routed networks. *The Journal of Supercomputing*, *53*(1), 196–211. doi:10.1007/s11227-010-0408-0

Bani Yassein, M., Khalaf, M., & Al-Dubai, A. (2010). A performance comparison of smart probabilistic broadcasting of ad hoc distance vector (AODV). *International Journal of Supercomputing*, *53*, 196–211. doi:10.1007/s11227-010-0408-0

Bani Yassein, M., & Khaoua, M. O. (2007). Application of Probabilistic Flooding in MANETs. *Ubiquitous Computing and Communication Journal*, *1*, 1–5.

Bani Yassein, M., Khaoua, M. O., Mackenzie, L. M., & Papanastasiou, S. (2006). Performance evaluation of adjusted probabilistic broadcasting in MANETs. *Proceeding of the 2nd IEEE International Symposium on Dependable, Autonomic and Secure Computing*. doi:10.1109/DASC.2006.39

Bani-Yassein, M., Khaoua, M. O., Mackenzie, L. M., & Papanastasiou, S. (2006). Performance analysis of adjusted probabilistic broadcasting in mobile ad hoc networks. *International Journal of Wireless Information Networks, 13*(2), 127–140. doi:10.1007/s10776-006-0027-0

Bani Yassein, M., Manaseer, S., Al-hassan, A. A., Taye, Z. A., & Al-Dubai, A. Y. (2010). A new probabilistic Linear Exponential Backoff scheme for MANETs. In *Proceeding of International Symposium on Parallel & Distributed Processing Workshops and Phd Forum (IPDPSW)*. Atlanta, GA: IEEE.

Bani Yassein, M., Nimer, S., & Al-Dubai, A. Y. (2010). The effects of network density of a new counter-based broadcasting scheme in mobile ad hoc networks. In *10th International Conference on Computer and Information Technology (CIT)*. Bradford, UK: IEEE.

Bani Yassein, M., Nimer, S. F., & Al-Dubai, A. Y. (2011). A new dynamic counter-based broadcasting scheme for mobile ad hoc networks. *Simulation Modelling Practice and Theory, 19*(1), 553–563. doi:10.1016/j.simpat.2010.08.011

Bani Yassein, M., Ould-Khaoua, M., Mackenzie, L. M., & Papanastasiou, S. (2005). Improving the performance of probabilistic flooding in MANETS. *Proceedings of International Workshop on Wireless Ad-hoc Networks*.

Bani Yassein, M., Ould Khaoua, M., Mackenzie, L. M., & Papanastasiou, S. (2005). The Highly Adjusted Probabilistic Broadcasting in Mobile Ad hoc Networks. *Proceedings of the 6th Annual PostGraduate Symposium on the Convergence of Telecommunications, Networking & Broadcasting*.

Bani Yassein, M., Ould-Khaoua, M., & Papanastasiou, S. (2005). Performance evaluation of flooding in MANETs in the presence of multi-broadcast traffic. *Proceeding of the 11th International Conference on Parallel and Distributed Systems*.

Dembla, D., & Chaba, Y. (2010). Performance Modeling of Efficient & Dynamic Broadcasting Algorithm in MANETs Routing Protocols. In *Proceeding of Second International Conference on Computer Research and Development*. Washington, DC: IEEE. doi:10.1109/ICCRD.2010.82

Gill, A., & Diwaker, Ch. (2012). Comparative Analysis of routing in MANET. *International Journal of Advanced Research in Computer Science and Software Engineering*, *2*, 309–414.

Jang, H.-C., & Ch, H. (2010). Direction based routing strategy to reduce broadcast storm in MANET. In *Proceeding of International Computer Symposium (ICS)*. Tainan, Taiwan: IEEE. doi:10.1109/COMPSYM.2010.5685471

Kalpana, Govindaswamy, & Punithavalli. (2012). Reliable broadcasting using efficient forward node selection for mobile ad-hoc networks. *The International Arab Journal of Information Technology*, *9*, 299–305.

Kalpana, G., Kumar, P. V., Aljawarneh, S., & Krishnaiah, R. V. (2017). Shifted Adaption Homomorphism Encryption for Mobile and Cloud Learning. *Computers & Electrical Engineering*. doi:10.1016/j.compeleceng.2017.05.022

Kanakaris, Venetis, Ndzi, Ovaliadis, & Yang. (2012). A new RREQ message forwarding technique based on Bayesian probability theory. *EURASIP Journal on Wireless Communications and Networking*, *318*, 1–12.

Khamayseh, Y., Bader, A., Mardini, W., & BaniYasein, M. (2011). A new protocol for detecting black hole nodes in Ad Hoc Networks. *International Journal of Communication Networks and Information Security, 3*, 36-47.

Khan, A. I., Madani, S. A., Anwar, W., & Hayat, K. (2011). Location based dynamic probabilistic broadcasting for MANETs. *World Applied Sciences Journal*, *13*, 2296–2305.

Liarokapis, D., & Shahrabi, A. (2011). Fuzzy-based probabilistic broadcasting in mobile ad hoc networks. In *Proceeding of Wireless Days (WD)*. Niagara Falls, Canada: IEEE.

Manickam, P., Baskar, T., Girija, M., & Manimegalai, D. (2011). Performance comparisons of routing protocols in mobile ad hoc networks. *International Journal of Wireless & Mobile Networks*, *3*(1), 98–106. doi:10.5121/ijwmn.2011.3109

Nand, P., & Sharma, S. C. (2011). Probability based improved broadcasting for AODV routing protocol. In *Proceeding of International Conference on Computational Intelligence and Communication Networks*. Gwalior, India: IEEE.

Natesapillai, K., Palanisamy, V., & Duraiswamy, K. (2010). Optimum density based model for probabilistic flooding protocol in mobile ad hoc network. *European Journal of Scientific Research*, 577-588.

Singh, A., Juneja, D., & Malhotra, M. (2015). A Novel Agent Based Autonomous Service Composition Framework for Cost Optimization of Resource Provisioning in Cloud Computing. In JKSU-CIS. Elsevier.

Singh, A., & Malhotra, M. (2015). Evaluation of a Secure Agent based optimized Resource Scheduling Framework in Cloud Environment. IJCAR, 188-198.

Singh, A., & Malhotra, M. (2016). Hybrid Two Tier Framework for Improved Security in Cloud Environment. India-Com, 1601-1606.

Singh, A., & Malhotra, M. (n.d.). A Novel Agent Based Framework for Cost Optimization in Cloud Computing Environment. *International Journal of Cloud Applications*, 53–61.

Vijayakumar, P., & Poongkuzhali, T. (2012). Efficient power aware broadcasting technique for mobile ad hoc network. *Procedia Engineering*, *30*, 782–78930. doi:10.1016/j.proeng.2012.01.928

Wang, Q., Shi, H., & Qi, Q. (2010). A dynamic probabilistic broadcasting scheme based on cross-layer design for MANETs. *International Journal of Modern Education and Computer Science*, *2*(1), 40–47. doi:10.5815/ijmecs.2010.01.06

Wu, X., Yang, Y., Liu, J., Wu, Y., & Yi, F. (2010). Position-aware counter-based broadcast for mobile ad hoc networks. In *Proceeding of the Fifth International Conference on Frontier of Computer Science and Technology (FCST)*. Changchun, China: IEEE. doi:10.1109/FCST.2010.42

Yassein, M. B., & Al-Dubai, A. Y. (2016). A Novel Broadcast Scheme DSR-based Mobile Adhoc Networks. *International Journal of Advanced Computer Science and Applications*, *7*, 563–568.

Yassein, M. B., Al-Dubai, A. Y., Khaoua, M. O., & Al-jarrah, O. M. (2009). New adaptive counter based broadcast using neighborhood information in MANETS (IPDPS 2009). In *Proceeding of the IEEE International Parallel and Distributed Processing Symposium*. Rome, Italy: IEEE.

Yassein, M. B., Khaoua, M. O., Mackenzie, L. M., & Papanastasiou, S. (2006). Performance evaluation of adjusted probabilistic broadcasting in MANETs. In *Proceeding of the 2nd IEEE International Symposium on Dependable, Autonomic and Secure Computing (DASC 2006)*. Glasgow. UK: IEEE. doi:10.1109/DASC.2006.39

Yassein, M. B., Oqaily, O. A., Min, G., Mardin, W., Khamayseh, Y., & Manaseer, S. S. (2010). Enhanced Fibonacci backoff algorithm for mobile Ad-hoc network. In *Proceedings of the 10th IEEE International Conference on Computer and Information Technology(CIT-2010), 7th IEEE International Conference on Embedded Software and Systems (ICESS-2010, ScalCom-2010)*. Bradford, UK: IEEE. doi:10.1109/CIT.2010.144

Yassein, M. B., Ould-Khaoua, M., & Papanastasiou, S. (2005). Performance evaluation of flooding in MANETs in the presence of multi-broadcast traffic. *Proceedings of the International Conference on Parallel and Distributed Systems*. doi:10.1109/ICPADS.2005.228

Chapter 14

Current Drift in Energy Efficiency Cloud Computing:
New Provocations, Workload Prediction, Consolidation, and Resource Over Commitment

Shivani Bajaj
Chandigarh University, India

ABSTRACT

Energy Efficiency can be defined as reduction of energy used by a given service or level of activity. In spite of scale and complexity of data centre equipment it can be highly difficult to define the proper activity that could be examined for the efficiency of energy. So there can be four scenarios which may define within the system where the energy is not utilised in an efficient manner. The main goal of Cloud service providers is creation of usage of Cloud computing resources proficiently for efficient cloud computing. Cloud computing has many serious issues such as load manager, security and fault tolerance. This chapter discusses the energy efficient approaches in cloud computing environment. The energy efficiency has become the major concern for the service providers. In this chapter, the major concern is the high lightly of resource allocation challenges and there are some which will be given in the data center energy consumption. The focus is done on the power management task and even the virtualization of saving the energy.

DOI: 10.4018/978-1-5225-3029-9.ch014

INTRODUCTION

Cloud computing is a materialize technology now-a-days that provides computing, storage resources and communication resources and it is that kind of technology which attracts the ICT (Information and communication Technology) services that provides huge distribution of online services. It provides a great infrastructure which involves large centers including the large amount of servers dealing with the requests given by the clients. There is rapid growth of demand for the power which computes the creation of large-scale data centers. The data centers consume a huge amount of electricity which results in carbon dioxide emission and high operational costs. The cloud computing is that kind of concept which gives an immediate action of many well researched domains like grid computing, cluster computing, distributed computing and virtualization (Singh, & Malhotra, (2016)). The data centers of cloud computing give many virtualization technologies that may allow the scheduling of workload on less number of servers which keeps the better utilization as the different kind of workload may give different kind of footprints. There are many companies which are offering cloud computing services for the expansion of cloud infrastructures such as Microsoft, Amazon, Go grid, vCloud Express, Layered Technologies, ENKI Prima Cloud. From the Google's point of view, there are five characteristics of cloud computing user centric, task centric, powerfulness, programmability and intelligence. Cloud computing gradually writes off the initial cost over the diversity of workloads, shared system operators and the distributed server's offers different kind of services based on computation and operational tasks (Aljawarneh, et al., 2017). There are many unique issues based on the cloud computing infrastructure such as standardization, dynamic scalability, debugging, reduction of operational costs, reduction of carbon emission and the most important privacy and security of Information and Communicational Technology resources. Now-a-days it has become the major concern of research that "How to reduce carbon emission". This is all because of the energy which is required by the large-scale data centers for its power supply, cooling, and operations. Therefore reduction of power consumption has become a major issue in this present time.

The popularity of cloud computing is growing day by day and making of the efficient energy usage in cloud data centers has a basic proposal which defines its characteristics.

Definition:

A Cloud is a collection of interconnected and the computers which are dynamically provisioned and even presented for computing the resources depending on the service-level agreements which are established for customers and providers.

MODELS

In the following section, there is a complete review of the cloud, its applications and energy models. In their description there is a detail presenting the model which particularly focuses on management of the resources, its characteristics and the issues which come through the cloud service providers.

Cloud Model

The Definite system which is being used for this model comprises of a set which can be identified by R of r resources and these resources can be connected internally in such a way that it a route is defined between them. Let us suppose that the resources are equivalent according to the maximum amount and the computing ability and its justification can be provided depending upon the technologies which are provided by the virtualization. At this present time many virtualization tools such as parallel desktop for Mac, VirtualBox, VMware and many more. On a single physical resource, there is no firm leap for the number of happening tasks. A cloud can range from one side to another side to the distributed locations. But according to the study of cloud model it can be setup to a particular location. The processor among the communications can be supposed to accomplish with a continuous and equivalent speed to all the channels which are in connection (Singh & Malhotra, (2014)). It has also been observed that the message can be conveyed from one resource side to another resource side which is even possible in many of the other systems when the task is being performed on the receiver side of the resource.

Figure 1.

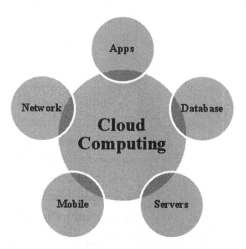

Application Model

There are many services which are being provided by the service providers like software as a service (SaaS), Platform as a service (PaaP) and infrastructure as a service (IaaS). When the instances are being regarding these services they can come under the category of computational tasks. These services are distinguished depending upon the services offered such as they can be defined in such a way IaaS follows the payment depending upon the hourly system whereas SaaS & Paas follows the payment according to the fixed time which is offered. But there exist some possibilities that the estimates can be taken depending upon the request given by the consumers supplied services. Suppose the service request which utilize the processors can be identified (Aljawarneh, et al., 2016). One more thing can be taken into this that the memory or the disk which are used can be correlated with the utilization of the processors. So therefore, we can say that the terms like applications, task and the services can be used interchangeably.

Task Consolidation Problem

The problem related to task consolidation can also be called as workload consolidation is that type of process which deals with the assigning of tasks as a set N of n tasks dealing to the set R of r as the resources of cloud. This thing properly works for the time constraints and properly aims at the maximization of the utilization of the resources (Vecchiola et al., 2009). There are certain time constraints which deals directly with the usage of the resources, and then these things are allocated directly with the tasks. For instance, the task associated with the resource utilization depends totally on the requirement which is being given as 60% and then this given allocation can be assigned to the resource usage particularly at the time of task's arrival is 50%.

Figure 2.

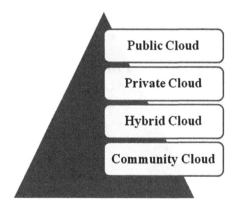

ENERGY EFFICIENCY IN CLOUD

Energy Efficiency is properly a reduction of energy used by the activities level or the provided service. In spite of scale and complexity of data center equipment it can be highly difficult to define the proper activity that could be examined for the efficiency of energy (Abdelsalam, et al., 2009)). So there can be four scenarios which may define within the system where the energy is not utilized in an efficient manner. The basic research on energy efficiency originated from the grid computing and the environments of data centers.

WHY AGNOIZE ABOUT ENERGY?

Energy efficiency is a major concern in the large-scale data centers. In US the data centers consumes about 1.5 percent of electricity in earlier time which is quite equal to the annual energy consumption. It costs a lot to around 4.5 billion per year, so the providers of data centers are searching the better way to save energy and low down the power consumption (Rivoire et al., 2007). Apart from this there are also many environmental issues that are also generalized to make call for the reduction of energy in large data centers. The carbon footprints and energy costs are increasing rapidly in data centers. All these factors are made on high priority to find out the solutions to slow down energy consumption in data centers and this practice has been given to the academia, industries and also the government agencies. There are many large data centers examples like the cloud data centers which offer the various services on certain devices.

The following equation is the proper amount of calculation which deals with the energy consumed by the data centers and there are two metrics which are being included and these are green grid & international consortium. The metrics are Power Usage Effectiveness (PUE) and Data Centre Infrastructure Efficiency (DCiE) as defined below:

$$PUE = Total\ Facility \frac{Power}{IT} Equipment\ Power \tag{1}$$

$$DCiE = \frac{1}{PUE} = \left(IT\ Equipment \frac{Power}{Total} Facility\ Power \right) \times 100\% \tag{2}$$

Figure 3.

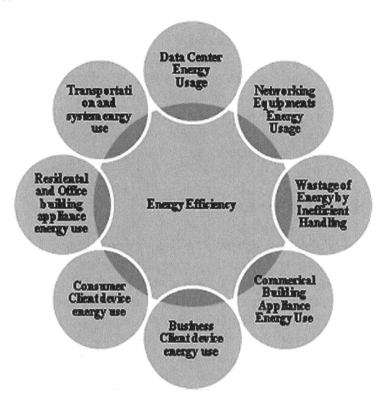

The equipment power of the IT which deals with the delivery of the load of all the computing hardware resources.

Important Factor: Energy Efficiency

There is one important factor which tells us about the calculation of energy consumption while cooling and during the overheads. There are certain metrics which come under the emerging technologies such as the power Usage Effectiveness (PUE) which actually tells us about the deployment of the energy versus the energy being spent overhead (Allman, et al., 2007). The effectiveness of power usage of a data center can be defined as the ratio of the consummated power facility which can be analyzed as the data or the switching center to the consummated power of the IT equipment those including the routers, servers and the storage areas. It keeps on varying from the data centers which totally depend upon the place where the data centers are located and the devices which are used in its construction part. So there are many data centers according to the research study which provide motivation to have the efficiency in energy.

CLOUD COMPUTING AND USAGE OF ENERGY

Applications Related to Cloud/Users

There is one important factor which actually covers up with the contribution of energy consumption and this deals with the software applications related to the design and implementation. The cloud computing is used for the applications which are being run and owned by the user those who are individual and offered by the cloud service providers with the usage of SaaS. When we talk about both these cases, then directly the energy consumption depends on the applications (Woods, 2010). Suppose the application is running for a very long time with the high speed memory and the central processing unit requirements, so depending upon these requirements, their execution will result with the matter of high energy consumption. So therefore, due to this the consumption of the energy can be calculated as directly proportional to the application's profile. There is one more fact that the resources which are being given as the allocation depending upon the maximum level of utilization of the CPU and the memory which will result in higher energy consumption than the requirement (Bash & Forman, (2007)). The inefficiency of the energy during the execution of application performs in such a way related to the design and implementation such as the algorithms of suboptimal and inefficient usage of the resources which are being shared and these resources cause contention leading to the higher CPU utilization with higher consumption of energy. So concluding this means that the factors like energy efficiency cannot be considered with the design of an application with the most applications domains including the example of the devices which are embedded like the mobile phones.

SaaS, PaaS, IaaS Level in Cloud Software Stack

The stack of the cloud software has the overhead in extra for the execution of the applications of the end users. For example, it is quite clear that the performance efficiency of physical server is much higher than the virtual machine. The general access related to the virtual machine can be done by the infrastructure providers (Garg et al., 2011). Adding onto this, the process related to the management which is in the form of accounting and monitoring may require the CPU power. As it is profit oriented so it keeps a regular check on the service level agreements (SLA) with their clients. The SLA's can purely relate work with time commitment. So according we can assume, the cloud service providers may need the extra resources to have better quality and the availability. The cloud service providers have to make several replicas across the whole data center network so that they can avoid any kind of failure, fast recovery process and reducing the response of time. So the web applications of work flow may require the sites which can give a better time of response to the end users and due to this its data can be replicated for servers across the world.

Network Devices

The network system is one of the major concerns with those which we studied earlier and this can consume the non-negligible fraction of the consumption of the power. The energy consumption may estimate the Vodafone fro up radio access network nearly up to 3TWh according to the study. In cloud computing the resources are being processed and accessed only with the help of the internet, both the data and the applications are in requirement form for transmitting to the compute node. So there is a huge requirement for the bandwidth of the communication and the personnel computer of the users including the cloud resources which require the execution of application. Suppose in some cases the data gets bigger then that data can be considered more for the carbon emission just to send the data by electronic mails instead of the internet.

What actually happens in cloud computing is that the data travels through many nodes before reaching to the data center which is its exact place to setup everything. Taking as example, the user of the computer may connect to the Ethernet so as to make a switch of the ISP in which there is efficiency of trafficin aggregation. The Ethernet switches can receive the authentication functions and the traffic management linking up to the Broadband Network Gateway (BNG). There are many BNG routers can directly connect to the internet routers depending on the provider's edge routers.

While talking about the energy it totally works upon the power consumption values and its efficiency power. There are many things which are to be kept in mind while the utilization of the energy i.e the network equipments and also the system design, design of topologies and the network design along with its protocols (Verma, et al., 2010). So, it can be said that the energy consumption of the devices remains same during the high time and idle time also. There is a scope of lot of improvement in the case of energy efficiency. For instance, during the periods which are on low utilization they can made in such a way that links of Ethernet and the packets can be routed either them. Many energy saving techniques are possible at hardware level too.

Datacenter

The facilities of hosting are quite different from the data center techniques. A data center which is included in cloud actually comprises of the thousands of the networked computers along with the storage and further the subsystems of the networking area available with power distribution, equipments used for cooling the infrastructures. Due to all these things the data centers release a large amount of carbon which is very dangerous. In can be observed that not only the servers and the storage parts of infrastructures consume the energy but the cooling equipments also release a large amount of energy. So to avoid this there is a need to make energy efficient while using them for the datacenters.

ENERGY CONSUMPTION

Energy Consumption has become an eloquent worry for the cloud service providers due to many environmental and financial factors. Due to this major concern, the cloud service providers are looking for many unconventional ways that can help them to reduce the amount of energy being used in the data centers (Song, et al., 2007). The deployment of data centers in cloud has put more and more computers in use every year which increases the energy pressure on the environment and the energy consumption. The recent research tells us about the to run a single 300 Watt server in one year can cost about $338 and can also emit about 1300kg of carbon dioxide, and this is apart from the cooling equipments being used.

Energy Consumption of Computing Servers

The server power consumption depends upon the utilization of CPU. A server which is ideal consumes 2/3 rd of the highest power consumption. This energy consumption by ideal server is because sever must keep the disks, modules of memory, I/O resources and other exterior operations even if not in use or no computations are performed on that. So when the load comes on the network the power consumption is increased.

$$P_s\left(l\right) = P_{fixed} + \frac{\left(P_{peak} - P_{fixed}\right)}{2}\left(1 + l - e^{-\frac{1}{a}}\right) \tag{1}$$

In equation 1, the following variables depict the meaning as follows:

P_{fixed} = Idle power consumption
P_{peak} = Power consumption at its peak load
l = Load of server
a = Utilization point at which server reaches linear consumption of power than the load offered.

Processor consumption of power is proportional to the $V^2 f$ in which

V= Voltage

f = Operating frequency

When the frequency downshift takes place the voltage is reduces at that time and infers a cubic relation from f. The equation inferred from the relation is as follows:

$$Pb2_s\left(l\right) = P_{fixed} + \frac{\left(P_{peak} - P_{fixed}\right)}{2}\left(1 + l^3 - e^{-\frac{l^3}{a}}\right)$$ (2)

On the basis of equation 2, the power management can adjust the frequency of operation during the ideal routine of server and leads to operational power consumption.

THE PATTERN FOLLOWED BY THE CLOUDS

In this, the company which offers the cloud service having the cloud center which may consist of several servers which can be known as the physical machines(PM) and those physical machines are further grouped into the multiple units which can be known as clusters, where each cluster controls and manages the several physical machines (Srikantaiah, et al., 2008). A cluster can be homogeneous or heterogeneous depending upon the resources or the capabilities requirement. Many resources are being given to the clients as a service by the cloud providers and depending upon their usage the clients are then charged accordingly. For the resource usage the request are being given to the cloud providers and according to that requests the virtual machines (VM) are setup. These virtual machines carry the entire request given by the client through the sources, it then chooses one of the clusters host the virtual machine and then assigns that virtual machine to the physical machine. Throughout the lifetime the virtual machine is connected to the commitment of the physical machines and the client request are further known as the VM requests.

New Provocations, New Scope

Energy efficiency is the significant subject which came into existence even before the defining the pattern of cloud data centers where the main focus was given on the saving of energy of laptops and other electronic devices just in order to save the lifetime of the battery. Many techniques were opted to save the energy such as dynamic voltage, power gating and frequenting scaling. Now, what the challenge is? The Challenge is the data centers includes a huge range of servers and those servers further contains the virtual machines and when these severs work there are many dynamic requests, on-demand resource provisioning where the clients can submit their request any time (Ranganathan, 2010). This dynamic provisioning nature of cloud computing makes the cloud computing dealing with energy efficiency concept a great one. Such kind of flexible nature give birth too many new challenges like managing the resources, scheduling the tasks and even the consumption of power. And the most important fact that the cloud provides commitment to give the quality of service to their clients which requires extreme eye on the techniques applied for energy saving. The good new fact about energy efficiency is the adoption of new opportunities related to the virtualization that brings the new deals with the energy saving which are not given by the non-virtualized environments. Furthermore, the cloud clusters can be distributed among the various geographical areas.

USING THE CLOUD IN ENERGY EFFICIENT MANNER

While working for the improvement of energy efficiency, the data centers which are being wrapped up in the whole cloud computing concept can make it perfect to improve the energy saving and consumption techniques. There are many separate techniques which are working upon the cloud computing concepts so instead of working on those individual techniques we can merge the techniques for the betterment of energy consumption (Raghavendre, et al., 2008). There are many energy efficiency models such as Clear Model developed by Lawrence Berkeley National Laboratory which provides an open access approach to analyze energy saving while moving to the clouds. Its estimate potential is up to 95% reduction in energy compared to the present day business software in use, which may include the customer relationship management, email software as well as the productivity. There can be concept of video streaming by the video industry as while streaming video on internet can save a lot of energy consumption around 15% compared to the shipment of it on CDs and DVDs. Using the infrastructure in cloud computing is a good concept along with this we can even use the flexible nature of computing that is technique of energy optimization. The techniques which are included under this i.e. powering on or off machines can be used for frequency regulation of the power network. Instead of only consuming energy, modern data centers are becoming the producers of energy with on-site power generators. Due to this approach it not only reduces the power consumption but also reduces the costs for the data centers and power losses due to the energy transfer and load on the energy grid.

Energy Saving

Energy saving is the major concern to work on energy efficiency. There are two approaches for making the data center consume lesser energy by shutting down the components and scaling down their performance. Both these approaches can be applied to the network switches and computing servers. While applying to the servers, the method which was used earlier, dynamic power management (DPM) which results in energy saving (Allenotor et al., 2008). When the combination of DPM and workload consolidated scheduler, it allows the maximizing of the servers which are idle and those can be put on sleep due to which the average load of the cloud computing system remains below 30%. There is one technology i.e Dynamic Voltage and Frequency Scaling (DVFS)which gives the relationship between power consumption p, Voltage v and operating frequency:

$$P = V^2 * f$$

The major factor of cloud computing is the performance of its applications like gaming, voice, video conferencing, online office, storage, backup files, networking which totally depends upon the efficiency of high performance resources. For high performance the physical infrastructure should be brought closer to the data resources which can optimize the resources used.

Data Replication

Data Replication optimizes the power consumption, network bandwidth, communication delay and network availability of the cloud computing (Allalouf, et al., 2009). The maintenance of replicas at multiple numbers of sites can enhance the performance by reducing the access delays and single point of failure.

Virtualization

Virtualization is another important technology which is widely used in the systems and it allows many VMs to be used effectively. In networking the virtualization can enable the implementation of different addressing and forwarding mechanisms.

ENERGY PRESERVATION TECHNIQUES

The most powerful management and conservation techniques, there are many questions which arise during the power management that How the challenges are being faced? How the challenges are being managed? How to explain the basic ideas related to behind the power preservation techniques? Now all these techniques focus on the limitations and the section tries to manage the entire cloud data centers. For the management of perfect cloud centers there are certain energy efficient techniques which can be divided into the following categories: Workload Prediction, VM Placement and Workload Consolidation and Resource Over commitment.

Workload Prediction

There is one main reason why a high rate of energy is being consumed in cloud data center because there are many servers which are having the energy but they are idle for that time so the energy is being wasted. According to the study, the energy consumed by the servers those who are categorized as idle is almost 50% of those servers which are in proper use. So when we talk about the energy saving, it purely comes down to the point that the server switches should be put on the sleep state when they are not in use. But this kind of act is when done, creates a lot of problem when we switch OFF the physical Machine and again put it as ON Physical Machine, it creates a lot of disturbance in the system and it incurs high energy as well as delay overheads.

As a result, the amount of energy consumed after switching the Physical Machine ON is more than 50% of the energy which was used during the physical machine ON. As to amount the various sharing resources (Memory, CPU, Bandwidth) the Physical machine are to be put ON and OFF depending upon the utilization. So this can properly help in saving the energy. There should be on-demand sharing of the resources and one predictor is needed to identify that when a virtual machine can be made in contact with the physical machine requests (Beloglazon et al., 2011). On the basis of this prediction, the specific and the efficient power management predictions can be taken so as to save the energy by making the machine ON and OFF according to the requests receiving that which particular VM or PM is to be kept ON for that request.

Different categories can be made to identify the IDLE and SLEEP mode machine. There are certain categories through which the classification of multiple categories can be done by the clustering techniques. The clustering techniques totally depend upon the data which is collected from the Google study.

Workload Consolidation and VM Placement

There are multiple clustering techniques and cloud centers which are present in different geographical locations. In this when a cloud service provider receives any kind of request in virtual machine VM, its scheduling device has to decide first that which particular cluster should be present to host the submitted request. As the electricity prices increase day by day it makes even tougher to make up with the major concerns of the valuable facts for temporal variations. There are certain sources of energy in clustering form and they can even make a beneficial aspect for the selection of clusters. When the cluster is selected another question arises with the physical machine which are used for the hosting the request sent by the users.

The virtual machine consolidation problem can work with online bin packing (OBP)to solve the optimization problems, which is having the virtual and the physical machines as the major objects. The objects can have the different sizes and the bins which may include physical machines having the different capabilities (Bianchini et al., 2004). The main problem can be identified as online bin packing and that can even include the NP-Hard problem and including this the problems related to the first fit, next fit and even the best fit can be proposed to solve the major issues of proposal. The idle physical machines and the virtual machines can be involved in ON and OFF depending on the values or request which are given by the users or the clients.

There is one more technique pertaining to the virtualization that may even turn into useful consolidation of the virtual migration. One major key problem can be identified as the technique virtual machine migration but the energy in involved in energy overhead. Rather than working on the virtual and physical machine individually we can have resorting of virtual and physical machine and can be addressed to the workload. The main idea can be given as the similarities which come under the virtual as well as the physical machine. And this can be identified as the client or they can even be predicted depending on the types of the task which are given for performing the perfect behavior of the client request.

The random request can be maintained depending on the work of the request and even the idle systems and the hosting. So concluding this can be saved as the energy efficiency and even the placement of the virtual machine and the consolidation of the work according to the load.

Resource Over Commitment

As discussed earlier, the two working techniques such as the prediction in the workload and the technique of virtual machine placement dealing with the consolidation of the workload are the considered to be the best techniques. Now the next techniques which for the over commitment of the resources can work on the cluster scheduling which allocates the request of the virtual machines during the entire releasing of the reserved resources which may come to the completion of the virtual machine requests. There is one major concern that how the energy can be saved during the commitment of the resources in data center. There is one study which indicates that the cloud resources can be reserved which may even lead to the substantial CPU utilization and saving the energy from wastage.

The clients on an average know the exact amount of the resources and their applications according to their need. One major concern is the utilization of the resources on the virtual machine and according to the resources they can work on the applications which are chosen for the different types of request for computing the resources.

The over commitment of the resources is that type of technique which can adopt the addresses and may vary depending on the time and can be equal to the peak time. It consists basically of the virtual as well as the physical machine allocation with the capacities and the capabilities of handling the workload. The process of over commitment has a best quality and it can be maintained well and result in great energy saving technology which may host the virtual machines. These virtual machines linking to the physical machines can allow the lower power states for working.

But apart from these entire positive things one major problem is the physical machine overload, where the overload can occur with an aggregate amount of resources and may even schedule the virtual machine request and can exceed the hosting capacity of the physical machines. When this condition occurs on the performance degradation it can come into existence and can solve the problem in such a way that there is violation of service level agreement. Defending on the SLA there is possibility to avoid any kind of conspiracy between the client and the cloud capability.

Based on this essence, there are two questions which can be answered while developing the resources

- What is the level for the over commitment which can be supported by the cloud?
- At what time the virtual machines should be used to reduce the physical machine overloading consequences?

The answer to these questions is that we can predict the future of the utilization of the resources and according they can be scheduled with the virtual machines. The predictions can even determine the level of over commitment to support the cloud. For the second question, one prediction can be made to avoid the incident of overloading (Garg et al., 2011). So on these predictions the virtual machines can avoid the overloading of the virtual machine migration. It can be avoided with the amount of request receiving by the physical machine while hosting the cloud.

So to sum up the over commitment of the resources, it can be said that to reduce the consumption of the energy in cloud centers has a great impact, but even this there is still a major requirement of the development of the resources which can manage the energy saving techniques.

The over commitment of the resources is not possible without the virtualization technology which actually enables it with the real, dynamic and the flexible time. Along with this the allocation of resources is a major concern for providing the authority to host the virtual machines for the ease of migration across the physical machines.

BASIC TERMINOLOGIES RELATED TO ENERGY EFFICIENCY AT DATA CENTER LEVEL INCLUDES COOLING, HARDWARE, NETWORK & STORAGE

Now-a-days we have some factors which need to value such as the cost savings factor. The providers of the cloud make this in such a way that the providers need to opt some practices. To work upon the energy efficiency we need to see many facts such as the energy improvisation. To improve the efficiency of each device we need to work on many things such as from the electrical to the processor level.

First level which needs to be kept in mind is the construction of small data centers and choosing the best of their location. Two factors are there which come under this level are: energy supply and efficiency of energy of equipments. So due to this the data centers are developed in such a way that that they can generate the renewable sources comprising of sun and wind. At this present time the geographical features come like climate, fiber-optic connectivity and access to the affordable energy supply. Today's major concern for the cloud is the business; the sources of energy are majorly seen in the terms of cost not for the carbon emissions.

The next level which comes under this process is the cooling system. Sometimes the temperature in data center may also lead to the decline of the data centers related to the IT systems. There are two types of approaching systems: air and the water. In both these approaches the cooling system of energy are based on the proposed liquid cooling and the nano fluid cooling systems. Due to this they don't have any direct contact with the outer atmosphere. There are many systems which have been constructed where the external cool air is usually used to remove the data center's heat.

Another important level is the power efficiency of the data center. Which is being addressed on the deployment of the power efficient severs and the processors

(Grobschadl et al., 2005). On important thing is there that the processors which are of low energy can even reduce the power usage of the systems in a very great degree.

The most important level is the power supply infrastructure which is to be designed as an energy efficient manner. The main task which can come under this is to feed the server resources with the power by converting the voltage of high alternating current from the grid of power to the voltage of low direct current and in this we need to install most electric currents. They come under the terminology of power supply unit (PSU) which mainly depends on the load, number of circuits installed and even the temperature conditions.

NETWORK INFRASTRUCTURE

According to the earlier discussion, there are two methods through which the energy needs to be identified i.e the network interface card (NIC) which is at the node level and other is at the infrastructure level including the switches and the nodes. The factors which come under energy efficiency issues can be named under the term Green Networking (GN). The term GN relates to the embedding energy-awareness in the design form which includes the devices and the rules related to the network. There are for classes which are to considered under this and can be offered under this in such a way naming the resource consolidation, virtualization, selective connectedness and proportional computing. The term resource consolidation includes the regrouping of the utilized devices just to reduce the energy consumption. Getting on to the similarity part the term selective connectedness of devices may lead to the distributed mechanism which directly goes for the idle systems. There is one very important difference between the resource consolidation and selective connectedness i.e. the consolidation is being to the devices which come under the process of network but the selective connectedness allows is turning off the devices which are not in use. The term virtualization may allow more than on service which can be made operational on the same hardware systems and thus they can improve the utilization.

CONCLUSION

In this chapter we discussed about energy efficiency and cloud computing as a useful paradigm of computing which has become a firm base for a varied array of organization and user applications. Many Providers give variable service sets that vary in configuration of resources and given services. A complete solution for allocation of resources is important to every cloud computing service supplier. In this modern era cloud computing has become very fast growing service in the environment of the networks of computer. The challenges and even the opportunities for saving the energy in data centers of the clouds are of major concern. While concluding we can say that the energy saving can be done in very proper and efficient manner by making more servers to the data centers into the low power states and even by increasing the utilization of the active servers in data centers. There are three different approaches which are being used workload prediction, placement of the virtual machine and the consolidation of the workload along with commitment of the resource. These techniques are highlighted to make energy more efficient in such a manner that it can save the energy, cost and even the carbon emissions are avoided. Basic terminologies are also defined so as to give a power to these techniques.

REFERENCES

Abdelsalam, H., Maly, K., Mukkamala, R., Zubair, M., & Kaminsky, D. (2009). Towards Energy Efficient Change Management In A Cloud Computing Environment. *Proceedings of 3rd International Conference on Autonomous Infrastructure, Management and Security.* doi:10.1007/978-3-642-02627-0_13

Aljawarneh, S., Aldwairi, M., & Yassein, M. B. (2017). Anomaly-based intrusion detection system through feature selection analysis and building hybrid efficient model. *Journal of Computational Science.* doi:10.1016/j.jocs.2017.03.006

Aljawarneh, S., Yassein, M.B., & Talafha, W.A. (2017). A multithreaded programming approach for multimedia big data: encryption system. *Multimed Tools Appl.* <ALIGNMENT.qj></ALIGNMENT>10.1007/s11042-017-4873-9

Aljawarneh, S. A., Alawneh, A., & Jaradat, R. (2017). Cloud security engineering: Early stages of SDLC. *Future Generation Computer Systems, 74,* 385–392. doi:10.1016/j.future.2016.10.005

Aljawarneh, S. A., Moftah, R. A., & Maatuk, A. M. (2016). Investigations of automatic methods for detecting the polymorphic worms signatures. *Future Generation Computer Systems, 60,* 67–77. doi:10.1016/j.future.2016.01.020

Aljawarneh, S. A., Vangipuram, R., Puligadda, V. K., & Vinjamuri, J. (2017). G-SPAMINE: An approach to discover temporal association patterns and trends in internet of things. *Future Generation Computer Systems, 74,* 430–443. doi:10.1016/j.future.2017.01.013

Allalouf, M., Arbitman, Y., Factor, M., Kat, R. I., Meth, K., & Naor, D. (2009). Storage Modelling For Power Estimation. *Proceedings of 2009 Israeli Experimental Systems Conference (SYSTOR '09).*

Allenotor, D., & Thulasiram, R. K. (2008). Grid resources pricing: A Novel Financial Option Based Quality Of Service-Profit Quasi-Static Equilibrium Model. *Proceedings of the 8th ACM/IEEE International Conference on Grid Computing*. doi:10.1109/GRID.2008.4662785

Allman, M., Christensen, K., Nordman, B., & Paxson, V. (2007). Enabling an Energy-Efficient Future Internet Through Selectively Connected End Systems. *Proceedings of the Sixth ACM Workshop on Hot Topics in Networks (HotNets-VI)*.

Baliga, J., Ayre, R., Hinton, K., & Tucker, R. S. (2010). Green Cloud Computing: Balancing Energy In Processing, Storage And Transport. *Proceedings of the IEEE*, 99(1), 149–167. doi:10.1109/JPROC.2010.2060451

Bash, C., & Forman, G. (2007). Cool job allocation: Measuring the power savings of placing jobs at cooling-efficient locations in the datacenter. *Proceeding of 2007 Annual Technical Conference on USENIX*.

Beloglazov, A., Buyya, R., Lee, Y. C., & Zomaya, A. (2011). A Taxonomy and Survey of Energy-Efficient Data Centers and Cloud computing Systems. In Advances in Computers. Elsevier.

Bianchini, R., & Rajamony, R. (2004). Power And Energy Management For Server Systems. *Computer*, 37(11), 68–74. doi:10.1109/MC.2004.217

Bianzino, P., Chaudet, C., Rossi, D., & Rougier, J. (2011). A Survey of Green Networking Research. *IEEE Communications Surveys and Tutorials*.

Buyya, R., Yeo, C. S., & Venugopal, S. (2008). Market-Oriented Cloud Computing: Vision, Hype, And Reality For Delivering It Services As Computing Utilities. *Proceedings of the 10th IEEE International Conference on High Performance Computing and Communications*. doi:10.1109/HPCC.2008.172

Garg, S. K., Yeo, C. S., Anandasivam, A., & Buyya, R. (2011). Environment-Conscious Scheduling Of HPC Applications On Distributed Cloud-Oriented Datacenters *Journal of Parallel and Distributed Computing*, 71(6), 732–749. doi:10.1016/j.jpdc.2010.04.004

Großschädl, Avanzi, R.M., Savas, E., & Tillich, S. (2005). Energy-Efficient Software Implementation Of Long Integer Modular Arithmetic. *Proceedings of 7th Workshop on Cryptographic Hardware and Embedded Systems*.

Kalpana, G., Kumar, P. V., Aljawarneh, S., & Krishnaiah, R. V. (2017). Shifted Adaption Homomorphism Encryption for Mobile and Cloud Learning. *Computers & Electrical Engineering*. doi:10.1016/j.compeleceng.2017.05.022

Kephart, J. O., Chan, H., Das, R., Levine, D. W., Tesauro, G., Rawson, F., & Lefurgy, C. (2007). Coordinating Multiple Autonomic Managers To Achieve Specified Power-Performance Tradeoffs. *Proceedings of 4th International Conference on Autonomic Computing*. doi:10.1109/ICAC.2007.12

Malhotra, M., & Malhotra, R. (2014). Cloud Adaptive Resource Allocation Mechanism for Efficient Parallel Processing. *International Journal of Cloud Applications and Computing*, 1–6.

Raghavendra, R., Ranganathan, P., Talwar, V., Wang, Z., & Zhu, Z. (2008). No "Power" Struggles: Coordinated Multi-Level Power Management For The Datacenter. *SIGOPS Operating. Systematic Reviews*, *42*(2), 48–59.

Ranganathan, P. (2010). Recipe For Efficiency: Principles Of Power-Aware Computing. *Communications of the ACM*, *53*(4), 60–67. doi:10.1145/1721654.1721673

Ranganathan, P., Leech, P., Irwin, D., & Chase, J. (2006). Ensemble Level Power Management For Dense Blade Servers. *SIGARCH. Computer Architecture News*, *34*(2), 66–77. doi:10.1145/1150019.1136492

Rawson, A., Pfleuger, J., & Cader, T. (2008). *Green Grid Data Center Power Efficiency Metrics*. Consortium Green Grid.

Rivoire, S., Shah, M. A., Ranganathan, P., & Kozyrakis, C. (2007). Joulesort: A Balanced Energy-Efficiency Benchmark. *Proceedings of the 2007 ACM SIGMOD International Conference on Management of Data*. doi:10.1145/1247480.1247522

Singh, A., Juneja, D., & Malhotra, M. (2015). A Novel Agent Based Autonomous Service Composition Framework for Cost Optimization of Resource Provisioning in Cloud Computing. In JKSU-CIS. Elsevier.

Singh, A., & Malhotra, M. (2015). Evaluation of a Secure Agent based optimized Resource Scheduling Framework in Cloud Environment. IJCAR, 188-198.

Singh, A., & Malhotra, M. (2016). Hybrid Two Tier Framework for Improved Security in Cloud Environment. India-Com., 1601-1606.

Singh, A., & Malhotra, M. (n.d.). A Novel Agent Based Framework for Cost Optimization in Cloud Computing Environment. *International Journal of Cloud Applications*, 53–61.

Singh, A., & Malhotra, M. (n.d.). A Novel Agent Based Framework for Cost Optimization in Cloud Computing Environment. *International Journal of Cloud Applications*, 53–61.

Song, Y., Sun, Y., Wang, H., & Song, X. (2007). An Adaptive Resource Flowing Scheme Amongst Vms In A VM-Based Utility Computing. *Proceedings of IEEE International Conference on Computer and Information Technology*. doi:10.1109/CIT.2007.16

Soror, A. A., Minhas, U. F., Aboulnaga, A., Salem, K., Kokosielis, P., & Kamath, S. (2008). Automatic Virtual Machine Configuration For Database Workloads. *Proceedings of ACM SIGMOD International Conference on Management of data*. doi:10.1145/1376616.1376711

Srikantaiah, S., Kansal, A., & Zhao, F. (2008). Energy Aware Consolidation For Cloud Computing. *Proceedings of HotPower '08 Workshop on Power Aware computing and Systems*.

Vecchiola, C., Chu, X., & Buyya, R. (2009). Aneka: A Software Platform For. NET-Based Cloud Computing. In High Performance & Large Scale computing. IOS Press.

Verma, A., Koller, R., Useche, L., & Rangaswami, R. (2010). Srcmap: Energy Proportional Storage Using Dynamic Consolidation. *Proceedings of the 8th USENIX conference on File and storage technologies (FAST'10)*.

Woods, A. (2010). Cooling The Data Center. *Communications of the ACM*, *53*(4), 36–42. doi:10.1145/1721654.1721671

Compilation of References

Abdelsalam, H., Maly, K., Mukkamala, R., Zubair, M., & Kaminsky, D. (2009). Towards Energy Efficient Change Management In A Cloud Computing Environment. *Proceedings of 3rd International Conference on Autonomous Infrastructure, Management and Security*. doi:10.1007/978-3-642-02627-0_13

Abdul-Rahman, A., & Hailes, S. (2000). Supporting trust in virtual communities. *Proceedings of 33rd Hawaii International Conference on System Sciences*, 777-780.

Aberer, K. (2001). P-grid: A self-organizing access structure for p2p information systems. *Proceedings of Ninth International Conference on Cooperative Information Systems*, 179-194.

Aberer, K., & Despotovic, Z. (2001). Managing trust in a peer-2-peer information system. *Proc. of 10th International Conference on Information and Knowledge Management*, 310-317. doi:10.1145/502585.502638

Ade S. A., & Tijare P.A. (2010). Performance comparison of AODV, DSDV, OLSR and DSR routing protocols in mobile ad hoc networks. *International Journal of Information Technology and Knowledge Management, 2*, 545-548.

Aegis. (2015). *Opportunities in Telecom Sector: Arising from Big Data*. School of Business and Data Science and Telecommunications

Agostinho, C., et al. (n.d.). Towards a sustainable interoperability in networked enterprise information systems: Trends of knowledge and model-driven technology. *Computers in Industry, 79*, 64-76.

Agrawal, D., El Abbadi, A., Das, S., & Elmore, A. J. (2011, April). Database scalability, elasticity, and autonomy in the cloud. In *Proceedings of the 16th Intl. conference on Database systems for advanced applications*. Springer-Verlag. doi:10.1007/978-3-642-20149-3_2

Ahmed, Xiang, & Ali. (2010). Above the Trust and Security in Cloud Computing: A Notion towards Innovation. *IEEE/IFIP International Conference on Embedded and Ubiquitous Computing*. doi:10.1109/CSCWD.2010.5471954

Al Hamed, T., & Alenezi, M. (2016). Business Continuity Management & Disaster Recovery Capabilities in Saudi Arabia ICT Businesses. *International Journal of Hybrid Information Technology, 9*(11), 99–126. doi:10.14257/ijhit.2016.9.11.10

Al-Ali & Aburukba. (2015). Role of the Internet of Things in the smart Grid. *Journal of Computer and Communications, 3*, 229-233.

Aleisa, N., & Renaud, K. (2016). *Privacy of the Internet of Things: A Systematic Literature Review (Extended Discussion).* arXiv preprint arXiv:1611.03340

Ali, Qadir, Rasool, Sathiaseelan, & Zwitter. (2016). *Big Data for Development: Applications and Techniques.* National University of Sciences and Technology (NUST).

Aljawarneh, S. (2011a). Cloud Security Engineering: Avoiding Security Threats the Right Way. *International Journal of Cloud Applications and Computing, 1*(2), 64-70. doi:10.4018/ijcac.2011040105

Aljawarneh, S., Yassein, M.B. & Talafha, W.A. (2017). A multithreaded programming approach for multimedia big data: Encryption system. *Multimed Tools Appl.* <ALIGNMENT.qj></ALIGNMENT>10.1007/s11042-017-4873-9

Aljawarneh, S. (2011b). _A web engineering security methodology for e-learning systems. *Network Security, 3*(3), 12–15. doi:10.1016/S1353-4858(11)70026-5

Aljawarneh, S. A., Alawneh, A., & Jaradat, R. (2017). Cloud security engineering: Early stages of SDLC. *Future Generation Computer Systems, 74*, 385–392. doi:10.1016/j.future.2016.10.005

Aljawarneh, S. A., Moftah, R. A., & Maatuk, A. M. (2016). Investigations of automatic methods for detecting the polymorphic worms signatures. *Future Generation Computer Systems, 60*, 67–77. doi:10.1016/j.future.2016.01.020

Aljawarneh, S. A., Vangipuram, R., Puligadda, V. K., & Vinjamuri, J. (2017). G-SPAMINE: An approach to discover temporal association patterns and trends in internet of things. *Future Generation Computer Systems, 74*, 430–443. doi:10.1016/j.future.2017.01.013

Aljawarneh, S. A., & Yassein, M. O. B. (2016). A Conceptual Security Framework for Cloud Computing Issues. *International Journal of Intelligent Information Technologies, 12*(2), 12–24. doi:10.4018/IJIIT.2016040102

Aljawarneh, S., Aldwairi, M., & Yassein, M. B. (2017). Anomaly-based intrusion detection system through feature selection analysis and building hybrid efficient model. *Journal of Computational Science.* doi:10.1016/j.jocs.2017.03.006

Aljawarneh, S., Yassein, M. B., & Telafeh, W. (2017). A resource-efficient encryption algorithm for multimedia big data. *Multimedia Tools and Applications*, 1–22.

Allalouf, M., Arbitman, Y., Factor, M., Kat, R. I., Meth, K., & Naor, D. (2009). Storage Modelling For Power Estimation. *Proceedings of 2009 Israeli Experimental Systems Conference (SYSTOR '09).*

Allenotor, D., & Thulasiram, R. K. (2008). Grid resources pricing: A Novel Financial Option Based Quality Of Service-Profit Quasi-Static Equilibrium Model. *Proceedings of the 8th ACM/IEEE International Conference on Grid Computing.* doi:10.1109/GRID.2008.4662785

Allman, M., Christensen, K., Nordman, B., & Paxson, V. (2007). Enabling an Energy-Efficient Future Internet Through Selectively Connected End Systems. *Proceedings of the Sixth ACM Workshop on Hot Topics in Networks (HotNets-VI).*

Alonso, V., & Arranz, O. (2016). *Big Data and e- Learning: A Binomial to the Future of the Knowledge Society.* Special Issue on Big Data and AI.

Alpár, G., Batina, L., Batten, L., Moonsamy, V., Krasnova, A., Guellier, A., & Natgunanathan, I. (2016, May). New directions in IoT privacy using attribute-based authentication. In *Proceedings of the ACM International Conference on Computing Frontiers* (pp. 461-466). ACM. doi:10.1145/2903150.2911710

Aly, , Elmogy, & Barkat. (2015). Mansoura university, Egypt, Big data on Internet of Things: Application Architecture, Technologies, Techniques and future directions. *International Journal on Computer Science and Engineering.*

Anvari-Moghaddam, A., Monsef, H., & Rahimi-Kian, A. (2015). Optimal Smart Home Energy Management Considering Energy Saving and a Comfortable Lifestyle. *IEEE Transactions on Smart Grid, 6*(1), 324–332. doi:10.1109/TSG.2014.2349352

Armbrust, M., Fox, A., Griffith, R., Joseph, A. D., Katz, R. H., & Konwinski, A. (2010). A View of Cloud Computing. ACM Communication, 53(4), 50–58.

Armbrust, M., Fox, A., Griffith, R., Joseph, A. D., Katz, R. H., & Konwinski, A. (2010). A view of cloud computing. ACM Communication, 53(4), 50–58. doi:10.1145/1721654.1721672

Armbrust, M., Fox, A., Griffith, R., Joseph, A., Katz, R., Konwinski, A., . . . Stoica, M. (2009). Above the Clouds: A Berkeley View Of Cloud Computing. UC Berkeley Reliable Adaptive Distributed Systems Laboratory, 1-23.

Armbrust, M., Fox, A., Griffith, R., Joseph, A., Katz, R., Konwinski, A., . . . Stoica, M. (2009). Above The Clouds: A Berkeley View of Cloud Computing. UC Berkeley Reliable Adaptive Distributed Systems Laboratory, 1-23.

Army Battle Command Systems (ABCS). (n.d.). Retrieved from http://www.dote.osd.mil/pub/reports/FY2005/pdf/ army/2005abcs.pdf

Ashwini Khadke, C. (2016). *Review on Mitigation of Distributed Denial of Service (DDOS).* Attacks in Cloud Computing. doi:10.1109/ISCO.2016.7726917

Asmuth, C. A., & Blakley, G. R. (1982, April). Pooling, splitting, and restituting information to overcome total failure of some channels of communication. In *Security and Privacy, 1982 IEEE Symposium on* (pp. 156-156). IEEE. doi:10.1109/SP.1982.10019

Atallah, M., Frikken, K., & Blanton, M. (2005). Dynamic and Efficient Key Management for Access Hierarchies. *Proceedings of ACM Conference Computer Communication Security*, 190–202. doi:10.1145/1102120.1102147

Baba, H., Adachi, I., Takabayashi, H., Nagatomo, N., Nakasone, S., Matsumoto, H., & Shimano, T. (2014). Introductory study on Disaster Risk Assessment and Area Business Continuity Planning in industry agglomerated areas in the ASEAN. *IDRiM Journal*, *3*(2), 184–195. doi:10.5595/idrim.2013.0069

Badger, L., Patt-Corner, R., & Voas, J. (2012). Draft cloud computing synopsis and recommendations of the national institute of standards and technology. *Nist Special Publication*, 146. Available at http://csrc.nist.gov/publications/drafts/ 800-146/Draft-NIST-SP800-146.pdf

Baliga, J., Ayre, R., Hinton, K., & Tucker, R. S. (2010). Green Cloud Computing: Balancing Energy In Processing, Storage And Transport. *Proceedings of the IEEE*, *99*(1), 149–167. doi:10.1109/JPROC.2010.2060451

Banerjee, C. (2012). Framework ON Service Based Resource Selection In Cloud Computing. *International Journal of Information Processing and Management*, *3*(1), 17–25. doi:10.4156/ijipm.vol3.issue1.2

Bani Yassein M., Al-Humoud S., Khaoua, & Mackenzie, L. (2007). *New counter based broadcast scheme using local neighborhood information in manets.* Academic Press.

Bani Yassein, M., Al-Rushdan, S., Mardini, W., & Khamayseh, Y. (2011). Performance of Probabilistic Broadcasting of Dynamic Source Routing Protocol. In *Proceeding of The Fourth International Conference on Communication Theory, Reliability, and Quality of Service*. Budapest, Hungary: IARIA.

Bani Yassein, M., Ould Khaoua, M., Mackenzie, L. M., & Papanastasiou, S. (2005). The Highly Adjusted Probabilistic Broadcasting in Mobile Ad hoc Networks. *Proceedings of the 6th Annual PostGraduate Symposium on the Convergence of Telecommunications, Networking & Broadcasting*.

Bani Yassein, M., Al-Dubai, A. Y., & Buchanan, W. (2010). A new adaptive broadcasting approach for mobile ad hoc networks. In *Proceeding of the Sixth Conference on Wireless Advanced (WiAD)*. London: IEEE.

Bani Yassein, M., Al-Dubai, A. Y., Khaoua, M., & Al-jarrah, O. (2009). New adaptive counter based broadcast using neighborhood information in manets. *Proceeding of the IEEE International Symposium on Parallel & Distributed Processing*.

Bani Yassein, M., Khalaf, M., & Al-Dubai, A. (2010). A new probabilistic broadcasting scheme for mobile ad hoc on-demand distance vector (AODV) routed networks. *The Journal of Supercomputing*, *53*(1), 196–211. doi:10.1007/s11227-010-0408-0

Bani Yassein, M., & Khaoua, M. O. (2007). Application of Probabilistic Flooding in MANETs. *Ubiquitous Computing and Communication Journal*, *1*, 1–5.

Bani Yassein, M., Khaoua, M. O., Mackenzie, L. M., & Papanastasiou, S. (2006). Performance evaluation of adjusted probabilistic broadcasting in MANETs. *Proceeding of the 2nd IEEE International Symposium on Dependable, Autonomic and Secure Computing.* doi:10.1109/DASC.2006.39

Bani Yassein, M., Manaseer, S., Al-hassan, A. A., Taye, Z. A., & Al-Dubai, A. Y. (2010). A new probabilistic Linear Exponential Backoff scheme for MANETs. In *Proceeding of International Symposium on Parallel & Distributed Processing Workshops and Phd Forum (IPDPSW)*. Atlanta, GA: IEEE.

Bani Yassein, M., Nimer, S. F., & Al-Dubai, A. Y. (2011). A new dynamic counter-based broadcasting scheme for mobile ad hoc networks. *Simulation Modelling Practice and Theory, 19*(1), 553–563. doi:10.1016/j.simpat.2010.08.011

Bani Yassein, M., Nimer, S., & Al-Dubai, A. Y. (2010). The effects of network density of a new counter-based broadcasting scheme in mobile ad hoc networks. In *10th International Conference on Computer and Information Technology (CIT)*. Bradford, UK: IEEE.

Bani Yassein, M., Ould-Khaoua, M., Mackenzie, L. M., & Papanastasiou, S. (2005). Improving the performance of probabilistic flooding in MANETS. *Proceedings of International Workshop on Wireless Ad-hoc Networks.*

Bani Yassein, M., Ould-Khaoua, M., & Papanastasiou, S. (2005). Performance evaluation of flooding in MANETs in the presence of multi-broadcast traffic. *Proceeding of the 11th International Conference on Parallel and Distributed Systems.*

Banirostam, H., Hedayati, A., Zadeh, A. K., & Shamsinezhad, E. (2013). A Trust Based Approach for Increasing Security in Cloud Computing Infrastructure. *15th International Conference on Computer Modelling and Simulation*, 717-721. doi:10.1109/UKSim.2013.39

Bani-Yassein, M., Khaoua, M. O., Mackenzie, L. M., & Papanastasiou, S. (2006). Performance analysis of adjusted probabilistic broadcasting in mobile ad hoc networks. *International Journal of Wireless Information Networks, 13*(2), 127–140. doi:10.1007/s10776-006-0027-0

Bansal, H. S., McDougall, G. H. G., Dikolli, S. S., & Sedatole, K. L. (2004). Relating e-satisfaction to behavioral outcomes: An emprical study. *Journal of Services Marketing, 18*(4), 290–302. doi:10.1108/08876040410542281

Barsoum & Hasan. (2012). Enabling Dynamic Data and Indirect Mutual Trust for Cloud Computing Storage Systems. *IEEE Transactions on Parallel and Distributed Systems.*

Bash, C., & Forman, G. (2007). Cool job allocation: Measuring the power savings of placing jobs at cooling-efficient locations in the datacenter. *Proceeding of 2007 Annual Technical Conference on USENIX.*

Bauman, E., Ayoade, G, & Lin, Z. (2015). A survey on hypervisor-based monitoring: Approaches, applications, and evolutions. *ACM Comput. Surv., 48*(1). DOI: 10.1145/2775111

Compilation of References

Becker, M., Goldszal, A., Detal, J., Gronlund-Jacob, J., & Epstein, R. (2015). Managing a Multisite Academic–Private Radiology Practice Reading Environment: Impact of IT Downtimes on Enterprise Efficiency. *Journal of the American College of Radiology*, *12*(6), 630–637. doi:10.1016/j.jacr.2014.11.002 PMID:25686641

Béguin, P., & Cresti, A. (1998). General information dispersal algorithms. *Theoretical Computer Science*, *209*(1-2), 87–105. doi:10.1016/S0304-3975(97)00098-4

Bella, G., Pistagna, C., & Riccobene, S. (2006). Distributed backup through information dispersal. *Electronic Notes in Theoretical Computer Science*, *142*, 63–77. doi:10.1016/j.entcs.2004.11.046

Beloglazov, A., Buyya, R., Lee, Y. C., & Zomaya, A. (2011). A Taxonomy and Survey of Energy-Efficient Data Centers and Cloud computing Systems. In Advances in Computers. Elsevier.

Berlekamp, E. R. (1968). *Algebraic coding theory*. Academic Press.

Bernabe, J. B., Ramos, J. L. H., & Gomez, A. F. S. (2016). TACIoT: Multidimensional trust-aware access control system for the Internet of Things. *Soft Computing*, *20*(5), 1763–1779. doi:10.1007/s00500-015-1705-6

Bestavros, A. (1994). An adaptive information dispersal algorithm for time-critical reliable communication. In Network Management and Control (pp. 423-438). Springer US. doi:10.1007/978-1-4899-1298-5_37

Beth, T., Borcherding, M., & Klein, B. (1994). Valuation of trust in open networks. In *Proc. of the 3rd European Symposium on Research in Computer Security*. Springer-Verlag.

Beyk Mohammadi, H. (2000). New outlook on the economic effects of tourism development by looking at Iran. Political-Economic Information, 248-253.

Bianchini, R., & Rajamony, R. (2004). Power And Energy Management For Server Systems. *Computer*, *37*(11), 68–74. doi:10.1109/MC.2004.217

Bianzino, P., Chaudet, C., Rossi, D., & Rougier, J. (2011). A Survey of Green Networking Research. *IEEE Communications Surveys and Tutorials*.

Bi, J., Zhu, Z., Tian, R., & Wang, Q. (2010). Dynamic Provisioning Modeling for Virtualized Multi-tier Applications in Cloud Data Center. In *3rd International Conference on Cloud Computing* (pp. 370-377). Miami, FL: IEEE. doi:10.1109/CLOUD.2010.53

Blakley, G. R. (1979). Safeguarding cryptographic keys. *Proc. of the National Computer Conference*, *48*, 313-317.

Bohtan, A., Vrat, P., & Vij, A. K. (2016). *Peculiarities of Disaster Management in a High-Altitude Area*. Managing Humanitarian Logistics. doi:10.1007/978-81-322-2416-7_19

Bonatti, P. A., & Olmedilla, D. (2005). Driving and monitoring provisional trust negotiation with metapolicies. In *IEEE 6th International Workshop on Policies for Distributed Systems and Networks (POLICY)*. Stockholm, Sweden: IEEE Computer Society. doi:10.1109/POLICY.2005.13

Bonatti, P. A., Shahmehri, N., Duma, C., Olmedilla, D., Nejdl, W., Baldoni, M., . . . Fuchs, N. E. (2004). Rule-based policy specification: State of the art and future work. *Report I2:D1, EU NoE REWERSE, 2*(14), 10.

Bonatti, P., & Samarati, P. (2000). Regulating service access and information release on the web. *Proc. of the 7th ACM conference on computer and communications security*, 134-143. doi:10.1145/352600.352620

Boukerche & Ren. (2008). A trust-based security system for ubiquitous and pervasive computing environments. *Computer Communications*.

Brazelton, N. C., & Lyons, A. M. (2016). Downtime and Disaster Recovery for Health Information Systems. In *Health Informatics-E-Book: An Interprofessional Approach*. Elsevier.

Brindley, C. (2017). *Supply chain risk*. Ashgate Publishing.

Build your business on Google Cloud Platform. (n.d.). Retrieved from https://cloud.google.com

Buyya, R., Yeo, C. S., & Venugopal, S. (2008). Market-Oriented Cloud Computing: Vision, Hype, And Reality For Delivering It Services As Computing Utilities. *Proceedings of the 10th IEEE International Conference on High Performance Computing and Communications*. doi:10.1109/HPCC.2008.172

Buyya, R., Yeo, C. S., Venugopal, S., Broberg, J., & Brandic, I. (2009). Cloud computing and emerging IT platforms: Vision, hype, and reality for delivering computing as the 5th utility. *Future Generation Computer Systems*, *25*(6), 599–616.

Buyya, R., Yeo, C. S., Venugopal, S., Broberg, J., & Brandic, I. (2009). Cloud computing and emerging IT platforms: Vision, hype, and reality for delivering computing as the 5th utility. *Future Generation Computer Systems*, *25*(6), 599–616. doi:10.1016/j.future.2008.12.001

Canedo. (2012). Trust Model for Private Cloud. *IEEE International Conference on Cyber Security, Cyber Warfare and Digital Forensic (CyberSec)*.

Canedo, E. D. (2012). Trust Model for Private Cloud. *IEEE International Conference on Cyber Security, Cyber Warfare and Digital Forensic (CyberSec)*, 380-389.

Caronni, G. (2000). Walking the web of trust. *Proceedings of 9th IEEE International Workshops on Enabling Technologies (WETICE)*, 153-158.

Chang, V., Ramachandran, M., Yao, Y., Kuo, Y. H., & Li, C. S. (2016). A resiliency framework for an enterprise cloud. *International Journal of Information Management*, *36*(1), 155–166. doi:10.1016/j.ijinfomgt.2015.09.008

Chanwick, A., & Mary, C. (2003). Interaction between states and citizens in the age of the internet: EGovernment and E-Governance. *An International Journal of Policy, Administration & Institutions*, *16*, 271–300. doi:10.1111/1468-0491.00216

Chatterjee, R., Ismail, N., & Shaw, R. (2016). *Identifying Priorities of Asian Small-and Medium-Scale Enterprises for Building Disaster Resilience*. Urban Disasters and Resilience in Asia. doi:10.1016/B978-0-12-802169-9.00012-4

Chen, Mao, & Liu. (2014). *Big Data: A Survey*. Springer.

Chen, K., Shen, M., & Zheng, W. (2005). Resources Allocation Schemas For Web Information Monitoring. *Tsinghua Science and Technology*, *10*(3), 309–315. doi:10.1016/S1007-0214(05)70074-2

Chen, M., Mao, S., & Liu, Y. (2014). Big Data: A Survey. *Mobile Networks and Applications*, *9*(2), 171–209. doi:10.1007/s11036-013-0489-0

Chen, R., Guo, J., & Bao, F. (2016). Trust management for SOA-based IoT and its application to service composition. *IEEE Transactions on Services Computing*, *9*(3), 482–495. doi:10.1109/TSC.2014.2365797

Corporate Partnership Board Report. (2015). *Big Data and Transport Understanding and assessing options*. OEC.

Coursey, D., & Norris, D. (2008). Model of e-Governance: Are they correct? An empirical assessment public administration overview. Academic Press.

Cui, W. (2011). Application and Developing Prospect of Cloud Computation in the Agricultural Informationization. *Agricultural Engineering*, *2*(1), 40–43.

Daniel, W. K. (2014). Challenges on privacy and reliability in cloud computing security. *Information Science, Electronics and Electrical Engineering (ISEEE), 2014 International Conference*, 1181-1187. doi:10.1109/InfoSEEE.2014.6947857

Danny, B. (1998). Mobile Objects And Mobile Agents: The Future Of Distributed Computing. *12th European Conference on Object-Oriented Programming*, *1445*, 1-12.

Daubert, J., Wiesmaier, A., & Kikiras, P. (2015, June). A view on privacy & trust in iot. In *2015 IEEE International Conference on Communication Workshop (ICCW)* (pp. 2665-2670). IEEE. doi:10.1109/ICCW.2015.7247581

De Santis, A., & Masucci, B. (2002). On information dispersal algorithms. In *Information Theory, 2002. Proceedings. 2002 IEEE International Symposium on* (p. 410). IEEE. doi:10.1109/ISIT.2002.1023682

Dembla, D., & Chaba, Y. (2010). Performance Modeling of Efficient & Dynamic Broadcasting Algorithm in MANETs Routing Protocols. In *Proceeding of Second International Conference on Computer Research and Development*. Washington, DC: IEEE. doi:10.1109/ICCRD.2010.82

Dias de Assunção, M., Cardonha, C. H., Netto, M. A. S., & Cunha, R. L. F. (2016). Impact of user patience on auto-scaling resource capacity for cloud services. *Future Generation Computer Systems*, *55*, 41–50. doi:10.1016/j.future.2015.09.001

DiStefano, B., & Hawkins, B. (2016). Achieving top-quartile reliability returns. *Asset Management & Maintenance Journal*, *29*(2), 18.

Doelitzscher, F., Reich, C., Knahi, M., Passfall, A., & Clarke, N. (2012). An Agent Based Business Aware Incident Detection System For Cloud Environments. *Journal of Cloud Computing: Advances Systems and Applications*, *1*(9), 239-246.

Dougherty, B., White, J., & Schmidt, D. C. (2012). Model-driven auto-scaling of green cloud computing infrastructure. *Future Generation Computer Systems*, *28*(2), 371–37. doi:10.1016/j.future.2011.05.009

Douligeris, C., & Mitrokotsa, A. (2004). DDoS attacks and defense mechanisms: Classification. *Computer Networks*, *44*(5), 643–666. doi:10.1016/j.comnet.2003.10.003

Doyle, R. P., Chase, J. S., Asad, O. M., Jin, W., & Vahdat, A. M. (2003). Model-based resource provisioning in a web service utility. In *4th conference on USENIX Symposium on Internet Technologies and Systems* (vol. 4, pp. 5-5). Seattle, WA: ACM.

Duma, C., Shahmehri, N., & Caronni, G. (2005). Dynamic trust metrics for peer-to-peer systems. *Proc. of 2nd IEEE Workshop on P2P Data Management, Security and Trust*, 776-781.

Dutta, S., Gera, S., Verma, A., & Viswanathan, B. (2012). SmartScale: Automatic Application Scaling in Enterprise Clouds. In *3rd International Conference on Cloud Computing* (pp. 221-228). IEEE. doi:10.1109/CLOUD.2012.12

Egger, R., & Buhalis, D. (2008). *E-tourism case studies: Management and marketing issues*. Elsevier Ltd.

Eisen, M. (2011). *Introduction to Virtualization*. The Long Island Chapter of the IEEE Circuits and Systems (CAS) *Society*.

Epstein, B., & Khan, D. C. (2014). Application impact analysis: A risk-based approach to business continuity and disaster recovery. *Journal of Business Continuity & Emergency Planning*, *7*(3), 230–237. PMID:24578024

eSkills UK. (2013). *Big Data Analytics Adoption and Employment Trends, 2012-2017*. Author.

Fayyad-Kazan, H., Perneel, L., & Timmerman, M. (2013). Full and Para-Virtualization with Xen: A Performance Comparison. *Journal of Emerging Trends in Computing and Information Sciences*, *4*, 719–727.

Feyzioglu, O., Buyukozkan, G., & Ersoy, M. S. (2017). Supply chain risk analysis with fuzzy cognitive maps. *Industrial Engineering and Engineering Management, 2007 IEEE International Conference*, 1447-1451.

Flavio, L., & Roberto, D. P. (2011). Secure Virtualization For Cloud Computing. *Journal of Network and Computer Applications*, *41*(1), 45–52.

Foster, I., Yong, Z., Raicu, I., & Lu, S. (2008). Cloud Computing And Grid Computing 360-Degree Compared. *Workshop on Grid Computing Environments*, 1-10. doi:10.1109/GCE.2008.4738445

Franke, U., Holm, H., & König, J. (2014). The distribution of time to recovery of enterprise IT services. *IEEE Transactions on Reliability, 63*(4), 858–867. doi:10.1109/TR.2014.2336051

Franke, U., Johnson, P., & König, J. (2014). An architecture framework for enterprise IT service availability analysis. *Software & Systems Modeling, 13*(4), 1417–1445. doi:10.1007/s10270-012-0307-3

Funmilade, F., Rami, B., & Georgios, T. (2012). A Dynamic Data Driven Simulation Approach For Preventing Service Level Agreement Violations In Cloud Federation. *International Conference on Computational Science Procedia of Computer Science*, 1167-1176.

Galante, G., & Luis Carlos, E. de Bona (2012). A Survey on Cloud Computing Elasticity. *IEEE/ACM Fifth International Conference on Utility and Cloud Computing*. doi:10.1109/UCC.2012.30

Gandomi, A., & Haider, M. (2015). Beyond the hype: Big data concepts, metho- ds, and analytics. *International Journal of Information Management*. doi:10.1016/j.ijinfomgt.2014.10.007

Garg, S. K., Yeo, C. S., Anandasivam, A., & Buyya, R. (2011). Environment-Conscious Scheduling Of HPC Applications On Distributed Cloud-Oriented Datacenters *Journal of Parallel and Distributed Computing, 71*(6), 732–749. doi:10.1016/j.jpdc.2010.04.004

Gartner. (2000). *Key issues in E-Government strategy and management*. Research Notes, key issues.

Gartner. (2017). Retrieved from www.gartner.com

Gasbarro, F., Iraldo, F., & Daddi, T. (2017). The drivers of multinational enterprises' climate change strategies: A quantitative study on climate-related risks and opportunities. *Journal of Cleaner Production, 160*, 8–26. doi:10.1016/j.jclepro.2017.03.018

Gavriloaie, R., Nejdl, W., Olmedilla, D., Seamons, K. E., & Winslett, M. (2004). No registration needed: How to use declarative policies and negotiation to access sensitive resources on the semantic web. In *1st European Semantic Web Symposium (ESWS 2004)*. Springer. doi:10.1007/978-3-540-25956-5_24

Gbadeyan, A., Butakov, S., & Aghili, S. (2017). IT governance and risk mitigation approach for private cloud adoption: Case study of provincial healthcare provider. *Annales des Télécommunications, 72*(5-6), 347–357. doi:10.1007/s12243-017-0568-5

Gebai, M., Giraldeau, F., & Dagenais, M. R. (2014). Fine Grained Preemption Analysis for Latency Investigation Across Virtual Machines. *Journal of Cloud Computing: Advances System and Applications, 3*(23), 1–15.

Gill, A., & Diwaker, Ch. (2012). Comparative Analysis of routing in MANET. *International Journal of Advanced Research in Computer Science and Software Engineering, 2*, 309–414.

Gong, Z., Gu, X., & Wilkes, J. (2010). PRESS: PRedictive Elastic ReSource Scaling for cloud systems. In *International Conference on Network and Service Management* (pp. 9 – 16). IEEE.

Gonnot, T., & Saniie, J. (2014). User Defined Interactions between Devices on a 6L- OWPAN Network for Home Automation. *IEEE International of Technology Management Conference*, 1-4.

Gonzalez N, Miers C, Redigolo F, Jr M, Carvalho T, Naslund M & Pourzandi M (2012). A quantitative analysis of current security concerns and solutions for cloud computing. *Journal of Cloud Computing: Advances, System and Applications*, 1-11.

Gonzalez, N., Miers, C., Redigolo, F., Carvalho, T., Naslund, M., & Pourzandi, M. (2012). A Quantitative Analysis Of Current Security Concerns And Solutions For Cloud Computing. *Journal of Cloud Computing: Advances, System and Applications*, 1-11.

Gouda, K. G., Patro, A., Dwivedi, D., & Bhat, N. (2014). Virtualization Approaches in Cloud Computing. *International Journal of Computer Trends and Technology*, *12*(4), 161–166. doi:10.14445/22312803/IJCTT-V12P132

Goyal, O., & Pandey, A. (2006). Attribute-based encryption for fine-grained access control of encrypted data. *ACM Conference Computer Communication Security*, 89–98.

Goyal, O., Pandey, A., & Sahai Waters, B. (2006). Attribute-Based Encryption For Fine-Grained Access Control Of Encrypted Data. *ACM Conference Computer Communication Security*, 89–98. doi:10.1145/1180405.1180418

Grandison, T., & Sloman, M. (2002). Specifying and analysing trust for internet applications. In *Towards the Knowledge Society: eCommerce, eBusiness, and eGovernment, The Second IFIP Conference on E-Commerce, E-Business, E-Government (I3E 2002), IFIP Conference Proceedings*. Lisbon, Portugal: Kluwer.

Grandison, T., & Sloman, M. (2002). Specifying and analysing trust for internet applications. In Towards The Knowledge Society: eCommerce, eBusiness, and eGovernment. In *The Second IFIP Conference on E-Commerce, E-Business, E-Government (I3E 2002), IFIP Conference Proceedings*. Lisbon, Portugal: Kluwer.

Grimes, J., Jaeger, P. J., & Lin, J. (2009). Weathering the storm: The policy implications of cloud computing. In *Proceedings of Conference*. University of North Carolina.

Großschädl, Avanzi, R.M., Savas, E., & Tillich, S. (2005). Energy-Efficient Software Implementation Of Long Integer Modular Arithmetic. *Proceedings of 7th Workshop on Cryptographic Hardware and Embedded Systems*.

Gupta, Kapur, & Kumar. (2016). Exploring disaster recovery parameters in an enterprise application. In *International Conference of Innovation and Challenges in Cyber Security (ICICCS-INBUSH)*. Greater Noida, India: IEEE.

Gu, Z. H., & Zhao, Q. L. (2012). A State-of-the-Art Survey on Real-Time Issues in Embedded Systems Virtualization. *Journal of Software Engineering and Applications*, *5*(4), 277–290. doi:10.4236/jsea.2012.54033

Hashem, Chang, Anuar, Adewole, Yaqoob, Gani, & Ahmed. (2014). *The role of big data in smart city*. University of Malaya.

Hashem, I. A. T., Yaqoob, I., Anuar, N. B., Mokhtar, S., Khan, A., & Gani, S. U. (2015). The rise of "big data" on cloud computing: Review and open research issues. *Information Systems*, *47*, 98–115. doi:10.1016/j.is.2014.07.006

Hassanalieragh, M., Page, A., Soyata, T., Sharma, G., Aktas, M., & Mateos, G. (2015). Health Monitoring and Management Using Iternet-of- Things (IoT) Sensing with Cloud-based Processing: Opportunities challenges. *IEEE International Conference on Service Computing*.

Herbst, N. R., Kounev, S., & Reussner, R. (2013). Elasticity in Cloud Computing: What It Is, and What It Is Not? *ICAC*, 23 – 27. Retrieved from https://sdqweb.ipd.kit.edu/publications/pdfs/HeKoRe2013-ICAC-Elasticity.pdf

Hernández-Ramos, J. L., Bernabe, J. B., Moreno, M., & Skarmeta, A. F. (2015). Preserving Smart Objects Privacy through Anonymous and Accountable Access Control for a M2M-Enabled Internet of Things. *Sensors (Basel)*, *15*(7), 15611–15639. doi:10.3390/s150715611 PMID:26140349

Hernandez-Ramos, J. L., Pawlowski, M. P., Jara, A. J., Skarmeta, A. F., & Ladid, L. (2015). Toward a lightweight authentication and authorization framework for smart objects. *IEEE Journal on Selected Areas in Communications*, *33*(4), 690–702. doi:10.1109/JSAC.2015.2393436

Herrera, F.Research Group on Soft Computing and Information Intelligent Systems. (2015). *Data Mining Methods for Big Data Preprocessing*. INIT/AERFAI Summer School on Machine Learning.

Hiller, M., Bone, E. A., & Timmins, M. L. (2015). Healthcare system resiliency: The case for taking disaster plans further—Part 2. *Journal of Business Continuity & Emergency Planning*, *8*(4), 356–375. PMID:25990980

Hossein, R., Elankovan, S., Zulkarnain, M. A., & Abdullah, M. Z. (2013). Encryption as a service as a solution for cryptography in cloud. *International Conference on Electrical Engineering and Informatics indexed in Science Direct*, 1202-1210.

Hossein, R., Elankovan, S., Zulkarnain, M. A., & Abdullah, M. Z. (2013). Encryption As A Service As A Solution For Cryptography In Cloud. *International Conference on Electrical Engineering and Informatics indexed in Science Direct*, 1202-1210.

Huang, J., & Nicol, D. M. (2013). *Trust mechanisms for cloud computing*. Retrieved from http://www.journalofcloudcomputing.com/content/2/1/9

Huang, J., & Nicol. (2013). *Trust mechanisms for cloud computing*. Retrieved from http://www.journalofcloudcomputing.com/content/2/1/9

Huang, Z. C., & Yuan, F. (2015). Implementation of 6LoWPAN and Its Application in Smart Lighting. *Journal of Computer and Communication.*, *3*(03), 80–85. doi:10.4236/jcc.2015.33014

Huatuco, L. H., Ullah, G. S., & Burgess, T. F. (2017). Supply Chain Major Disruptions and Sustainability Metrics: A Case Study. *International Conference on Sustainable Design and Manufacturing*, 185-192. doi:10.1007/978-3-319-57078-5_18

Huiqi, X., Shumin, G., & Keke, C. (2014). Building Confidential And Efficient Query Services In The Cloud With Rasp Data Perturbation. *IEEE Transactions on Knowledge and Data Engineering*, *26*(2), 322–335. doi:10.1109/TKDE.2012.251

Hung, Hu, & Li. (2012). Auto-Scaling Model for Cloud Computing System. *International Journal of Hybrid Information Technology, 5*(2).

Hurwitz, J., Bloor, R., Kaufman, M., & Halper, F. (2010). *Cloud Computing for Dummies*. Wiley.

Intel IT Center (2015). *Big data in the cloud convergenging technologies, big data in the cloud*. Unpublished.

Intel. (2015). *Ultra-Wideband (UWB) Technology Enabling high-speed wireless personal area networks*. Intel.

Iqbal, W., Dailey, M. N., Carrera, D., & Janecek, P. (2011). Adaptive resource provisioning for read intensive multi-tier applications in the cloud. *Future Generation Computer Systems*, *27*(6), 871–879. doi:10.1016/j.future.2010.10.016

Ivanov, D., Dolgui, A., Sokolov, B., & Ivanova, M. (2017). Literature review on disruption recovery in the supply chain. *International Journal of Production Research*, 1–17. doi:10.1080/00207543.2017.1343507

Jan Kremer Consulting Services (JKCS). (2015). *Cloud Computing & Virtualization*. White Paper. Author.

Jang, H.-C., & Ch, H. (2010). Direction based routing strategy to reduce broadcast storm in MANET. In *Proceeding of International Computer Symposium (ICS)*. Tainan, Taiwan: IEEE. doi:10.1109/COMPSYM.2010.5685471

Javadi, B., Kondo, D., Iosup, A., & Epema, D. (2013). The Failure Trace Archive: Enabling the comparison of failure measurements and models of distributed systems. *Journal of Parallel and Distributed Computing*, *73*(8), 1208–1223. doi:10.1016/j.jpdc.2013.04.002

Jechlitschek. (2015). *A survey paper on Radio Frequency Identification*. Academic Press.

Jungwoo, R., Syed, R., William, A., & John, K. (2013). Cloud Security Auditing: Challenges And Emerging Approaches. *IEEE Security and Privacy*, 1–13.

Jungwoo, R., Syed, R., William, A., & John, K. (2013). *Cloud Security Auditing: Challenges and Emerging Approaches*. IEEE Security and Privacy.

Kalpana, G., Kumar, P. V., Aljawarneh, S., & Krishnaiah, R. V. (2017). Shifted Adaption Homomorphism Encryption for Mobile and Cloud Learning. *Computers & Electrical Engineering*. doi:10.1016/j.compeleceng.2017.05.022

Kalpana, Govindaswamy, & Punithavalli. (2012). Reliable broadcasting using efficient forward node selection for mobile ad-hoc networks. *The International Arab Journal of Information Technology, 9*, 299–305.

Kanakaris, Venetis, Ndzi, Ovaliadis, & Yang. (2012). A new RREQ message forwarding technique based on Bayesian probability theory. *EURASIP Journal on Wireless Communications and Networking, 318*, 1–12.

Kephart, J. O., Chan, H., Das, R., Levine, D. W., Tesauro, G., Rawson, F., & Lefurgy, C. (2007). Coordinating Multiple Autonomic Managers To Achieve Specified Power-Performance Tradeoffs. *Proceedings of 4th International Conference on Autonomic Computing.* doi:10.1109/ICAC.2007.12

Khajuria & Srivastava. (2013). Analysis Of The DDOS Defence Strategies In Cloud Computing. *International Journal Of Enhanced Research In Management & Computer Applications,* (2), 1-5.

Khamayseh, Y., Bader, A., Mardini, W., & BaniYasein, M. (2011). A new protocol for detecting black hole nodes in Ad Hoc Networks. *International Journal of Communication Networks and Information Security, 3*, 36-47.

Khan, A. I., Madani, S. A., Anwar, W., & Hayat, K. (2011). Location based dynamic probabilistic broadcasting for MANETs. *World Applied Sciences Journal, 13*, 2296–2305.

Kim, Sung-Han-sim, Cho, Yun, & Min. (2016). *Recent Rand D activities on structural health monitoring in Korea.* Pukyoung National University.

Klafft, M., & Ziegler, H. G. (2014). A concept and prototype for the integration of multi-channel disaster alert systems. *Proceedings of the 7th Euro American Conference on Telematics and Information Systems, 20.* doi:10.1145/2590651.2590669

Kotikela & Gomathisankaran. (2012). CTrust: A framework for Secure and Trustworthy application execution in Cloud computing. *International Conference on Cyber Security.*

Krawczyk, H. (1993a, August). Secret sharing made short. In *Annual International Cryptology Conference* (pp. 136-146). Springer Berlin Heidelberg.

Krawczyk, H. (1993b, September). Distributed fingerprints and secure information dispersal. In *Proceedings of the twelfth annual ACM symposium on Principles of distributed computing* (pp. 207-218). ACM. doi:10.1145/164051.164075

Krishnatej, K., Patnala, E., Narasingu, S. S., & Chaitanya, J. N. (2013). Virtualization Technology in Cloud Computing Environment. *International Journal of Emerging Technology and Advanced Engineering, 3.*

Kristo, Filipovic, & Cingula. (n.d.). Methodological aspects of measuring business resilience. *Economic and Social Development Proceedings.*

Krumm, J. (2009). A survey of computational location privacy. *Personal and Ubiquitous Computing, 13*(6), 291–399. doi:10.1007/s00779-008-0212-5

Kshetri, N., Fredriksson, T., & Torres, D. C. R. (2017). *Big Data and Cloud Computing for Development: Lessons from Key Industries and Economies in the Global South.* Taylor & Francis.

Kumarswamy. (2009). Cloud Security And Privacy: An Enterprise Perspective On Risks And Compliances. Academic Press.

L'Hermitte, C., Tatham, P., Brooks, B., & Bowles, M. (2016). Supply chain agility in humanitarian protracted operations. *Journal of Humanitarian Logistics and Supply Chain Management, 6*(2), 173–201. doi:10.1108/JHLSCM-09-2015-0037

Lakshminarayanan, Kumar, & Raju. (2014). *Cloud Computing Benefits for Educational Institutions.* Higher College of Technology. Retrieved from https://ai2-s2-pdfs.s3.amazonaws.com/d3dc/566 db2811b61776d0216ccf9c55d55c0101c.pdf

Lamb, C. C., & Heileman, G. L. (2012). Content Centric Information Protection In Cloud Computing. *International Journal of Cloud Computing and Services Science, 2*(1), 28–39.

Lam, J. (2014). *Enterprise risk management: from incentives to controls.* John Wiley & Sons. doi:10.1002/9781118836477

Lee, J. Y., Lin, W. C., & Huang, Y. H. (2014, May). A lightweight authentication protocol for internet of things. In *Next-Generation Electronics (ISNE), 2014 International Symposium on* (pp. 1-2). IEEE. doi:10.1109/ISNE.2014.6839375

Levy, J., Yu, P., & Prizzia, R. (2016). Economic Disruptions, Business Continuity Planning and Disaster Forensic Analysis: The Hawaii Business Recovery Center (HIBRC) Project. Disaster Forensics, 315-334. doi:10.1007/978-3-319-41849-0_13

Li, Chinneck, Wodside, & Litoiu. (2009). Fast Scalable Optimization To Configure Service System Having Cost And Quality Of Service Constraints. *IEEE International Conference on Autonomic System Barcelona*, 159-168 doi:10.1145/1555228.1555268

Li, N., Mitchell, J. C., & Winsborough, W. H. (2002). Design of a role-based trust-management framework. In *Security and Privacy, 2002. Proceedings. 2002 IEEE Symposium on.* IEEE.

Li, N., Mitchell, J. C., & Winsborough, W. H. (2002). Design of a role-based trust-management framework. *Security and Privacy, 2002. Proceedings. 2002 IEEE Symposium on.*

Li, Q. (2016). *Estimation of the costs of information system downtime in organisations: underlying threats, effects and cost factors* (Master's thesis). University of Twente.

Liarokapis, D., & Shahrabi, A. (2011). Fuzzy-based probabilistic broadcasting in mobile ad hoc networks. In *Proceeding of Wireless Days (WD).* Niagara Falls, Canada: IEEE.

Li, G., Zhang, Q., Feng, Z., & Wang, W. (2016). A disaster recovery solution based on heterogeneous storage. *Journal of Intelligent & Fuzzy Systems, 31*(4), 2249–2256. doi:10.3233/JIFS-169065

Li, T., Lin, C., & Ni, Y. (2010). Evaluation of User Behavior Trust in Cloud Computing. *International Conference on Computer Application and System Modeling.*

Lockamy, A. III. (2014). Assessing disaster risks in supply chains. *Industrial Management & Data Systems, 114*(5), 755–777. doi:10.1108/IMDS-11-2013-0477

Loke, S. W (1999). A Technical Report On: Mobile Agent Technology For Enterprise Distributed Applications: An Overview And An Architectural Perspective. *CRC for Distributed Systems Technology*, 1-45.

Lyu, H., Li, P., Yan, R., Qian, H., & Sheng, B. (2016). High-availability deployment for large enterprises. *Progress in Informatics and Computing (PIC), 2016 International Conference,* 503-507.

Macecevic, D. (2014). Enterprise risk management-priority of export-oriented firm in emerging economy. *Economic and Social DevelopmentProceedings*.

Madakam, , Ramaswamy, & Tripathi. (2015). Internet of Things (IoT): A Literature Review. *Journal of Computer and Communications., 3*, 164–173. doi:10.4236/jcc.2015.35021

Mahmoud, R., Yousuf, T., Aloul, F., & Zualkernan, I. (2015, December). Internet of things (IoT) security: Current status, challenges and prospective measures. In *2015 10th International Conference for Internet Technology and Secured Transactions (ICITST)* (pp. 336-341). IEEE.

Maler, E., Catalano, D., Machulak, M., & Hardjono, T. (2016). *User-Managed Access (UMA) Profile of OAuth 2.0.* Academic Press.

Malhotra, L., Agarwal, D., & Jaiswal, A. (2014). Virtualization in Cloud Computing. *Journal Information Technology & Software Engineering, 4*(2), 136. doi:10.4172/2165-7866.1000136

Malhotra, M., & Malhotra, R. (2014). Cloud Adaptive Resource Allocation Mechanism for Efficient Parallel Processing. *International Journal of Cloud Applications and Computing*, 1–6.

Manekar & Pradeepin. (2015). A review on cloud Based Big data analytics. *Journal on Computer Networks and communications, 1*.

Manickam, P., Baskar, T., Girija, M., & Manimegalai, D. (2011). Performance comparisons of routing protocols in mobile ad hoc networks. *International Journal of Wireless & Mobile Networks, 3*(1), 98–106. doi:10.5121/ijwmn.2011.3109

Mao, M., Li, J., & Humphrey, M. (2010). *Cloud Auto-scaling with Deadline and Budget Constraints.* Brussels: IEEE. doi:10.1109/GRID.2010.5697966

Mardini, W., Khamayseh, Y., Jaradatand, R., & Hijjawi, R. (2012). Interference problem between ZigBee and WiFi. *International Proceedings of Computer Science and Information Technology*, 133-138.

Matos, M., Sousa, A., Pereira, J., & Oliveira, P. (2009). Clon: Overlay Network For Clouds. *Third Workshop on Dependable Distributed Data Management.* doi:10.1145/1518691.1518696

Mell, P., & Grance, T. (2011). *The NIST Definition of Cloud Computing.* Tech. rep., U.S. National Institute of Standards and Technology (NIST), Special Publication 800-145. Retrieved from http://csrc.nist.gov/publications/nistpubs/800-145/SP800-145.pdf

Mell, P., & Grace, T. (2009). *The NIST Definition of Cloud Computing*. National Institute of Standards and Technology.

Microsystems, S. (2009). *Introduction to Cloud Computing Architecture*. White paper.

Miller, H. E., & Engemann, K. J. (2015). Threats to the electric grid and the impact on organisational resilience. *International Journal of Business Continuity and Risk Management, 6*(1), 1–16. doi:10.1504/IJBCRM.2015.070348

Mogul, J. C., Mudigonda, J., Renato Santos, J., & Yoshio Turner, Y. (2012). *The NIC is the Hypervisor: Bare-Metal Guests in IaaS Clouds*. HP Labs.

Mohammed Falatah, M., & Batarfi, O. (2014). Cloud scalability considerations, Saud Arabia. *International Journal of Computer Science & Engineering Survey, 5*(4).

Mohammed, A. B., Altmann, J., & Hwang, J. (2010). *Cloud computing Value: Understanding Businesses and Value Creation in the Cloud*. Economic Models and Algorithms for Distributed Systems.

Mohan Murthy, Ameen, Sanjay, & Yasser. (2013). Software licensing models and benefits in Cloud Environment: A Survey. In *International Conference on Advances in Computing (vol. 174*, pp. 645-650). Springer. doi:10.1007/978-81-322-0740-5_76

Mohan Murthy, M. K., Ashwini, J. P., & Sanjay, H. A. (2012). Pricing Models and Pricing Schemes of IaaS Providers: A Comparison Study. In *International Conference on Advances in Computing, Communications and Informatics* (pp. 143-147). ACM. doi:10.1145/2345396.2345421

Mohan Murthy, M. K., & Sanjay, H. A., & Anand, J. (2014). Threshold Based Auto Scaling of Virtual Machines in Cloud Environment. In Lecture Notes in Computer Science: Vol. 8707. *IFIP International Conference on Network and Parallel Computing* (pp. 247-256). Springer. doi:10.1007/978-3-662-44917-2_21

Mohan, S., & Bakshi, N. (2017). Supply Chain Resilience-Epidemiological Characterization. *History (London)*.

Moharana, S. S., Ramesh, R. D., & Powar, D. (2013). Analysis Of Load Balancers In Cloud Computing. *Computing in Science & Engineering, 2*(2), 101–108.

Montshiwa, A. L., Nagahira, A., & Ishida, S. (2016). Modifying Business Continuity Plan (BCP) Towards an Effective Auto-Mobile Business Continuity Management (BCM): A Quantitative Approach. *Journal of Disaster Research, 11*(4), 691–698. doi:10.20965/jdr.2016.p0691

Morikawa, T., & Ikebe, M. (2011). Proposal And Evaluation Of A Dynamic Resource Allocation Method Based On The Load Of Vms On Iaas. *4th IFIP International Conference on New Technologies, Mobility and Security, 5*(6), 1–6.

Muchahari & Sinha. (2012). A New Trust Management Architecture for Cloud Computing Environment. *IEEE International Symposium on Cloud and Services Computing (ISCOS)*.

Muchahari, M. K., & Sinha, S. K. (2012). A New Trust Management Architecture for Cloud Computing Environment. *IEEE International Symposium on Cloud and Services Computing (ISCOS)*, 136-140. doi:10.1109/ISCOS.2012.30

Mukherjee, S., & Shaw, R. (2016). *Big Data Concepts, Applications, Challenges and Future Scope. International Journal of Advanced Research in Computer and Communication Engineering.*

Murnane, Simpson, & Jongman. (n.d.). Understanding risk: what makes a risk assessment successful? *International Journal of Disaster Resilience in the Built Environment, 7*(2), 186-200.

Nagurney, A., Masoumi, A. H., & Yu, M. (2015). *An integrated disaster relief supply chain network model with time targets and demand uncertainty* (pp. 287–318). Regional Science Matters. doi:10.1007/978-3-319-07305-7_15

Nakayama, M. K., & Yener, B. (2001). Optimal information dispersal for probabilistic latency targets. *Computer Networks, 36*(5), 695–707. doi:10.1016/S1389-1286(01)00184-0

Nand, P., & Sharma, S. C. (2011). Probability based improved broadcasting for AODV routing protocol. In *Proceeding of International Conference on Computational Intelligence and Communication Networks*. Gwalior, India: IEEE.

Närman, P., Franke, U., König, J., Buschle, M., & Ekstedt, M. (2014). Enterprise architecture availability analysis using fault trees and stakeholder interviews. *Enterprise Information Systems, 8*(1), 1–25. doi:10.1080/17517575.2011.647092

Natesapillai, K., Palanisamy, V., & Duraiswamy, K. (2010). Optimum density based model for probabilistic flooding protocol in mobile ad hoc network. *European Journal of Scientific Research*, 577-588.

Neisse, R., Steri, G., & Baldini, G. (2014, October). Enforcement of security policy rules for the internet of things. In *2014 IEEE 10th International Conference on Wireless and Mobile Computing, Networking and Communications (WiMob)* (pp. 165-172). IEEE. doi:10.1109/WiMOB.2014.6962166

Neto. (2014). *A brief history of cloud computing*. Retrieved on December 16, 2017, https://www.ibm.com/blogs/cloud-computing/2014/03/a-brief-history-of-cloud-computing-3/

Neves, Schmerl, Bernardino, & Cámara. (2016). *Big Data in Cloud Computing: features and issues*. Academic Press.

Noh, H. W., Kitagawa, K., & Oh, Y. S. (2014). Concepts of Disaster Prevention Design for Safety in the Future Society. *International Journal of Contents, 10*(1), 54–61. doi:10.5392/IJoC.2014.10.1.054

Noran, O. (2014). Collaborative disaster management: An interdisciplinary approach. *Computers in Industry, 65*(6), 1032–1040. doi:10.1016/j.compind.2014.04.003

Obasuyi, G. C., & Sari, A. (2015). Security Challenges of Virtualization Hypervisors in Virtualized Hardware Environment. *International Journal Communications. Network and System Sciences*, *8*, 260–273. doi:10.4236/ijcns.2015.87026

OCDA. (2012). *Master Usage Model: Compute Infratructure-as-a-Service.* Tech. rep., Open Data Center Alliance. Retrieved from http://www.opendatacenteralliance.org/docs/ODCA_Compute_IaaS_MasterUM_v1.0_Nov2012.pdf

Ogata, W., Kurosawa, K., & Tsujii, S. (1993). Nonperfect secret sharing schemes. In Advances in Cryptology—AUSCRYPT'92 (pp. 56-66). Springer Berlin/Heidelberg. doi:10.1007/3-540-57220-1_52

Ojha, D., Salimath, M., & D'Souza, D. (2014). Disaster immunity and performance of service firms: The influence of market acuity and supply network partnering. *International Journal of Production Economics*, *147*, 385–397. doi:10.1016/j.ijpe.2013.02.029

Orellana, L., Silva, D., & Castineira, F. (2010). Privacy For Google Docs: Implementing A Transparent Encryption Layer Cloud Views. *International Conference on Cloud Computing*, 41-48.

Organisation for Economic Co-operation and Development. (2002). *OECD Guidelines on the Protection of Privacy and Transborder Flows of Personal Data.* OECD Publishing.

Ouaddah, A., Mousannif, H., Elkalam, A. A., & Ouahman, A. A. (2017). Access control in The Internet of Things: Big challenges and new opportunities. *Computer Networks*, *112*, 237–262. doi:10.1016/j.comnet.2016.11.007

Pal, A. (2015). Internet of things: Making the hype a reality. *IT Professional*, *17*(3), 2–4. doi:10.1109/MITP.2015.36

Papadopoulos, T., Gunasekaran, A., Dubey, R., Altay, N., Childe, S. J., & Fosso-Wamba, S. (2017). The role of Big Data in explaining disaster resilience in supply chains for sustainability. *Journal of Cleaner Production*, *142*, 1108–1118. doi:10.1016/j.jclepro.2016.03.059

Papageorgiou & Salmeron. (2014). Methods and algorithms for fuzzy cognitive map-based modeling. *Fuzzy Cognitive Maps for Applied Sciences and Engineering*, 1-28.

Paper, W. (2010). *Introduction to Cloud Computing.* Retrieved from http://www.thinkgrid.com/docs/computing-whitepaper.pdf

Paper, W. (2012). Cloud 101: Developing a cloud-computing strategy for higher education. *Proceedings of the International Conference on Transformations in Engineering Education.* Retrieved from www.cisco.com/c/dam/en/us/solutions/.../cloud.../cloud_101_higher_education_wp.p

Pearson, S., & Benameur, A. (2010). Privacy, security and trust issues arising from cloud computing. *Proceedings of the 2nd IEEE International Conference on Cloud Computing Technology and Science,* 693-702. doi:10.1109/CloudCom.2010.66

Philipp, H., Rolf, W., Joachim, S., & Thomas, B. (2013). Virtual Fort Knox: Federative Secure And Cloud Based Platform For Manufacturing. *46th Conference on Manufacturing System indexed in Science Direct*, 527-532.

Popek, G. J., & Goldberg, R. P. (1974). Formal requirements for virtualizable third generation architectures. *Communications of the ACM*, *17*(7), 412–421. doi:10.1145/361011.361073

Prasad, S., Su, H. C., Altay, N., & Tata, J. (2015). Building disaster-resilient micro enterprises in the developing world. *International Journal of Production Economics*, *39*(3), 447–466. PMID:25546436

Putri & Mganga. (2011). *Enhancing Information Security in Cloud Computing Services using SLA Based Metrics*. School of Computing, Blekinge Institute of Technology.

Puttaswamy, K. P. N., Kruegel, C., & Zhao, B. Y. (2011). Silverline: Toward Data Confidentiality in Storage-Intensive Cloud Applications. *Proc. Second ACM Symp. Cloud Computing (SOCC '11)*, 10:1-10:13. doi:10.1145/2038916.2038926

Qian, K. (2012). The Application of Cloud Computing in Agricultural Management Information System. *Hubei Agricultural Sciences*, *5*(1), 159–162.

Qian, W., Cong, W., Kui, R., Wenjing, L., & Jin, L. (2011). Enabling Public Auditability And Data Dynamics For Storage Security In Cloud Computing. *IEEE Transactions on Parallel and Distributed Systems*, *22*(5), 847–859. doi:10.1109/TPDS.2010.183

Quan, Z., Chunming, T., Xianghan, Z., & Chunming, R. (2015). A Secure User Authentication Protocol For Sensor Network In Data Capturing. *Journal of Cloud Computing: Advances System and Applications*, *4*(6), 1–12.

Rabin, M. O. (1989). Efficient dispersal of information for security, load balancing, and fault tolerance. *Journal of the Association for Computing Machinery*, *36*(2), 335–348. doi:10.1145/62044.62050

Rabin, M. O. (1990). The information dispersal algorithm and its applications. In *Sequences* (pp. 406–419). Springer New York. doi:10.1007/978-1-4612-3352-7_32

Raghav, C. I. (2013). Intrusion Detection and Prevention in Cloud Environment. *Systematic Reviews*, (24), 21–30.

Raghavendra, R., Ranganathan, P., Talwar, V., Wang, Z., & Zhu, Z. (2008). No "Power" Struggles: Coordinated Multi-Level Power Management For The Datacenter. *SIGOPS Operating. Systematic Reviews*, *42*(2), 48–59.

Ramanathan, A. (2015). *A Multi-Level Trust Management Scheme for the Internet of Things*. Academic Press.

Ranganathan, P. (2010). Recipe For Efficiency: Principles Of Power-Aware Computing. *Communications of the ACM*, *53*(4), 60–67. doi:10.1145/1721654.1721673

Ranganathan, P., Leech, P., Irwin, D., & Chase, J. (2006). Ensemble Level Power Management For Dense Blade Servers. *SIGARCH. Computer Architecture News, 34*(2), 66–77. doi:10.1145/1150019.1136492

Rawson, A., Pfleuger, J., & Cader, T. (2008). *Green Grid Data Center Power Efficiency Metrics.* Consortium Green Grid.

Ribeiro, Silva, & Rodrigues da Silva. (2015). Data Modeling and Data Analytics: A Survey from a Big Data Perspective. *Journal of Software Engineering and Applications*, 617-634.

Rieser, H., Dorfinger, P., Nomikos, V., & Papataxiarhis, V. (2015). Sensor interoperability for disaster management. *Sensors Applications Symposium (SAS)*, 1-6.

Rivera, D., Cruz-Piris, L., Lopez-Civera, G., de la Hoz, E., & Marsa-Maestre, I. (2015, October). Applying an unified access control for IoT-based Intelligent Agent Systems. In *Service-Oriented Computing and Applications (SOCA), 2015 IEEE 8th International Conference on* (pp. 247-251). IEEE. doi:10.1109/SOCA.2015.40

Rivoire, S., Shah, M. A., Ranganathan, P., & Kozyrakis, C. (2007). Joulesort: A Balanced Energy-Efficiency Benchmark. *Proceedings of the 2007 ACM SIGMOD International Conference on Management of Data.* doi:10.1145/1247480.1247522

Rizwana Shaikh, M. (2012, April). Cloud Security issues: A Survey. *International Journal of Computers and Applications.*

Rizzardi, A., Miorandi, D., Sicari, S., Cappiello, C., & Coen-Porisini, A. (2015, October). Networked smart objects: moving data processing closer to the source. *2nd EAI International Conference on IoT as a Service.*

Robinston, Starr, & Vass. (2016). *Implementation of Radio Frequency Identification in hospitals.* Academic Press.

RougerS. F. (2012). Retrieved from http://www.akamai.com/dl/akamai/akamai-ebook-guide-to-multilayered-web-security.pdf

Rouse, M. (n.d.). *Virtualization.* Retrieved on March 1, 2017, from http://searchservervirtualization. techtarget.com/definition/virtualization

Safiriyu, E., Olatunde, A., Ayodeji, O., Adeniran, O., Clement, O., & Lawrence, K. (2011). A User Identity Management Protocol For Cloud Computing Paradigm. *Int J Commun Network Syst Sci, 1*(4), 152–163.

Sahebjamnia, N., Torabi, S. A., & Mansouri, S. A. (2015). Integrated business continuity and disaster recovery planning: Towards organizational resilience. *European Journal of Operational Research, 242*(1), 261–273. doi:10.1016/j.ejor.2014.09.055

Salmeron, J. L., & Lopez, C. (2012). Forecasting risk impact on ERP maintenance with augmented fuzzy cognitive maps. *IEEE Transactions on Software Engineering, 38*(2), 439–452. doi:10.1109/TSE.2011.8

Saltoglu, R., Humaira, N., & Inalhan, G. (2016). Scheduled maintenance and downtime cost in aircraft maintenance management. *International Journal of Mechanical, Aerospace, Industrial, Mechatronic and Manufacturing Engineering, 10*(3), 580–585.

Samani, A., Ghenniwa, H. H., & Wahaishi, A. (2015). Privacy in Internet of Things: A model and protection framework. *Procedia Computer Science, 52*, 606–613. doi:10.1016/j.procs.2015.05.046

Sapuntzakis, C., Brumley, D., Chandra, R., Zeldovich, N., Chow, J., Lam, M., & Rosenblum, M. (2008). Virtual appliances for deploying and maintaining software. *17th USENIX Conference on System Administration*, 181–194.

Sapuntzakis, C., Brumley, D., Chandra, R., Zeldovich, N., Chow, J., Lam, M., & Rosenblum, M. (2008). Virtual Appliances For Deploying And Maintaining Software. *17th USENIX Conference on System Administration*, 181–194.

Sarmiento, J. P., Hoberman, G., Jerath, M., & Jordao, G. F. (2016). Enterprise engineering and management at the crossroads. *Computers in Industry, 79*, 87–102. doi:10.1016/j.compind.2015.07.010

Sato, H. (2016). Practical Correctness in ICT Environments. *IT Professional, 18*(6), 4–8. doi:10.1109/MITP.2016.107

Sato, H., Kanai, A., Tanimoto, S., & Kobayashi, T. (2016, March). Establishing Trust in the Emerging Era of IoT. In *2016 IEEE Symposium on Service-Oriented System Engineering (SOSE)* (pp. 398-406). IEEE. doi:10.1109/SOSE.2016.50

Saxena, A., Duraisamy, P., & Kaulgud, V. (2015, November). SMAC: Scalable Access Control in IoT. In *Cloud Computing in Emerging Markets (CCEM), 2015 IEEE International Conference on* (pp. 169-176). IEEE.

Science Definition Team Report. (2016). *Enhancing STScls astronomical data science capabilities over the next five years.* Academic Press.

Sedaghat, M., Hernandez-Rodriguez, F., & Elmroth, E. (2013). A Virtual Machine Re-packing Approach to the Horizontal vs. Vertical Elasticity Trade-off for Cloud Autoscaling. In *Proceedings of the ACM Cloud and Autonomic Computing Conference.* Miami, FL: ACM. doi:10.1145/2494621.2494628

Shaikh & Sasikumar. (2012). Cloud Security issues: A Survey. *International Journal of Computers and Applications.*

Shaikh, & Sasikumar. (2012). Trust Framework for Calculating Security Strength of a Cloud Service. *IEEE International Conference on Communication, Information & Computing Technology (ICCICT)*, 1-6.

Shaikh, R., & Sasikumar, M. (2012). Trust Framework for Calculating Security Strength of a Cloud Service. *IEEE International Conference on Communication, Information & Computing Technology (ICCICT)*, 1-6. doi:10.1109/ICCICT.2012.6398163

Shamir, A. (1979). How to share a secret. *Communications of the ACM, 22*(11), 612–613. doi:10.1145/359168.359176

Shamsolmoali. (2014). CDF: High rate DDOS filtering method in Cloud Computing. *Computer Network and Information Security*, 43-50.

Shawish & Salama. (2014). *Cloud Computing: Paradigms and Technologies*. Academic Press.

Shawish, A., & Salama, M. (2013). Cloud computing: Paradigms and technologies. *Studies in Computational Intelligence, 495*, 39–67. doi:10.1007/978-3-642-35016-0_2

Shekarpour, S., & Katebi, S. D. (2010). Modeling and evaluation of trust with an extension in semantic web. *Journal of Web Semantics, 8*(1), 26–36. doi:10.1016/j.websem.2009.11.003

Shen, Z., Subbiah, S., Gu, X., & Wilkes, J. (2011). CloudScale: elastic resource scaling for multi-tenant cloud systems. In *2nd ACM Symposium on Cloud Computing*. Cascais, Portugal: ACM doi:10.1145/2038916.2038921

Shilendra, Jain, & Sustal. (2007). E-Government and E-Governance: Definition and status around the world. *ICEG*.

Shuyuan Jin, C. (2004). A Covariance Analysis Model for DDOS Attack Detection. IEEE.

Sicari, S., Rizzardi, A., Grieco, L. A., & Coen-Porisini, A. (2015). Security, privacy and trust in Internet of Things: The road ahead. *Computer Networks, 76*, 146–164. doi:10.1016/j.comnet.2014.11.008

Sicari, S., Rizzardi, A., Miorandi, D., Cappiello, C., & Coen-Porisini, A. (2016). Security policy enforcement for networked smart objects. *Computer Networks, 108*, 133–147. doi:10.1016/j.comnet.2016.08.014

Singh, A., & Malhotra, M. (2015). Evaluation of a Secure Agent based optimized Resource Scheduling Framework in Cloud Environment. IJCAR, 188-198.

Singh, A., & Malhotra, M. (2016). Hybrid Two Tier Framework for Improved Security in Cloud Environment. India-Com, 1601-1606.

Singh, A., & Malhotra, M. (2016). Hybrid Two Tier Framework for Improved Security in Cloud Environment. India-Com., 1601-1606.

Singh, A., Juneja, D., & Malhotra, M. (2015). A Novel Agent Based Autonomous Service Composition Framework for Cost Optimization of Resource Provisioning in Cloud Computing. In JKSU-CIS. Elsevier Publisher.

Singh, A., Juneja, D., & Malhotra, M. (2015). A Novel Agent Based Autonomous Service Composition Framework for Cost Optimization of Resource Provisioning in Cloud Computing. In JKSU-CIS. Elsevier.

Compilation of References

Singh, J., Pasquier, T. F. M., & Bacon, J. (2015, April). Securing tags to control information flows within the Internet of Things. In *Recent Advances in Internet of Things (RIoT), 2015 International Conference on* (pp.1-6). IEEE. doi:10.1109/RIOT.2015.7104903

Singh, Singh, Garg, & Mishra. (n.d.). Big Data: Technologies, Trends and Applications. *International Journal of Computer Science and Information Technologies, 6,* 4633-4639.

Singh, A., & Malhotra, M. (2012). Analysis For Exploring Scope Of Mobile Agents In Cloud Computing. *International Journal of Advancements in Technology, 3*(3), 172–183.

Singh, A., & Malhotra, M. (2015). Analysis of security issues at different levels in cloud computing paradigm: A review. *Journal of Computer Networks and Applications, 2*(2), 41–45.

Singh, A., & Malhotra, M. (2015). Analysis Of Security Issues At Different Levels In Cloud Computing Paradigm: A Review. *Journal of Computer Networks and Applications, 2*(2).

Singh, A., & Malhotra, M. (n.d.). A Novel Agent Based Framework for Cost Optimization in Cloud Computing Environment. *International Journal of Cloud Applications,* 53–61.

Singh, P. K., & Chudasama, H. (2017). Assessing impacts and community preparedness to cyclones: A fuzzy cognitive mapping approach. *Climatic Change,* 1–18.

Song, Y., Sun, Y., Wang, H., & Song, X. (2007). An Adaptive Resource Flowing Scheme Amongst Vms In A VM-Based Utility Computing. *Proceedings of IEEE International Conference on Computer and Information Technology.* doi:10.1109/CIT.2007.16

Soror, A. A., Minhas, U. F., Aboulnaga, A., Salem, K., Kokosielis, P., & Kamath, S. (2008). Automatic Virtual Machine Configuration For Database Workloads. *Proceedings of ACM SIGMOD International Conference on Management of data.* doi:10.1145/1376616.1376711

Spinner, S., Herbst, N., Kounev, S., Zhu, X., Lu, L., Uysal, M., & Griffith, R. (2015). Proactive Memory Scaling of Virtualized Applications. In *8th International Conference on Cloud Computing* (pp. 277-284). New York: IEEE.

Srikantaiah, S., Kansal, A., & Zhao, F. (2008). Energy Aware Consolidation For Cloud Computing. *Proceedings of HotPower '08 Workshop on Power Aware computing and Systems.*

Staab, Bhargava, Lilien, Rosenthal, Winslett, Sloman, … Kashyap. (2004). The pudding of trust. *IEEE Intelligent Systems, 19*(5), 74–88.

Staab, S., Bhargava, B. K., Lilien, L., Rosenthal, A., Winslett, M., Sloman, M., & Kashyap, V. et al. (2004). The pudding of trust. *IEEE Intelligent Systems, 19*(5), 74–88. doi:10.1109/MIS.2004.52

Subashini, S., & Kavitha, V. (2011). A survey on security issues in service delivery models of cloud computing. *Journal of Network and Computer Applications, 34*(1), 1–11. doi:10.1016/j.jnca.2010.07.006

Sullivan, J. (2017). Considering employee needs during a catastrophe requires innovative recovery plans: Why traditional workplace recovery solutions are outdated. *Journal of Business Continuity & Emergency Planning, 10*(3), 259–267. PMID:28222849

Sun, H. M., & Shieh, S. P. (1994, December). Optimal information dispersal for reliable communication in computer networks. In *Parallel and Distributed Systems, 1994. International Conference on* (pp. 460-464). IEEE.

Szwed, P., Skrzynski, P., & Chmiel, W. (2016). Risk assessment for a video surveillance system based on Fuzzy Cognitive Maps. *Multimedia Tools and Applications, 75*(17), 10667–10690. doi:10.1007/s11042-014-2047-6

Tabikh, M. (2014). *Downtime cost and Reduction analysis: Survey results* (Thesis of Master degree). Mälardalen University, School of Innovation, Design and Engineering, Innovation and Product Realisation.

Takabi, H., Joshi, J. B. D., & Ahn, G.-J. (2010). Security and privacy challenges in cloud computing environments. *IEEE Security and Privacy, 8*(6), 24–31. doi:10.1109/MSP.2010.186

Takakuwa, S. (2013). *A perspective on manufacturing and environmental management.* Daaam International Scientific.

Tammepuu, A., Kaart, T., & Sepp, K. (2016). Emergency preparedness and response in ISO 14001 enterprises: An Estonian case study. *International Journal of Emergency Management, 12*(1), 55–69. doi:10.1504/IJEM.2016.074879

Timperio, G., Panchal, G. B., De Souza, R., Goh, M., & Samvedi, A. (2016). Decision making framework for emergency response preparedness: A supply chain resilience approach. *Management of Innovation and Technology (ICMIT), 2016 IEEE International Conference, 78*-82. doi:10.1109/ICMIT.2016.7605011

Topuz, Ç. (2016). Crisis management and strategies in tourism industry. *Proceedings Book.*

Ukil, A., Bandyopadhyay, S., & Pal, A. (2014, April). IoT-privacy: To be private or not to be private. In *Computer Communications Workshops (INFOCOM WKSHPS), 2014 IEEE Conference on* (pp. 123-124). IEEE.

UNESCO Institute for Information Technologies in Education (IITE) Report. (2010). *Cloud Computing in Education.* Author.

Urgaonkar, B., Shenoy, P., Chandra, A., & Goyal, P. (2005). Dynamic provisioning of multi-tier internet applications. In *Second International Conference on Autonomic Computing* (pp. 217 – 228). Seattle, WA: IEEE. doi:10.1109/ICAC.2005.27

Urgaonkar, B., Shenoy, P., Chandra, A., Goyal, P., & Wood, T. (2008). Agile dynamic provisioning of multi-tier Internet applications. *ACM Transactions on Autonomous and Adaptive Systems, 3*(1), 1–25. doi:10.1145/1342171.1342172

Vaquero, L. M., Rodero-Merino, L., & Morán, D. (2011). Locking the sky: A survey on IaaS cloud security. *Computing*, *91*(1), 93–118. doi:10.1007/s00607-010-0140-x

Vecchiola, C., Chu, X., & Buyya, R. (2009). Aneka: A Software Platform For. NET-Based Cloud Computing. In High Performance & Large Scale computing. IOS Press.

Verma, A., Koller, R., Useche, L., & Rangaswami, R. (2010). Srcmap: Energy Proportional Storage Using Dynamic Consolidation. *Proceedings of the 8th USENIX conference on File and storage technologies (FAST'10)*.

Vijayakumar, P., & Poongkuzhali, T. (2012). Efficient power aware broadcasting technique for mobile ad hoc network. *Procedia Engineering*, *30*, 782–78930. doi:10.1016/j.proeng.2012.01.928

Villalpando, L. E. B., April, A., & Abran, A. (2014). Performance Analysis Model For Big Data Applications In Cloud Computing. *Journal of Cloud Computing*, *4*, 3–19.

Virtualization Special Interest Group PCI Security Standards Council Report. (2011). *Information Supplement*. PCI DSS Virtualization Guidelines.

VMWare. (2007). *Understanding Full Virtualization, Paravirtualization and Hardware Assist*. Retrieved from http://www.vmware.com/files/pdf/VMware_paravirtualization.pdf

Wang, B., Li, B., & Li, H. (2013). Panda: Public Auditing For Shared Data With Efficient User Revocation In The Cloud. *IEEE Transaction*, 1-14. Retrieved from http://www.thinkgrid.com/docs/computing-whitepaper.pdf

Wang, Ramasamy, Harper, Plattier, & Viswanathan. (2015). Experiences with Building Disaster Recovery for Enterprise-Class Clouds. In *Dependable Systems and Networks (DSN), 45th Annual IEEE/IFIP International Conference*. Rio de Janeiro, Brazil: IEEE.

Wang, Q., Shi, H., & Qi, Q. (2010). A dynamic probabilistic broadcasting scheme based on cross-layer design for MANETs. *International Journal of Modern Education and Computer Science*, *2*(1), 40–47. doi:10.5815/ijmecs.2010.01.06

Wei, Z., Lu, L., & Yanchun, Z. (2008). Using fuzzy cognitive time maps for modeling and evaluating trust dynamics in the virtual enterprises. *Expert Systems with Applications*, *35*(4), 1583–1592. doi:10.1016/j.eswa.2007.08.071

Wiese, L. (2014). Clustering Based Fragmentation And Data Replication For Flexible Query Answering In Distributed Databases. *Journal of Cloud Computing*, *2*, 3–18.

Wi-Fi Alliance. (2014). Connect your life: Wi-Fi and the Internet of Everything. *International Journal on Recent Innovation Trends in Computing and Communication*, *4*(1), 86-189.

Wikipedia. (n.d.). *Software as a Service*. Retrieved on December 1, 2016, from http://en.wikipedia.org/wiki/Software_as_a_service

Williams, P. (1993). Information technology and tourism: a dependent factor for future survival. In World Travel and Tourism Review: Indicators, Trends and Issues (2nd ed.; vol. 3, pp. 200-205). CAB International.

Witty, R. J. (2016). *Cool Vendors in Business Continuity Management and IT Resilience, 2016. IT Regular Report.* Gartner.

Wolski, R. (2011). *Cloud Computing and Open Source: Watching Hype Meet Reality.* Retrieved from http://www.ics.uci.edu/~ccgrid11/files/ccgrid-11_Rich_Wolsky.pdf

Woods, A. (2010). Cooling The Data Center. *Communications of the ACM, 53*(4), 36–42. doi:10.1145/1721654.1721671

Wu, X., Yang, Y., Liu, J., Wu, Y., & Yi, F. (2010). Position-aware counter-based broadcast for mobile ad hoc networks. In *Proceeding of the Fifth International Conference on Frontier of Computer Science and Technology (FCST).* Changchun, China: IEEE. doi:10.1109/FCST.2010.42

Wu, J., Liang, Q., & Bertino, E. (2009). Improving Scalability of Software Cloud for Composite Web Services. In *International Conference on Cloud Computing* (pp. 143 - 146). Bangalore, India: IEEE. doi:10.1109/CLOUD.2009.75

Yan, Huang, & Yi. (2015). *Is Apache Spark Scalable to Seismic Data Analytics and Computations?* Academic Press.

Yang, H., & Tate, M. (2009). Where Are We At Cloud Computing? A Descriptive Literature Survey. Association for Information System, 807-819.

Yang, Jia, Ren, Zhang, & Xie. (2013). DAC-MACS: Effective Data Access Control for Multiauthority Cloud Storage Systems. *IEEE Transaction on Information Forensics and Security,* 1790-1801.

Yang, Jia, Ren, Zhang, & Xie. (2013). DAC-MACS: Effective Data Access Control for Multiauthority Cloud Storage Systems. *IEEE Transaction on Information Forensics and Security.*

Yang, H., & Tate, M. (2009). Where are we at with Cloud Computing?: A Descriptive Literarure Review. *Proceedings of 20th Australasian Conference on Information Systems,* 807-819.

Yang, K., & Jia, X. (2013). An Efficient And Secure Dynamic Auditing Protocol For Data Storage In Cloud Computing. *IEEE Transactions on Parallel and Distributed Systems, 24*(9), 1717–1726. doi:10.1109/TPDS.2012.278

Yang, Z., Qiao, L., Liu, C., Yang, C., & Guangming, W. (2010). A Collaborative Trust Model of Firewall-through based on Cloud Computing. *14th International Conference on Computer Supported Cooperative Work in Design.*

Yassa, M. M., Hassan, H. A., & Omara, F. A. (2012). New Federated Collaborative Network Organization Model (FCNOM). *International Journal of Cloud Computing and Services Science, 1*(1), 1–10.

Yassein, M. B., Al-Dubai, A. Y., Khaoua, M. O., & Al-jarrah, O. M. (2009). New adaptive counter based broadcast using neighborhood information in MANETS (IPDPS 2009). In *Proceeding of the IEEE International Parallel and Distributed Processing Symposium*. Rome, Italy: IEEE.

Yassein, M. B., Mardini, W., & Khalil, A. (2016, September). Smart homes automation using Z-wave protocol. In *Engineering & MIS (ICEMIS), International Conference on* (pp. 1-6). IEEE.

Yassein, M. B., Oqaily, O. A., Min, G., Mardin, W., Khamayseh, Y., & Manaseer, S. S. (2010). Enhanced Fibonacci backoff algorithm for mobile Ad-hoc network. In *Proceedings of the 10th IEEE International Conference on Computer and Information Technology(CIT-2010), 7th IEEE International Conference on Embedded Software and Systems (ICESS-2010, ScalCom-2010).* Bradford, UK: IEEE. doi:10.1109/CIT.2010.144

Yassein, M. B., & Al-Dubai, A. Y. (2016). A Novel Broadcast Scheme DSR-based Mobile Adhoc Networks. *International Journal of Advanced Computer Science and Applications*, 7, 563–568.

Yassein, M. B., Ould-Khaoua, M., & Papanastasiou, S. (2005). Performance evaluation of flooding in MANETs in the presence of multi-broadcast traffic. *Proceedings of the International Conference on Parallel and Distributed Systems.* doi:10.1109/ICPADS.2005.228

Ye, N., Zhu, Y., Wang, R. C., & Lin, Q. M. (2014). *An efficient authentication and access control scheme for perception layer of internet of things.* Academic Press.

Yeboah, Feng, Daniel, & Joseph. (2014). Agricultural Supply Chain Risk Identification-A Case Finding from Ghana. *Journal of Management and Strategy*, 5(2), 31.

Youseff, L., Botrico, M., & Silva, D. D. (2008). Towards a unified Ontology of Cloud Computing. *Proc. Of Grid Computing Environments Workshop.*

Yuefa, D., Bo, W., Yaqiang, G., Quan, Z., & Chaojing, T. (2009). Data Security Model For Cloud Computing. *International Workshop on Information Security and Application New York*, 141-144.

Yuefa, D., Bo, W., Yaqiang, G., Quan, Z., & Chaojing, T. (2009). Data security model for cloud computing. *International Workshop on Information Security and Application*, 141-144.

Yu, G., Li, F., & Yang, Y. (2017). Robust supply chain networks design and ambiguous risk preferences. *International Journal of Production Research*, 55(4), 1168–1182. doi:10.1080/00207543.2016.1232499

Zafari & Christidis. (2015). *Micro-location for Internet of Things equipped Smart Buildings.* IEEE.

Zargar, S. T., Joshi, J., & Tipper, D. (2013). A Survey of Defense Mechanisms Against Distributed Denial of Service (DDOS)Flooding. *IEEE Communications Surveys and Tutorials*, 1–24.

Zhang, Q., & Cheng, L. (2010). Cloud computing: state-of-the-art and research challenge. *Raouf Boutaba J Internet Serv Appl*, 7-18.

Zhang, Q., & Cheng, L. (2010). Cloud Computing: State-Of-The-Art And Research Challenge. *Raouf Boutaba J Internet Serv Appl*, 7-18.

Zhang, C., & Sterck, H. D. (2009). Cloudwf A Computational Workflow System For Cloud Based For Hadoop. *Lecture Notes in Computer Science*, *5391*, 393–404. doi:10.1007/978-3-642-10665-1_36

Zhang, Q., Cheng, L., & Boutaba, R. (2010). *Cloud computing: state-of-the-art and research challenges* (Vol. 7). Springer.

Zhang, W., Zhu, Y., & Zhao, Y. (2016). Fuzzy Cognitive Map Approach for Trust-Based Partner Selection in Virtual Enterprise. *Journal of Computational and Theoretical Nanoscience*, *13*(1), 349–360. doi:10.1166/jctn.2016.4812

Zhen, C., Fuye, H., Junwei, C., Xin, J., & Shuo, C. (2013). Cloud Computing-Based Forensic Analysis For Collaborative Network Security Management System. *Tsinghua Science and Technology*, *18*(1), 40–50. doi:10.1109/TST.2013.6449406

Zissis, D., & Lekkas, D. (2012). Addressing Cloud Computing Security Issues. *Future Generation Computer Systems*, *28*(3), 583–592. doi:10.1016/j.future.2010.12.006

About the Contributors

Shadi A. Aljawarneh is an associate professor, Software Engineering, at the Jordan University of Science and Technology, Jordan. He holds a BSc degree in Computer Science from Jordan Yarmouk University, a MSc degree in Information Technology from Western Sydney University and a PhD in Software Engineering from Northumbria University-England. He worked as an associate professor in faculty of IT in Isra University, Jordan since 2008. His research is centered in software engineering, web and network security, e-learning, bioinformatics, Cloud Computing and ICT fields. Aljawarneh has presented at and been on the organizing committees for a number of international conferences and is a board member of the International Community for ACM, Jordan ACM Chapter, ACS, and IEEE. A number of his papers have been selected as "Best Papers" in conferences and journals.

Manisha Malhotra working as an Associate Professor in University Institute of Computing, Chandigarh University, India. She has credible record of various degrees like Ph.D (Computer Science & Applications), MCA (With Distinction), BSC (Computer Science). She has published more than 20 research papers in various National / International Conferences, International Journal having indexed with Sci, Elsevier, Scopus, ACM. Dr. Malhotra is the members of various professional bodies like IEEE, CSI, IAENG. She also has the members of editorial boards of various journals. She has been awarded as Young Faculty in the field of Cloud Computing. Dr. Malhotra research area includes Cloud Computing, Agent Technology, and Information Retrieval.

* * *

Reema Abdulraziq is a master student of Computer Science at Jordan University of Science and Technology. Reema Abdulrazaq received his B.Sc. in computer Science from Jordan University of Science and Technology, Jordan in August 2015. She worked with two of the best doctors of the university Dr. Muneer and Dr. Shadi, she published this book chapter that is extended from an article about how to secure LEACH routing protocol. Reema continue this domain in writing about the Metaheuristics with the groundwater optimization and protein to protein interaction project. This domain is continued to be extended to an article of how to deal with children and how to build their characteristics, this work will be completed sooner. She tries to make a balance between her courses and the research and publish as she can during her program of master. Her future will be for the Doctorate program of the same department at Amman, Jordan. Her gain to be a popular Doctor at her university of bacalerous and master programs. Abdulrazaq was working as Teacher Assistant for one year in department of computer science at Jordan University of Science and Technology. Abdulrazaq will complete her master in Computer Science in August 2018 from Jordan University of Science and Technology. Her main research interests include Wireless sensor networks and Internet of Things.

Muneer Masadeh Bani Yassein received his B.Sc. degree in Computing Science and Mathematics from Yarmouk University, Jordan in 1985 and M. Sc. in Computer Science, from Al Al-bayt, University, Jordan in 2001. And PhD degrees in Computer Science from the University of Glasgow, U.K., in 2007, He is currently an associate professor in the Department of Computer science at Jordan University of Science and Technology (JUST), Muneer served as Chairman of the department of Computer science from 2008 to 2010, as Vice Dean of the Faculty of Computer and Information Technology from 2010 to 2012, and from2013-2014.Muneer is currently conducting research in Mobile Ad hoc Networks, Wireless sensors Networks, Cloud Computing, simulation and modelling, development/analysis of the performance probabilistic flooding behaviours in MANET, optimizations and the refinement of service discovery and routing algorithms for mobile device communications in heterogeneous network environments. Bani Yassein has published over 90 technical papers in well reputed international journals and conferences. During his career, he has supervised more than 50 graduate and undergraduate students. Dr. Bani Yassein is member of IEEE and he is a member of the technical programs of several journals and conferences.

B. Deepika obtained her B.E degree in A.C.College of Engineering and Technology, Karaikudi and M.E degree in Thiagarajar College of Engineering, Madurai. Her research interest includes Cloud computing and Networks.

Gamoura is an Associate Professor at French universities and Business Schools (University of Strasbourg, University of Saint Etienne, University Lyon 3), and IT Project Manager in IT Worldwide companies. PhD in Information Systems and Management, specialized in advanced modelling and artificial intelligence. She was graduated engineer in information systems with a Master degree in computer science and systems. Dr. Gamoura has over 10 years' experience in technical management, research & development, and operational business positions, in French, European, and worldwide companies including Hewlett Packard, Total, EDF, Atos, SCNF, Adecco, and so forth. Also, she has broad experience in industrial project management and technical teams' coordination. Researches and scientific communication of Dr. Gamoura are focused on the topic of Data science, management and advanced programming. She has over 15 years' experience in teaching, providing a wide range of courses, mainly in in management, modelling, data bases, Big data, software programming.

Sanjay H. A. received the BE degree in Electrical and Electronics Engineering from the University of Kuvempu, India, in 1996 and the M.Tech. degree in Computer Science and Engineering from Visvesvaraya Technological University, India, in 2001. He has done his Ph.D. in Supercomputer Education and Research Center at Indian Institute of Science (IISc), Bangalore. His Research interests include Grid Computing, Cloud computing, Parallel Computing, Distributed Systems, and Performance Modeling of parallel applications. He is having several research publications in reputed international journals & conferences. Based on his research works he has filed 3 patents. He is working on a couple of research projects funded by Government of India, VTU, Government of Karnataka, and KSCST-UNESCO. He has also served as a reviewer for the reputed International Journals and Conferences like IEEE Transactions on Cloud Computing, International Journal of High-Performance Computing and Networking, Journal of Parallel & Distributed Computing, HiPC. He is currently working as Professor & Head in the Department of Information Science & Engineering at Nitte Meenakshi Institute of Technology, Bangalore. He is also serving as a member of Board of Directors for the Indian Subsidiary of TGE Global Ventures, USA. He has served as a BOE member of VTU and Jain University.

Rohit Kumar is a PhD Research Scholar at India's Premiere Panjab University Chandigarh and Assistant Professor at Chandigarh University, Gharaun, Mohali, India. He holds his Master of Engineering degree in computer science and engineering from U.I.E.T. Panjab University, Chandigarh. He has published more than 30 research papers in referred journals and conferences. He also has three patents in the field of computer science and electronics to his credit. He has also written a book on programming language C and has been working on similar other projects. His core research areas include system programming and ad-hoc networks.

Thangavel M. is an Assistant Professor presently working in the Department of Information Technology at Thiagarajar college of Engineering, Madurai. He presently holds 3 years of Teaching and Research experience in Thiagarajar College of Engineering, Madurai and 2 years of Teaching and Research experience in Madras Institute of Technology, Anna University – Chennai. He graduated as a B.E. Computer Science and Engineering from M.A.M College of Engineering, Trichy (Anna University – Chennai) and as an M.E. Computer Science and Engineering from J.J. College of Engineering and Technology, Trichy (Anna University – Chennai) and Pursuing his PhD from Madras Institute of Technology, Chennai under Anna University – Chennai. He is a Gold Medalist in UG and Anna University – First Rank Holder with Gold Medal in PG. His specialization is Cloud Computing and Information Security. His Areas of Interest include Educational technology, DNA Cryptography, Ethical Hacking, Compiler Design, Computer Networks, Data Structures and High-Performance Computing. He has published 4 articles in International Journals, 5 book chapters in International Publishers, 11 in the proceedings of International Conferences and 3 in the proceedings of national conferences /seminars. He has attended 40 Workshops / FDPs/Conferences in various Higher Learning Institutes like IIT, Anna University. He has organized 21 Workshops / FDPs over the past 5 years of experience. He has been recognized by IIT Bombay & SAP CSR as SAP Award of Excellence with a cash reward of Rs.5000/- for the best Participation in IITBombayX: FDPICT001x Use of ICT in Education for Online and Blended Learning. He shows interest in student counseling, in motivating for better placements and in helping them design value-based lifestyle.

Mohan Murthy M. K. currently works as Senior Consultant at IBM, USA. He is also a research scholar working on his thesis under Vishveshvaraya Technological University. He holds BE and MTech degrees in Computer Science and Engineering from Vishveshvaraya Technological University, India. Mr. Mohan Murthy's research work focuses on effective resource utilization in cloud computing environment and to develop strategies to maximize the profit of the vendors and end users in the cloud market. His research interests include Cloud Computing, Big Data, and Network Management System. Based on his research work two patents have been filed. Also, he has published several papers in reputed International conferences. He has served as a reviewer for the journals and international conferences. Apart from his technical background Mr. Mohan Murthy is interested in literature, and he holds the Master of Arts degree in Kannada from Karnataka State Open University.

Wail Mardini is an Associate professor of Computer Science at Jordan University of Science and Technology (JUST)/ Jordan since 2006. Dr. Mardini received his Masters and Ph.D. degree in Computer Science from University of New Brunswick/

Canada at 2001 and University of Ottawa/Canada at 2006, respectively. Dr. Mardini research interests include Wireless Mesh Networks, Wireless Sensor Networks, Optical Network Survivability, WiMax Technology, Scheduling in Parallel Computing, and Intrusion Detection in database Techniques.

Jameson Mbale holds a PhD in Computer Science and Application. Currently, he is serving as the Inaugural Director for the Directorate of Research, Innovation and Consultancy (DRIC) at the Copperbelt University, in Zambia. He is also the founder and serving as Deputy Centre Leader for the Copperbelt University Africa Centre of Excellency in Sustainable Mining (CBU-ACESM), a project funded by World Bank. He lectures / teaches the following computer science courses: Introduction to Computer Engineering, Multimedia Computing and Web Services, Advanced Mobile Computing and Networking, Internet Technologies, Wireless and Mobile Computing, Mobile Networks and Ubiquitous Computing, Telecommunications, and Compiler Construction and Theory of Automata. His research interest is in wireless and mobile computing; network security and cloud computing; and multimedia. He has published scientific papers at both international journals and conferences. Currently he has also published six (6) book chapters.

N. Narmadha is Assistant Professor in M.Kumarasamy college of Engineering,Karur,India. Before this she obtained her B.Tech degree in Sethu Institute of Technology, Virudhunagar, and M.E degree in Thiagarajar college of Engineering, Madurai.Her research interest includes Cloud Computing and Network Security.

Mohammed Q. Shatnawi received his undergraduate degree in computer science from Yarmouk University/ Jordan in 1995. Shatnawi joined the Ahli National Bank/ Amman as programmer in 1999 for a year. After completing his master and D.Sc. studies at the George Washington University/ DC, in January 2007 he joined the Faculty of Computer and Information Technology/ Jordan University of Science and Technology. He is currently working in the computer information systems department. His research interests are in information retrieval, supply chain management systems, natural languages, data mining, algorithms, and text analytics.

Aarti Singh is presently working as Asstt. Prof. in G.N.G. College, Yamuna Nagar, Haryana. She has a credible academic record, with various degrees like Ph.D. (Computer Science), M.Phil. (Computer Science), MCA, M.Sc. (Computer Science) and B.Sc. (Computer Science). Dr. Singh owes the credit of 72 published research papers in various International Journals of repute, with one Best Paper in an IEEE Conference. She has also participated in many International conferences within India and abroad. She is associated with many international conferences as editor and review committee member. Dr. Singh is associated with many journals as editorial board member and reviewer. Her research interests include Semantic Web, Agent Technology & Web Personalization.

Gurpreet Singh, ISTE AWARDEE, is presently managing the University Institute of Computing (UIC)-Chandigarh University, in the designation of Head of Department. He has received his Master of Computer Applications from Punjabi University, Patiala and his primary research interests lie in Web Mining, Genetic Algorithm, Cloud Computing, Artificial Intelligence and Intelligent Systems. Holding a lifetime membership of the Computer Society of India, he has been awarded with the Best Teacher by Indian Society of Technical Education (ISTE) twice, for the year's 2013-2014 and 2015-2016.

Makhan Singh received his B.E degree in Computer Science & Engineering from Punjab Technical University, Jalandhar, Punjab, India in 2000 and M.Tech degree in Computer Science from University of Indore in 2002. Currently he is working as an Assistant Professor in Computer Science and Engineering department at UIET, Panjab University, Chandigarh, India. His research interests include Distributed Systems, Privacy and Storage Management in Distributed Systems and Information dispersal in Cloud Computing.

Sarbjeet Singh received his B.Tech degree in Computer Science and Engineering from Punjab Technical University, Jallandhar, Punjab, India in 2001 and M.E. degree is Software Engineering from Thapar University, Patiala, India in 2003. He also received Ph.D degree in Computer Science and Engineering from Thapar University, Patiala, India in 2009, working on grid security systems architecture. Currently he is Associate Professor in Computer Science and Engineering at UIET, Panjab University, Chandigarh, India. He has more than 30 research publications in international journals and conferences to his credit. His research interests include parallel and distributed systems, distributed security architectures, distributed services like grid and web services, privacy and trust related issues in distributed environments. Dr. Singh is a life member of Computer Society of India and Indian Society for Technical Education.

Index

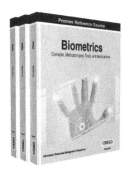

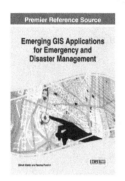

Printed in the United States
By Bookmasters